Research wi

This second, fully updated edition of *Research with Children* brings together both leading and new researchers within the social studies of childhood to explore some central questions arising in empirical research with children. Demonstrating the links between theory and practice, the authors illustrate questions of methodology and epistemology by drawing on research with children in different social and cultural contexts.

Covering a wide range of subjects, such as ethics and reflexivity in research with children, quantitative and qualitative approaches and children as researchers, it stresses the importance of adopting both comparative and intergenerational perspectives to account for the commonality and diversity of childhood, children's empowerment and children as subjects and partici-pants in the research process.

The new edition of this respected text has been fully updated and includes new chapters on topics in the area including:

- Research with children living in war-affected areas
- Research with children living on the streets
- Gendered aspects of the research process

The theoretical perspectives and practical questions are clear and well-argued, appealing both to the newcomer to childhood studies and to experienced researchers in the field.

Pia Christensen is Professor of Anthropology and Childhood Studies at the University of Warwick, UK. She is Director of Childhood Studies and, as a leading ethnographer in the field, she has published widely.

Allison James is Professor of Sociology and Director of the Centre for the Study of Childhood and Youth at the University of Sheffield, UK. As a pioneer of the new social sudies of childhood, she has researched extensively in children's culture.

Research with Children

Perspectives and Practices

Second Edition

Edited by Pia Christensen and
Allison James

Routledge
Taylor & Francis Group
NEW YORK AND LONDON

First published 2000 by

This edition published 2008
by Routledge
2 Park Square, Milton Park, Abingdon, Oxon OX14 4RN

Simultaneously published in the USA and Canada
by Routledge
270 Madison Ave, New York, NY 10016

Routledge is an imprint of the Taylor & Francis Group, an informa business

Transferred to Digital Printing 2009

© 2000, 2008 Pia Christensen and Allison James for editorial material and
selection; individual chapters, the contributors

Typeset in Garamond by Keyword Group Ltd.

All rights reserved. No part of this book may be reprinted or reproduced or
utilized in any form or by any electronic, mechanical, or other means, now
known or hereafter invented, including photocopying and recording, or in
any information storage or retrieval system, without permission in writing
from the publishers.

British Library Cataloguing in Publication Data
A catalogue record for this book is available from the British Library

Library of Congress Cataloging in Publication Data
A catalog record has been requested for this book

ISBN10: 0-415-41683-3 (hbk)
ISBN10: 0-415-41684-1 (pbk)
ISBN10: 0-203-96457-8 (ebk)

ISBN13: 978-0-415-41683-2 (hbk)
ISBN13: 978-0-415-41684-9 (pbk)
ISBN13: 978-0-203-96457-6 (ebk)

This book is dedicated to Josefine, Tobias, Peter and Daniel, who have been both our keenest informants and strongest critics

Contents

Notes on Contributors

SOUTH BIRMINGHAM COLLEGE
6 JUL 201
095484
305.23 CHR
LIBRARY HALL GREEN

Priscilla Alderson is Professor of Childhood Studies at the Social Science Research Unit, Institute of Education, University of London. She is interested in children's competence and wisdom. Recent ethnographic research includes a study of premature babies' rights and contributions to their neonatal care, and the experiences of children aged under 3 years in a new children's centre. Recent publications include Alderson, P. Morrow, V., *Ethics, Social Research and Listening to Children and Young People* (Barnardo's, 2004), and the second edition of *Young Children's Rights* (Jessica Kingsley/Save the Children, 2007).

Pia Christensen is Professor of Anthropology and Childhood Studies at the University of Warwick. Her extensive ethnographic research with children and young people has been conducted in families, schools and in local communities in Denmark and the UK, and currently includes innovative mixed-methods research into children's mobility in the city. Her theoretical interests focus on how agency is constituted in children's everyday lives, how concepts of the life course can be used in and developed through the study of children, and in ethical questions in research with children. She has published widely on children's understanding of and agency in health, learning, risk engagement, food, time, and space. She is co-editor of *Children in the City: Home, Neighbourhood and Community* (RoutledgeFalmer, 2003).

Paul Connolly is Professor of Education at Queen's University Belfast and also Director of the NFER at Queen's Centre for Educational Research. He has researched and published extensively on issues of diversity and social inclusion in the early years. His previous books include: *Racism, Gender Identities and Young Children* (Routledge, 1998); *Too Young to Notice?: The Cultural and Political Awareness of 3-6 Year Olds in Northern Ireland* (Northern Ireland Community Relations Council, 2002); and *Boys and Schooling in the Early Years* (Routledge, 2004). He has just Published a book in 2007 (with J. Hayden and D. Levin) on the role of early childhood services in building peace in conflict-affected societies.

William A. Corsaro is Robert H. Shaffer Class of 1967 Endowed Professor of Sociology at Indiana University, Bloomington, USA. His main interests relate to the sociology of childhood, children's peer cultures, early childhood education, and ethnographic research methods. He is the author of *Friendship and Peer Culture in the Early Years* (Ablex, 1985), *We're Friends, Right: Inside Kids' Culture* (Joseph Henry Press, 2003), *The Sociology of Childhood*, 2nd Edition (Pine Forge Press, 2005), and *I Compagni: Understanding Children's Transition from Preschool to Elementary School* (with Luisa Molinari, Teachers College Press, 2005).

Sarah Cunningham-Burley is Professor of Medical and Family Sociology at the University of Edinburgh, where she has worked since 1990. She is based in the Division of Community Health Sciences (Public Health Sciences section) within the College of Medicine and Veterinary Medicine and also at the Centre for Research on Families and Relationships (CRFR), where she is one of its co-directors. She has been conducting research in the sociology of health and illness and family sociology for many years. Her research interests include sociological aspects of genetics and health; public engagement in science; young people, children and health; families, relationships and health. She is a member of the Human Genetics Commission, the UK Government's advisory body on new developments in human genetics, and social, legal and ethical issues.

John Davis is Head of Department in Educational Studies, at the School of Education of the University of Edinburgh. He has been carrying out research in relation to primary/secondary education, community education, disability, leisure, out of school care, early years and child/family services. His work in the field of social justice and inclusion has been recognized internationally and involves in-depth experience of developing participatory approaches in hospitals, schools, voluntary organizations, mental health services, out of school clubs, and respite care centres. He has produced books, journal articles, policy reports, curriculum materials, and practical guides for practitioners. His most recent work include Tisdall, K., Davis, J.M., Hill, M. and Prout, A. (eds) *Participation For What: Children, Young People and Social Inclusion* (Policy Press, 2006).

Mathijs Euwema is a child psychologist and currently works as senior programme manager with International Child Development Initiatives (www.icdi.nl), a Dutch-based INGO which activities focus on addressing the root causes of problems of marginalized children. In the last six years Mathijs has been involved in management, needs assessments, and impact measurements of War Child Holland's programmes in Kosovo, Bosnia, Sierra Leone, Sudan, Eritrea, Israel/Palestine, and the Caucasus. At ICDI he is now coordinating the development of a psychosocial indicator instrument for 5-year-old children.

Dorothy Faulkner is a senior lecturer in the Educational Dialogue Research Unit within the Centre for Research in Education and Educational Technology at The Open University. She is a developmental psychologist with expertise in the area of the psychology of education. Her current research interests include literacy development, the impact of friendships and peer relationships on collaborative learning, creative teaching and learning, and children as researchers. Dorothy is a member of the Children's Research Centre at the Open University and is engaged in a number of projects supporting children to carry out research on social and educational issues that directly impact on their lives. Recent books and publications include *Creativity and Cultural Innovation in Early Years Education*, a special issue of the *International Journal of Early Years Education*, 2006, 14 (3) (D. Faulkner, E. Coates, A. Craft and B. Duffy, eds).

Roy Gigengack is Departmental Lecturer in Development Anthropology at the Queen Elizabeth House, Department of International Development, University of Oxford. A street ethnographer of profession, Roy's main research interests include drugs users, sex workers, informal street traders, gangs, and police. He has a particular interest in street children, inhalant users and child labourers, and Roy has done extensive research on these issues in Mexico City. He has published a number of articles on street children, and is rewriting for publication his PhD dissertation *Young, Damned and Banda: The World of Young Street People in Mexico City, 1990–1997*. A second book, which will be called *The City of the Glue Sniffers*, is as well in the making.

Donatien de Graaff is a social psychologist and works as methodology specialist at the Programme Development & Methodology Department of War Child Holland in Amsterdam (www.warchild.org). She has been involved in research studies in Sierra Leone, Sudan and Kosovo, measuring the effect of War Child interventions. Within War Child, she is currently working on the assessment of indicators of resilience, and the development of a participatory psychosocial well-being inventory to measure psychosocial well-being of war-affected children

Harry Hendrick teaches modern British history at the University of Southern Denmark, Odense. His specialist interest is the history and sociology of childhood and youth. His book publications include *Images of Youth, 1880–1920* (Clarendon Press, 1990); *Child Welfare, England 1982–1989* (Routledge, 1994); *Children, Childhood and English Society, 1880–1980* (CUP, 1997); *Child Welfare. Historical Dimensions, Contemporary Debate* (Policy Press, 2003); *Child Welfare and Social Policy: An Essential Reader* (Policy Press, 2005). He has also published articles on the Edwardian school medical service, post 1945 day-care, historical constructions of childhood, and hospital visiting and children's emotions. He is currently working on a history of child/adult age relationships since the eighteenth century.

Ans de Jager is a child psychologist and cultural anthropologist, she works as Head of the Programme Development & Methodology Department of War Child Holland in Amsterdam. War Child develops and implements psychosocial programmes for children in war-affected areas. In her job she is responsible for the development and updating of policies on War Child's programmatic areas. Among other things, she has been involved in the development of War Child's Methodological Frame Work, in the War Child Planning, Monitoring and Evaluation policy and toolkit, programme reviews and evaluations in Sierra Leone, Colombia, and the Caucasus.

Allison James is Professor of Sociology at the University of Sheffield. As one of the pioneers of the new social studies of childhood she has carried out empirical and theoretical research into children's culture, children as social actors, child health, children's time use, and the cultural politics of childhood. She also has research interests in identity, the life course and food. Her current research projects include children's perceptions of hospital space and children's perspectives on food. Author of numerous books and articles, her most recent work is *Constructing Childhood: Theory, Policy and Social Practice* (joint authored with A.L. James, Palgrave, 2004).

Brechtje Kalksma-van Lith works in Colombia as War Child Holland's country representative. Within the line of this work she wrote a State of the Art in Psychosocial Interventions with children in war-affected areas. She also has been involved in baseline and evaluation studies in the Caucasus and Sierra Leone. As part of her current work she is supporting Colombian partner organizations to closely monitor their work with children in war-affected areas, and to study the effect of their programmes. Mrs Kalksma-van Lith holds a postgraduate degree in Advanced Development Studies.

Berry Mayall is Professor of Childhood Studies at the Institute of Education, University of London. She has carried out many studies with parents and children, with a focus on their use of services. In recent years she has worked on the sociology of childhood, and her most recent work includes several contributions to European handbooks on the topic and a book exploring the social status of childhood *Towards a Sociology for Childhood* (Open University Press, 2002).

Luisa Molinari is Associate Professor of Developmental Psychology at the Department of Psychology of the University of Parma, Italy. Her main interests concern social development, parental representations of education, and processes of microtransitions within families. Her most recent publications are *Rappresentazioni e Affetti* (with Francesa Emiliani, Cortina, 1995),

Psicologia dello Sviluppo Sociale (Il Mulino, 2002), *I Compagni: Understanding Children's Transitions from Preschool to Elementary School* (with William Corsaro, Teachers College Press, 2005).

Claire O'Kane is an experienced child participation and protection practitioner, researcher, and advocate with more than a decade of international experience in South and Central Asia, UK, and Uganda. She was the researcher for the 'Children and Decision-Making Study' in University of Swansea Wales from 1996 to 1998. She worked with Butterflies Programme of Street and Working Children in India from 1998 to 2001. She then worked with Save the Children from 2001 to 2005 and is the author of Save the Children's South and Central Asia regional flagship publication *Children and Young People as Citizens: Partners for Social Change* (2003). Claire is currently working as a freelance child rights consultant.

Jens Qvortrup is Professor of Sociology at Norwegian University of Science and Technology, and a former director of Norwegian Centre for Child Research. Since the mid-eighties, he has been engaged in establishing and developing social studies of childhood, both substantively and organizationally. He directed the path-breaking sixteen-country study *Childhood as a Social Phenomenon (1987–1993)*, one result of which was the book *Childhood Matters* (Avebury, 1994); he was Founding President of International Sociological Association's Research Committee on Sociology of Childhood (RC53); he is currently a co-editor of the journal *Childhood* (Sage). Qvortrup has published widely in the field; his most recent publication, as an editor, is *Studies in Modern Childhood* (Palgrave, 2005).

Helen Roberts is Professor of Child Health at the Social Science Research Unit, University of London Institute of Education. Up until 2001, she spent a decade as head of research and development at Barnardo's. Her main academic interests are in developing the evidence base for intervening in children's lives, research-informed advocacy, and methodological work on synthesizing complex bodies of research.

Jacqueline Scott is Professor of Empirical Sociology at the University of Cambridge and a Fellow of Queens' College. She was formerly the research director of the British Household Panel Study at the University of Essex. Her research interests are concerned with family and household change, youth at risk, and gender inequalities across the life course. She is the Director of the ESRC Research Priority Network on Gender Inequalities in Production and Reproduction (see www.genet.ac.uk).

Nick Watson is Professor of Disability Studies and Director of the Strathclyde Centre for Disability Research at the University of Glasgow. He has published widely on a number of disability related issues including disability and childhood, disability and identity, and disability theory. His more recent work has focused on the history of the wheelchair.

Martin Woodhead is Professor of Childhood Studies at The Open University. His research and publications cover early childhood development, education and care, child labour, and children's rights, including theoretical and policy studies as well as extensive international work. He pioneered Childhood and Youth Studies as an undergraduate degree at The Open University, including co-editing three major textbooks, *Understanding Childhood*, *Childhoods in Context* and *Changing Childhoods* (Wiley, 2003) He is co-editor of the journal *Children & Society* and a member of the Editorial Board for *Childhood*.

Foreword to the Second Edition

Since its first publication in 2000, *Research with Children* has deservedly become an indispensable source on methodological practice and debate in childhood research, useful to students and researchers alike and the leading source of insight on it for an international readership. Reflecting the thinking of many of the best childhood scholars from around the world, the First Edition had numerous strengths that this new edition further develops. It avoids giving recipes for doing research with children, promoting instead the idea that researchers need to be aware of broad methodological problems, explore them in the specific circumstances of their work and think creatively about the particular solutions they might adopt. Related to this is the encouragement it gives to avoiding any artificial boundary-in-principle between research with children and that with adults. This, it is suggested, would lead researchers back to misleading and reified ideas about children by making the lazy assumption that unique methods for researching children are needed. In fact, it is difficult to think of any characteristic (such as being subordinated in a system of power relations or lacking literacy) that are not also shared by some groups of adults. This fact gives powerful support to the editors' view that the study of children does not require 'special' techniques, but rather simply a rigorous application of a general methodological requirement, applicable whether studying adults or children, and that the techniques used in a study should reflect the concrete particularities of the children being studied. Viewing children through this lens has led Christensen especially to argue that researchers should pay particular attention to the 'culture of communication' of children as a way of guiding their work to the most appropriate methodological practice.

Like its predecessor this volume covers a wide range of modes and genres of research, continuing to encourage the adoption of mixed method practices that during the period since the publication of the First Edition have become more appreciated generally across the social sciences. The volume accomplishes this without trying to impose a new orthodoxy and without minimizing the real differences of theoretical and methodological perspective between its diverse group of contributors. However, whilst the Second Edition builds on the strengths of the original, it also adds to them. Chapters have been revised and brought up to date, with new insights woven through what is in some cases a thoroughly rethought way of understanding the issues it discusses. Other chapters have had postscripts added, in which authors have reflected on and extended their previous thinking. Excitingly some new chapters have been added, taking the range of discussion found in the Second Edition into areas not previously explored, giving greater depth to the book's treatment of reflexivity, of race and gender as part of childhood experience and enlarging its discussion of 'street children' living in the South and to the important (including ethical) questions facing researchers working with children affected by war. This Second Edition adds these new elements whilst enhancing its original purposes. For this, I warmly welcome it and wish it great continuing success.

Alan Prout
Director, Institute of Education
University of Warwick
August, 2007

Introduction

Researching Children and Childhood Cultures of Communication

Pia Christensen and Allison James

Introduction

When we brought together the chapters for the first edition of this book, discussions about research with children as central informants of their own life worlds were relatively uncommon and were scattered through a diverse literature. Our focus was on research *with*, rather than, *on* children, in our desire to position children as social actors who are subjects, rather than objects of enquiry. Since that time, however, research *with* children has not only grown in volume, but, in doing so, has also generated a more engaged discussion of the particular methodological and ethical issues that this raises for social researchers. In this second edition, therefore, we have invited our contributors to reflect on these recent developments in relation to their particular fields of enquiry and we have also included three additional chapters in the collection. Together, these bring some new conceptual and theoretical problems into the methodological debate. Through drawing on research with children across a range of different contexts and exploring different aspects of the research process, this second edition provides an updated and comprehensive discussion of the methodological and ethical issues that should be of central concern to childhood researchers within the human and social sciences.

Our engagement with these issues is not straightforward, however, for despite its coverage of a variety of methods and a range of disciplinary perspectives, this book does not present a Cook's tour of *how* best to carry out research with children. Indeed, in some ways, its intention is completely other – no rules of sociological method are to be found here! And there are no well tested recipes with formulas guaranteeing a successful result. Rather, the book sets out to explore the complexity of the epistemological and methodological questions that arise in contemporary research practices with children. Exploring such issues is, we suggest, critical in a field of study where researchers are increasingly having to address the theoretical and policy implications of treating children as social actors in their own right in contexts where, tradi- tionally, they have been denied those rights of participation and their voices have remained unheard (James and Prout 1990; Alderson 1995; Alderson and Morrow 2004). These issues are also critical to the action-oriented research with children that is now being carried out by NGOs and others working directly to intervene, beneficially, in the lives of children. This concern with the links between epistemology and methods does not mean, however, that there will be no practical guidance about conducting research with children to be found – throughout the chapters in the book many insightful lessons can be gained.

This book is, therefore, not a book about methods but about methodologies. It represents a rich collection of contributions from authors with a wide range of disciplinary backgrounds, research practices and theoretical perspectives. We have deliberately chosen this broad diversity in order to represent the, by now, wide field of study which comprises research with children and to illustrate the knowledges that are being produced not only about children's lives through research but also, and importantly, about the process of researching those lives. However, as editors of this volume, we have not chosen to produce a set of chapters that adhere to a particular consensus. In the interest of furthering the academic debates about research with children, we have ensured that a wide span of differing views about the central questions in childhood research is represented here. The hope is, then, that the individual contributions may challenge the readers' thinking through the range of questions and arguments presented here, as they have done our own, in order to further the development of good practice in research with children.

Conceptualising children in research

The book begins from the assumption that to carry out research with children does not *necessarily* entail adopting different or particular methods – as the individual chapters reveal, like adults, children can and do participate in structured and unstructured interviews; they fill in questionnaires; they use new media; they are involved in action-research; and, on their own terms, they allow the participant observer to join with them in their daily lives. Thus, although some research techniques might sometimes be thought to be more appropriate for use with children, with regard to particular research contexts or the framing of particular research questions, there is, we would argue, nothing particular or indeed peculiar to children that makes the use of any technique imperative. In this sense, this book continues the effort to deconstruct the essentialism with which the study of children and childhood has often been – and sometimes still is – approached. This process is manifested in the shifts in dominant methodological approaches used in childhood research (Woodhead and Faulkner, Chapter 1; Christensen and James, Chapter 7 this volume).

Traditionally, childhood and children's lives have been explored solely through the views and understandings of their adult caretakers who claim to speak for children. This rendered the child as object and excluded him/her from the research process. In part, this view was challenged by the perspective which sees children as possessing distinctive cognitive and social developmental characteristics with which the researcher, wishing to use child informants, must consider in his/her research design and methodology. Although avowedly child-focused, such approaches, however, do little to enable us to learn from children's own perspectives on their everyday lives and experiences. Furthermore, children are not recognized as integral to the process and practice of research nor acknowledged as reflexive participants. Instead, their participation is conditional upon their age and cognitive competences, thereby continuing to exclude particular groups/ages of children from participating in the research process (cf. Scott, this volume). The chapters in this volume demonstrate, by contrast, that research with children 'requires a re-examination of the conceptual frameworks that influence children's representation' (Christensen 1994: 4) and participation. For example, as Solberg argued in justifying her decision to ignore 'age' as a significant marker in her research into child work,

> our concept of such qualities should not influence ways of approaching children in social science research, It should be open to empirical investigation to explore the significance of age and status within different contexts and situations, to explore 'doing' rather than 'being'.
>
> (1996: 63–4)

The tradition within which this book can be located is one that suggests that research with children should not take the age-based adult/child distinction for granted as it occurs in these other approaches described above. Instead, it argues that what is important is that the particular methods chosen for a piece of research should be appropriate for the people involved in the study, for its social and cultural context and for the kinds of research questions that are being posed. This volume provides insights into the framing of research questions in childhood research, the production and interpretation of data and the experience of the research process from different researchers' points of view. In this way the individual contributions go some way towards identifying the central methodological planks upon which future research with children can build.

In this book the authors of each chapter set out to reflect on and identify how they conceptualize children and child agency, and the ways in which this shapes the research they carry out. They represent a variety of different disciplinary and epistemological positions – psychology, history, sociology, anthropology and applied research in a variety of policy and practice fields and in contexts where interventions and action research projects are used to assist children in difficult circumstances. The differences and similarities that can be found in their contributions signal the wide variety of theoretical, practical, moral and ethical issues that arise when working with children.

For example Alderson, as do others, argues strongly for research with children to be carried out with equality, insight and respect. Her standpoint being the primacy of 'alike studying alike' she advocates for children to be best suited to research children's experiences. In Alderson's conceptualization children have in common their life course position and share a subordinate status in society delegated to them by adult ignorance of children's competences and maturity to understand matters that concern them. In this approach is a tendency to essentialize the identity of child *vis-à-vis* adult, over and above other social identities. In her chapter, Mayall mirrors this emphasis on the adult–child distinction. She considers how she, as an adult, belongs to a different generation to the children she is studying and how generational issues have become central therefore to the way she undertakes her research. Consequently, she sensitively asks children to help her, as an adult, to understand 'what it means to be a child?' Corsaro and Molinari, on the other hand, show the ways in which they negotiated their entry into children's everyday lives and domains, forming long-term research relationships of trust with them. They argue that it was their commitment to a longitudinal ethnographic approach that enabled them to gain detailed understanding of children's perspectives. Each of these contributions illustrate how the different emphasis and significance the researchers give to the adult–child distinction influence the way they choose to carry out their research and, ultimately, how they, as the other contributors to the volume, aim to accomplish the art of learning from children themselves about their lives.

Other issues of children's identity are also important in research. Connolly, in this volume, argues that childhood identities and binary opposites built around race and gender – such as black/white, boys/girls or adult/child – are not fixed universal categories. Neither are they essential. They change across and within contexts, thus reflecting the way power relations, including those inherent to the research process, relationships and struggles are being reconfigured over time and across space. Thus, he demonstrates how not only his own identity as an adult white male researcher but also the gender and race identities of the children were actively challenged, worked out, resisted and new subject positions created by children through drawing on wider discourses of race, gender and childhood. In the same vein he concludes that there is not one true and authentic account of children's lives to be found, only a diverse range of accounts. In the same vein Roberts draws attention to the diversity of children's experiences, arguing that they do not speak with one voice. To argue that they do, she suggests, risks socially excluding children yet again. In this way, Connolly and Roberts, in their different ways, challenge the collectivization of children within a minority status, advocated in Alderson's and Mayall's accounts.

However, the study of childhood as a segment in the life course and as a structural feature of society remains an important strand of childhood studies. In his chapter Qvortrup argues that it is essential to maintain and further develop macro-comparative perspectives on childhood through understanding the commonality of the social, cultural and economic circumstances that derives from children's minority status and living conditions. These, he argues, enable the more qualitative and micro-analysis of children's everyday lives to be situated, both locally and globally. Through citing in-depth examples of large-scale statistical studies Qvortrup is able to extrapolate factors which contribute to the diversities of childhood and therefore of children's daily lives. In doing so, he points to the importance of adopting a generational perspective when considering societal inequalities and socio-political and economic change. This view is confirmed by Scott in her chapter. She emphasizes the importance of such macro and generational perspectives to understand social continuities and change in children's lives. To this end, she advocates the collection of large-scale data sets through the use of quantitative methods developed specifically for children that build upon children's competences and use of new technologies.

Recounting paradigm shifts in childhood research

Most contributors to this volume demonstrate in their accounts of researching childhood how a distinct paradigm shift has had implications for the ways in which they undertake their research work within their own particular field of study or in their professional expertise and practice. This shift has involved repositioning children as the subjects, rather than objects of research. While for some this move to recognizing children as social actors is implicit and taken-for-granted, other authors have made this shift a distinctive focus for their chapter through revealing the complexities and obstacles that have occurred in this process within their particular discipline. Their accounts testify to the close scrutiny and revamping of earlier research methods and practices which have had to occur in order to facilitate this paradigmatic shift.

Woodhead and Faulkner's chapter, for example, provides a broad overview of the shifts which have and still are taking place within developmental psychology, noting the obstacles and epistemological barriers which such changes confront. Hendrick's chapter argues that lessons from the new social studies of childhood – for example that children are social actors in their own right and thus participants in the shaping of social, political, cultural and economic structures – can and must be drawn on by historians, if a new era within childhood history is to be furthered. He also argues that historians should address the ethical questions involved in childhood research. These have a particular significance since children have an apparent silence, and appear powerless, in historical sources.

Within the field of policy and practice Roberts' account reveals how shifting the perspective on children has manifested itself in children's organizations, with government bodies beginning to involve children themselves in research and consultation processes in innovative ways (see also Alderson). In drawing a subtle distinction between 'listening' to children and 'hearing' what they say, Roberts argues that although earlier so-called child-focused approaches may have 'listened' to children, researchers and practitioners may often not have 'heard' them. In this way Roberts also draws attention to the important link between theory and practice in order to ensure that the process and outcomes of research, including the evaluation of interventions and practices, are of real benefit and value to children through identifying 'what works' for them. In this way, Roberts shows that children are experts on their own lives and that therefore we need to find meaningful ways to consult with them.

Drawing on research about interventions for children living in war-affected areas, Euwema, de Graaf, de Jager and Kalksma-Van Lith similarly question prevailing paradigms through exploring the kinds of psychosocial interventions that currently are delivered. They argue that we still do not know enough about the impact of suffering on children's psychosocial development and mental well-being over time, and neither do we know whether the interventions themselves make a difference. They call, therefore, for action research that can both evaluate the interventions, systematically, while also helping children in distress by catering for their material as well as psychological needs. They set out guidelines to show how this might be done in order to ensure the best quality of life for children and to ensure, through involving local stake-holders, its sustainability. Central to this, they suggest, is war-affected children's participation in the design and implementation of the research so that these children are no longer seen as 'charity cases' but as 'rights holders'.

In his account of research with street children, Gigengak, also draws attention to the ways in which different and competing paradigms of governments, NGOs and social activists have shaped the understanding of how young street people see, experience and act in their world. This, he argues, has deflected attention from the destructive reality of street children's lives through seeing them as either victims and social problems, or as agentic survivors. Gigengak suggests, therefore, that a counter-balance to these institutional and activist perspectives are the insights to be gained from the research practices and concepts of the street ethnography literature. This 'older' paradigm enables the reality of the everyday lives and deaths of street people, old and young, to be documented and an understanding of how they experience their position in society to be gained through an emphasis on longitudinal ethnography. As Gigengak argues their lives are embedded within the power relations of the political economy that engender various kinds of self-destructive behaviours.

Reflexivity in studying children

Reflexivity is now widely regarded as a methodological necessity in research. However, for the study of children, the potential lies also in the recognition that reflexivity is not only common to the discourse and practice of researchers but is also a stance adopted by the children who participate in the research. That such a dual process of reflexivity takes place and makes an important contribution to the understanding and analysis of children's everyday lives is central to Corsaro and Molinari's account. They describe how in the process of ethnographic participation in an Italian school the male researcher, through interactions with the children and through paying attention to their conventions, language and practices, was made conscious of the significance of his status as an adult, as foreign and as a man. In their account the children are similarly shown to be reflexive. They reflect upon their experiences and practices and consider the importance of the involvement of the researcher in their everyday lives at school. In this way the children not only appear as respondents but as also actively interpreting and shaping the research process. Similarly, Connolly shows in some interactions, children would reflexively relate to him as a white, adult male. For Connolly this means that the conversations he has with the children have to be understood within the specific parameters of the context in which the research took place.

In their chapter Christensen and James also highlight this reflexive involvement of children in research. In a detailed analysis of the use of a particular graphic research technique with groups of children in schools they show that it was the technique itself which enabled children to become reflexive interpreters of their own use and understanding of time and social experience. The technique, which required children's direct participation to produce a visual representation of their everyday time use, worked to mediate the communication between the researcher and the children and allowed the children to literally see for themselves how they spent their time and how that knowledge could be represented and interpreted.

Davis et al. and Corsaro and Molinari show that reflexivity on the part of the ethnographer is particularly crucial at the point of entry into the field and the importance of acknowledging and, as Gigengack does, they stress the importance of working with any preconceptions brought to the study. In their discussion of carrying out participant observation research with disabled children Davis et al. argue that, at this point in the research process, the researcher needs to understand the ways in which she or he is being accepted by the children, and by adults too, as a particular kind of presence in their normal everyday lives which, for the researcher, constitutes the research context. In research with children, forming relationships in which children feel they want to participate throughout the research process is particularly important in order to keep up a continuing dialogue over which children, as well as researchers, feel they have control.

Mediating communication and power relations with children

In all research the relations and contexts within which communication takes place fundamentally shape the nature and outcome of the research. It has been argued, for example, that the inherent power relations between researcher and researched in childhood studies must be seen as reinforced by more general cultural notions of the power relations which exist between children and adults (Alderson 1995). In her chapter Mayall takes up this theme to argue that it is something which must and can be worked with. In this way she offers a view rather different from that earlier suggested by Mandell in her claim that 'even physical differences can be so minimised when participating with children as to be inconsequential in interaction' (1991: 40). In arguing for the 'complete involvement, research role ... of least-adult' Mandel succeeds to ignore the subtleties of the adult–children relationship (1991: 40). These Mayall, on the other hand, makes central to her account and in this way her chapter offers a radical challenge to the position adopted by Mandell and others within childhood research through her insistence that the power relations inherent between children and adults cannot be ignored.

O'Kane's chapter addresses directly this question of the differential power of adults and children in her account of conducting emancipatory work with children. The research project, that she describes, explored children's involvement in decision-making during foster care placements and through using techniques that can empower children. O'Kane offered the children a way in which to reflect and comment on their involvement in the decisions which were being made about their lives. The techniques she used enabled the children to both objectify and to translate the difficult and emotional context surrounding foster care placement into something which they could talk about and discuss.

In their work with disabled children, Davis, Watson and Cunningham-Burley give examples of how particular research techniques can be developed *in situ* to mediate communication with children who cannot verbalize their views and understandings. Christensen and James, on the other hand, show how children are enabled to discuss abstract notions of time through using the graphic design of a circle as a mediating device. The children communicated their views in different ways – through drawing; through writing; through mathematical skills; and through talking. In a comparable way, Scott argues in her chapter, that the careful design and sensitivity in the use of interactive questionnaire techniques can empower children as respondents in large-scale surveys, thereby ensuring that children's own views are articulated.

Conclusion

The particularities of the cultures of communication that are established between, mainly, adult researchers and child participants are a key focus for many of the chapters in this book. It is an overarching theme which insists that researchers pay attention to the importance of a 'practical engagement with the local cultural practices of communication' used among children (Christensen 2004). This means paying attention to children's 'language use, their conceptual meanings and their actions to piece together a picture of the social interactions and the connections between people through getting to know about different codes of conduct and communication' (Christensen 2004). The individual chapters in this book – whether using participatory group work techniques, structured interviews, questionnaires or participant observation – testify to this need. Children are not adults. Researchers need therefore, not to adopt different methods *per se*, but to adopt practices that resonate with children's own concerns and routines. This is what makes the research *participant* friendly, rather than child friendly (Fraser 2004). Additionally, as this book demonstrates, attention must be given to the wider discourses of childhood, to the power relations, organizational structures and social and inequalities which, in large part, shape children's everyday lives. To better understand childhood and represent a faithful account of children's everyday lives we need to be able to explore and explain through our methodologies the commonalities and diversities in their social experience across time and space.

In his book, *The Little Prince*, (1945) Antoine de Saint-Exupery writes that grown ups cannot, on their own, understand the world from the child's point of view and therefore they need children to explain it to them. This is wise advice indeed for childhood researchers. Only through listening and hearing what children say and paying attention to the ways in which they communicate with us will progress be made towards conducting research with, rather than simply on, children.

References

Alderson, P. (1995) *Listening to Children: Children, Ethics and Social Research*, London: Barnardo's.

Alderson, P. and Morrow, G. (2004) *Ethics, Social Research and Consulting with Children and Young People*, Ilford: Barnadis.

Christensen, P. (1994) 'Children as the cultural other', *Kea Zeitscrift*.

Christensen, P. (2004) 'Children's participation in ethnographic research: issues of power and representation', *Children and Society*, 18: 165–176.

Fraser, S. (2004) 'Situating empirical research', in S. Fraser, V. Lewis, S. Ding, M. Kellett and C. Robinson (eds) *Doing Research with Children and Young People*, London: Sage/Open University Press.

Hardman, C. (1973) 'Can there be an anthropology of children?', *Journal of the Anthropology Society of Oxford*, 4 (1): 85–99.

James, A. and Prout, A. (1990;1997) (eds) *Constructing and Reconstructing Childhood*, Basingstoke: Falmer Press.

Mandell, N. (1991) 'The least-adult role in studying children', in F. Waksler (ed.) *Studying the Social Worlds of Children*, London: Falmer Press.

Solberg, A. (1996) 'The challenge in child research: from "being" to "doing", in J. Brannen and M. O'Brien (eds) *Children in Families: Research and Policy*, London: The Falmer Press.

1 Subjects, Objects or Participants?

Dilemmas of Psychological Research with Children

Martin Woodhead and Dorothy Faulkner

Introduction

As a novice researcher in the early 1970s one of us (Martin) was assigned the task of carrying out psychological tests on 4-year-old children in a nursery school. The aim was to measure the impact of 'cognitive style' on socially disadvantaged children's learning. The study was part of a wider programme of experimental intervention research to test (at that time) contested claims about the long-term outcomes of preschool education (Woodhead 1976). The site of fieldwork was a nursery school on a new housing estate. The head teacher had allocated a small room where I could test the children undisturbed. In the days leading up to the research I familiarized myself with nursery routines and with the children who had been selected as subjects of the research – as well as observing their behaviour as they worked on jigsaw puzzles, scrambled over the climbing frame and played in the home corner.

Finally the moment came to show one of my new 'friends' the attractive set of 'games' designed to test for cognitive style. I invited her into the room, shut the door, sat her down and took my place at the opposite side of the table. This first child carried out the tests all right, but she seemed uncomfortable throughout and eager to return to the main playroom. My next recruit was a boy, who refused point-blank even to enter the room. A third seemed equally apprehensive. I can still recall my feelings of inadequacy, faced with the prospect of going back to the office with only one completed set of data sheets. I couldn't think of anything from the methodology textbooks to explain the children's reluctance to do the tests. Eventually I plucked up courage to admit my failure to the head teacher. She paused for a moment and then reassured me in a motherly way: 'Oh don't worry, it's probably because the children think of that as "the naughty room". You'd better use a different room.' My research credibility was redeemed, although I've always wondered about the real or imagined fate that awaited children sent to the 'naughty room'.

We start with this anecdote as a way of introducing some of the key issues for anyone working in psychological research with children:

- about the appropriateness of applying principles of experimental design and laboratory measurement as tools for understanding and shaping children's lives;

- about the constructions of childhood associated with various kinds of psychological enquiry, as these compare with other disciplinary approaches to research with children;
- about the importance of enquiring how children themselves construe the research context, the tasks set and the interactions initiated by the investigator;
- about power relationships between researcher and researched that are implicit within scientific procedures of psychological testing, systematic observation, controlled intervention and evaluation;
- about the ethical dilemmas raised by this kind of child research, especially research that involves experimental procedures and may involve a degree of deception about the researcher's purposes;
- more broadly, about the status of children who are the subject of a scientific discipline primarily concerned with the description and explanation of psychological and developmental processes through objective observation, experimentation and explanation.

Psychological theory and research related to children has grown into a major area of university research and teaching since its establishment little more than a century ago. Developmental theories, especially, have been a major source of insight for improving child care and education (Schaffer 1990), and a significant influence on policy and professional training. The significance of the child development paradigm is highlighted in UK government's identification of 'knowledge about child and young person development' as one of the six areas of expertise that make up the 'common core of skills and knowledge' for the children's workforce, covering 'physical, intellectual, linguistic, social and emotional growth and development of babies, children and young people' (DfESa 2005).

At the same time, critical views have been expressed since the 1970s, about the ways developmental psychology constructs its subject 'the child', (Ingleby 1974; Henriques et al. 1984), about the role of child study in regulating children's lives (Rose 1989), and about the ethics of social research with children (Morrow and Richards 1996; Alderson 1995; Alderson and Morrow 2004). 'Deconstructing' and 'reconstructing' developmental psychology (Burman 1994, Woodhead 1999a) has most often been linked to the reassertion of children as subjectivities, as meaning-makers, as social actors and as rights bearing citizens (e.g. Bruner and Haste 1987; Bradley 1989; Morss 1996; Stainton-Rogers and Stainton-Rogers 1992; Woodhead 2004).

Some of these critiques and reconceptualizations of the 'developing child' arose from within the discipline. Others have been part of the move towards more interdisciplinary 'childhood studies', building on the recognition that children have been 'muted voices' in much conventional social science research, and society (Hardman 1973) and asserting children's agency as a central theme (James and Prout 1990).

Re-valuing the child in 'Child Development' – a challenge and a caution

Contemporary child researchers can now draw on a refreshingly diverse array of frameworks and methods (see Lewis et al. 2003; Fraser et al. 2003; and other chapters in this volume). Even so, psychological studies of development remain highly influential in research, in policy and in professional training. The scale of research, publishing, media and teaching activity is huge, with numerous professional associations, journals, textbooks and courses at all levels.

This chapter was first drafted in 1999, as a commentary on some major trends in psychological research, with particular attention to the way the child is positioned in theory and in research practices: as subject, as object or as participant. The status, role and rights of children was becoming a subject of debate in all areas of society, including research. *The Children Act*, 1989 was a catalyst for policy change within the UK, as was the *United Nations Convention on the Rights of the Child*, 1989 at an international level. In the intervening years, the momentum of child-focused research, official reports and legislation has intensified; for example, in the UK through major reforms in the wake of the government's *Every Child Matters* initiative, and the *Children Act, 2004* (Parton 2005). Safeguarding children, early intervention and prevention have been major policy priorities, but an increasing emphasis on recognizing the child as the principal stakeholder in their own well-being, with a right to express their views and feelings, and to be consulted on matters that affect them, is gradually becoming embedded in legal and social work practice. Internationally, the UN Committee on the Rights of the Child identified the right to express views and feelings, and be heard (UNCRC, Article 12) as one of four general principles, along with the right to survival and development, the right to non-discrimination and the primacy of the best interests of the child (UN Committee 2003).

Davie (1993) was amongst the first to draw attention to the implications of these developments for professional psychology in a keynote lecture in 1991, presented to the Education Section of the British Psychological Society. Entitled *'Listen to the child: a time for change'*, the paper argued that children's perspectives should be given due weight in all areas of psychological work, (Davie 1993; see also Davie and Galloway 1996, and Davie et al. 1996). At first sight, appealing to psychologists to make sure they listen to children may seem a little puzzling. Surely, amongst all the professional groups who work with children, psychologists might be expected to be most experienced and skilled in 'listening to the child'. In one sense this is of course true, especially for those engaged in clinical, therapeutic and counseling work. And those engaged in academic research, which is our emphasis here, offer a very substantial body of expertise, founded on generations of painstaking work to refine methods of interviewing and observation, as well as any number of techniques for eliciting children's sense of self, moral awareness, understanding of the world, interpersonal sensitivities, etc. Much of this research expertise is all about empathizing with children's experiences, understanding their beliefs and respecting their concerns.

But in another sense this research is not about 'listening to the child'. While research transcripts are often rich in this kind of material, they are generally analysed and interpreted in terms of more abstract questions which, as a rule, reflect the beliefs and priorities of researchers, rather than children. 'Child Development' is a body of knowledge constructed for the most part by adults, for other adults to use in order to make sense of, regulate, and promote children's lives, growth and well-being. Most commonly this has meant interpreting children's situation, behaviour, feelings and thoughts in terms of theories and hypotheses, for example about cognitive or memory processes, stages of relative competence, normality, deviation and pathology:

> Most research directly on children is devoted to measuring them, using the model of animal research to measure their growth, disease or behaviour. Such research can bring great benefits to children's health and education. Yet it is largely impersonal. If children's views are collected, this is usually to atomise and process them through the grid of adult designed research.
>
> (Alderson 1995: 40)

Put crudely, while 'listening carefully' has always been considered basic good practice in psychological research, alongside 'observing systematically' and 'recording accurately', these research values have for the most part been a means to an end, not an end in themselves. Child research projects have conventionally been framed in terms of any number of academic, policy or professional agendas, but rarely child agendas. Exceptions to the rule are increasing, but are mostly initiated by researchers in other areas of child research (e.g. Hill et al. 1996; Boyden and Ennew 1997; Jones 2003; Kellett et al. 2004). It is still the case within psychological, child development studies that research questions and methods are designed and carried out by researchers, not by children (especially in the case of structured, laboratory procedures). The research product is 'data', which is usually interpreted in relation to adult discourses about children's development, albeit often framed in terms of protecting their welfare and promoting the quality of their care and education. In short, power relationships in the research process are traditionally weighted towards the researcher as the expert on children, and on how to study children, on what to study about children and about how to interpret what children say and do.

These practices are reflected in the way topics are framed, for example as about investigating: the formative significance of infancy for later psychological functioning; the cognitive processes of communication and language, learning and teaching, thinking and reasoning; the evidence for developmental stages in the processes of psychological change; individual differences in children's abilities, personality, etc.; the positive or negative impact of environmental influences (methods of parenting, teaching approaches, etc.); and the potential impact of interventions (parent-training, preschool education, etc.).

It is hard to imagine how developmental research could be conducted in a radically different way without abandoning many of these overarching themes that define the discipline.

Before accepting the proposal that developmental psychology be consigned to the dustbin of history (James et al. 1998), it may be worthwhile looking more into the complexities underlying that simple appeal to 'listen to the child'. To begin with, it seems important to assert the obvious, that developmental research is not a singular enterprise. On the contrary, it encompasses a wide range of stances towards children and childhood, according to the questions being asked and the methods being employed. Moreover, doing research requires individual researchers to adopt multiple discourses of relationship with their subject. In the course of carrying out fieldwork, it is our experience that developmental researchers engage with children at a personal level in ways that are at least as warm, respectful and humane as might be observed for children's encounters with significant adults during their lives at home and at school. Yet when it comes to thinking about and writing about these same children, the scientific paradigm imposes different standards. Generations of aspiring developmental researchers have been exhorted to be objective, dispassionate, and adopt the technical rigours of hypothesis testing, experimental and control groups, and so on. Their subject – the child – is thereby transformed into a de-personalized object of systematic enquiry, their individuality evaporated into a set of measurable independent and dependent variables, and then condensed into general laws of behaviour. The particularities of the enterprise vary, as does the terminology, but the overall vision is little changed. For example, according to a new grand theory of development reported in the journal *Child Development* (2006): 'the infant is viewed as an integrated system consisting of multiple reciprocally coupled components ... embedded within a specific context, (Spencer et al. 2006: 1534).

For many professional researchers, objectification, universalization and abstraction indicate the sophistication of a modern scientific discipline, rather than a signal heralding its imminent demise. In this respect, psychological research with children might be seen as no different from medical research, where the capacity of the clinician to switch communication register between the bedside and seminar room is a highly valued skill. In the same vein, the complex roles and relationships between psychological researcher and researched require to be articulated, not assumed, far less dismissed. The critique of psychological research is, however, more far reaching than research methods and professional practices. It also links to the way childhood has been theorized, as a process of 'development':

> Perhaps the most fundamental assumption concerning an overall picture of individual development is that of progress. Derived from or at least legitimated by biological sources, the notion that the individual gets better and better as time passes has been central to most developmental thinking.
>
> (Morss 1990: 173)

Development as a positive, progressive process is one side of the story. The other side of the story is about the relative status of the researched child. As Verhellen (1997) puts it, within the developmental paradigm, children are in a state of 'not yet being'. They are a set of 'potentials', a 'project' in the making, researched within an evaluative frame that is mainly interested in their position on the stage-like journey to mature, rational, responsible, autonomous, adult competence (James 1998; James et al. 1998). The dominant child image is of a 'human becoming' rather than a 'human being' (Qvortrup et al. 1994), illustrated by a book on early development published in 1991, co-edited by the first author under the title *Becoming a Person* (Woodhead et al. 1991). With hindsight, this title clearly denigrates children's status as persons from the beginning of life, but at the time it appeared to reflect the growing research literature on the social processes through which young children construct skills and identity.

As we shall see, critics within and outside the psychological community have increasingly scrutinized research paradigms that were commonly applied with children in the past, but are now considered ethically unacceptable, and/or methodologically unsound and/or theoretically unsatisfactory. To ensure this process is productive, account should be taken of the historical/cultural contexts in which psychological research has been carried out, the specific issues that it has most successfully informed and the significant role it has played in educational and social reform during the one hundred years or so of its existence. If psychological research and discourse may sometimes appear (by contemporary standards) to have been negligent of the rights, feelings and potential of young participants as social actors, such practices can be understood (but not condoned) as reflecting taken-for-granted assumptions about inter-generational relationships at the time. Research that may with hindsight appear insensitive to children's role and status was often at the forefront of social reform towards more enlightened, child-centred ways of treating children. The impact of Bowlby's studies of separation and attachment for the care of children in hospitals and nurseries during the 1940s and 1950s, or the impact of Piaget's studies of children's thinking on primary education practices in the 1960s and 1970s both illustrate the point. Contemporary psychologists have inherited a legacy of theoretical understanding and allied research procedures that are still practised in modified form to this day. These continue to pose dilemmas to those who practise them, as we will elaborate further.

In the rest of this chapter we discuss children's role and status in two respects: within the research process; and within the theories of child development that inform that research. We are cautiously optimistic that psychologists are well able to reconstruct developmental research in ways that are both respectful to children and their cultural context as well as articulating and promoting their status as the principal stakeholder in child research. Indeed, we will argue that some recent insights from within developmental psychology have a positive role to play in elaborating the concepts that underpin the re-valuation of childhood, about children as 'social actors', about children as 'participants' and about the importance of listening to children's 'perspectives'.

Children in research

The physical and biological sciences have strongly shaped the ways developmental research relates to its subject. One introductory textbook author writing in the early 1990s affirmed the dominant view:

> Developmental psychology today is a truly objective science ... Today a developmentalist determines the adequacy of a theory by deriving hypotheses and conducting research to see whether the theory can predict the observations he or she has made. There is no room for subjective bias in evaluating ideas; theories of human development are only as good as their ability to account for the important aspects of children's growth and development.
>
> (Shaffer 1993: 38)

While underlying scientific principles endure, as does their widespread application in educational and clinical work, the study of development has been transformed in recent years. Major shifts include increasingly sophisticated research technologies and an emphasis on more ecologically valid methods. Rigorous research ethics protocols now regulate all research involving human participants. At the same time, developmental psychologists are increasingly willing to recognize that research is a cultural practice, marked by specific patterns of adult–child relationship through which children's nature is constructed as much as it is revealed (see for example Bradley 1989: Stainton-Rogers and Stainton-Rogers 1992; Burman 1994; Gergen et al. 1996; Morss 1996 and Woodhead 1999a). Ingleby's account of 'The psychology of child psychology' (Ingleby 1974), along with Kessen's essay on the 'American child and other cultural inventions' stand as landmarks in this respect. Kessen challenged 1970s orthodoxy thus:

> Most expert students of children continue to assert the truth of the positivistic dream – that we have not yet found the underlying structural simplicities that will reveal the child entire, that we have not yet cut nature at the joints – but it may be wise for us developmental psychologists to peer into the abyss of the positivistic nightmare – that the child is essentially and eternally a cultural invention and that the variety of the child's definition is not the removable error of an incomplete science.
>
> (Kessen 1979: 815)

Accepting the scale, eclecticism and changing character of research activity in developmental psychology, our aim in this section is to highlight some of the ways psychologists have engaged with their subject, as revealed through a selection of popular research methodologies.

Closely observed children

The origins of systematic developmental research are most often traced to Charles Darwin, who famously compiled a day-to-day record of the behaviour of his eldest son (see Woodhead 2003). The biological-evolutionary orientation of observational work was most strongly reinforced by ethology, with its emphasis on meticulous recording of animal behaviours, often using complex coding systems (Tinbergen 1951; Blurton Jones 1972). And more general principles of developmental research – identifying age-linked, universal features of growth, behaviour and psychological functioning through rigorous scientific enquiry – remain deeply embedded in the developmental paradigm.

For example, the 1970s saw a burgeoning of interest in the role and function of play in children's development. Observational methodologies predominated, many originating from the comparative, evolutionary and ethological sciences. In one of the most influential collections of papers on play from the 1970s (Bruner et al. 1976) the sections headed 'Play and the world of objects and tools' and 'Play and the social world' contained one and a half as many papers on play in apes and other sub-human primates as papers on play in children. The underlying assumption was that methods appropriate to studying chimpanzees, stumptail monkeys and Japanese macaques in the wild, and the experimental techniques used on these animals in the laboratory, were also appropriate to the study and interpretation of play behaviour in children.

For the observational researcher working within these traditions, the less subjects are aware of being studied the better. In numerous classic studies, the observer may be found backed-up against the corner of the classroom or playground, trying to ignore children's invitations to join in the game, and at worst – kidding themselves they can appear like the metaphoric 'fly on the wall'. Increasingly the video camera has displaced the observation checklist, as David Shaffer noted in his introductory child development textbook:

> Observers must try to minimize the influence they are likely to have on the behaviour of their subjects ... Videotaping is particularly effective at minimizing the influence of an observer if the taping is done from a concealed location ... If videotaping is not feasible, observers can minimize their influence by mingling with the children in their natural habitats before the actual conduct of the study. In this way, children become accustomed to the observers' presence and therefore are less likely to 'perform' for them or alter their behaviour in any significant way.
>
> (Shaffer 1993: 19)

Another influence on the development of observational methodologies came from ecological studies, such as those of Barker and Wright (1951), who studied children in communities throughout post-war USA, including one American 7-year-old tracked in every context and interaction from the moment he woke up to the moment he went to sleep.

While these studies emphasized the importance of observing natural behaviour, the influence of the physical sciences encouraged psychologists to consider the potential of collecting observational data under more controlled conditions. Treating 'the child' as an unproblematic unit of observation, experimentation and analysis was rarely questioned, as Greene noted:

> The object of knowledge for mainstream child psychologists of the twentieth century has been 'the child'. This objectification of children has been the inevitable consequence of the emulation of the natural sciences and the associated quest for universal laws... Since for most of this century, mainstream child psychology conceptualized the child in much the same way as a chemist conceptualizes an interesting compound, it made absolute sense for the psychologist to take the child into a laboratory for closer inspection and testing.
>
> (Greene 1998: 257–258)

The test-tube child

Principles of close observation combined with systematic experimentation enabled hypotheses to be tested about children's psychological functioning. Objectification was commonplace as in the following textbook author's advice about how to 'find out what children are like':

> There are many ways to test hypotheses. Researchers can find out what children are like by observing them in natural settings, or by experimenting with them in a laboratory ... Unlike naturalistic observation, an experiment tests a hypothesis in a controlled situation, that is a situation in which the relevant variables are limited and therefore can be manipulated by the experimenter. Typically the experimenter exposes a group of children to the particular variable that is under investigation (for instance a new teaching method, or a particular behaviour on the part of the caregiver, or a novel stimulus of some kind) and then evaluates how they react.
>
> (Berger 1991: 22)

Dr Arnold Gessell was one of the pioneers of laboratory-based child study. Working at Yale during the 1920s and 1930s, his meticulous observations guided generations of parents and professionals about the 'normal' milestones of physical, social and intellectual development. A famous photograph of Gessell at work shows a giant 'test-tube' dome, within which the solitary infant sits in a cot, illuminated by spotlights and viewed by observers and camera-man through glazed panels. Gessell stands alongside the cot (attired in white lab. coat), apparently testing the baby's reaction to a new object:

> It is surely something quite remarkable that this small creature should have become the focus of this complex apparatus. The child is here

caught-up within a complicated arrangement that will transform it into a visible, observable and analysable object, within a particular rational scientific discourse ... It is these traces or inscriptions that have been accumulated, combined, correlated, graded, and consolidated into the object of developmental psychology.

(Rose 1989: 143-4)

Gessell's continuing legacy is evident in the laboratories and observation rooms that are considered essential university research facilities, with ubiquitous one-way screen and ever more sophisticated computer-linked video recording equipment. Our own department is no exception.

Objects, subjects or participants?

The objectified status of the child in research was clearly signalled in traditional scientific discourse, through being identified as experimental 'subjects'. The same applied to research with adults. But by 1991, guidelines issued by the *British Psychological Society* (BPS) signalled a policy shift, in favour of referring to 'participants':

. . . psychologists owe a debt to those who agree to take part in their studies . . . people who give up their time should be able to expect to be treated with the highest standards of consideration and respect.

(BPS Code of Ethical Principles 1991: 5)

The code of 1991 related to research with all human participants, covering issues of informed consent, avoidance of deception and harm, confidentiality, and debriefing. It is notable that very little of the code related specifically to psychological research with children, whereas four pages were given over to ethics of animal research. The BPS has progressively elaborated ethical guidelines, most recently through a revised 'Code of Ethics and Conduct' (2006) and detailed guidance is also available on specific topics via the BPS website (www.bps.org.uk). In the USA, the 'Ethical Principles of Psychologists and Code of Conduct' issued by the *American Psychological Association* (APA, 2002) is augmented by a set of 'Ethical Standards for Research with Children' issued by the *American Society for Research in Child Development* (SRCD), (www.srcd.org/ethicalstandards). These emphasize that children's rights have priority over the interests of the investigator and stress the importance of informing children about features of the research that might affect their willingness to participate. They also stress that procedures that may harm children physically or psychologically are unacceptable (see also Stanley and Sieber 1992). These trends are of course one reflection of the demand for strong standards of ethical conduct and ethical scrutiny, affecting all areas of research, and signalled for example by the emergence of a specialist journal *Research Ethics Review*.

Increasing sensitivity to ethical issues is also mirrored in the advice given by authors of child development textbooks: in his 1996 textbook, Rudolf Schaffer emphasized the ethical unacceptability of experiments that were once standard items on undergraduate reading lists. For example, so-called 'resistance to temptation' experiments were still being reported in the prestigious journal *Child Development* in the early 1970s. In these laboratory based studies, children were tantalized with a toy they were told they were not allowed to touch and observed to see If temptation got the better of them. In some extreme examples, they were then punished with a loud noise or some other unpleasant experience. Such research is now considered indefensible on at least two counts. Far from being asked to give their consent, children were deceived and spied on by the investigators; second, the procedure was at best confusing, and at worst distressing. Ironically, researchers carried out such studies in order to measure children's capacities for moral behaviour!

A strange situation

Despite these signs of progress, we believe ethical dilemmas are still insufficiently acknowledged in relation to some procedures that are still routinely used in contemporary research. To conclude this section we offer just one example, known as the Strange Situation. Originating from Bowlby's theory about emotional attachments in young children, and the impacts of early deprivations, and developed by Ainsworth et al. (1978), the Strange Situation procedure has become a key tool in infancy research, in clinical studies, and in cross-cultural comparisons (e.g. Van IJzendoorn and Kroonenberg 1988). One of its most controversial uses has been as an indicator of the impact of day care on young children (Belsky 1988; Clarke-Stewart 1989).

Typically, the researcher or clinician invites a parent or other primary caregiver to bring the young child into a laboratory playroom where their behaviour can be observed/video-recorded. In practice, in most studies this means the mother. The procedure involves several episodes. Initially mother sits with her infant, then a stranger enters and tries to engage with the child. At a signal the mother leaves the room, and the stranger tries to comfort the child. The child's reaction to being alone with the stranger is observed, as well as the reaction to the mother's return as she attempts to comfort the child. Several more episodes of separation and reunion follow, including the child being left entirely on their own for a short time (Ainsworth et al. 1978). At each stage the infant's behaviour, level of distress and reaction to mother as well as stranger is observed through a one-way screen and subsequently classified in terms of three (and increasingly four) categories: 'secure', 'anxious/avoidant', 'anxious/ambivalent', 'disorganized'. (For an overview see Oates 2005).

The procedure is highly instructive about the relative status of adults versus children in research procedures – especially those involving very young, pre-verbal children. One issue concerns the ethics of placing children in a strange room, leaving them with a stranger, as well as entirely alone, whilst dispassionately measuring the level of their distress in terms of crying, sobbing and other expressions of panic. It is arguable – from the child's point of view – the procedure involves deception, withdrawal of consent and harm. Deception is involved because the infant has no way of knowing they are not at serious risk of abandonment, and they are taking part in a research procedure. Withdrawal of consent is clearly signalled by the infant's distress during the earliest episodes of separation. Yet the baby's wishes are overridden (albeit very briefly) in the interests of completing the procedure. Third, the procedure involves inflicting pain, in that children are intentionally placed in a situation that it is anticipated will cause them distress. Despite these concerns, this 'minimal risk' procedure is defended on the grounds that the parent has given consent, and is free to terminate the procedure at any stage. Moreover, it is argued that the stress involved is very brief, is quickly followed by comforting, and is no different from the kinds of brief separation experiences infants often have to cope with during the normal round of daily life. (For a discussion of the developmental dimensions of so-called 'minimal risk situations' see Thompson 1992). The child might not agree with this analysis during that moment of separation distress where the presence of a stranger offers little comfort or consolation.

To highlight this point, we ask students to imagine they are asked to conduct the ethical review of a proposal for a variant on the Strange Situation paradigm, this time where the experimenter is mainly interested in measuring parents' rather than children's emotional attachments. The procedure would involve enlisting children's cooperation in triggering a brief episode of separation distress in their parent. For example, during a school outing to the zoo, children would be encouraged to lead their parent around the zoo, admiring the lions and tigers, snakes and gorillas until – at a predetermined signal – the child would slip away into the crowd and out of sight of their parent. The researchers would be interested to observe evidence of parental distress on 'losing' their child and their reactions to the child's equally sudden reappearance. They would also be interested in the impact of a stranger offering comfort, and how long it took for the parent to compose themselves on reunion with their child.

The separation anxiety experienced by a parent faced with experimentally manipulated separation from their child might be expected to engage very powerful adult emotions, just as it does for an infant who is experimentally separated from their parent. But cultural attitudes to experimental interventions involving children versus adults are very different. Whereas inflicting distress in young children is justified because the distress is minor, commonplace and carried out with parental consent, a contrived procedure that intentionally causes distress to their parent would be considered highly unethical.

To highlight the issues further, it is also instructive to ask how social attitudes towards experimentally induced distress might shift according to the age of the participant. The Strange Situation typically involves very young participants, under two years of age, who have little power to influence what happens to them. Would the procedure be equally acceptable if the child were three or four or five years old, able to articulate their distress in words, or try to run after their parent and escape the unwelcome attention of a strange person in a strange setting?

So far we have focused on the ethical dilemmas associated with the Strange Situation. A second concern relates to the ecological validity of this approach to researching children's emotional lives. A human emotional reaction cannot be measured as if it were a chemical reaction. Unlike the chemist's raw materials, even very young children try to make sense of the 'strange-situation' in relation to their experiences of separations and reunions and the cultural meanings that attach to those experiences. For example, if day-care children show a different reaction to the procedure compared with home-reared children, does that show they are pathologically insecure, or that they have known very different experiences of separations and reunions during their daily lives? If they react in an identical way to home-reared children, can we assume they are experiencing the situation in an identical way (Clarke-Stewart 1989)?

Bronfenbrenner (1979) famously described many laboratory experiments involving children as studies of 'the strange behaviour of children in strange situations with strange adults for the briefest possible periods of time' (p. 19). His challenge to laboratory procedures has been widely heeded and there is much greater emphasis in contemporary developmental research on carrying out research in real-life settings, and, where experimental procedures are used, in asking what sense children make of the situation, the researcher's behaviour, instructions or question. Some examples of shifts in research paradigm will be explored in the next section, as we turn to questions about the underlying images of children's status, capacities and competencies that shape research into their development. It is one thing for children to be recognized as participants in research. But how far are they recognized as participants in their own development?

Children in development

Undergraduate psychology students are perennially asked to, 'Compare and contrast two major theories about children's learning – Behaviourism versus Constructivism'. In this section we take a look at these major theories of development and learning and consider the image that each portrays of children's activity, competence and status in the processes involved in learning, thinking and reasoning. The contrast between the two theories could hardly be greater – in terms of ways of researching as well as ways of conceptualizing children's developing abilities.

The managed child

In their introduction to Behaviourism, textbook authors are fond of citing an experiment by the American pioneer of this approach, J.B. Watson. In order to demonstrate that children's fears of animals are not innate, but shaped by the environment, Watson and Rayner (1920) showed a 9-month-old child a series of toy animals. At first the child was happy to play with them. Then in the second stage of the procedure, the investigators hit a steel bar above the baby's head every time he reached for the rabbit. The noise was so loud it made the baby cry. By the time the procedure had been repeated several times, the sight of the rabbit was sufficient to induce fear in the baby. Moreover the baby's fear became generalized to other furry objects. In the language of behaviourism, the experimenters had induced a 'conditioned response' in their subject. Regrettably, they did not report any steps to reverse the procedure, and decondition the fears induced in their hapless young subject.

This way of treating children in research has long been condemned as ethically untenable. Yet the behaviourist legacy is still reflected in some areas of applied research, especially in contexts where modifying unacceptable behaviour is the psychologists' explicit goal. Skinner's influential experimental work with rats and pigeons was carried out mainly in the 1960s, and informed his view of a utopia where children are cared for by specialists in operant conditioning. Like so many celebrated developmental psychologists, Skinner saw his own offspring as an opportunity to test his theories. In one of his papers, entitled 'Baby in a box' Skinner describes how he designed '… an inexpensive apparatus in which our baby daughter has now been living for eleven months …' Having extolled the virtues of this labour-saving, hygienic, air-conditioned, sound-regulated device, Skinner goes on to discuss how

> … a more interesting possibility is that her routine may be changed to suit our convenience. A good example of this occurred when we dropped her schedule from four to three meals per day. The baby began to wake up in the morning about an hour before we wanted to feed her. This annoying habit, once established, may persist for months. However, by slightly raising the temperature during the night we were able to postpone her demand for breakfast.
>
> (extracts from Skinner 1972: 567-571)

The basic principles of operant-conditioning proposed by Skinner are still influential in some branches of clinical work and education. For example, Forehand and McMahon (1981) pioneered the so-called 'parent–child game' to help parents regulate the behaviour of severely disruptive 3–8-year-olds. Parents are taught to offer positive reinforcement to acceptable behaviour, give clear commands and operate a 'time-out' system for unacceptable behaviour. It is claimed that implementing clear rules and positive rewards combined with increased positive parental interactions with children in ways that enhance the quality of their relationship results in more positive parental perceptions of parents towards children and an enhanced probability that parents will be able to 'tune in' to and 'listen to' their children (Jenner 1992).

Behavioural approaches to working with children are also reflected in major textbooks. For example, Durkin (1995) cites the work of Aronfreed (1968):

> Punishment, according to Aronfreed, results in conditional anxiety becoming associated with the behavioural and cognitive precursors of a

particular act ... This promotes alternative courses of action, including preference for non-punished behaviour and suppression of any inclination towards the punished act. Aronfreed [...] provides an excellent review of the effects of punishment upon rats, children, and other behaviorally challenging creatures.

(Durkin 1995: 468)

We can only presume that the final phrase was intentionally provocative! Fortunately, more recent approaches to 'behaviorally challenging creatures' emphasize that it is just as necessary for parents to modify their behaviour and parenting practices as it is for them to attempt to manage their children's behaviour (e.g. Cavell 2000).

The developing child

Constructivist approaches offer a very different image of children's development, and very different ways of carrying out research with children. Jean Piaget's theories are the most influential example of this paradigm. For most of his life, Piaget's principal goal was the elaboration of an epistemological theory rather than a theory that explained how children came to think and reason like adults. He is regarded as a developmental psychologist, however, because he held that it was necessary to trace the origins of mature logical, mathematical, scientific and moral thinking from infancy through to adolescence and beyond in order to answer questions about the nature of knowledge. This inspired a life-long research effort directed towards discovering and explaining changes in children's thinking from infancy onwards.

Piaget did not ascribe to the nativist view that knowledge is innate, nor did he accept the environmentalist position that children develop more mature ways of thinking by virtue of direct instruction and knowledge transmission. Instead he claimed that the human intellect is constructed through individual children's actions on the environment that lead them to discover certain logical truths about the properties of objects and the physical world. To test this claim Piaget questioned children closely about their explanations of and solutions to a series of carefully constructed scientific and logical problems. These experimental tasks were for decades considered the litmus test for assessing the maturity of children's reasoning. He was also a keen observer of children's play and games. By asking how they understood the difference between pretence and reality and by taking part in their games Piaget was able to give an account of how children's understanding of social reality developed and changed over time.

Piagetian studies have been a major focus of the critiques of the developmental paradigm mentioned at the beginning of the chapter. A central plank of the argument is that developmentalism inevitably serves to diminish the status of the immature child when measured against adult standards of thinking and reasoning. What such critiques frequently fail fully to acknowledge, however, is that Piaget had a deep respect for children. He listened to them closely and did not belittle their explanations as examples of inferior (non-adult) ways of thinking. In *'The Moral Judgement of the Child'*, he states that:

> It is of paramount importance [...] to play your part in a simple spirit and to let the child feel a certain superiority at the game [...] In this way the child is put at ease, and the information he gives as to how he plays is all the more conclusive. [...] The interrogatory, moreover, requires extremely delicate handling; suggestion is always ready to occur, and the danger of romancing is ever present. It goes without saying that the main thing is simply to grasp the child's mental orientation.
>
> (Piaget 1932/75: 14–16)

Piaget's use of the 'clinical' or 'interrogatory' interview as a research method with its emphasis on encouraging children to talk freely, thus allowing their thinking to unfold and reveal itself to an attentive researcher, was highly innovatory at the time. As a young clinical psychologist, Piaget worked in the Binet laboratory in Paris, assisting in the standardization of intelligence tests. In later life, however, Piaget became much less interested in measuring children's relative competence and much more interested in what the mistakes they made revealed about their mental processes. Instead of dismissing children's words and deeds as due to ignorance, Piaget's goal was to encourage greater respect for young children's ways of thinking and behaving.

Piagetian approaches to studying child development were dominant in Europe and to a lesser extent USA during the 1960s and 1970s. One of the virtues of the paradigm was in encouraging teachers and parents (as well as researchers) to become more child-centred. But developmental research does not end with Piaget. His theory concerning the stage-like nature of the development of children's thinking and his explanations concerning the biological, or adaptive nature of the mechanisms responsible for this development have been subject to sustained re-examination. In the late 1960s, questions also began to be raised about the validity of the classic 'litmus paper' tasks and their correct interpretation.

Making sense to children

During the 1970s a research team led by Margaret Donaldson carried out a major reappraisal of the classic studies on which Piaget constructed his theories. She argued that Piaget's experimental context and tasks were so out of the ordinary compared to children's normal, everyday experience that they found them difficult to relate to and understand. She also argued that the design of the tasks made it impossible for young children to reveal their true competencies. The tasks made little 'human sense' to children. Donaldson and her colleagues devised several ingenious modifications of Piaget's original experimental tasks in ways that made them much more meaningful (Donaldson 1978). They showed that under these more favourable circumstances, young children's reasoning was demonstrably more sophisticated than Piaget claimed.

Take, for example, one of Piaget's classic tasks designed to see whether children of different ages understand the principle that two numerically identical sets of objects will always be equal provided that nothing is added to, or taken away from one or other of the sets. Piaget assessed children's knowledge of this principle by carrying out a series of transformations on two rows of counters which were initially arranged in one-to-one correspondence. He would then make one row appear longer or shorter than the other row, and ask 'Now is this row the same as that row?' Of course, perceptually, it isn't and under these circumstances young children typically respond that the second row is not the same as the first row. Piaget argued that children make progress with this particular concept when they recognize that they should ignore the perceptual evidence and only consider the logical evidence, something they are not capable of doing before the age of about seven. In McGarrigle and Donaldson's (1974) version of the task, children see naughty teddy accidentally rearrange the counters. Under these 'accidental' circumstances young children no longer argue that the two rows are not equivalent.

Experiments where naughty teddies appeared to run riot amongst the testing materials, where children were asked where would be the best place to hide from a policeman, or where they were asked to help a toy panda to learn how to speak grammatically helped developmental psychologists recognize that children's true competencies are only revealed in situations which make sense to them. Comparing Piaget's original experiments with more child-friendly versions revealed that Piaget's experiments made situational demands on children's perception, verbal comprehension, memory and social understanding which served to mask the very reasoning processes they were designed to reveal. More importantly, it came to be recognized by Donaldson and others (e.g. Bryant 1974; Harris 1983) that what appears to be 'faulty', immature reasoning actually indicates children's ingenious attempts to create sensible meanings for what are, to them, nonsensical situations and contexts.

By taking the children's perspectives into consideration, Donaldson and her followers demonstrated that carefully crafted experiments can offer important insights about young children's capacities. Nevertheless, the experimental approach still relied on the isolation and control of variables that are not of immediate interest to the researcher concerned. As a result, important aspects of children's thinking such as imagination and pretence may be marginalized or ignored. In her recent book, *Real Kids: Creating Meaning in Everyday Life*, the American developmental psychologist, Susan Engel argues that observational studies of children in more natural contexts reveals that just like adults, children have complex inner lives and that their thinking is multifaceted. It is not always governed by logic and reason, contrary to what Piagetian approaches would have us believe.

> It may be that because we are scientists, we tend to assume that that's what children are trying to be too, able to think about a certain problem and put everything else (personal lives, immediate visceral reactions and

fantasies) aside. In trying to isolate their more scientific or rational thinking from other aspects of their experience, we may get a distorted view of the phenomenon. [...] The goal of more descriptive, naturalistic research is not simply to test the relative influence of a given variable on a specific outcome or behaviour, but more importantly to develop well articulated descriptions of the processes children use when encountering the world.

(Engel 2005: 41–42)

Children as social actors in cultural contexts

The developing child's capacities for thinking and reasoning have been a major field for psychological investigation for more than 50 years. During much of this period Piagetian approaches dominated developmental psychology. The research emphasis was on investigations of how the child actively constructed knowledge through individual action and exploration. Since the 1970s, however, an alternative theoretical paradigm began to compete with the view of the child as a 'lone actor' or 'miniature scientist' (Cannella and Viruru 2004, cited in Smidt 2006: 26). Psychologists began to articulate the extent to which children are social communicators and meaning-makers from the beginning of life, trying to make sense of their social world, in the various cultural contexts they inhabit (Bruner and Haste 1987). This new socio-cultural paradigm was shaped by the insights of L.S. Vygotsky. Vygotsky's research on the nature of human cognition was carried out in the 1920s and 30s during a time of great social and political change in the then Soviet Union (e.g. Vygotsky 1978). Like his contemporary Piaget, he used experimental methods to study children's mental processes. Importantly, however, Vygotsky was a former teacher and many of his investigations were carried out in applied educational contexts. This led him to propose that knowledge is socially constructed between people; children develop sophisticated cognitive competencies through interaction with adults who are available as teachers or models to guide the child and help her make sense of her experience. This view marked a break from conventional cognitive theories of development, as Jerome Bruner explained: 'The child does not enter the life of his or her group as a private and autistic sport of primary processes, but rather as a participant in a larger public process in which public meanings are negotiated' (1990:13).

The socio-cultural paradigm inspired by Vygotsky's writing has been enthusiastically embraced by leading developmental psychologists such as Bruner (1990), Cole (1996), Dunn (1988) and Rogoff (1990, 2003) who have spearheaded major research programmes comparing the contribution of family and peer relationships and schooling to children's development. Central to this activity is the view that children are social actors in the cultural contexts or 'developmental niches' (Super and Harkness 1986) that constitute their particular worlds. We will offer a few contrasting examples of this research and newer methodological approaches that have, in Engel's words, attempted to 'develop well articulated descriptions of the processes children use when encountering the world' (Engel 2005: 42).

Active members of family worlds

Our first example is concerned with the way preschool children achieve social understanding in family contexts. Judy Dunn carried out a series of studies drawing attention to children negotiating disputes, teasing and joking with adults and siblings, and sharing in conversations about social and moral issues from a very early age. She argued that:

> Children are motivated to understand the social rules and relationships of their cultural world because they need to get things done in their family relationships. What we see ... is the child's increasing subtlety as a member of a cultural world – a subtlety achieved in part because of the pressure of the individual's needs and relationships within that world.
>
> (Dunn 1988: 189)

Much of Dunn's research has been based on detailed observational studies in family contexts, in sharp contrast to a very different paradigm for studying children's capacities for social understanding that has dominated the attention of many developmental psychologists in recent years. So-called 'theory of mind' research is centred mainly on Piagetian-style clinical interviews with children. In classic 'false-belief' studies a story about two characters with different beliefs about the existing state of their world is presented to children using dolls as props. The story is designed to reveal the age at which children are capable of seeing a situation from another's point of view (Wimmer and Perner 1983). Young children appear much less competent as social actors when they are asked to apply their skills in this experimental setting than when observed in everyday life. Dunn makes the discrepancy explicit thus:

> If preschool children are so limited in their ability to understand others, how do they manage to function effectively in the complex world of the family? Is it possible that there are differences between children's under-standing of others... in their intimate emotional family world, on the one hand, and their ability to reflect on and talk about the minds and actions of the hypothetical others that are the focus of most experimental studies, on the other hand?
>
> (Dunn 1998: 102)

Guided participants

A second example offers powerful evidence on the way children's emerging competencies are structured, supported and amplified within supportive relationships. Based on an extensive, naturalistic observation of family communities in several cultural contexts, (Rogoff 1990; Rogoff et al. 1993) elaborated a model of 'guided participation'. Instead of being about how children become competent to participate, it is about how they grow in competence *through* participation. Emphasizing that learning is primarily a social not an individual process, Rogoff built on another key concept in socio-cultural work, 'intersubjectivity', (Trevarthen 1998). This concept emphasizes the shared history, communicative strategies and purposes in a learning relationship that facilitate joint focus and effective collaboration. Laboratory studies of how children learn are often based on children working alone on a new task or skill. In everyday life, such complete novelty is rare. Rogoff argues that when teachers and learners encounter a new situation one of the first things they try to do is to make sense of it in terms of their past experiences. Teachers play a vital bridging role for children which:

> Involves assisting children in understanding how to act in new situations by provision of emotional cues regarding the nature of the situation, non-verbal models of how to behave, verbal and non-verbal interpretations of behaviour and events, and verbal labels to classify objects and events.
>
> (Rogoff 1990)

Over the past 20 years or so, Rogoff's work with children and families in cultural contexts as diverse as India, Turkey, Guatemala and the USA has highlighted the way caregivers structure children's environment and interactions according to perceived goals for children's development and expectations about children's participation in community activities. In a seminal book entitled *'The Cultural Nature of Human Development'*, Rogoff proposes that development should be regarded as 'transformation of participation in socio-cultural activity'. This view does not restrict development to children. Rogoff argues that children and adults jointly engage in a process of changing participation in the socio-cultural activities of their communities. The process of development is transformative both for individuals and for their cultural communities because 'as people develop through their shared use of cultural tools and practices they simultaneously contribute to the transformation of cultural tools, practices and institutions' (Rogoff 2003: 52). It is unlikely that she would have arrived at this sophisticated view of development had she confined herself to studies of children and their caregivers in tightly controlled experimentally contrived settings that attempt to control for inconvenient factors such as cultural variability.

Collaborative learners

Our next example is drawn from studies of children's collaborative learning in educational contexts. As outlined earlier, while Piaget offered an image of the child as a 'lone scientist' who constructed new knowledge through individual action, Vygotsky provided us with an image of the 'collaborative child' *socially* constructing knowledge through talk and collaborative activity.

This theory has been incorporated into the pedagogy of British classrooms (e.g. Kutnick et al. 2005; Light and Littleton 1999), along with the neo-Piagetian notion that engaging in socio-cognitive conflict leads to significant cognitive gain, (e.g. Mercer 1995; Howe et al. 2005). In other words, children will make more intellectual progress when their own thoughts and ideas are challenged by children holding alternative, contradictory or opposing ideas.

The majority of early studies on collaborative learning followed a conventional experimental design, assigning children to pairs and groups on the basis of gender, age or ability depending on the variable of most interest to the psychologist (e.g. Doise and Mugny 1984; Howe et al. 1992; Light and Glachan 1985). While these studies offered insight into how knowledge is socially constructed between children they did not take into account the ways different interpersonal relationships influence this process. For example, Light et al. (1994) showed that the mere presence of another child significantly affects children's performance on a simple computer task. This has led developmental psychologists to explore how interpersonal relationships such as friendships influence the social construction of knowledge between children (e.g. Azmitia 1998; Miell and MacDonald 2000). These studies reinforce the view that the creation of shared meanings and new understandings between children in classroom and educational contexts requires conditions of genuine intersubjectivity such as those which exist between parent and child, between siblings or amongst friends (e.g. Dunn 1988; Göncü 1998; Azmitia 1998). These insights cannot be achieved through traditional short-term experimental designs. They require longitudinal and observational studies that track how children's relationships change over time and how they develop the intersubjective understanding that underpins effective collaboration and shared problem-solving.

An alternative approach harnesses already existing relationships (see Hartup 1996 for a review). For example, Faulkner and Miell (1993) established that young children work better when paired with their best friend than when paired with an acquaintance. In these studies care was taken to select genuine friendship pairs using both conventional sociometric techniques and friendship interviews. The interviews encouraged children to talk about their friendships and dislikes and were used to confirm the sociometry. Thus the children's own judgements largely determined the selection of the friendship pairs who took part in the observational and experimental phases of the studies.

Faulkner and Miell (1993) also carried out longitudinal observations of children's naturally occurring classroom interactions over the course of three months to supplement observations of friendship and non-friendship pairs carrying out collaborative tasks under more contrived experimental conditions. This multiple methods approach added weight to the conclusion that children's pre-existing interpersonal relationships can have a powerful effect on collaborative learning. Multiple method approaches have become increasingly popular in recent years (Faulkner and Miell 2004; Kutnick and Kington 2005) as have ethnographic and participatory approaches (e.g. Smith, Taylor and Gollop 2000).

Unfortunately, just as children have little control over the learning experiences they encounter in schools, they have little control over whether or not they wish to participate in experimental school-based interventions designed by psychologists. In spite of an accumulation of studies by developmental psychologists concerning the influence of children's relationships on collaborative learning in school settings, we still know next to nothing about how children *feel* about being required to work with an acquaintance (or even someone they may deeply dislike), when they may normally prefer to work with a best friend or to work alone. While researchers generally seek parental and school consent for children to participate in classroom-based studies, the children themselves are still relatively passive in decisions about the goals, design and methods of research, and their willingness to be considered part of an experimental or control group, is somewhat taken for granted.

A notable exception has been the research by Anne Smith and her colleagues in New Zealand on children's perspectives on their own learning. In these studies, listening to children's voices and encouraging their active participation is integral to the research process (Smith et al. 2000). For the most part, however, in the interests of generating 'scientific' knowledge, researchers assume the power and authority to impose certain 'experimental' ways of working on children rather than listening to their views or respecting their preferences. This is regrettable nearly 20 years after ratification on the UN Convention on the Rights of the Child, 1989, which asserts children's right to be consulted a basic principle. The same principle is embodied in the *European Charter for Democratic Schools without Violence* (2004) that states that: all members of the school community have the right to a safe and peaceful school. Everyone has the responsibility to contribute to creating a positive and inspiring environment for learning and personal development.

Like the studies by Smith and her colleagues cited earlier, the research studies described next have made significant progress in developing ways of working with children and young people that will eventually enable the principles enshrined in this charter to become reality.

Peer supporters

While numerous strategies are employed by teachers to tackle bully/victim problems, Helen Cowie's research is distinctive in harnessing children's own energies and competencies in the process (1998; 2004). Her starting-point is an understanding of the power of peer relationships in young people's lives. Conventionally, attention is focused on 'victims' who experience rejection, bullying and harassment, and 'bullies' who base their social relationships on an abuse of power. Cowie asks about the role of other members of the peer group – 'bystanders' who may collude, either actively or passively in bullying incidents, or attempt to intervene in a variety of ways. Cowie has argued that these young people can play an active part in reducing bullying, to the benefit of bullies, victims and themselves, provided school systems are willing to recognize young people not just as part of 'a problem' but as a key to its solution. Cowie has worked with young people themselves to initiate, offer training, support and evaluation to a range of school-based peer support systems (Sharp and Cowie 1998; Cowie 2004). She argues that where schools have implemented these strategies the emotional climate of the school undergoes a marked change. Instead of being based on competition, distrust and rivalry, the ethos becomes more oriented to care and responsibility for the needs and rights of all pupils in the school. Taking account of students' own perspectives on the process has been an important feature of the research. For example one secondary school student reported:

> There was initial resistance from the staff. They were unwilling to give students the responsibility. The staff didn't really understand what we were doing, so we gave a small presentation in a staff meeting which helped to rectify this. But communication with staff has been a big problem.
>
> (Cited by Cowie 1998: 145)

Consulting with children

Participatory principles, such as those embraced by Cowie, have encouraged increasing numbers of researchers to recognize the importance of valuing children's experiences and perspectives as important areas of study in their own right (Greene and Hogan 2005), and as an essential basis for developing genuinely child-centred policies. One salient example concerns the treatment of working children in Majority World contexts. Woodhead carried out a study of children's perspectives on their working lives in Bangladesh, Ethiopia, The Philippines and Central America. The main aim was to inform the debate about eliminating hazardous child labour with the voices of the children themselves. In a policy context dominated by protectionist views about children's needs, and their vulnerability to exploitation, the research elicited the experiences and feelings of those most affected by childhood work, and most affected by any interventions implemented 'in their best interests' (Woodhead 1998; 1999b; 2004). The starting point for the study was the UN Convention on the Rights of the Child, Article 32, which is framed as about protecting children's 'development' from 'hazard' and 'harm'. Woodhead argued that conventional research into the harmful psychological effects of work is of limited value unless account is taken of children's active role in shaping their working lives:

> With the possible exception of extreme cases of forced or bonded labour, children are not simply passive victims adversely affected by their work. They are social actors trying to make sense of their physical and social world, negotiating with parents and peers, employers and customers, and making the best of the difficult and oppressive circumstances in which they find themselves. They shape their working lives as well as being

shaped by it. Work does not simply affect young people. It is part of their activity and it becomes part of their identity.

(Woodhead 1998: 19)

Workshops were set-up involving groups of young people engaged in lead mining, fireworks manufacture, weaving, brick-chipping, domestic work, market work, portering, street vending, shoeshine, fishing and associated trades, plantation work and various other types of agricultural work. Young people were encouraged to represent their feelings and beliefs in whatever ways were most meaningful to them, including drawings, mapping, role play as well as group discussion. At the heart of the protocol were a series of semi-structured activities and games focusing on key themes in children's lives, about family circumstances and parental expectation, experiences of work and school (positive and negative), self-esteem and personal identity. As far as possible children's own words shaped the preparation of the report, helping break down stereotypic views of childhood by illustrating diverse children's perspectives on the place of work in their development (Woodhead 1998; 1999b):

> A neighbour ... took me away from the village to Dhaka ... I didn't want to go ... but ... my mother forced me to. The night before ... I cried a lot.
>
> (Domestic – Bangladesh)

> Our parents make us work. They tell us that we must go picking. That's what we're here for ... to help with the work.
>
> (Farm work – Guatemala)

> No one forced me. I learned myself, out of curiosity... I had some friends, they went to get the material with their mother, I went with them and saw how they did the work, since then I've been working in my house on my own.
>
> (Fireworks – Guatemala)

> To work is a natural thing to do. Our friends do it. My parents work. My brothers work so why shouldn't I work? Even schooling is not an excuse not to work.
>
> (Fishing – The Philippines)

The importance of consulting with children is now taken for granted in child labour research (e.g. Hungerland 2007), as it is in many other areas of social research (Alderson and Morrow 2004). Participatory principles have been taken even further when children themselves research child issues (e.g. Kellett 2005 and other chapters in this volume).

Conclusion

At the beginning of this chapter we identified six broad issues facing anyone carrying out psychological research with children. We have been able to sketch in only some of the ways psychologists have been addressing these issues, and some of the ways they continue to face dilemmas that are in many ways inherent to the discipline. Principles of experimental design, measurement and statistical analysis remain central to undergraduate research methods courses. Moreover, each major topic of research tends to have constructed a repertoire of procedures specific to the questions being addressed. For example, whereas Piagetian 'conservation' tasks dominated research on children's reasoning during the 1960s and 1970s (Flavell 1963), the so-called 'false-belief' paradigm was in the ascendant during the 1980s and 1990s, associated with growing interest in how children develop 'theory of mind' (Wimmer and Perner 1983). Considerable inertia to methodological diversification must also be acknowledged, mainly due to the status accorded these and other research procedures, which come to define legitimate approaches to enquiry. Another clear example is the Strange Situation, discussed earlier in the chapter.

More positively, some broadening of psychologists' approach to research is evidenced in the content of recent research methods textbooks. Increasingly these include some treatment of qualitative alongside quantitative approaches, ethnographic research alongside structured observation and discourse analysis alongside attitude scales (e.g. Breakwell et al. 1994; Coolican 1994). The Fourth Edition of one of the most widely used Child Development textbooks includes a brief section on 'Children as Researchers' alongside sections covering more conventional experimental methods, (Smith et al. 2003).

In part these trends represent a willingness to look beyond the traditional disciplinary insularity of developmental research and are of value in themselves, in enriching our understanding of childhood issues. But methodological diversification also bears directly on the themes of this chapter insofar as alternative images of childhood are offered that might provoke developmental psychologists to adopt a more reflexive relationship to their subject, and become more explicit about the assumptions being made, and power relationships being played out through the research process (James 1998).

While we have acknowledged that much research continues to work within traditional scientific paradigms which treat the child as the subject of the research, new lines of research have opened up that place much greater emphasis on children as social and cultural actors. The studies we have cited as examples of this demonstrate that significant knowledge gains result when children's active participation in the research process is deliberately solicited and when their perspectives, views and feelings are accepted as genuine, valid evidence. In addition, these studies demonstrate that psychologists must acknowledge the status and power differentials which shape (or have the potential to distort) the processes involved in carrying out research *with* children.

These methodological and attitudinal innovations are closely linked to social changes in the status of children described at the beginning of the chapter. The image of the child as subject (or object) is gradually being replaced by the notion of child as participant. We noted that the British Psychological Society Ethical Code clearly marked the shift from 'subjects' to participants in the 1991 edition, but this was not consistently applied within the house-style of the *British Journal of Developmental Psychology* until 1996. Even at the end of 1998, one issue of the *International Journal of Behavioural Development* included some articles referring to children as 'subjects', along-side others that talked about 'participants'. It is a moot point how far these are merely rhetorical label changes, and how far they represent a more profound shift in frameworks of thinking about children's status in research.

Finally, we would caution that displacing an image of the developing child as subject or object with an image of the child as social actor, and active participant, must not result in the neglect of differences between younger and older human beings, in all their diverse expression. We must not throw out the baby with the developmental bathwater. Children are 'becomings' at the same time as they are 'beings', something which children themselves are very aware. Looking beyond the dichotomy is more productive than perpetuating it (see Uprichard 2007). Respect for children's status as social actors does not diminish adult responsibilities. It places new responsibilities on the adult community to structure children's environment, guide their behaviour and enable their social participation in ways consistent with their understanding, interests and ways of communicating, especially in the issues that most directly affect their lives.

References

Ainsworth, M.D.S., Blehar, M.C., Water, E. and Wall, S. (1978) *Patterns of Attachment: A Psychological Study of the Strange Situation*, Hillsdale, NJ: Erlbaum.

Alderson, P. (1995) *Listening to Children: Children, Ethics, and Social Research*, Barkingside: Barnardo's.

Alderson, P. and Morrow, V. (2004) *Ethics, Social Research and Consulting with Children and Young people*, London: Barnardo's.

Aronfreed, J. (1968) *Conduct and Conscience: The Socialization of Internalized Control Over Behavior*, New York: Academic Press.

Azmitia, M. (1998) 'Peer interactive minds: developmental, theoretical and methodological issues' in D. Faulkner, M. Woodhead, and K. Littleton (eds) *Learning Relationships in the Classroom*, London: Routledge.

Barker, R.G. and Wright, H.F. (1981) *One Boy's Day: A Specimen Record of Behaviour*, New York: Harper.

Belsky, J. (1988) 'The "effects" of daycare reconsidered', *Early Childhood Research Quarterly* 3: 235–72.

Berger, K.S. (1991) *The Developing Person Through Childhood and Adolescence*, 3rd edn, New York: Worth.

Blurton Jones, N. (1972) *Ethological Studies of Child Behaviour*, Cambridge: Cambridge University Press.

Boyden, J. and Ennew, J. (1997) *Children in Focus: A Manual for Participatory Research with Children*, Stockholm: Radda Barnen.

Bradley, B. (1989) *Visions of Infancy: A Critical Introduction to Child Psychology,* Cambridge: Polity.

Breakwell, G.M., Hammond, S. and Fife-Schaw, C. (1994) *Research Methods in Psychology,* London: Sage.

British Psychological Society (1991) *Code of Conduct, Ethical Principles and Guidelines*, Leicester, UK: The British Psychological Society.

Bronfenbrenner, U. (1979) *The Ecology of Human Development*, Cambridge, MA: Harvard University Press.

Bruner, J.S. (1990) *Acts of Meaning*, Cambridge, MA: Harvard University Press.

Bruner, J.S. and Haste, H. (eds) (1987) *Making Sense: The Child's Construction of the World.* London: Methuen.

Bruner, J.S., Jolly, A. and Sylva, K. (eds) (1976) *Play: Its Role in Development and Evolution*, Harmondsworth: Penguin.

Bryant, P. (1974) 'Learning theory and deductive inferences', in *Perception and Understanding in Young Children*, London: Methuen.

Burman, E. (1994) *Deconstructing Developmental Psychology*, London: Routledge.

Cavell, T.A. (2000) *Working with Parents of Aggressive Children: A Practitioner's Guide*, Washington, DC, US: American Psychological Association.

Clarke-Stewart, A. (1989) 'Infant day care: maligned or malignant?' *American Psychologist* 44: 266–73.

Cole, M. (1996) *Culture in Mind*, Cambridge, MA: Harvard University Press.

Coolican, H. (1994) *Research Methods and Statistics in Psychology*, 2nd edn, London: Hodder and Stoughton Educational.

Council of Europe (2004) *European Charter for Democratic Schools without Violence*, available at http://www.coe.int/t/e/integrated_projects/democracy/02_activities/15_European_ School_Charter/ accessed 01-05-07.

Cowie, H. (1998) 'Children in need: the role of peer support', in M. Woodhead, D. Faulkner and K. Littleton (eds) *Making Sense of Social Development*, London: Routledge.

Cowie, H. (2004) 'Peer influences', in C.E. Sanders and G.D. Phye (eds) *Bullying: Implications for the Classroom*, San Diego, CA: Elsevier Academic Press.

Davie, R. (1993) '*Listen to the Child: a Time for Change*', *The Psychologist* June 1993: 252–57.

Davie, R. and Galloway, D. (1996) *Listening to Children in Education*, London: David Fulton.

Davie, R, Upton, G. and Varma, V. (eds) (1996) *The Voice of the Child: A Handbook for Professionals*, London, Falmer Press.

Department for Education and Science (2005) *Every Child Matters*, available at http://www.everychildmatters.gov.uk/publications/ accessed 12-05-07.

Doise, W. and Mugny, G. (1984) *The Social Development of the Intellect*, Oxford: Pergamon Press.

Donaldson, M. (1978) *Children's Minds*, London: Fontana Press.

Dunn, J. (1988) *The Beginnings of Social Understanding*, Oxford: Blackwell.

Dunn, J. (1998) 'Young children's understanding of other people: evidence from observations within the family', in M. Woodhead, D. Faulkner and K. Littleton (eds) *Cultural Worlds of Early Childhood*, London: Routledge.

Durkin, K. (1995) *Developmental Social Psychology*, Oxford: Blackwell.

Engel, S.L. (2005) *Real Kids: Creating Meaning in Everyday Life*, Cambridge, MA: Harvard University Press.

Faulkner, D. and Miell, D. (1993) 'Settling in to school: The importance of early friendships for the development of children's social understanding and communicative competence', *International Journal of Early Years Education* 1: 23–45.

Faulkner, D. and Miell, D. (2004) 'Collaborative story telling in friendship and acquaintance-ship dyads', in K. Littleton, D. Miell and D. Faulkner (eds) *Learning to Collaborate, Collaborating to Learn*, New York: Nova Science Publishers Inc.

Flavell, J.H. (1963) *The Developmental Psychology of Jean Piaget*, Princeton, NJ: Van Nostrand.

Forehand, R. and McMahon, R. (1981) *Helping the Non-Compliant Child: A Clinician's Guide to Parent Training*, London: Guilford Press.

Fraser, S., Lewis, V., Ding, S., Kellett, M. and Robinson, C. (eds) (2003) *Doing Research with Children and Young People*, London: Paul Chapman Publishing.

Gergen, K.J., Gulerce, A., Lock, A. and Misra, G. (1996) 'Psychological science in cultural context', *American Psychologist* 51 (5): 496–503.

Göncü, A. (1998) 'Development of intersubjectivity in social pretend play', in M. Woodhead, D. Faulkner and K. Littleton (eds) *Cultural Worlds of Early Childhood*, London: Routledge.

Greene, S. (1998) 'Child development: old themes, new directions', in M. Woodhead, D. Faulkner and K. Littleton (eds) *Making Sense of Social Development*, London: Routledge.

Greene, S. and Hogan, D. (eds) (2005) *Researching Children's Experience: Approaches and Methods*, London: Sage.

Hardman, C. (1973) 'Can there be an anthropology of childhood?', *Journal of the Anthropological Society of Oxford* 4 (1): 85–99.

Harris, P.L. (1983) 'Children's understanding of the link between situation and emotion', *Journal of Experimental Child Psychology* 36: 490–590.

Hartup, W.W. (1996) 'Co-operation, close relationships, and cognitive development', in W.M. Bukowski, A.F. Newcomb and W.W. Hartup (eds) *The Company They Keep; Friendship in Childhood and Adolescence*, Cambridge UK: Cambridge University Press.

Henriques, J., Hollway, W., Urwin, C., Couze, V. and Walkerdine, V. (1984) *Changing the Subject, Psychology, Social Regulation and Subjectivity*. London and New York: Methuen.

Hill, M., Laybourn, A. and Borland, M. (1996) 'Engaging with primary-aged children about their health and well-being: methodological considerations', *Children and Society* 10 (2): 129–44.

Howe, C., McWilliam, D. and Cross, G. (2005) 'Chance favours the prepared mind: Incubation and the delayed effects of peer collaboration', *British Journal of Psychology* 96 (1): 67–93.

Howe, C., Tolmie, A. and Rogers, C. (1992) 'The acquisition of conceptual knowledge in science by primary school children: Group interaction and the understanding of motion down an incline', *British Journal of Developmental Psychology* 10: 113–30.

Hungerland, B., Liebel, M., Milne, B. and Wihstutz, A. (2007) *Working to be Someone: Child Focused Research and Practice with Working Children*, London: Jessica Kingsley.

Ingleby, D. (1974) 'The psychology of child psychology', in M.P.M. Richards (ed.) *Integration of a Child into a Social World*, London: Cambridge University Press.

James, A. (1998) 'Researching children's social competence: methods and models', in M. Woodhead, D. Faulkner and K. Littleton (eds) *Making Sense of Social Development*, London: Routledge.

James, A. and Prout, A. (eds) (1990, 1997) *Constructing and Reconstructing Childhood*, London: Falmer Press.

James, A., Jenks, C. and Prout, A. (1998) *Theorising Childhood*, Cambridge: Polity Press.

Jenner, S. (1992) 'The assessment and treatment of parenting skills and deficits: within the framework of child protection', *Association for Child Psychology and Psychiatry Newsletter* 14: 228–33.

Jones, A. (2003) 'Involving children and young people as researchers', in S. Fraser, V. Lewis, S. Ding, M. Kellett and C. Robinson (eds) *Doing Research with Children and Young People*, London: Paul Chapman Publishing.

Kellett, M. (2005) 'Children as active researchers: a new research paradigm for the 21st century?' Published online by ESRC National Centre for Research Methods, NCRM/003 www.ncrm.ac.uk/publications

Kellett, M., Forrest, R., Dent, N. and Ward, S. (2004) 'Just teach us the skills please, we'll do the rest: Empowering ten-year-olds as active researchers', *Children and Society* 18 (5): 329–43.

Kessen, W. (1979) 'The American child and other cultural inventions', *American Psychologist* 34: 815–20.

Kutnick, P. and Kington, A. (2005) 'Children's friendships and learning in school: Cognitive enhancement through social interaction?', *British Journal of Educational Psychology* 75 (4): 521–38.

Kutnick, P., Blatchford, P. and Baines, E. (2005) 'Grouping of pupils in secondary school classrooms: Possible links between pedagogy and learning', *Social Psychology of Education* 8 (4): 349–74.

Lewis, V., Kellett, M., Robinson, C., Fraser, S. and Ding, S. (eds) (2003) *The Reality of Research with Children and Young People*, London: Paul Chapman Publishers.

Light, P. and Glachan, M. (1985) 'Facilitation of problem solving through peer interaction', *Educational Psychology* 5: 217–25.

Light, P. and Littleton, K. (1999) *Social Processes in Children's Learning*, New York: Cambridge University Press.

Light, P., Littleton, K., Messer, D. and Joiner, R. (1994) 'Social and communicative processes in computer-based problem solving', *European Journal of Psychology of Education* 9: 93–109.

McGarrigle, J. and Donaldson, M. (1974) 'Conservation accidents', *Cognition* 3, 341–50.

Mercer, N. (1995) *The Guided Construction of Knowledge*, Clevedon: Multilingual Matters.

Miell, D. and MacDonald, R. (2000) 'Children's creative collaborations: The importance of friendship when working together on a musical composition', *Social Development* 9: 348–69.

Morrow, V. and Richards, M. (1996) 'The ethics of social research with children: An overview', *Children and Society*, 10: 28–40.

Morss, J.R. (1990) *The Biologising of Childhood*, Hove: Erlbaum.

Morss, J.R. (1996) *Growing Critical: Alternatives to Developmental Psychology*, London: Routledge.

Moscovici, S. (1984) 'The phenomenon of social representations', in R.M. Farr and S. Moscovici (eds) *Social Representations*, Cambridge, UK: Cambridge University Press.

Oates, J. (2005) 'First relationships', in J. Oates, C. Wood and A. Grayson (eds) *Psychological Development and Early Childhood*, Oxford: Blackwell Publishing.

Parton, N (2005) *Safeguarding Children: Early Intervention and Surveillance in a Late Modern Society*, London: Palgrave Macmillan.

Piaget, J. (1932/75) *The Moral Judgement of the Child*, London: Routledge and Kegan Paul.

Qvortrup, J., Bardy, M., Sgritta, G. and Wintersberger, H. (eds) (1994) *Childhood Matters: Social theory, Practice and Politics*, Aldershot: Avebury.

Rogoff, B. (1990) *Apprenticeship in Thinking: Cognitive Development in Social Context*, New York: Oxford University Press.

Rogoff, B. (2003) *The Cultural Nature of Human Development*, Oxford, UK: Oxford University Press.

Rogoff, B., Mistry, J., Göncü, A. and Mosier, C. (1993) 'Guided participation in cultural activity by toddlers and caregivers', *Monograph of the Society for Research in Child Development* 58 (7, Serial no. 236).

Rose, N. (1989) *Governing the Soul: The Shaping of the Private Self*, London: Routledge.

Schaffer, H.R. (1990) *Making Decisions about Children: Psychological Questions and Answers*, Oxford: Blackwell Publishing.

Shaffer, D.R. (1993) *Developmental Psychology* (3rd edn), Pacific Grove, CA: Brooks/Cole Publishing Company.

Sharp, S. and Cowie, H. (1998) *Understanding and Supporting Children in Distress*, London: Sage.

Skinner, B.F. (1972) *Cumulative Record: A Selection of Papers* (3rd edn), New York: Appleton-Century-Crofts.

Smidt, S. (2006) *The Developing Child in the 21st Century: A Global Perspective on Child Development*, London: Routledge.

Smith, A., Taylor, N. and Gollop, M. (2000) *Children's Voices: Research Policy and Practice*, Auckland, NZ: Pearson Education.

Smith, P. Cowie, H. and Blades, M. (2003) *Understanding Children's Development*, Oxford: Blackwell.

Spencer, J., Clearfield, M., Corbetta, D. *et al.* (2006) 'Moving toward a grand theory of development: in memory of Esther Thelen', *Child Development* 77 (6): 1521–38.

Stainton-Rogers, R. and Stainton-Rogers, W. (1992) *Stories of Childhood: Shifting Agendas of Child Concern*, Hassocks: Harvester.

Stanley, B. and Sieber, J.E. (1992) *Social Research on Children and Adolescents*, London: Sage.

Super, C.M. and Harkness, S. (1986) 'The developmental niche: A conceptualisation at the interface of child and culture', *International Journal of Behavioural Development* 9: 545–69.

Thompson, R. (1992) 'Developmental changes in research risk and benefit', in B. Stanley and J.E. Sieber (eds) *Social Research on Children and Adolescents*, London: Sage.

Tinbergen, N. (1951) *The Study of Instinct*, Oxford: Oxford University Press.

Trevarthen, C. (1998) 'The Child's need to learn a culture', in M. Woodhead, D. Faulkner and K. Littleton (eds) *Cultural Worlds of Early Childhood*, London: Routledge.

UN Committee (2003) 'General measures of implementation for the Convention on the Rights of the Child', *General Comment 5*, Geneva, OHCHR.

Uprichard, E (2007) 'Children as being and becomings: Children, childhood and temporality', *Children & Society* (online).

Van IJzendoorn, M.H. and Kroonenberg, P.M. (1988) 'Cross-cultural patterns of attachment: A meta-analysis of the strange situation', *Child Development* 59: 147–56.

Verhellen, E. (1997) *Convention on the Rights of the Child*, Leuven: Garant Publishers.

Vygotsky, L.S. (1978) *Mind in Society: The Development of Higher Psychological Processes*, Cambridge: Harvard University Press.

Watson, J.B. and Rayner, R. (1920) 'Conditioned emotional reactions', *Journal of Experimental Psychology* 3: 1–14.

Wimmer, H. and Perner, J. (1983) 'Beliefs: representations and constraining function of wrong beliefs in young children's understanding of deception', *Cognition* 13: 103–28.

Woodhead, M. (1976) *Intervening in Disadvantage: A Challenge for Nursery Education*, Berks: NFER Publishing.

Woodhead, M. (1998) *Children's Perspectives on their Working Lives: A Participatory Study in Bangladesh, Ethiopia, The Philippines, Guatemala, El Salvador and Nicaragua*, Stockholm: Radda Barnen.

Woodhead, M. (1999a) 'Reconstructing developmental psychology: some first steps', *Children and Society* 13: 1–17.

Woodhead, M. (1999b) 'Combating child labour: listen to what the children say', *Childhood* 7: 27–49.

Woodhead, M. (2003) 'The child in development', in M. Woodhead and H. Montgomery (eds) *Understanding Childhood: an Interdisciplinary Approach*, Chichester: Wiley.

Woodhead, M. (2004) 'Children's rights and children's development: rethinking the paradigm', in Children's Rights Centre, *Ghent Papers on Children's Rights*, Ghent: University of Ghent.

Woodhead, M., Carr, R. and Light, P. (eds) (1991) *Becoming a Person*, London: Routledge.

2 The Child as a Social Actor in Historical Sources

Problems of Identification and Interpretation

Harry Hendrick

what historians do best is make connections with the past in order to illuminate the problems of the present and the potential of the future.
(Appleby quoted in Jenkins 1997)

Introduction

This chapter has two objectives. First, to provide an overview of some of the main developments, issues and approaches to be found in histories of childhood and in those of the much less widely researched topic, 'children'. My second objective is to make a number of suggestions as to how we historians might proceed to incorporate children as *social actors* into our accounts, with all that this implies for the writing of history, since they are not usually treated in such a manner. I suspect that many readers will find aspects of the argument presented here to be provocative, if not downright muddle-headed. Nevertheless, I hope that the following pages will stimulate discussion and encourage sceptical colleagues to be more conscious of what, in my opinion, are often their ageist assumptions and sympathies.

After a brief introduction, which draws attention to the particularity of children within childhood, the chapter provides a survey and commentary on the range and nature of historical studies to date. It then proceeds to examine sources in relation to identification and interpretation. These matters always pose difficulties, but they are especially acute where children and childhood are concerned, if only because the historian has to be constantly aware of the differences between *childhood*, as a concept, and *children*, as people. The chapter then looks at how the problems might be overcome. In broad terms, it argues for a politically sensitive 'child-centred' approach, which would be a further development in making the discipline more inclusive and, therefore, more democratic. The specific recommendation is that we look seriously at the relevance of feminist perspectives and analyses for this infant enterprise, while simultaneously informing ourselves about sociological theories of age and generation.

Childhood and children

If historical sources are to be used properly, we have to be clear as to our objectives: are we trying to write about childhood or children, and what issues does the distinction raise in relation to identification and interpretation? It is commonplace to define childhood, in a socio-historical context, as a structural feature of society – with its own social space – which largely determines the experiences of children or at least shapes their commonality (Qvortrup et al. 1994; James et al. 1998; Corsaro 1997). Generally speaking, 'age', as a category, is *the* distinguishing criterion for identifying childhood, despite the influences on its meaning of class, gender and historical period (Jordanova 1989: 5). At any one time, throughout society there is usually a dominant overarching notion of 'childhood', albeit one that encompasses a variety of perceptions. As will be shown, historians have tended to focus on the *concept* of childhood rather than on the lives of children. This is not surprising since the former involves fewer methodological posers than the latter. But perhaps it also reflects adult interest in defining age groups so that generational matters may be effectively ordered.

It is worth noting, however, exactly what purpose childhood, as a 'unitary structural phenomenon' (James et al. 1998: 135), serves *vis-à-vis* meanings and understandings. I mean here that 'childhood' tends to conceal a range of birth points, many of which are at odds with one another in terms of capabilities, needs, vulnerability, knowledge and so on. Similarly, 'children' are often referred to as if they were an undifferentiated collective. Yet in common speech we normally fragment childhood (and children) into a number of different identities: babies, toddlers, nursery children, juniors, secondary school pupils and young adolescents; alternatively, we may use categories favoured by psychologists: 'infants', 'young children', 'middle childhood' and 'pre and early adolescence' (Levine 1998: 102–31). This vocabulary permits us to insert 'children' into prescribed serial places. To record these dissimilarities is not to lapse into the 'stages' approach of conservative developmental psychology (James et al. 1998: 173–4), rather it is to recognize the different degrees of competence hidden within childhood which does, after all, involve 'a complex sequence of transitions' (Magnusson 1995: 300). In an ideal world, each transition would receive individual historical examination, though within the realm of childhood as a structural form. Unfortunately, in practice, they are thoughtlessly lumped together into a mêlée of age generalizations, resulting in flawed analyses. All this suggests that there is something of a tension, or perhaps it is a duplicity of meaning, between the nouns *childhood* and *children*. The former often assumes the latter without our knowing how or why. We need to remember such ambiguity (or is it ambivalence) in our reading, our research and our writing.

When we look at children, we are not looking at an idea but at *people* who, in many respects, cannot but be active in history, if only in the sense of how they deal with their daily situations (James et al. 1998: 78, 138; Corsaro

1997: 18). However, in the past, the majority of historians have had little explicit intellectual sympathy for children. Indeed (as will be shown), there are those who doubt that children can have a history; they argue that we can only ever understand childhood as a *cultural* construction. Such a view, if it were correct, would leave real, live children to the ethnographers. This discussion offers a more optimistic prognosis.

My basic premise is twofold: children are social actors and informants in their own right and childhood is a structural feature of all societies; it is not merely the early period of the life course (Hardman 1973; James 1998; Qvortrup et al. 1994). With this in mind, it should be understood that producing the history of children involves far more than the identification and interpretation of sources available for different historical periods. It is also necessary to practise theorizing childhood in order to see the interplay between 'childhood' as a concept and its place in the process of social theory. Of equal importance, if not more so, recognition has to be given to the fact that historians adopt what are in effect ideological positions with respect to age relations involving children. On this point, postmodernists are correct when they claim that historians are not outside the 'ideological fray' (Jenkins 1991: 20). Where history is concerned, then, sources are only one problem among many others. The crucial matter concerns the politics of age relations, which is instructed by adultism (Alanen 1992: 59),[1] meaning, in this regard, a view of children as naturally 'less' than adults in so far as they are in a state of becoming (adults), rather than being seen as complete and identifiable persons. Consequently, in much of the published work to date, children have been denied both a voice and, an essential feature of human identity, a rational standpoint.

The historiographical tradition

It is only since the 1960s that anything like a history of children and childhood has begun to emerge.[2] It was the well-documented publication of Ariès's *Centuries of Childhood* (English translation 1962), and the emergence of the 'new' social history in the late 1960s and early 1970s, that made the study of the family a popular research topic and gave rise to several controversies, some of which involved children. Ariès initiated a debate about childhood, rather than children, claiming that as an idea it was subject to historical change. He was especially interested in the development of the relationship between meanings and relations of childhood and the evolution of the family, arguing that since the seventeenth century the former had become the focus of the latter. For him the crucial influence was the emergence of the school as an age-graded institution, which segregated children from adults while subjecting them to new forms of order and discipline. Ariès's work opened up two main themes: the variability of concepts of childhood and (more implicitly) the experiences of children. Both were firmly placed within, on the one hand, the family and its evolution and, on the other, the relationship between the family and agents in the broader society, such as moralists, pedagogues and philanthropists.

By the 1970s, the family and its children were the focus of much attention. Three studies in particular, although very different from one another in scope and ideology, became standard works (deMause 1976; Shorter 1976; Stone 1977). Together, they served to highlight the fluidity of ideas concerning families, parenthood and childhood, in particular parental attitudes and patterns of childrearing. The 'psychogenic' theory of history (DeMause 1976) claimed that parent–child relations became more liberal and humane as they progressed through a number of modes: infanticidal, abandonment, ambivalence, intrusion, socialization and, currently, helping. Shorter (1976) emphasized the rise of the 'modern' family, paying particular attention to the mother–baby relationship, which he saw as a crucial factor in the move from the traditional to the 'modern' family form. In a famous (or infamous) passage he asserted:

> Good mothering is an invention of modernization. In traditional society, mothers viewed the development and happiness of infants younger than two years with indifference. In modern society, they place the welfare of their small children above all else.
>
> (Shorter 1976: 168)

Stone (1977) focused his attention on middle- and upper-class sections of society in the earlier period (1500–1800), seeing this as a time during which 'affective bonding of the nuclear core at the expense of neighbours and kin', one of the defining features of the modern family, came to set the pace for family relations in general (Stone 1977: 105). The importance of Stone for our purposes is his claim that the parent–child relationship evolved from being 'usually fairly remote' (1450–1630), through 'the great flogging age' (1550–1700), to the more affectionate relationships of the period 1640–1800. Although he infers children's experiences, he is primarily concerned with ideas and attitudes, as are deMause and Shorter. The central thesis of these authors (sometimes known as the 'pessimists' for the bleak picture they paint of pre-modern family life) is that notions of family and of childhood have progressed over time, resulting in more humane treatment of children. (More or less the same conclusion was reached by Plumb 1975; Trumbach 1978; Slater 1984.)

The received orthodoxy of the pessimistic school was challenged in the 1980s by a number of scholars who objected to the historical parent–child relationship being portrayed as one marked by indifference, beatings and insensitivity. Instead, so they argued, it had always witnessed mixed and often conflicting attitudes but, broadly speaking, parents loved their children, grieved at their early deaths and did their best for them (Pollock 1983; Wrightson 1982; MacFarlane 1979, 1984; Houlebrooke 1984). Several of these writers also denied that parent–child relations were characterized by discontinuity (historical change resulting from new ideas, economic developments, social movements, or great turning points such as the Enlightenment and the industrial revolution); they preferred to emphasize continuity: biological determinism, with parents attending to their children's nurturing needs (Pollock 1983; Hanawalt 1993; Shahar 1990; for a perceptive critique, see Lesnik-Oberstein 1998: 8–18; Johansson 1987). Almost alone among the critics, Anderson (1980) accepted the significance of discontinuity, while pointing to what he saw as methodological weaknesses in the research of Stone and Shorter (he refused to discuss the psycho-historical stance of DeMause), especially their lack of attention to economic matters.

Further accounts provided much invaluable detail about children's lives. Paul Thompson's (1975) classic oral history of social change in Edwardian Britain contextualized childhood; Burnett's (1982) edited collection of autobiographies informed us about schooling and wage labour; Dyhouse (1981), a feminist scholar, dealt with the domestic and school life of Edwardian girls; Roberts (1984, 1995), another feminist, looked at childrearing in her oral account of the lives of working-class women; and Walvin, in noting children's 'marginal place in the historians' reconstruction of past time' (Walvin 1982: 11), described the composition of their 'social world'. Other studies included a broad-sweeping history from ancient times to the present (Sommerville 1982); a survey of twentieth-century childhood, based on oral testimonies (Humphries et al. 1988); and a descriptive portrayal of Victorian and Edwardian schoolchildren (Horn 1974, 1989).

From the 1960s, scholars were also beginning to explore the history of welfare services for children. Some of the early findings were decidedly Whiggish (Heywood 1959; Pinchbeck and Hewitt 1969–73), but many were more critical (Pritchard 1963; Middleton 1971; Packman 1981; Behlmer 1982; Dwork 1987; Hendrick 1994). The first Marxist work was Humphries' (1981) important and controversial oral study, which tried to retrieve the experiences of resistance by children and youths in schools and reformatories and on the streets. Humphries theorized the subject through a vigorous use of Marxist revisionism – Gramsci's concept of hegemony – in order to 'penetrate the altruistic rhetoric of the social welfare and school teaching professions' (Humphries 1981: 2). But as his emphasis is on *class* conflict, so the children become figures in a power struggle in which the importance of *age* is obscured.

During the 1990s interest in the history of children and childhood continued to grow and, broadly speaking, publications became more ambitious in scope, as well as more analytical. Cunningham (1991) examined a variety of concepts of childhood in order to show how 'a proper childhood', previously the prerogative of middle-and upper-class children, came to be thought desirable for all children (Cunningham 1991: 1). Similarly, Steedman (1990, 1995) argued for a 'remaking' of working-class childhood in the late nineteenth and early twentieth century and for seeing childhood as an index of adults' concepts of the self. Other scholars tried to focus on the different meanings of childhood and to provide a synthesis of attitudes, practices and social policies from which a wide range of children's experiences might be extrapolated (Hendrick 1990, rev. edn 1997a; Shahar 1990; Rose 1991; Cooter 1992; Hanawalt 1993; Hopkins 1994; Horn 1994; Cunningham 1995; Mahood 1995; Davin 1996; Hendrick 1997b).

Clearly, neither children nor childhood have been ignored by historians. But we have not always been certain as to how to deal with real human beings, as opposed to the anatomical motifs. We are still without a sharp methodological understanding of what constitutes their history and, as has been mentioned, there are those who feel that while a history of childhood as a changing form is possible, that of children, by virtue of their apparent 'silence' as subjects, can never be satisfactorily written. Even so, a number of studies have tried to find a place for the child's voice or, as second best, to imagine the condition of childhood from a position of informed sympathy (Davin 1996; Hanawalt 1993; Walvin 1982; Graff 1995; Rose 1991; Cunningham 1991; Humphries 1981; Hendrick 1994, 1997b).

Sources: Identification and Interpretation

Broadly speaking, sources can be any kind of evidence of the presence of human beings: written words, artefacts, the lay of landscapes, pictorial images or oral testimonies. It was Ranke, the nineteenth-century German historian, who established history as an academic and professional discipline, and who told more than a generation of practitioners that the sources were sacrosanct and that, if properly used, would recreate the past – history could be written so as 'to show how things actually were'. Few contemporary scholars now believe that this is possible. The sanctity of the sources, however, remains inviolate, except for those of certain postmodernist persuasions (Jenkins 1997).

Identification

Put simply, prior to the process of interpretation, a number of sources must be identified; usually a combination will be selected from among, for example, printed parliamentary papers, government papers in the Public Record Office, oral testimonies, school log books, child-rearing manuals, moral and medical treatises, parish registers, memoirs, family correspondence, legal transcripts and the minute books of local and national charities. To a large extent this selection is dictated by the objectives (questions) of the historical inquiry. However, although a wide range of sources may be used, the evidence is not evenly distributed throughout the subject areas. Certain aspects of childhood, such as education, employment and health, are well covered in official sources (both printed and manuscript), at least in several institutional respects. Other aspects, which did not arouse official or philanthropic interest at the time, are more sparse: 'The inner life of the family and its relationships, the extent and meaning of family violence (including sexual abuse), and the children's own views on their lives, on work and school or on childhood itself, are not easy to discover or to generalize about', especially for the period prior to the 1900s, after which oral material becomes available (Davin 1996: 7).

It is obvious that where children are either dimly or not at all recognized as historical actors, historians will have difficulty in finding them in the records, of whatever kind. If children are not immediately visible, then it becomes problematic to ask relevant questions of sources. This is an important consideration because the questions asked not only help to determine the choice of sources, but also affect the way in which they are interpreted. Furthermore, the raw materials are often not identified until questions have been so framed as to make them relevant; alternatively, there are occasions when new questions can be asked of well-known materials, thereby giving them a whole new significance. 'Records', it has been said, are 'like the little children of long ago, they only speak when they are spoken to, and they will not talk to strangers' (Cheney quoted in Tosh 1991: 56). Needless to say, the manner and framing of questions and hence the identification of sources, as well as their subsequent interpretation, is always governed by the historian's ideological and methodological stance. Scholars who deny that children have a voice and or see them only as passive figures against the backdrop of adult life, will fail to ask relevant questions relating to their presence and, therefore, will exclude them from history. Eric Hobsbawm (1997), the influential Marxist historian, has confessed to an 'embarrassed astonishment' that his essay on social history, first published in 1970, 'contained no reference at all to women's history'. At the time, he was not, he admits, 'aware of the gap' (Hobsbawm 1997: 71). We are no longer unaware of children, but there is still some way to go before they are seen and heard.

Whatever the nature of the sources, it is axiomatic among historians that they have to be viewed with a sceptical eye *vis-à-vis* the intentions and prejudices of their authors. Such scepticism is particularly necessary when writing about children since the records at our disposal will in all probability reflect an adultist outlook. Thus, if we are to be honourable practitioners, we need to be conscious of this bias so that the evidence may be interrogated by 'minds trained in a discipline of attentive disbelief' (E.P. Thompson quoted in Tosh 1991: 70). After all, documents can be read in a variety of ways (Evans 1997: 84).

But the problem is not simply one of adultist bias, it is that children are without an authorial voice. Consequently, they have little or no opportunity to contest adult accounts. Of course, it could be argued that other 'minority groups' are at a similar disadvantage where documentary material is involved. However, their *actions* provide a kind of public record – through strikes, uprisings, riots and demonstrations. Moreover, the participants often give their view of events to newspapers, social investigators, charity workers and the courts and in this way provide themselves with an obvious political identity, which facilitates their inclusion in the collective historical memory.

Children are almost never in such a position; depending on their age, they have limited scope for *public* action, being as they are more restricted to the private domain (within the home and among their peers). Only very occasionally – in school strikes, playing games and as 'delinquents' – have children appeared through their *direct* actions in historical accounts (Humphries 1981; Opie and Opie 1984; Mahood 1995).

Since children as *people* experience difficulty in gaining access to the public record, so their perspectives (where they are to be found) are rarely examined. It may well be that their voices will always be muffled to a certain extent, and much of what they said in the past will have to be heard through adult conversations, just as their actions will have to be recorded through association with grown ups. This makes it even more imperative that 'adult' sources be treated as 'witnesses in spite of themselves' (Bloch quoted in Tosh 1991: 34) in order to reveal their 'unwitting testimony' (Marwick 1989).

Interpretation: Objectivity and ethical values

Besides the problem of authorship, there is that of *interpretation*. As Qvortrup has observed: 'the question of objectivity is [acute] because children ... have to leave the interpretation of their own lives to another age group, whose interests are potentially at odds with those of themselves' (Qvortrup quoted in Morrow and Richards 1996: 99). To say 'potentially' probably underestimates the degree to which children's interests are at odds with certain groups of adults, especially those in positions of power: parents, teachers, social workers and medical personnel. However, it is true that among many social scientists the emerging perception of children as social actors has begun to undermine the traditional 'principles of certainty by which people in Western culture "know" that children are natural, universal creatures who, eventually, simply "grow up"' (James et al. 1998: 196). Whether the same awareness is widespread among historians is doubtful.

The issues surrounding interpretation have received some critical discussion (Bellingham 1988; A. Wilson 1979; Jordanova 1990), but more often than not events and relationships have been described from the adult perspective. This is clearly demonstrated in family history with respect to the high child death rate and the general fragility of child life in the eighteenth century, where 'the interpretative energy of most recent historians has been directed more fully at the fears and mourning of their parents than at a comprehensive analysis of the way the children themselves perceived death and accepted the suffering of disease' (Schulz 1985: 69). Shahar, for example, exhorts us to interpret the sources concerning childhood experience and family relationships with 'empathy, a feeling for nuances, and objectivity', and to make a 'deliberate attempt to set aside one's own cultural assumptions' (Shahar 1990: 5; see also S. Wilson 1984). 'We should' she continues, 'endeavour to comprehend what we find unacceptable, or consider physically or emotionally harmful or even cruel, against the background of the character of the society, its weaknesses, and its inner contradictions'. This sounds reasonable, but where it leaves the bodily and emotional integrity of the child is not made clear.

Shahar is by no means alone in expounding this view. With reference to the corporal punishment of the children of the poor, Davin (1996) writes:

> For the particular child, the significance of being beaten probably varied with the context. For some it was a recurrent terror . . . For others it was occasional, more a ritual assertion of continuing adult authority . . . Much would depend on the relationship between adult and child, the spirit in which the beating was given ... and whether the child accepted it as deserved . . . To understand what corporal punishment meant in a particular historical context we may have to hold back our late twentieth-century indignation and rejection of it.
>
> (Davin 1996: 9)

There is some truth in the detail of this assertion, though its logic is flawed: understanding is not necessarily incompatible with either indignation or rejection. Moreover, not only does the sentiment conceal the misery and pain of those who were beaten, but also its implications are alarming for historical judgement where the oppressed and downtrodden are involved.

Similarly, in her critique of 'implicit moral values', Jordanova (1989) distinguishes between those scholars who

> either deny the validity of the evidence or the interpretative procedures applied to it – for example, by appealing to the untypical nature of infanticide – or they can seek other explanations – such as citing the ubiquity of poverty as a cause of harsh treatment of children.
>
> (Jordanova 1989: 80)

Jordanova appears to opt for a third approach, namely, one where historians take 'the phenomena (infanticide, abandonment, murder, labour, and so on), accept their evidence, and then seek to interpret them in terms of the value system of the time' (Jordanova 1989: 8–9). This might be thought adequate if the intention were simply to produce a partial explanation – I say 'partial' because 'the value system of the time' was not one in which children had any part in constructing.

Explanation cannot be separated off from interpretation; however informed and objective it may be, it is ultimately 'a matter of value judgements, moulded to a greater or lesser degree by moral and political attitudes' (Tosh 1991: 144). When Pollock (1983) claimed that 'parents have always tried to do what is best for their children within the context of their culture' (quoted in Horn 1994: 46), she was effectively rebutted by Horn, who wrote: 'To youngsters harshly disciplined . . . it was doubtless small consolation to know that this was taking place within the context of their culture' (Horn 1994: 46). The significant issue is the universalism of the anguish of the oppressed (whatever the differences in its form), not the apparent integrity of cultural relativism. Scholars would do well to have a '(critical) sympathy with the victims . . . and a skepticism about the claims of the victorious' (Barrington Moore quoted in Kaye 1990: 259).

Thus, while it is methodologically correct to examine a culture within its context, an 'objective' historical interpretation must also try to include children's view of the culture (even if it is only an informed assessment of how they *might* have felt). Otherwise, children are denied their standpoint as social actors in the making of history. As the previous section argued, their inclusion necessitates asking a new set of questions. We could do worse than take note of those asked by feminist scholars in pursuit of more egalitarian interpretations of women's past (Scott 1988; Lerner 1997: 119) and by left-wing historians, such as Christopher Hill, E.P. Thompson and colleagues in the History Workshop movement, who went in search of the voices of the people (Samuel 1981).

If the inquiries are made appropriate to children, the answers will almost certainly alter the nature of the interpretation. In respect of parent-child relations, for instance, we would be forced to recognize that 'Not only do family members of different ages have diverse functions, but they also receive unequal rewards. There are differences in power, privilege, and prestige . . . These inequalities can generate age-related dissension' (Foner quoted in Graff 1995: 13).[3] This reminds us that when writing about children, 'culture' has to be seen as 'a field of contention' in which the key words are 'change, experience, conflict and struggle' (Rosaldo in Kaye 1990: 105). Our purpose, as historians, is not simply to describe – however 'objectively' – past cultures, it is to unmask the hidden and apparently 'natural' structures of inequalities that existed (and continue to exist) between adults and children, to show how these affected the latter as historical subjects, to examine their influence on the evolution of age relations and to illustrate their significance for the varying concepts of childhood.

Perhaps the most explicit acknowledgement of children as viewholders has come from Harvey Graff (1995), who draws attention to the exclusion of 'the voices and actions of those growing up'. Usually, he says, historians ignore the fact that 'growing up is hard to do . . . meeting the multiple, contradictory challenges of biology, psychology, culture, and society is never an easy task'. The history of growing up is

> a history of conflicts, of conflicting paths . . . Conflicts exist within the developing self in pursuit of the maturity and competence appropriate to its era and station; the dialectical dance of the generations within and without the family; tradition and change. They confront developing institutions and expectations, as well as class, gender, race, geography, ethnicity, and age itself. They criss-cross and overlay other conflicts that stem from socialization, authority, morality, ideology, and historical circumstances. In personal as in social, cultural, economic, and political terms, growing up is a conflict defined, conflict-ridden, and conflict-bound historical process.
>
> (Graff 1995: 6–7, 11)

We do not have to accept the omnipotence of conflict relations to see that such a view offers numerous possibilities for the identification of children as socially engaged persons in the historical process.

Interpretation: Social relevance and commitment

Any discussion of interpretation sooner or later raises the connected issues of social relevance and commitment. This is not the place to go into the different arguments concerning the uses and abuses of history (for a good general account see Tosh 1991; for a postmodernist discussion see Jenkins 1991; for a critique see Evans 1997), but it is appropriate to note the concern expressed by many historians whenever they come across works which they feel focus upon social relevance. In its extreme form, these scholars see history as being either for its own sake, or 'to make the dead live'. Probably the majority of historians feel that in addition to recreating the past, we must explain it. However, behind the claim of 'scholarly objectivity' and seeing the past in its own terms, there can hide an unwillingness to question conventional beliefs. It is worth remembering that 'history' often legitimizes the coherence of the 'in-group'; it makes distinctions between 'us' and 'them' appear to be 'natural'. No wonder that to those in power, history has always mattered (Lerner 1997: 201–2).

This conservatism was not fully countered until the 1960s with the rise of the new social histories, especially those of the working class, women, blacks, gays and lesbians. The familiar charge made against this kind of 'relevant' or 'oppositional' history is that it risks being distorted and 'propagandist'.[4] In certain circumstances such criticisms may be valid, but they are not necessarily so. As Tosh (1991: 26) has countered: 'Our priorities in the present should determine the questions we ask of the past, but not the answers' (see also Evans 1997: 192–6). Moreover, the issue of relevance is linked to a wider social responsibility. Since all of us are of the past, we are obliged to understand it in relation to contemporary analyses of social, economic and political problems. And, like it or not, to write in this way is to be critical, thereby implying a commitment to social change. In the words of E.P. Thompson:

> as we argue about the past so also we are arguing about – and seeking to clarify the mind of the present which is recovering from the past. Nor is this an unimportant part of the mind of the present. For some of the largest arguments about human rationality, destiny and agency, must always be grounded there: in the historical record.
>
> (E.P. Thompson quoted in Kaye 1990: 264)

It has been said that Thompson wrote 'with continual human reference, affirming certain values over and against others' and that he tried 'to make his readers active valuing agents as they think about history and politics'

(Rediker quoted in Kaye 1990: 264). I hope that it will not come as too much of a shock to colleagues if I suggest that in order to surmount adultism in the historical record, we historians have to become 'valuing agents', engaging ourselves in sifting and sorting moral values. If 'morality is always potentially subversive of class and power' (Walzer quoted in Kaye 1990: 262), so it should be of adultism and power. After all, history without judgement is mere window-gazing at the past.

However, it is also vital to 'develop a detached mode of cognition, a faculty of self-criticism and an ability to understand another person's point of view' (Evans 1997: 252).[5] Nor should the cautionary remarks of Peter Burke, the cultural historian, be overlooked:

> although I consider myself a socialist and a historian, I'm not a socialist historian; that is, I don't believe in socialist history. I believe that to use history as a weapon in political struggle is counter-productive. One comes to believe one's own propaganda, to over-dramatise the past, and hence to forget the real complexity of the issues at any time. One comes to idealise one's own side, and to divide human beings into Us and Them.
>
> (Burke 1981: 8)

Clearly, it is essential that a balance be maintained between appreciating 'the real complexity of the issues' to be found in age relations and in viewing children as conscious social actors in order to give them a voice in the evaluative process. I see no contradiction between having this as an objective while simultaneously striving to 'understand how the past happened as it did' (Burke 1981: 8).

Overcoming the problems

By now it should be clear that the crucial matters relating to children as historical social actors cannot be dealt with through a consideration of the sources alone: methodology and ideology are also central to the task. The difficulties are not confined to history and can be found throughout the social sciences. But there has been a greater willingness to confront them within sociology (and anthropology), particularly in the work of the new social studies of children and childhood, than in other disciplines. This has raised the significance for child studies of one of the principal dichotomies of sociology, namely, structure and agency, and though both are connected through a continuum, there is currently a new emphasis upon agency:

> Whilst recognising variations between children (by gender, class, cultural and other differences), this approach [children as social actors] also recognises that children have a particular view and experience of the social, organisational, material and environmental circumstances of their lives. Children are regarded as a population group whose social

conditions and lives can be compared to other groups. Questions are
asked about children's influence on society as well as its influence on
them – they are not viewed as passive products.

>   (ESRC, 'Children 5–16: Growing into the Twenty-First Century',
>   publicity sheet; see also James et al. 1997: 200–2)

Achieving an historical identity for children

How have other traditionally repressed groups come to possess a proper
historical identity, one that recognizes their participation in 'agency'? We have
seen how the poor and the dispossessed made their presence felt through their
actions (which usually produced a multitude of written records) and how they
have attracted – and continue to attract – sympathetic historians who bring to
their task a highly developed political consciousness, which may be reflected in
active political engagement.[6] This sympathy is usually accompanied by that
crucially important sense of commitment, to which reference has already been
made; this often manifests itself in the search for 'politically useful knowledge'
(Kaye 1990: 263).[7] Consequently, these scholars come to their studies with a
set of critical assumptions and a sense of history regarding their subjects, and
each reinforces and informs the other. There is, then, a kind of theoretical and
empirical basis which not only serves as a departure point, but also exhibits an
awareness of the political and contested nature of the historical undertaking:
while claiming objectivity, the scholarship involved makes little or no pretence
at ideological neutrality. Alas, where children are concerned, critical awareness
has been largely absent as historians have tended to work

> from commonly held assumptions about age relations, without attending
> to the constraints – moral, cultural, and linguistic [and, it should be
> added, 'political'] – on their own frameworks.
>
>   (Jordanova 1989: 7)

The example of feminism

> women [like minority groups] cannot afford to lack a consciousness of
> collective identity, one which necessarily involves a shared awareness of
> the past. Without this, a social group suffers from a kind of collective
> amnesia, which makes it vulnerable to the impositions of dubious
> stereotypes, as well as limiting prejudices about what is right and proper
> for it to do or not to do.
>
>   (S.R. Johannson quoted in Tosh 1991: 8)

In order to continue to develop a complex history of children and childhood,
which is free of adultism, it is instructive to learn from feminist historical
scholarship (Scott 1988, 1996; Scott in Burke 1991; see also Davis in
Scott 1996; Hufton et al. in Gardiner 1988; Lerner 1997). Given that women

'as a social group have suffered a variety of controls and restrictions on their lives which need to be explored historically' (Hannam 1993: 309), feminist scholars are in no doubt about their objective. It is 'to point out and change inequalities between women and men' (Scott 1988: 3). The scale of the enterprise is obvious:

> Inspired . . . by the political agenda of the women's movement, historians have not only documented the lives of average women in various historical periods but they have charted as well changes in the economic, educational, and political positions of women in various classes in city and country and in nation-states.
>
> (Scott 1988: 15; see also Hannam 1993; Gardiner 1988)

It is clear that these historians have looked to confront and change existing distributions of power. Critical analysis of past and present is seen as a 'continuing operation' for 'history can interpret the world while trying to change it' (Scott 1988: 6). The common purpose here is 'to make women a focus of inquiry, a subject of the story, an agent in the narrative', to construct them 'as historical subjects', and this process has 'generated a search for terms of criticism, conceptual reorientations, and theory' which are the preconditions for feminist rewritings of history (Scott 1988: 18). The ultimate purpose of this history is to explain how 'gender hierarchies are constructed, legitimated, challenged, and maintained' (Scott 1988: 3).

In pursuit of this objective, many feminists have drawn upon the notion of sexual difference.[8] Perhaps the most important point here is that 'gender' (meaning knowledge about sexual difference) is the 'social organization' of this difference. But this does not mean that gender simply reflects an existing reality, rather it is 'the knowledge that establishes meanings for bodily differences'. Thus, sexual difference is not 'the originary cause from which social organization ultimately must be derived. It is instead a variable social organization that itself must be explained' (Scott 1988: 2; see also Lerner 1997: 148, 209). As Scott argues, historians who assume 'that women have inherent characteristics and objective identities consistently and predictably different from men's, and that these generate definable female needs and interests' are implying 'that sexual difference is a natural rather than a social phenomenon'. Accordingly, 'the search for an analysis of discrimination gets caught by a circular logic in which "experience" explains gender difference and gender difference explains the asymmetries of male and female "experience"' (Scott 1988: 4). This could hardly be more apposite to children since their 'experience' is conventionally held to explain their childhood, just as their childhood is said to explain their 'childish' experience. It is, of course, really a matter of 'the play of force involved in any society's construction and implementation of meanings', in other words *politics*: 'the process by which plays of power and knowledge constitute identity and experience' (Scott 1988: 4–5).

Although sex and age differences are obviously not directly analogous, there are sufficient similarities to warrant suggesting that 'age' (or 'generation') suffers from the same sort of *naturalist* assumptions of so many historians whose work reinforces and perpetuates the normalization of adult-child power inequalities (the 'naturalness' of which ensures that they go unnoticed). Just as 'history's representations of the past help to construct gender for the present' so they do with respect to 'age' in relation to our notions of children and childhood. 'History' can do this because it is the product of sets of power relationships which define these ideas in accordance with the demands of adult-governed structures. Consequently, analysing how historians construct childhood for the present

> requires attention to the assumptions, practices, and rhetoric of the discipline, to things either so taken for granted or so outside customary practice that they are not usually a focus for historians' attention . . . the notions that history can faithfully document lived reality, that archives are repositories of facts, and that categories like man and woman [children/adult] are transparent. They extend as well to examinations of the rhetorical practices of historians, the construction of historical texts, and the politics – that is, the power relationships – constituted by the discipline.
>
> (Scott 1988: 2–3)

(For the dangers in using 'gender' in a postmodern linguistic analysis, see Evans 1997: 216–17 and Downs 1993: 414–37.)

I do not mean to endorse all of Scott's postmodernist affiliations to 'language' (which she seems to see as constituting social being), but it is important to recognize the interplay between 'history' as a discourse and the ideology of childhood. It is not that the former is the sole influence on the latter (which comprises many component parts), but it *is* involved in the making of childhood; it is not innocent. In writing about children as social actors, we have to remember 'power', 'conflict' and 'contest'. We need a broad understanding of politics, one that sees all 'unequal relationships as somehow "political" because involving unequal distributions of power, and [asks] how they were established, refused, or maintained' (Scott 1988: 26).

Is there an authentic voice of children?

While feminism may be able to offer historians a framework in which they can develop their own methodological and theoretical approaches to the history of childhood, can it do the same for children as social actors? In Jordanova's (1989) opinion we can study 'childhood' through 'the law, medicine, social policy, and so on'. Yet, she says, 'there is something unsatisfactory about studying the history of childhood without any reference to specific historical personages'. Thus historians continue to look for the voice of the child. Such a search, however,

> is based on an illusion about both the nature of childhood and of history. Children . . . are constructed in particular social settings, there can be no

authentic voice of childhood speaking to us from the past because the adult world dominates that of the child. Thus, while we can study particular children, provided suitable materials exist, and examine general ideas about childhood, we cannot capture children's past experiences or responses in a pure form.

(Jordanova 1989: 5)

Jordonova also maintains that we cannot see children as 'other' in the same way as women and workers are so perceived, which is as outside the 'mainstream culture and separate from dominant social groups'. The 'otherness' of women 'is based on the depth of gender which . . . can readily be seen as constitutive of social relations in general'. There is a 'profound gulf' between men and women. Where children are involved, however, 'the otherness we assign . . . is paradoxical in that we have all experienced childhood – hence to make the child other to our adult selves we must split off a part of our past, a piece of ourselves'. And she continues:

it may be that women and workers have simply spoken with the voices of the dominant discourse, although many historians would deny this. Children . . . have inevitably done so, since there is no alternative for them.

(Jordanova 1989: 6)

This is a strange argument: is not the age gulf between children and adults based on a depth of age (or *generation*), which is embedded throughout social relations? Does not this age-depth impinge itself upon the practice of dependences and interdependences? And this reference to 'a piece of ourselves' – what does it mean beyond the implicit appeal to nostalgia? What is the reality, as opposed to the relativity, of the remark? It would seem to forever lock children into *our* experience, thereby further denying them an independent self. Anyway, surely ageism (meaning prejudice and oppression) forcibly separates children from adults, thereby constituting a 'profound gulf' of a kind? Children, then, are as much 'Other' to adults as women are to men, and not least in that their 'Otherness' is defined partly by their bodily differences. James (1993) has noted how height, weight and appearance have been used to create children as 'Othered' in western cultures. True, children are intimidated by a 'dominant discourse', but it does not necessarily follow that they *have* to speak 'with the voices' of this discourse. It is not inevitable: they may speak *through* the discourse, thereby altering it in subtle ways. All dominant discourses contain within them resistant themes. To suggest otherwise is to deny children any potential for their own voices.[9] It refuses the oppressed the agency to impact upon 'power' and, consequently, to make a difference (Kaye 1990: 260).

Sociological theories of age and generation

Notwithstanding Jordanova's pessimism, and in addition to adopting the committed and interrogative stance of feminism, another way of overcoming the obstacles in identifying and interpreting children as social actors in historical sources is for historians to familiarize themselves with a certain amount of sociological theory, in particular theories involving age and power. We could begin by looking at the concept of *ageism* which investigates 'the cultural, political and socio-economic bases of discrimination against people on the basis of age'; and it should not be forgotten that ageism also exacerbates the powerlessness inherent in being oppressed by virtue of social class, gender and race (Franklin and Franklin 1990: 1– 2). Historians writing about children and childhood need to understand not only that power is an expression of a relationship between individuals, but also that power relations tend to become routinized to the extent that opposition between dominant and subordinate persons is limited. As Franklin and Franklin (1990: 5) observe: 'The most effective exercise of power is a quiet affair in which individuals and groups may be ignorant of their subordination'. It is worth keeping this silence in mind when examining relations between teachers and pupils, parents and children and child subjects of social policies.

Besides thinking in terms of ageism, the social theories outlined by Pilcher (1995: 16–30) are also relevant: those of the life course, cohort and generational theory, functionalism and political economy, and interpretive perspectives (including symbolic interactionism and phenomenology). The interpretive perspective, in emphasizing the beliefs and interpretations of social actors, of 'agency' 'rather than the determination of social behaviour by systems of social organisation', has been particularly influential in bringing children to the attention of the new sociology (Alanen 1992; James 1993; James and Prout 1990; James et al. 1998; Jenks 1982b, 1996; Mayall 1994, 1996; Qvortrup et al. 1994; Corsaro 1997).

A sociological approach with enormous potential for advancing historical inquiry is that of Alanen (1992: 59–72; see also Jenks 1982a; James et al. 1998) who, in her exposition of 'generational analytics' via the concept of the 'relational', claims that the ontological questions 'What is a child?' and 'How is the child possible as such?' can be answered if 'the powerful asymmetrical configuration of childhood/adulthood' is seen as 'a general principle of social organization just like gender'. What Alanen (1992) terms this 'generational ordering' functions in the realms of the 'public' and the 'private' for children as 'childhood' orders them into the 'private' world of the home and the family, at each point differentiating them from the economy, politics and adults. This makes visible a 'generational system' which is analogous to 'the gender system . . . a social order composed of, but also constraining and coordinating children's relations in the social world in a systematical way' (Alanen 1992: 65; see also Mayall 1996).

Other helpful perspectives include Hood-Williams's application of Weber's theory of patriarchal authority – 'the probability that a command with a specific content will be obeyed by a given group of persons' – to age-patriarchy in order to explain the structure of adult-child relations (Hood-Williams in Chisholm et al. 1990). Second, Oldman's (1994a, 1994b) identification of 'childhood as a mode of production' and 'adult-child relations as class relations' offers rich but complex possibilities for historical analysis. Oldman argues that children are more than a 'minority group'. He suggests that adults and children be seen 'as constituting *classes*, in the sense of being social categories which exist principally by their *economic* opposition to each other and in the ability of the dominant class (adults) to exploit economically the activities of the subordinate class (children)' (Oldman 1994b: 44). This argument is resonant with opportunities for children's history in areas of parent-child relations, education, welfare and labour. Third, the phenomenological studies of Waksler (1996; see also Dunn 1988; Corsaro 1997; Borland et al. 1998) on children's worlds – 'the hard times of childhood and children's strategies for dealing with them' – are critical in assisting historians to see children as social actors who do indeed have their own 'strategies'.

Those readers with a social-scientific background will probably find much of this rather banal. Historians, however, are not so knowledgeable, and certainly not with regard to social theory in relation to children's lives. None of this is to say that we should uncritically submerge ourselves in social-scientific theory (any more than we should be confined by the relativism of postmodernism). But we do need to understand the insights and issues raised by the new social studies of childhood. An awareness of the 'implicit natural-izing of age' might dissuade historians from accepting the unimaginative 'stages of life' approach in which the differences between one age group and another are seen as an 'unmediated function of developmental change, of progression through the life course, an indication of the benefits (or dangers) of simply becoming older' (James et al. 1998: 174). A more social construc-tionist perspective (without being exclusively so), in which children are seen as social agents, recognizes that they have their own understandings, meanings, intentions, relationships and so on.

Conclusion

If there is one lesson that historians of children should learn from feminists it is that *standpoint* matters. As Alanen (1992) has written, there is no 'Archimedean perspective' or 'God's eye view' 'that is disinterested, impartial, value-free or detached from the particular historical situations in which every-one participates . . . knowledge always contains a perspective from one or another location, a *standpoint* from which the world is known'. As traditional sociology was dominated by men and, therefore, expressed the standpoint of men who ruled, so it responded to questions 'that men wanted answered' and these questions have 'all too often arisen from desires to pacify, control, exploit or manipulate women and to glorify forms of masculinity by understanding women as different from, less than . . . men' (Alanen 1992: 50–1). So it remains for children with respect to the *adultist* historical establishment.

It is important to understand that children neither present themselves, nor are they usually presented by adults, as political figures. Instead, they are seen as *natural* – meaning broadly of limited capabilities and weighed down by more than a measure of irrationality. The absence of a universally recognized political condition for children is crucial in explaining the kind of history to which they have been subjected to date. It influences so many of our assumptions and responses as we identify and interpret the records. Not only does this absence affect the way in which we 'see' children, but also because we rarely listen to them, we often do not hear them *speaking* to us. If this situation is to be rectified, we have to be extraordinarily sensitive to their *standpoint*, rather than those of their parents, school teachers, social workers and others. We need to recognize that throughout the discourse, adult opinions and interests are always dominant; they are the ones which *we* know off by heart. As a consequence of this dominance, children are at an inherent disadvantage when talking to us and when they try to present themselves as self-conscious actors. Only when the mentality of adultism has been overcome will it be possible to hear a more authentic and, probably, unsettling set of voices – because there will certainly be many occasions when children contest and contradict our views.

It hardly needs to be said that if children are to be seen as social actors, they first have to be seen as being *capable* of social action; second, those areas in which children *are* socially active have to be identified, and third, we have to see ourselves as being in a *relationship* with children, rather than simply possessing roles assured by the principle of governance. These recognitions are not currently widespread among historians, the majority of whom probably do not see children as historically active, but rather as, on the one hand, *becomings* who grow into adulthood – thus their existence at any one moment is seen as transitional; and on the other, as objects who can be understood by simply activating images derived from developmental psychology and the sociology of socialization, coupled with a dose of age prejudice. To this extent, personhood is always associated with adulthood. Since children are not adult, they are excluded from sets of understandings as to what is possible and desirable in human relationships. What I mean is that adults do not feel that they have to inquire into the nature of their relationships with children since their understanding of them is that they lack rational capacity. Thus they are easily denied agency and, therefore, disenfranchised as people. This allows adults to put children – subjects of paternalism – outside the definition of personhood.

But this chapter should not conclude on a pessimistic note. At the risk of offending those colleagues who find explicit moral assertions unscholarly and/or embarrassing, were historians to show a greater degree of commitment to children as social beings who are in possession of their own standpoint, rather than simply to perceive their existence through the lens of adultist assumptions, it would be possible to *include* them in what would be a more democratic history, one in which they were allowed to enter into the human marketplace, where all the best bargains are struck.

Notes

1 Alternative terms include 'adult-centric': children are not seen in their own right, but in terms of being socialized into adults, and 'adult chauvinist' (see Pilcher 1995: 31; Alanen 1992: 55).
2 This section is primarily concerned with works that focus on British children and childhood, although a few other accounts are mentioned.
3 It is perhaps significant that in citing an authority for his approach, he refers not to a historian but to Anne Foner, the sociologist, who has written about conflict in family life (see Foner 1978: 347).
4 Another criticism is that present-mindedness rakes through the past for evidence of the present – as Ariès is alleged to have done – that it is anachronistic, rather than simply trying to understand the past on its own terms (see A. Wilson 1979; S. Wilson 1984).
5 For example, the child's point of view.
6 'The recovery of the history of oppressed groups has had far more to do with the desire to expose fundamental structures of inequality in society than with any attempt to bolster political, social, ethnic or gender identities in the present' (Evans 1997: 212–13). This view may be open to question. Probably many historians see themselves as serving both the cause of exposure and the giving of respectful identities to the oppressed.
7 Of course, bearing in mind the remarks of Peter Burke it may be argued that politically useful knowledge is always bad history. There is certainly a risk that this will be the case. Ultimately, however, it depends on the integrity and talent of the historian. On 'Knowledge and Power' see Scott (1988) and Evans (1997: 191–223).
8 If gender is the 'social organization of sexual difference', what is the social organization of age difference? The problem is that there is no comparable term to 'gender'. Sexual difference is fairly straightforward: male-female. Age difference is much less easy to define since there are traditionally at least 'seven ages'. For references to 'generation' as an answer to this problem see Alanen (1992: 64–71).
9 Sociological and anthropological work certainly suggests that children can speak through the dominant discourse (see e.g. James 1993; Waksler 1996). The reference to 'dominant discourse' implies that the real lives of children must always be beyond our reach. But one study claims that wage-earning children were conscious social actors as 'agents operating on the labour market in cooperation with and in opposition to the adults'. These children were not only agents within the world of childhood, but also members of a working-class culture (de Coninck-Smith et al. 1997: 13; see also Davin 1996).

References

Alanen, L. (1992) *Modern Childhood? Exploring the Child Question in Sociology*, Research Report 50, Jyvaskyla, Finland: University of Jyvaskyla.
Anderson, M. (1980) *Approaches to the History of the Western Family, 1500–1900*, London: Macmillan.
Ariès, P. (1962) *Centuries of Childhood: A Social History of Family Life*, New York: Vintage.
Behlmer, G.K. (1982) *Child Abuse and Moral Reform in England, 1870–1908*, Stanford, CA: Stanford University Press.
Bellingham, B. (1988) 'The history of childhood since the "invention of childhood": some issues in the eighties', *Journal of Family History* 13: 347–58.
Borland, M. et al. (1998) *Middle Childhood: The Perspectives of Children and Parents*, London: Jessica Kingsley.
Burke, P. (1981) 'People's history or total history', in R. Samuel (ed.) *People's History and Socialist Theory*, London: Routledge and Kegan Paul.

Burke, P. (ed.) (1991) *New Perspectives on Historical Writing*, Cambridge: Polity.

Burnett, J. (ed.) (1982) *Destiny Obscure: Autobiographies of Childhood, Education and Family from 1820s to the 1920s*, London: Allen Lane.

Chisholm, L. *et al.* (eds) (1990) *Childhood, Youth, and Social Change: A Comparative Perspective*, London: Falmer Press.

Cooter, R. (ed.) (1992) *In the Name of the Child: Health and Welfare, 1880–1940*, London: Routledge.

Corsaro, W.A. (1997) *The Sociology of Childhood*, Thousand Oaks, CA: Pine Forge Press.

Cunningham, H. (1991) *The Children of the Poor: Representations of Childhood since the Seventeenth Century*, Oxford: Blackwell.

Cunningham, H. (1995) *Children and Childhood in Western Society since 1500*. London: Longman.

Davin, A. (1996) *Growing Up Poor: Home School and Street in London, 1870–1918*, London: Rivers Oram Press.

de Coninck-Smith, N., Sandin, B. and Schrumpf, E. (1997) *Industrious Children: Work and Childhood in the Nordic Countries, 1850–1990*, Odense, Denmark: Odense University Press.

DeMause, L. (ed.) (1976) *The History of Childhood*, London: Souvenir.

Downs, L.L. (1993) 'If "Woman" is just an empty category, then why am I afraid to walk alone at night? Identity meets the postmodern subject', *Comparative Studies in Society and History* 35: 414–37.

Dunn, J. (1988) *The Beginnings of Social Understanding*, Oxford: Blackwell.

Dwork, D. (1987) *War is Good for Babies and Other Young Children: A History of the Infant and Child Welfare Movement in England, 1898–1918*, London: Tavistock.

Dyhouse, C. (1981) *Girls Growing Up in Late Victorian and Edwardian England*, London: Routledge and Kegan Paul.

Evans, R.J. (1997) *In Defence of History*, London: Granta.

Foner, A. (1978) 'Age stratification and the changing family', in J. Demos and S. Spence Bocock (eds) *Turning Points: Historical and Sociological Essays on the Family*, Chicago: University of Chicago Press.

Franklin, B. and Franklin, A. (1990) 'Age and power', in T. and M. Smith (eds) *Young People, Inequality and Youth Work*, London: Macmillan.

Gardiner, J. (ed.) (1988) *What is History?*, London: Macmillan.

Graff, H. (1995) *Conflicting Paths: Growing Up in America*, Cambridge, MA: Harvard University Press.

Hanawalt, B. (1993) *Growing Up in Medieval London*, Oxford: Oxford University Press.

Hannam, J. (1993) 'Women, history and protest', in V. Robinson and D. Richardson (eds) *Introducing Women's Studies*, London: Macmillan.

Hardman, C. (1973) 'Can there be an anthropology of childhood?', *Journal of the Anthropological Society of Oxford* 4(1): 85–99.

Henderson, J. and Wall, R. (eds) (1994) *Poor Women and Children in the European Past*, London: Routledge.

Hendrick, H. (1994) *Child Welfare, England, 1872–1989*, London: Routledge.

Hendrick, H. ([1990] 1997a) 'Constructions and reconstructions of British childhood: an interpretative survey, 1800 to the present', in A. James and A. Prout (eds) *Constructing and Reconstructing Childhood: Contemporary Issues in the Sociological Study of Childhood*, rev. edn, London: Falmer Press.

Hendrick, H. (1997b) *Children, Childhood and English Society, 1880–1990*, Cambridge: Cambridge University Press.

Heywood, J. (1959) *Children in Care: The Development of Services for the Deprived Child*, London: Routledge and Kegan Paul.

Hobsbawm, E. (1997) *On History*, London: Weidenfeld and Nicolson.

Hopkins, E. (1994) *Childhood Transformed: Working-Class Children in Nineteenth-century England*, Manchester: Manchester University Press.

Horn, P. (1974) *The Victorian Country Child*, Kineton: Roundwood Press.

Horn, P. (1989) *The Victorian and Edwardian Schoolchild*, Gloucester: Alan Sutton.

Horn, P. (1994) *Children's Work and Welfare, 1780–1880*, Cambridge: Cambridge University Press.

Houlebrooke, R. (1984) *The English Family*, London: Longman.

Humphries, S. (1981) *Hooligans or Rebels? An Oral History of Working-Class Childhood and Youth*, Oxford: Blackwell.

Humphries, S., Mack, J. and Perks, R. (1988) *A Century of Childhood*, London: Sidgwick and Jackson.

James, A. (1993) *Childhood Identities: Self and Social Relationships in the Experience of the Child*, Edinburgh: Edinburgh University Press.

James, A. (1998) 'From the child's point of view: issues in the social construction of childhood', in C. Panter-Brick (ed.) *Biosocial Perspectives on Children*, Cambridge: Cambridge University Press.

James, A., Jenks, C. and Prout, A. (1998) *Theorising Childhood*, Cambridge: Polity.

James, A. and Prout, A. (1990) 'A new paradigm for the sociology of childhood? Provenance, promise and problems', in A. James and A. Prout (eds) *Constructing and Reconstructing Childhood: Contemporary Issues in the Sociological Study of Childhood*, London: Falmer Press.

Jenkins, K. (1991) *Re-Thinking History*, London: Routledge.

Jenkins, K. (ed.) (1997) *Postmodern History Reader*, London: Routledge.

Jenks, C. (1982a) 'Constructing the child', in C. Jenks (ed.) *The Sociology of Childhood: Essential Readings*, London: Batsford Academic.

Jenks, C. (ed.) (1982b) *The Sociology of Childhood: Essential Readings*, London: Batsford Academic.

Jenks, C. (1996) *Childhood*, London: Routledge.

Johansson, S.R. (1987) 'Centuries of childhood/centuries of parenting: Philippe Ariès and the modernization of privileged infancy', *Journal of Family History* 12: 343–65.

Jordanova, L. (1989) 'Children in history: concepts of nature and society', in G. Scarre (ed.) *Children, Parents and Politics*, Cambridge: Cambridge University Press.

Jordanova, L. (1990) 'New worlds for children in the eighteenth century: problems of historical interpretation', *History of the Human Sciences* 3: 69–83.

Kaye, H.J. (1990) 'E.P. Thompson, the British Marxist historical tradition and the contemporary crisis', in H.J. Kaye and K. McClelland (eds) *E.P. Thompson: Critical Perspectives*, Cambridge: Polity.

Lerner, G. (1997) *Why History Matters*, New York: Oxford University Press.

Lesnik-Oberstein, K. (1998) 'Childhood and textuality: culture, history, literature', in K. Lesnik-Oberstein (ed.) *Children in Culture*, London: Macmillan.

Levine, R.A. (1998) 'Child psychology and anthropology: an environmental view', in C. Panter-Brick (ed.) *Biosocial Perspectives on Children*, Cambridge: Cambridge University Press.

MacFarlane, A. (1979) 'The family, sex and marriage in England, 1500–1800 by Lawrence Stone', *History and Theory* 18: 103–26.

MacFarlane, A. (1984) *Marriage and Love in England, 1300–1840*, London: Routledge and Kegan Paul.

Magnusson, S.G. (1995) 'From children's point of view: childhood in nineteenth-century Iceland', *Journal of Social History* 29(2): 295–324.

Mahood, L. (1995) *Policing, Gender, Class and Family: Britain 1850–1940*, London: UCL Press.

Marwick, A. (1989) *The Nature of History*, London: Macmillan.

Mayall, B. (ed.) (1994) *Children's Childhoods Observed and Experienced*, London: Falmer Press.

Mayall, B. (1996) *Children, Health and the Social Order*, Buckingham: Open University Press.

Middleton, N. (1971) *When Family Failed*, London: Gollancz.

Morrow, V. and Richards, M. (1996) 'The ethics of social research with children: an overview', *Children and Society* 10(2): 90–105.

Oldman, D. (1994a) 'Childhood as a mode of production', in B. Mayall (ed.) *Children's Childhoods Observed and Experienced*, London: Falmer Press.

Oldman, D. (1994b) 'Adult-child relations as class relations', in J. Qvortrup *et al.* (eds) *Child Matters: Social Theory, Practice and Politics*, Aldershot: Avebury.

Opie, I. and Opie, P. (eds) (1984) *Children's Games in Street and Playground*, Oxford: Oxford University Press.

Packman, J. (1981) *The Child's Generation: Child Care Policy from Curtis to Houghton*, 2nd edn, Oxford: Blackwell.

Pilcher, J. (1995) *Age and Generation in Modern Britain*, Oxford: Oxford University Press.

Pinchbeck, I. and Hewitt, M. (1969–73) *Children in English Society*, 2 vols, London: Routledge and Kegan Paul.

Plumb, J.H. (1975) 'The new world of children in eighteenth-century England', *Past and Present* 67: 64–93.

Pollock, L. (1983) *Forgotten Children: Parent-Child Relations from 1500 to 1900*, Cambridge: Cambridge University Press.

Pritchard, D.G. (1963) *Education and the Handicapped, 1760–1960*, London: Routledge and Kegan Paul.

Qvortrup, J., Bardy, M., Sgritta, S. and Wintersberger, H. (eds) (1994) *Childhood Matters: Social Theory, Practice, Politics*, Aldershot: Avebury.

Roberts, E. (1984) *A Woman's Place: An Oral History of Working-Class Women, 1890– 1940*, Oxford: Blackwell.

Roberts, E. (1995) *Women and Families: An Oral History, 1940–1970*, Oxford: Blackwell.

Rosaldo, R. (1990) 'Celebrating Thompson's heroes: social analysis in history and anthropology', in H. Kaye and K. McClelland (eds) *E.P. Thompson, Critical Perspectives*, Cambridge: Polity.

Rose, L. (1991) *The Erosion of Childhood: Child Oppression in Britain, 1860–1918*, London: Routledge.

Samuel, R. (ed.) (1981) *People's History and Socialist Theory*, London: Routledge and Kegan Paul.

Schulz, C.B. (1985) 'Children and childhood in the eighteenth century', in J.M. Hawes and N.R. Hiner (eds) *American Childhood: A Research Guide and Historical Handbook*, Westport, CT: Greenwood. Scott, J.W. (1988) *Gender and the Politics of History*, New York: Columbia University Press.

Scott, J.W. (1996) *Feminism and History*, Oxford: Oxford University Press.

Shahar, S. (1990) *Childhood in the Middle Ages*, London: Routledge.

Shorter, E. (1976) *The Making of the Modern Family*, London: Collins.

Slater, M. (1984) *Family Life in the Seventeenth Century*, London: Routledge and Kegan Paul.

Sommerville, J. (1982) *The Rise and Fall of Childhood*, London: Sage.

Steedman, C. (1990) *Childhood, Culture and Class in Britain: Margaret McMillan, 1860–1931*, London: Virago.

Steedman, C. (1995) *Strange Dislocations: Childhood and the Idea of Human Inferiority, 1780–1930*, London: Virago.

Stone, L. (1977) *The Family, Sex and Marriage in England, 1500–1800*, London: Weidenfeld and Nicolson.

Thompson, P. (1975) *The Edwardians: The Remaking of British Society*, London: Weidenfeld and Nicolson.

Tosh, J. (ed.) (1991) *The Pursuit of History*, London: Longman.

Trumbach, R. (1978) *The Rise of the Egalitarian Family*, London: Academic Press.

Waksler, F.C. (1996) *The Little Trials of Childhood and Children's Strategies for Dealing with Them*, London: Falmer Press.

Walvin, J. (1982) *A Child's World: A Social History of English Childhood, 1800–1914*, Harmondsworth: Penguin.

Wilson, A. (1979) 'The infancy of the history of childhood: an appraisal of Philippe Ariès', *History and Theory* 18: 103–26.

Wilson, S. (1984) 'The myth of motherhood: the historical view of European child-rearing', *Social History* 9: 181–98.

Wrightson, K. (1982) *English Society, 1580–1680*, London: Hutchinson.

Postscript

Raising the ethical dimension in writing the history of childhood and children

By 'ethics' I mean morality in the sense of dealing with values, with the practices of right and wrong, good and bad: 'We cannot avoid involvement in ethics, for what we do – and what we don't do – is always a subject of possible ethical evaluation' (Singer 1993: v. See also LaFollette 2003: 1–11). Broadly speaking, however, historians do not appear to have given much thought to the place of 'ethics' in writing the history of either childhood or children. This might seem surprising at first glance, but given the apparent resistance of many historians to varieties of social theory (e.g. postmodernism), their relative indifference to the paradigmatic frame of 'age relations', and the seeming reluctance to look beyond traditional 'historical' sources (in this case, to the 'new' social studies of childhood), then ignorance of social scientific and philosophical writings on ethics is probably only to be expected.

Of course, unlike historians, social scientists face fewer methodological obstacles in prioritizing 'moral principles and rules of conduct' (Morrow and Richards 1996: 90) with regard to their research subjects. Moreover, only recently have professional bodies become sensitive to the ethical issues involved in conducting research *with* children (as opposed to 'on' them), such as consent, confidentiality and collaboration, and many organizations are still without child-centred research guidelines (Wyness 2006: 194–99). What is particularly important, however, is that in their communication with children 'in the present' contemporary researchers (certainly those doing ethnographic studies), who are increasingly obliged to obtain consent from their subjects, meet the children as 'real people' (not as unseen historical personages), and their relationship with them is one that allows for the interrogation of adult suppositions, interpretations and conclusions.

Clearly, in composing the history of childhood and children, the creative tension between author and subject is completely different from that found in the social sciences. In labouring alone, the historian is not compelled to engage with the 'humanness' of children in the past who, unlike their modern counterparts, as noted above, can neither question the ageist assumptions of the scholar nor, equally important, those *reflected* in the sources (keeping in mind the deceitful nature of reflections as they *appear* to be natural and true). These 'ways of seeing', characterized by ambiguity and ambivalence, generally regard children as vulnerable, incompetent, undisciplined, ignorant, unreliable, annoying and innocent. Accordingly, when faced with child subjects, historians often lack 'objectivity' coming as they do laden with what is an unconscious baggage of feelings and impulses which, as this chapter has argued, so often result in a failure to *see* that children have a standpoint and to *hear* their voices (which are usually muffled and indistinct). Consequently, historians are inclined to simplify the structure and subjectivity of individual child/adult relations and, therefore, not only misunderstand their nature, but also fail to see their significance in being constitutive of the age relationship itself.

What, then, of ethics for historians of childhood and children? We could begin by owning up to our personal opinions. Writing ethically requires us to 'de-centre' ourselves not merely in the sense of the words we use, but with respect to a kind of 'self-reflexivity' or 'self-monitoring'/'self-confrontation' (Beck et al. 2003: 5, 115–16). As Gramsci wrote: 'The starting point of critical elaboration is the consciousness of what one really is, and "knowing thyself" as a product of the historical process to date, which has deposited in you an affinity of traces, without leaving an inventory ... (therefore) it is imperative at the outset to compile such an inventory' (quoted in Brown 2005: 132–33).

Second, where the author/subject relationship is concerned, we should recognize the particular power of the author to silence the child subject in a number of ways, notably by ignoring children's perspectives but also, indirectly (and perhaps unconsciously), by subverting their standpoint in preference to adult interests, as was the case with much of the family history of the 1970s and 1980s – a practice that remains evident in several recent texts. Put simply, an ethical approach means acknowledging our authorial responsibilities in order to guard against creating tokenistic children, just as in the last half century, guided by a sympathy with 'history from below', we have learned to do with other previously ignored, neglected and repressed historical subjects (Macraild and Taylor 2004: 118–30).

Third, as part of our responsibility to children (ethically speaking), we should become better informed about their worlds, which means reading outside conventional 'historical' sources, acquainting ourselves with developmental psychology, cultural anthropology, social geography and, not least, theoretical, empirical and comparative sociological studies. The purpose here is not merely to extend our range of references in some pretentious manner, but to fulfil an 'ethical' obligation to prepare ourselves intellectually for the task of providing children with a just historical validity. Unfortunately, many historians do not feel the need to 'know' children (as they would were they writing about gender, ethnicity, gay/lesbian culture or working class lives). Instead, they rely on limited personal relationships, popular partialities and, that most treacherous of allies, diffused memory.

Fourth, we need to consider the controversial matter of historical 'objectivity'/'subjectivity' as it influences our moral position (Brown 2005; Evans 1997; Jenkins 1999; Marwick 2001). Regardless of where we stand in the debate (somewhere between brute empiricist and ardent postmodernist), the perception of children in history urgently requires to be theorized. Indeed, we have to *think* much more carefully about the viability of the *concept* of the history of children (not forgetting the philosophical distinction between 'concept' and 'conceptions'). Wherever we begin in the process, 'objectivity'/'subjectivity' and their environmental neighbours – neutrality, certainty, reliability, truth, relativism and commitment – will have to be clarified if the ethical quality of historical writing is to be improved. The essential issue is not so much *how* we clarify this galaxy of problematics, but rather that we recognize and understand the nature of the bond between our ethical stance and the obligation to our subjects. Writing the history of children poses particularly acute problems in this respect, for in their power-lessness, their *apparent* silence and their enforced distance from us, they are the 'absent referent', the archetypal 'Other' – and yet not entirely, for they are who once we were, but no longer quite know.

References

Beck, U., Giddens, A. and Lasch, S. (2003) *Reflexive Modernization,* Cambridge: Polity Press.

Brown, C.G. (2005) *Postmodernism for Historians*, Harlow: Pearson Education.

Evans, R.J. (1997) *In Defence of History*, London: Granta Books.

Jenkins, K. (1999) *Why History? Ethics and Postmodernity*, London: Routledge.

LaFollette, H. (ed.) (2003) *The Oxford Handbook of Practical Ethics*, Oxford: OUP.

Macraild, D.M. and Taylor, A. (2004) *Social Theory and Social History*, Basingstoke: Palgrave Macmillan.

Marwick, A. (2001) *The New Nature of History*, Basingstoke: Palgrave.

Morrow, V. and Richards, M. (1996) 'The ethics of social research with children and young people – an overview', *Children & Society* 10 (2): 90–105.

Singer, P. (ed.) (1993) *A Companion to Ethics*, Oxford: Blackwell.

Wyness, M. (2006) *Childhood and Society*, Basingstoke: Palgrave Macmillan.

3 Macroanalysis of Childhood

Jens Qvortrup

> When I look back on my childhood I wonder how I survived at all. It was, of course, a miserable childhood: the happy childhood is hardly worth your while. Worse than the ordinary miserable childhood is the miserable Irish childhood, and worse yet is the miserable Irish Catholic childhood. People everywhere brag and whimper about the woes of their early years, but nothing can compare with the Irish version: the poverty; the shiftless loquacious alcoholic father; the pious defeated mother moaning by the fire; the English and the terrible things they did to us for eight hundred long years. Above all – we were wet.
>
> (McCourt 1997: 9)

Introduction

What Frank McCourt is saying on the very first page of *Angela's Ashes* is that Irish childhood was a wet childhood. He was probably wrong. I feel pretty sure that many sociologists and anthropologists would immediately present to him a sample of children who were not wet, only half wet, or merely wet during the night. Yet, McCourt gives us an impression of Irish childhood, which is quintessentially real: its Irish-ness, its Catholic-ness, miserable-ness, and above all, its wet-ness. Although not applicable for each and every child in Ireland, it conveys a picture which Irish children at the time could recognize and which justified talking – as McCourt does – about an Irish version of childhood. This Irish version achieved its distinction in comparison with what childhood was like in other countries; no one other childhood possessed the features which brought about the Irish childhood. Did one find a wet childhood elsewhere? If so, not one that was Catholic and wet, and for sure not Irish and Catholic and wet. Though McCourt did not think of it, he is actually using a particular method for coming to terms with his childhood, indirectly comparing it with other (national or cultural) childhoods so as to make it as distinct as possible.

His methods, if one may use such a clinical term, for coming to this insight, probably come close to the comparative method of analysis. We would not have become wiser if he had not had the courage to generalize his insight.

No one – besides himself and his many siblings – had such a childhood, but nevertheless he dared to abstract from these particularities to reach his conclusion about a miserable childhood which was Irish, Catholic and above all – wet; had he pondered upon his childhood's particularity his book would still have been entertaining and moving, but we would not have been as wise.

It is sometimes suggested by researchers that it is dangerous to generalize, because we lose information; this is indeed true, but, I would suggest, losing information in a controlled way is the very idea of research. It was never the task of researchers to tell everything they knew; on the contrary, the task was always to sort out the most important features and findings, and one crucial criterion is to meet the demand for commonality. If this is not met, one fails to be able to classify – and what cannot be classified according to selected research problems, we should leave on our shelves as impressionistic memories.

Generalized insight presupposes causal factors; McCourt is – perhaps unwittingly – giving us them as well: nationality, religion, alcoholism, poverty, history and geo-politics – perhaps even pious defeated mothers. These were the factors that constructed Irish childhood. They have not been subjected to scientific scrutiny, and researchers might have chosen others, but this is not the point. The point is, once again, the method, which in principle is a correct one. Researchers must look for boundaries within which similarities are exceeding differences and, through that, locate those parameters which have explanatory value.

From my vantage point, as one with experience of a large-scale international and comparative project – Childhood as a Social Phenomenon – the trend in the paradigm for the social studies of childhood seems, however, to have been drifting towards a micro-orientation[1] following Prout and James' recommendation that

> Ethnography is a particularly useful methodology for the study of childhood. It allows children a more direct voice and participation in the production of sociological data than is usually possible through experimental or survey styles of research.
>
> (Prout and James 1990: 8-9 and unchanged in
> Prout and James 1997: 8).[2]

This is, indeed, an important methodology, provided one has the courage to generalise from the cases collected; to this end we need as many cases with as much information as possible. I am however more reluctant to accept their thesis if any prioritizing of methodologies is intended for there are many ways of collecting information about children's lives and childhood. No one method alone can produce all knowledge needed. In fact, much of the insight we have about children we have from sources in which children of flesh and blood are conspicuously distant, such as statistics collected at an aggregate level. Moreover, we are often forced to make inferences from knowledge about apparently childhood-alien topics in order to learn about children's life worlds. This is mostly the case when we are mapping the life conditions of adults or political, economic, social and cultural realms in general. These are the realms, I suggest, which more than any others are forming and forging childhood in any given national or cultural context; they are largely independent variables as far as childhood is concerned, but are due themselves to variation in an historical or intercultural comparative perspective.

I do not find it particularly useful to argue about the preponderance of either material or cultural factors; at the end of the day, both are structural factors, the former unequivocally so, the latter will enjoy the same status as they eventually achieve hegemonic influence, and both are subjected to secular changes. Which are the more or less influential in contributing to the architecture of childhood, nobody knows. The point is that no child can evade the impact of economic or spatial forces, nor ideologies about children and the family – let alone political and economic ideologies and realities (see Davis, Watson and Cunningham-Burley, this volume). Discussions of either structure or agency seem similarly abortive. Children are of course actors in a diversity of arenas, even where this is not visible to the ethnographic gaze; yet, they are born into economic and cultural circumstances which cannot be explained away. The overwhelming majority of Irish children – to refer for a last time to McCourt – could not help being impacted by religion and poverty and nationality, the latter imprinted by century-long traumatic experiences with a mighty neighbouring nation, whose children, *grosso modo*, obviously had other experiences.

The purpose of this chapter is therefore to explore the variability of child-hood as a macro-phenomenon. As such, childhood is a variable, the contours of which are determined by an ensemble of parameters pertaining to a given society or any other macro-units 'defined as all those units the majority of whose *consequences* affect one or more societies, their combinations, or their sub-units' (Etzioni 1968: 49; my italics). This ensemble of parameters is what John Stuart Mill (1950: 211) in his comparative methodology calls an *instance* within which the *phenomenon* – e.g. childhood – does or does not occur, or according to which it assumes more or less distinct values compared with other instances. While taking a dialectical relationship between instances and phenomena for granted, it is assumed that the 'instance' stands in a supra-sub relationship to the 'phenomenon' – that, in other words, we are dealing with a hierarchical relationship, theoretically speaking (Qvortrup 1989: 19).

What *is* important for macroanalysis, thus, is to look for strong explanatory instances; society, mode of production, culture, or – more vaguely – historical periods are such instances, while the phenomenon may be any kind of sub-unit *vis-à-vis* this instance. As abstractions (a necessary ingredient of comparative methodology), they are too crude to explain everything, but they do empirically influence phenomena such as education, wealth, health, housing, institutional-ization, urbanization.[3] The instances mentioned are explanatory strong in that they enable us to make predictions with a high degree of certainty; as supra-units they impose on their sub-units limits which can only at pains be transgressed by individuals. Industrialization, for example, has formed a new architecture of life conditions compared with the general life circumstances preceding it; it has influenced not merely the most basic survival phenomena and indicators, but a whole framework of life.

There is no doubt that such variables – whatever their weight relative to each other – have played a part historically in producing the kind of society we know in the Western world today. Basically, these variables have only exceptionally been invented or developed with any view to producing childhood in any society; indeed, children themselves were hardly allotted a role as agents in inaugurating modernity, although to some extent they have been the objects of thoughts and plans and instrumentalized for safeguarding the wealth and prosperity of these countries' futures (de Lone 1979) or for embodying parents' own pasts and futures (Jenks 1996: 97ff.; Beck 1986: 193). Finally, the interaction of any variables, which were brought into play, has not infrequently produced unintended consequences as powerful as those which have been planned for.

However, which of the *instances* or elements of modernity has been most influential in changing the *phenomenon* of childhood historically is of less importance for my argument than the assumption that it has been historically altered and formed in accordance with the demands of prevailing instances. Ariès' (1962) proposition that childhood was a cultural invention is important in the sense that it suggests a non-incidental modality in the shape of childhood due to the changing requirements of society. The importance of his study was its ability to make intelligible a historical change in both the architecture of and the attitudes towards childhood, while rendering its diversification due to time and place relatively immaterial. Thus he seems to concur with Bloch's methodological statement that 'the unity of place is only disorder; only the unity of problem makes a center' (Bloch 1934: 81; translated and quoted in Skocpol 1994: 89).

Of the numerous possibilities to demonstrate the power of macro-conditions in producing childhoods and thus children's life worlds, I shall select merely three, which necessarily involve comparisons, (i) historically and inter-culturally, (ii) between countries, and (iii) between generations. The latter differs from the former two in that it applies most conveniently (although not by way of principle) to intra-societal relations.

Historical and intercultural comparisons: the variability of childhood

In their important discussion of whether childhood researchers should focus on one or several/many childhoods, James et al. (1998) in their influential book rightly draw our attention to differences between countries with large variations in their scores on a number of basic survival indicators. Despite the fact that the figures they quote are eye-catching in their *systematic* variations between countries, they conclude, that 'in sum, what these accounts point to is that it is quite misleading to think about childhood in the developing world as homogeneous' (1998: 130). They support this conclusion with a number of facts which actually do demonstrate many differences between children within and between the developing as well as industrial countries, and one could easily add many more in support of their conclusion. Yet, I wonder if their conclusion is one which I would have drawn. My reason for not wanting to do so is that I would, by that, increase the risk for overlooking the reality and systematic influence of such large socio-economic factors, which presumably account for fundamental variations of everybody's life worlds and thus also those of children.

The sources cited by the authors actually do show significant variation to an extent that it recommends the conclusion that childhoods differ systematically, depending on socio-economic development. In Table 3.1, I quote the most recent figures from UNICEF, while at the same time presenting them with a slightly different categorization (compare James et al. 1998, Table 1, p. 129, in which the figures are grouped according to four levels of under-5 mortality rates [very high, high, medium, and low].

The assumption that children's life conditions and prospects first and foremost depend on the level of socio-economic development does not deny a diversity of children's life worlds; neither does it deny that there are both rich and poor children in each and every country. This being so, one could hypothesize that children of rich parents – wherever they live – may have more in common with each other than with poor children in their own country. This hypothesis may be attractive, but is hardly tenable. Although there is no guarantee, to say the least, that inequality disappears as nations become richer, I would suggest, first, that the *likelihood* that children will come to lead a more prosperous life – measured in absolute terms – is unquestionably higher if they live in an industrial rather than a developing, not to say a least developed nation; second, the inequality is qualitatively different given the fact that it is situated in dramatically different environments or 'opportunity spaces'[4] (Zeiher and Zeiher 1994: 86). In other words, the level of societal

Table 3.1 – UNICEF basic indices for children grouped according to level of development 2005

	Under-5 mortality rate (annual deaths per 1,000 live births)	Infant mortality rate (annual deaths under 1 year per 1,000 live births)	Life expectancy at birth (years)	% of population below 1 $ a day (most recent data 1994–2004)
Industrialized countries	6	5	79	no data
Developing countries	83	57	65	22
Least developed countries	153	97	53	41

Source: UNICEF, 2007: 105, 129.

development has importance for the welfare and well-being of people in general, inclusive of children.[5]

What I am arguing, therefore, is that although the degree of socio-economic development is far from being a sufficient factor for explaining or predicting children's life conditions in any detail, it nevertheless has a great deal of explanatory value in accounting for the general level of living and for determining, by and large, childhood as a historically and culturally variable social form. If, in other words, a country – according to its gross national product (GNP) – is industrialized, we can be pretty sure that most of its children score high on a number of other indicators, which we normally accept as positive for children.

When James, Jenks and Prout in another summary write that '... it is the *specificity* of childhoods which emerges as a predominant theme through comparative analysis' (1998: 132, my italics), this statement is likely to be valid merely if small and specific units are compared – such as families within a homogeneous context. If we avail ourselves of macro-units in our comparative analysis it will, in all likelihood, be the *generality* of childhoods which emerges as a predominant theme. As soon as we make efforts to discriminate by means of larger and more encompassing *instances*, such as mode of production, modernity, industrialization, or merely a nation, we will be producing *similarities of phenomena within each of these instances*, because they exert dominant influence on the overall life of the peoples living within their orbit. At the same time we are creating *systematic differences of phenomena between the instances*, which will distinguish themselves *vis-à-vis* another. Indeed, one important insight accruing from comparative research is that specificities are waning to the advantage of more general characteristics; the more we specify our variables, the less able we are to arrive at common denominators and the more we jeopardize comparative results.

The important question therefore is: at which level is one permitted to talk about there being a childhood? If one cannot talk about British childhood, can one talk about a London childhood – a Chelsea childhood, a working class childhood? If one would allow merely individual childhoods to be spoken of, one would at the same time deem quite a number of parameters superfluous, because they do not discriminate between these individual childhoods. My point is that although macro instances such as modernity are likely to lack sufficient discriminatory power in explaining differences between British childhoods, they do by the same token work as instances enabling us to discriminate between British childhood and, say, Nigerian childhood. Herein lies exactly the power of comparative analyses: without such comparisons we would have to discard modernity as a parameter, which makes a difference both historically and inter-culturally.

As a matter of fact, it is quite popular to talk about modernity; indeed, even 'modern childhood' is not an uncommon phrase. This usage presupposes generality and commonness in childhood, although some uneasiness may be aired. There seems to be much less reflection, however, as we talk about pre-industrial childhood, although this was diversified and thus ostensibly unwarranted to speak of in the singular (see Hendrick, this volume). Provided one is able to specify the instances 'modernity' and 'pre-modernity' (or industrialism and pre-industrialism), it is not only permitted to talk in such general terms, it is, I would suggest, also necessary.

Many historians have made the historicity of childhood a plausible claim. Although most of them are giving accounts of childhood and its variation in a given historical period, the underlying assumption is more or less implicitly that historical childhood differs from modern childhood (and for that matter future childhood). Apart from obvious changes in terms of industrialization, urbanization, secularization and individualization, which in themselves and in conjunction have changed completely the 'opportunity spaces' for each and every child – although admittedly to varying degrees – at least the following propositions appear to be valid for changes in the social forms of childhood specifically over the last century: (1) childhood has in numerical terms become relatively much smaller – i.e. children have become relatively fewer due to a declining birth rate and a longer life expectancy; (2) childhood has become less stable due to an increase of family forms; (3) childhood has become more and more institutionalized and organized; (4) children are more exposed to the risk of becoming relatively poor; and (5) children's chances of obtaining subject or individual status have increased (see Wintersberger 1997).

The relativity of these propositions refers to their historicity, i.e. comparisons are made with childhood in previous eras. None of them can be seen as independent from the others; they are closely connected with each other as they are all a result of the secular changes which our societies have undergone. Hardly any childhood is unaffected by these changes, and, moreover, current childhood (plural or singular) is impacted by these developments in the same direction. Thus, due to this overall tendency – this massive societal construction of modern childhood – there are good reasons to suggest that, historically, we are dealing with two different social forms of childhood. Although, as I have said, this does not imply that these two forms of childhood might not at a lower level of generality consist of a plethora of (local and/or individual) childhoods. First, none of them will, as a general rule, contradict the prevailing mode of production; rather, all of them are subsumed under their respective supra-unit (in Britain one would hardly find anything like a late nineteenth-century childhood in the late twentieth century). Second, what is important is that we cannot do without the explanatory parameters at the societal level, (a) if we want to understand the modalities of the secular changes, and (b) if we want to understand what major forces account for childhood's common features presently. The latter point may be more important than the former, because the risk we are running at present, if we restrict our efforts to merely accounting for children's particular lives, is to underline an assumption that there is little that is common to the many childhoods which have been so admirably detailed; a further, but more fateful corollary, is that we risk being left ignorant or oblivious of variables that are strategic for changing the life worlds for all or any age group of children.

Since the five propositions mentioned are very broad, let me focus on some aspects which are closer to the everyday life of children. In German childhood research, which unfortunately is not well known in the English-speaking world, two concepts have been of importance in characterizing the influence of modernity on childhood, namely *domestication* (Verhäuslichung) and *insularization* (Verinselung). Both these concepts are related to children's space; *domestication* refers to the observation that, historically, there has been a general trend towards having children removed from streets and other open areas and their being confined to limited spaces protected by fences, walls, etc. (see Zinnecker 1990). Institutionalization is only a special case of this trend. *Insularization* makes reference to another secular trend, namely that children's open and greater mobility have been replaced by 'islands' in different parts of the city due to a growing differentiation of functions (see Zeiher and Zeiher 1994: 17ff.).

These trends are clearly a result of major changes in society in general, not least the new demands of infrastructure and traffic intensity. Children have got little chance to escape them and their concomitant new regimes of control. Thus they are truly phenomena of instances of a higher order, and, at the same time, themselves instances which, in turn, impact phenomena at levels on a smaller scale. Both are processual in nature and therefore their salience can be detected only by making historical or intercultural comparisons; the movement from one end point to another represents a movement from one social form of childhood to another, both of which at given historical periods were by and large encompassing all children. All other differences between them remain untold, but these other differences do not detract from or invalidate the commonness and generality of domestication and insularization. Indeed, the particularization of spaces and the ensuing particularization of children's social relations are *general features*, an important parameter of childhood in its modern social form (see Zeiher and Zeiher 1994: 28).

Countries as instances

A straightforward and instructive illustration of 'country as an instance' might be comparisons of the two Germanies, the much more so since many new studies in Germany provide rich sources of knowledge. Strictly speaking, 'the two Germanies' are now one country, but due to its recent unification it still makes sense to analytically deal with them as two. Inter-German comparisons represent cases which are a mixture of historical, cross-country and within-culture comparisons: as it may be remembered, before 1989, the Germans talked about two states, but one nation, to indicate, on the one hand, the political-economic divide, and on the other, the common cultural heritage. Already basic information, such as fertility rates, institutionalization of children, and employment of mothers alerts us to look for deeper causes, because they exhibit large, partly surprising and dramatic differences and changes (see for instance Ditch et al. 1998: 27; Nauck 1995: 42; Braun and Klein 1995: 243–4 and 233; for a more recent account, see Jurczyk et al. 2004).

An early 1990's study of modernization of childhood in East Germany, West Germany and the Netherlands, firmly based within social studies of childhood, collected empirical data from the three regions – in cities, towns and rural areas – including interviews with children. They concluded that childhood was most modernized in West Germany, whereas childhood in the Netherlands seemed to lag behind even East German childhood. Core variables ('phenomena') such as individualization, autonomy, children's activities and networks were used. The 'victorious' modernization in West Germany is explained – in terms of 'instances' – by a more favourable infrastructure in urbanized areas and higher material standards when compared with East Germany; although the Netherlands shared these instances, children in this country were more traditional than even their East German mates, due to the persistence of a classical wife and mother role. For example, the Netherlands have systematic lower female employment, longer school hours and at the same time a more cosy and child friendly climate (see du Bois-Reymond et al. 1994: 270-71; for an English summary, see du Bois-Reymond et al. 1995).

The attraction of this rich study lies in its effort to establish micro-macro links and its successful attempt to explain the everyday lives of children and their changes by macro-economic, social and cultural forces to the extent that it makes sense to talk about more or less distinct childhoods in each of these three countries. It certainly adds to the value of the study that it also examines variables such as gender, urbanization, social class background, etc. However, at the same time as it clearly demonstrates the importance of locating particular explanatory instances, the study is nevertheless an encouragement for us to look deeper into causes of this systematic variation.

Exactly this is done in a study by Dieter Kirchhöfer (1998). He made a longitudinal study of 10-14-year-old children from East Berlin during the transition from socialism to capitalism; the first interviews were made in 1990, the second ones in 1994. The differences between previous East German and present German childhoods are many and mainly predicated on the fact that in East Germany childhood was not regarded as a private matter, whereas this is the case in the old as well as the new Federal Republic of Germany (FRG). This meant, says the author, that while East German parents saw a common interest with the authorities as far as their children were concerned, the social construction of childhood is presently a result of conflicting interests, for instance between parents and the school.

During the transition the schools have become severed from the family. Under these new conditions it is not the business of teachers to interfere with children's homework or leisure time, whereas parents' rights as far as children's work in school is concerned have legal priority. The opposite was more or less the case before the transition; cooperation between schools, family, municipality and even firms made sure that no child was left in the lurch.

In the German Democratic Republic children were deliberately and from an early age drawn – perhaps dragged – into the public sphere. They were present at demonstrations and celebrations, and there was a broad network of relations to organisations and firms. This involvement implied that children gained an acquaintance with and a confidence in public institutions, which has now been lost. There is now no encouragement at all to parents and children to participate in any public arrangements and their experiences are increasingly alienated from political and administrative institutions. New institutions for children, such as a 'child traffic parliament' or a 'children's bureau' are not taken seriously. 'Childhood appears presently to have been taken out of political structures or political structures seem no longer to function in childhood', which increases the risk of childhood becoming a convenient toy for political ambitions (Kirchhöfer 1998: 226).

After the unification, children in the sample expressed a growing distrust towards other adults, i.e. strangers. It was apparently a new situation. They were warned against having contacts with others, speaking to others, or keeping their company; they were not supposed to receive or offer help and were asked to avoid any confrontation in public. In other words, the new images of socialization were mirrored in a 'new type of discretion', which in this form had so far been unknown. Yet this plays with the fact that there was previously another type of silence concerning openness about politically sensitive issues. A paradox seems to have arisen in which 'the private space closes its doors to public behaviour in an open society, whereas in the closed society the private space leaves the door open to public behaviour' (Kirchhöfer 1998: 227).

The mechanisms of control also changed. From having been partly institutionalized by means of people living in children's areas and partly taken care of by common adults, parents of school mates, etc., a new kind of control has appeared: doors remain locked, people have become more alert to personal property rights, electronic devices are monitoring children even in their neighbourhoods and in department stores and shops. As far as parents' work is concerned, this was previously well known to children, who often went to visit them there; the stability of workplace implied that parents' colleagues were also friends of the family and thus of children as well, whereas the much more insecure present work relations and an increasing change in parents' employment currently seem to dilute such relations. In this connection the institutionalized arrangements by firms for holidays also meant that many colleagues spent their vacation together, including their children. Nowadays, children make no statements about the social relations between parents and their colleagues (see Kirchhöfer 1996: 39-42).

Kirchhöfer's study, *nota bene*, uses a qualitative methodology; he has asked children at two points of time and has on this basis made meticulous conceptualizations (inspired by the model of Zeiher and Zeiher 1994). The point is not if one agrees with his conclusions or not. The importance – at least for my purpose – lies in the fact that he has been able convincingly to capture two different kinds of childhood, the variation between which is caused by societal parameters. In this case, there is no doubt that diverging political-economic ideologies have accounted for the fundamental differences between childhood in German Democratic Republic and childhood in current Federal Republic of Germany. As it has repeatedly been underlined, these common frameworks do not rule out a host of other underlying differences between children within each of the countries, but it is suggested that they constitute frameworks which are largely obligatory for all children in the respective countries.

Intergenerational comparisons

The last major dimension I want to take up is that of intergenerational comparison. It seems logical to suggest that different population groups within a given country are fundamentally exposed to the same set of national and international macro parameters. This is the thesis I have been seeking to make plausible above by comparing childhoods at other levels. Although one must expect important within-differences in micro analyses, a relatively high level of generality holds, I suggest, for different classes and ethnic groups and for both sexes as well as for different generations. Precisely because everybody is influenced by macro parameters – or instances, as Mill (1950) called them – they are often overlooked or deemed less important. The temptation to dive into the variation within one of the large units is of course justified if, *but only if*, in the final analysis it is not forgotten that the within-variation takes place in a larger framework which presses towards relative commonness. The eminent worth of comparative analysis lies in its ability to heighten the awareness of macro parameters, which may be overlooked because they appear to be – and in a sense are – constant factors. However, what comparative analysis suggests is that they are likely to be the most powerful parameters of conditions and behaviour, exactly because their influence is widespread.

In this section I add to my argument, then, the suggestion that different population groups – *in casu* generations – are not necessarily impacted in the same way or equally strong. Indeed they are for a number of reasons likely to be differently influenced. This is, to be sure, one way of focusing on variation within one macro unit; at the same time it presupposes systematic differences between relative distinct instances within this macro unit, typically a country.

The concept of generation is of fundamental importance. For the study of childhood it assumes the same methodological status as the concept of class does in accounting for social exploitation, gender for patriarchal domination, and ethnicity for alerting us to racial and cultural discrimination. However, to the extent that these approaches, important as they are, fail to address and cross boundaries of dominance within a macro-unit, they fail to elucidate structural reasons for inequality and discrimination between classes, sexes and ethnic groups. So, I believe, is the case also in generational studies, in which childhood assumes the status of being a dominated category, while its dominating category is adulthood.[6]

To the extent that it is plausible that childhood is discriminated against in terms of resources and privileges (see Wirth 1945), there is a case for speaking of childhood as a minority group or category.[7] A softer version might be that negative discrimination does not take place in general terms; in this case one would not speak of a minority category. However, if there is evidence showing systematic differences between generations, one would nonetheless have a case for talking about a distinct category, the modalities of which can only be sorted out in comparison with other groups with, in principle, the same needs (assuming ontological sameness of children and adults) and circumstances[8].

It is important for my argument to assume that the category childhood has enough assertive power so as to assume that defining characteristics of subgroups of children are secondary to its categorical status. That is, by analogy, if patriarchalism is strong enough as a theory about male dominance, it does not weaken this theory that a number of women are not objectively or do not subjectively see themselves as dominated; if the theory of class is sound, it is not rendered invalid if some working class members enjoy different life conditions than others; and ethnic discrimination remains theoretically plausible even if some differences between ethnic groups can be ascertained.

Now, what speaks in favour of regarding childhood as a category which distinguishes itself from other generational categories?[9] Oldman suggests that there are 'three sets of influences on the nature of childhood (which) we might loosely call the structural, the normative, and the regulative' (Oldman 1991: 1). These criteria have the advantage of indisputably being applicable to all population groups.

First, the most obvious influence is *regulative*: there is undoubtedly a systematique in legal regulations according to age, and, in most countries, persons who have reached the age of 18 are entitled to enjoy all rights of personhood, whereas those who are minors do not enjoy all of them. Besides the polity's support of majority law, it also has the normative backing of most adults. It may even be supported by children themselves, if they were asked. An argument to the effect, that the majority rule is an advantage to children (see Blackstone 1979: 441, 452) in that, for instance, it protects them, does not change its distinctiveness and its universal validity for one group *vis-à-vis* other groups, which are not protected to the same measure.

A universal rule, but not quite as strong as that of majority regulation, is children's duty to attend schools. It is less strong in the sense that its implementation varies from country to country in a number of respects.[10] The empirical fact, however, is that practically all children are enrolled in schools for 8-12 years, depending on national legislation. The formative power of schooling thus is presumably one of the most forceful ones, and decisive in distinguishing children from other generations (as well as from those children who historically had no schooling).

Second, it is not easy to make a clear distinction between regulative and *normative* influences,[11] for in fact, regulative factors have often grown out of norms, when it becomes risky to leave the latter to people's discretion. Besides, many norms are rooted in ideologies or moral conceptions which, from time to time, have been underpinned by claiming the status of scientific theories of the child (Oldman 1991: 1). Basically, much of what we call normative factors aim at regulating behaviours whether it is legislated for or not. Ideas about the child's level of maturity, competence and vulnerability, for example, and commonly held views of the proper attitudes to and social-ization of children may be valid or not; however, they exist and they work, although their modes of existence and functioning change (see Benedict 1955 [1938]: 21–2; Wolfenstein 1955).

From the point of view of children, normative factors oscillate between protective and participatory measures, and what is normatively positive or negative for one generation may assume the opposite values for the other. This phenomenon is aptly caught in the concept of status offence: children are protected against/prevented from seeing certain movies, they are protected against/prevented from participating in outdoor activities during the evening,[12] or protected/prevented from drinking beer, for example. There is however nothing wrong as such about movies, outdoor play, or beer; neither do we know for sure about their differential perils for children and/or adults, but they are simply perceived as adults' domain. A better example, perhaps, has to do with norms about children's gainful work. The general resistance among adults (including legal prohibitions) against child labour is rooted in views of children's vulnerability, coupled with concern for their school attendance. It is however more than that; it also reflects adults' suspicion that children cannot properly deal with money (lack of competence); it therefore also denies children access to certain provisions procured by themselves (lack of recognition); it prevents them from gaining the kind of new experiences which is connected with possession of money earned by themselves; finally, it denies them the enjoyment of respect which cannot be obtained by using pocket money handed over to them by parents (see Ward 1994: 147–8).

Third, the differential use of norms and their generation-specific applica-tion may be to the advantage or disadvantage of children (and adults). The point is, however, that they are *distinctively different over age and generation*; they therefore assume generation specific imprints that make it reasonable to talk about them in quasi-structural terms. As such they assume an influence which hardly falls short of structural influences as they are conventionally known from economic, political, social and technological realms. I shall here choose only two dimensions for discussing differential access between generations in *structural* terms: economic and spatial dimensions.

Children have, as other social groups, benefited historically from and been enjoying the fruits of welfare development as regards basic survival indicators. Yet, it is less clear whether they have kept pace or whether they have been or are being discriminated against, if we look at it from a generational perspective. That is, to what extent have children, for instance, achieved shares of resources in the same measure as other parts of society, such as for instance adults and elderly people? We have barely sufficient data to document this question convincingly in a historical perspective; even today it is uncommon to find systematic information about generational discrimination (see Ringen 1997; Rainwater and Smeeding 1995; Ditch et al. 1998; Vleminckx and Smeeding 2001).[13]

The reduction of children's disposable incomes compared with those of adults has, though, been observed by Coleman for the USA over the last hundred years (see Coleman 1990: 590). This intergenerational relationship has also been documented as a current problem on several occasions and seminally presented by Preston (1984). By that it has gained a particular importance, raising new questions about causes; it is no longer sufficient to refer to parents' responsibility and social class background (see Krüsselberg 1987); nor to think merely in terms of the feminization of poverty (see Smith 1989). The generational profile of poverty makes it more reasonable to speak of the pauperization of childhood (Jensen 1994), as has been documented for a long time in the United States.

A number of reports have shown the incidence of poverty among children, most recently from the European Union. According to data from Eurostat (2004), 20 per cent of the member states' children were living in poor households, if the 60 per cent cut-off point is used (the so-called at-risk-of-poverty-rate after tax and transfer) – ranging from around 10 per cent in the Nordic countries to 26 per cent in Italy and 22 in the UK. This rate, which the European Union eventually prefers to use, gives though an impression of a general high level compared to the 50 per cent cut-off point which was used until recently. For 2001, the figures for children – using the 50 per cent cut-off point – were for UK and Italy around 16 per cent, whereas for the Nordic countries it oscillated around 3 per cent (Förster and d'Ercole 2005). On the other hand, the impression of a lower poverty rate for children has strengthened after a change of equivalence scale which gives a lower weight to persons of second parity (from 0.7 to 0.5) and third and higher parity persons (mostly children – from 0.5 to 0.3). Contrarywise, the impression of higher poverty among the elderly has become much more pronounced. Currently the level for the under 16-year-olds and persons between 66 and 75 is relatively equal (Förster and d'Ercole 2005), whereas prior to the change of definition, children's risk of poverty was comparatively speaking much higher than for the elderly. Given the changes in definition and also the change of cut-off point, it is for the moment difficult to make conclusive statements of how children and the elderly compare with each other.

Based on information mainly from New Zealand and United Kingdom, Thomson (1996) has sought to demonstrate in a thorough analysis of intergenerational relations during most of this century, that welfare states have moved from being youth-oriented in the 1930s and 1940s to being more and more favourable to older generations, which thus have succeeded in being beneficiaries through all phases of the welfare state since around the Second World War.

A market economy, in which achievement (and not need) is the basic distributive mechanism, is bound to create inequalities, which can only be countered by compromising the market principle through state intervention. Such compromising does take place, but to various degrees in different countries (see Rainwater and Smeeding 1995; see also Sgritta 1997). The fact, however, that its extent varies considerably between nations is evidence of (a) that nation is an important variable, since the regulations are state-specific and thus valid for all children within one nation; (b) that children do not have a right to expect state-interventions (for Sweden, see Björnberg 1996: 115; see also Hammarberg 1994; Stephens and Huber 1995; for Finland, see Salmi 1995a, 1995b; Qvortrup 2007), a point which indicates a difference to adults, that is, it is typically families that are targeted rather than children.

In this sense, childhood seems to be more vulnerable than other generational categories, not only economically, but also politically: children do not, either as individuals or as a collectivity, possess rights or powers to ensure distributive justice. The increased subjectivity of children as expressed for instance in the UN Convention of the Rights of the Child, has hardly changed this reality.

Similarly, children's access to and enjoyment of the environment is limited compared with adults. By giving supremacy to the idea and practice of protecting children in all imaginable ways, one is justifying this solicitous mood, irrespective of its encroachments on other wishes children might have; for instance a desire to have new experiences on their own or for recognition (see Thomas 1966). In increasingly more dominant urban environments, dictated by adult economic interests, children's life worlds are squeezed, their degrees of freedom reduced and their opportunities for autonomous explorations more and more beyond their reach (cf. Matthews 1998; Zeiher and Zeiher 1994; Zinnecker 1990).

Urban worlds, as they are increasingly found in this century, are primarily therefore adults' worlds, or perhaps better, the worlds of adulthood, leaving childhood contexts as protected residues. Thus, statistics from 1970 to 1992 show that the number of children killed in road accidents fell dramatically in Britain – from around 1,000 to just over 300 (Central Statistical Office 1994: 52); at face value an extremely positive development. At the same time a study from 1971 and replicated in 1990 showed that more and more children were no longer licensed to move around on their own. For instance, the percentage of English junior children (aged 7-11) who were allowed to cross roads alone fell from 72 to 51, those permitted to visit leisure parks alone plummeted from 63 to 37 per cent (Hillman et al. 1990: 131; see also O'Brien et al. 2000). It is hard not to conclude that the price for reducing the number of children killed on the roads was partly paid by children themselves. In Thomas' (1996) terminology, the adult wish for security was achieved at the cost of children having new experiences. It was, in other words, a change in the internal book-keeping on children's own account, without compromising adults' demands and interests – or a trade-off between protection and participation to the disadvantage of the latter. The potential conflict of interests between adults and children becomes clear, when the car is seen by (male) adults as the ultimate epitome of freedom, while for children it almost literally means curfew.

Conclusion

Sociological research is about looking for commonalities among persons and groups of persons; research in childhood is no exception to this rule. To find commonalities presupposes insight in both interpersonal relations at a local level and in the macro-structures, of which they are necessarily a part. It goes without saying that without a dialectic approach to social realities we will not be able to finalize our intellectual journey convincingly.

Personally I am attracted by the methodological programme of the Annales-school, the outstanding French group of historians to whom among others Marc Bloch and Fernand Braudel belonged. The latter contended that it was at the '"microscopical" level that one hopes to perceive structural laws of the most general kind' (Braudel 1972: 33). The programme of the Annales-school was to create the long view in history on the basis of minute studies of daily life, but this could not be done without the ever present reality of the macro-world. The intersection of the micro-events and the macro-perspective is what Braudel calls a conjuncture, which is the point at which we must finally arrive.

> In my view, [he explains] research must constantly move between social reality and the model, in a succession of readjustments and journeys ever patiently reviewed. Thus the model is both an attempt to explain a given structure, and an instrument with which one can examine it, and compare it, and test its solidity and its very life. If I constructed a model, starting from contemporary reality, I should want to locate it at once in reality, then make it move back over time, right to its birth, if possible. After that I should calculate its probable life-span as far as its next breaking point according to the concomitant movement of other social realities. In other ways, using it as an element of comparison, I can move it through time and space in search of other realities capable of being illuminated by it.
> (Braudel 1972: 33)

Experience shows that there are no good reasons to argue about the paramountcy of either a micro- or macro-level approach; neither is it demanded that each and everybody must in his or her research capture all levels. The choice is partly made by inclination and/or temperament. In the end it is nonetheless a requirement that our research problem – childhood – be seen from as many fruitful angles as possible.

My inclination is towards elucidating structures of childhood – be they economic, social, political or ideological; these constitute frameworks that cannot be discounted, their salience and their being made intelligible depending on the insight they provide into children's everyday life. This means among other things that insight from one level must not contradict insight from another level within any chosen instance.

One way of reaching this goal is by using a comparative methodology in the sense of crossing boundaries between what Mill (1950) called instances, because it enables us to see realities which otherwise remain opaque, because we are too close to our research object; if the new social studies of childhood does not meet the challenge of dialectically connecting – in a conjuncture – different levels of reality, it will hardly come of age, become a household member of the scientific community or be seen as useful for understanding and possibly changing realities of childhood(s).

Notes

1   This is not to say, that this 16-country project (1987–1992 – see Bardy et al., 1990–1993; Qvortrup et al., 1994; Qvortrup 1993) and its orientation have not received attention, on the contrary; the bulk of new projects and studies though appears to belong to what is now called the agency-perspective rather than the structural perspective; this can be seen for instance in the British programme Children 5–16 – Growing into the Twenty-first Century, in similar Norwegian and Danish programmes, as well as in the almost 70 contributions to the recent Sociology of Childhood session at the International Sociological Association's Congress in Montreal, 1998.

2   The thesis remained unchanged despite the authors' acknowledgement in the new preface to the second edition that 'In retrospect, however, our claims for the primacy of ethnography seem somewhat one-sided as others have begun to grapple with ways of including children in survey and other methodologies' (James and Prout 1997b: xv).

3   These phenomena may in turn at the next level be instances *vis-à-vis* a new set of phenomena or sub-units.

4   'Opportunity space' is translated from the German 'Möglichkeitsraum'; it indicates that persons have a limited number of options, determined by their objective circumstances; the subjectivity of the concept lies in persons' opportunity to choose among those options.

5   There is of course no reason to believe that the quoted authors disagree in this statement; the crucial question is, however, if one is giving major weight to within- or between-differences as far as instances are concerned; any choice will produce different results which are all needed. The discussion is, I trust, about safeguarding that none of the approaches is forgotten.

6   There is of course nothing wrong in studying gender or class or race issues among children, but one has to be aware that such choices are by the same token not addressing generational questions, i.e. they may be unwarrantedly assuming similarities among children or in childhood to be second to their differences. In analogy with class, race and gender studies, I believe the opposite – to give analytic primacy to similarities – is most conducive to the progress of childhood studies. In this vein Coles made an important point when he observed that 'in a sense white and Negro children have more in common with each other than with their parents' (Coles 1967: 322).

7   For a discussion of childhood as a minority group, see Qvortrup 1987, and Sgritta and Saporiti 1990. For another interpretation, see James et al. 1998.

8   '... two conditions are necessary to make a comparison, historically speaking, possible: there must be a certain similarity between the facts observed – an obvious point – and a certain dissimilarity between the situations in which they have arisen' (Bloch 1967: 45).

9　There are many criteria for categorizing people (see Spencer 1911: 6; Thomas 1966: xxxix and 117ff.; Hirschman 1970). It is interesting and symptomatic in itself that these criteria appear to have been established with merely adults in mind.

10　For instance as to whether it is schooling or education, which is obligatory; whether the schools are merely national schools or some kind of opt-out or free schools; at which ages children are obliged to attend school; whether it is children's or parents' duty and responsibility that children receive education.

11　See James and James (2004) who to the same effect makes a distinction between 'Law' and 'law'.

12　Cf. the new curfew act in Britain.

13　One reason for this lacuna is the fact that children – despite recent improvements (see Jensen and Saporiti 1992; Qvortrup 1997) – are seldom dealt with as statistical units of observation.

References

Ariès, P. (1962) *Centuries of Childhood: A Social History of Family Life*, New York: Vintage Books.

Bardy, M., Qvortrup, J., Sgritta, G. and Wintersberger H. (eds) (1990–1993) *Childhood as a Social Phenomenon – A Series of National Reports*. (Introduction, 16 National Reports and Statistical Appendix). Eurosocial 36 and 36.1–36.17. Vienna: European Centre.

Beck, U. (1986) *Risikogesellschaft. Auf dem Weg in eine andere Moderne*, Frankfurt: Suhrkamp.

Benedict, R. (1955) 'Continuities and discontinuities in cultural conditioning', in M. Mead and M. Wolfenstein (eds) *Childhood in Contemporary Cultures*, Chicago and London: The University of Chicago Press, [Originally in: *Psychiatry*, I (2), 1938].

Björneberg, U. (1996) 'Children's Rights in a Dual-Earner Family Context in Sweden', in H. Wintersberger (ed.) *Children on the Way from Marginality towards Citizenship. Childhood Policies: Conceptual and Practical Issues*, Eurosocial Report 61. Vienna: European Centre.

Blackstone, W. (1979) *Commentaries on the Law of England*. Vol. I [A facsimile of the First Edition of 1765-1769]. Chicago: University of Chicago Press.

Bloch, M. (1934) 'Une Étude Régionale: Géographie ou histoire?'. *Annales d'Histoire Economique et Sociale*, 6, (Janvier): 81–85.

Bloch, M. (1967) 'A contribution towards a comparative history of European aocieties', in M. Bloch (ed.) *Land and Work in Mediaeval Europe*, London: Routledge & Kegan Paul.

Bois-Reymond, M du, Büchner, P., Krüger, H.H. (with others) (1994) *Kinderleben: Modernisierung von Kindheit im interkulturellen Vergleich*, Opladen: Leske & Budrich.

Bois-Reymond, Manuela du, Büchner, P. and Krüger, H.H. (1995) 'Growing up in three European regions', in L. Chisholm *et al.* (eds) *Growing Up in Europe: Contemporary Horizons in Childhood and Youth Studies*, Berlin/New York: Walter de Gruyter.

Bradshaw, J. (1998) *'The Prevalence of Child Poverty in the United Kingdom: A Comparative Perspective'*. Paper to the Conference Children and Social Exclusion, Centre for the Social Study of Children, University of Hull, 5–6 March.

Braudel, Fernand (1972) 'History and the Social Science', in P.Burke (ed). *Economy and Society in Early Modern Europe. Essays from Annales*, New York: Harper & Row.

Braun, U. and Thomas Klein, T. (1995)'Der berufliche Wiedereinstieg der Mutter im Lebensverlauf der Kinder', in B.Nauck und H. Bertram (eds) *Kinder in Deutschland. Lebensverhältnisse von Kindern im Regionalvergleich*, Deutsche Jugend Institut: Familien-Survey 5. Opladen: Leske and Budrich.

Central Statistical Office (1994) *Social Focus on Children*, HMSO: London.

Coleman, J.S. (1990) *Foundations of Social Theory*, Cambridge, MA and London: Belknap Press of Harvard University Press.

Coles, R. (1967) *Children of Crisis. A Study of Courage and Fear*, Vol. I. London: Faber & Faber.

De Lone, R. (1979) *Small Futures: Children, Inequality, and the Limits of Liberal Reform*, New York and London: Harcourt Brace & Jovanovich.

Ditch, J., Barnes, H., Bradshaw, J. and Kilkey, M. (1998) *A Synthesis of National Family Policies 1996*, European Observatory on National Family Policies. Published by the European Commission. The University of York.

Etzioni, A. (1968) *The Active Society*, New York: The Free Press.

Eurostat (2004) http://epp.eurostat.ec.europa.eu/portal/page?_pageid=1996,39140985&_dad= portal&_schema=PORTAL&screen=detailref&language=en&product=sdi_ps&root=sdi_ps/ sdi_ps/sdi_ps_mon/sdi_ps1112

Förster, M. and Mira d'Ercole, M. (2005) *Income Distribution and Poverty in OECD Countries in the Second Half of the 1990s*, Paris: OECD Social, Employment and Migration, Working Paper 22.

Hammarberg, T. (1994) *Rika länder sviker barnen* [Rich countries are betraying children], Dagens Nyheter, 21 April 1994.

Hillman, M., Adams, J. and Whitelegg, J. (1990) *One False Move ... A Study of Children's Independent Mobility*, London: Policy Studies Institute.

Hirschman, A. O. (1970) *Exit, Voice and Loyalty*, Cambridge MA.: Harvard University Press.

James, A. and James, A.L. (2004) *Constructing Childhood: Theory, Policy and Social Practice*, Basingstoke: Palgrave Macmillan.

James, A. and Prout, A. (1997a) *Constructing and Reconstruction Childhood. Contemporary Issues in the Sociological Study of Childhood*, London: Falmer Press.

James, A. and Prout, A. (1997b) 'Preface to second edition', in A. James and A. Prout (eds) *Constructing and Reconstruction Childhood. Contemporary Issues in the Sociological Study of Childhood*, London: Falmer Press.

James, A., Jenks, C. and Prout, A. (1998) *Theorizing Childhood*, Cambridge: Polity Press.

Jenks, C. (1996) *Childhood*, London: Routledge.

Jensen, A-M. (1994) 'The feminization of childhood', in J. Qvortrup *et al.* (eds) *Childhood Matters. Social Theory, Practice and Politics*, Avebury: Aldershot,

Jensen, A-M. and Saporiti, A. (1992) *Do Children Count?* Childhood as a Social Phenomenon: A Statistical Compendium. Eurosocial Report 36/17, Vienna: European Centre.

Jurczyk, K., Olk, T. and Zeiher, H. (2004) 'German children's welfare between economy and ideology', in A-M. Jensen *et al.* (eds) *Children's Welfare in Ageing Europe*, Volume II, Norwegian Centre for Child Research: Trondheim, pp. 703–70.

Kirchhöfer, D. (1996) 'Veränderungern in der alltäglichen Lebensführung Ostberliner Kinder', in *Aus Politik und Zeitgeschichte* B11/96, 8 (March): 31–45.

Kirchhöfer, D. (1998) *Aufwachsen in Ostdeutschland. Langzeitstudie über Tagesläufe 10- bis 14 jähriger Kinder*, Weinheim und München: Juventa Verlag.

Krüsselberg, H-G. (1987) 'Vita capital policy and the unity of the social budget: economic prospects of a social policy for childhood', *International Journal of Sociology*, 17 (3): 81–97.

Matthews, H. (1998) 'The right to be outdoors', *Family Policy Bulletin*, Summer.

McCourt, F. (1997) *Angela's Ashes*, New York: Simon & Schuster (A Touchstone Book).

Mill, J.S. (1950) *Philosophy of Scientific Method*, New York: Hafner.

Nauck, B. (1995) 'Kinder als Gegenstand der Sozialberichterstattung – Konzepte, Methoden und Befunde im Überblick', in B. Nauck and H. Bertram (eds) *Kinder in Deutschland. Lebensverhältnisse von Kindern im Regionalvergleich*, Deutsche Jugend Institut: Familien-Survey 5. Opladen: Leske & Budrich.

O'Brien, M., Jones, D., Rustein, M. and Sloan, D. (2000) 'Children's independent spatial mobility in the urban public realm', *Childhood*, 7 (3): 257–77.

Oldman, D. (1991) *'Conflict and accomodation between ideologies in the regulation of children's rights'*. Paper to the Conference Social Policies for Children and Adolescents, Florence, 1991; printed as 'I diritti del bambino: conflitto e compromesso tra ideologie', pp. 107–20 in *Politiche Sociali Per l'Infanzia e l'Adolescenza*, Milano: Edizioni Unicopli.

Preston, Samuel H. (1984) 'Children and the elderly: Divergent paths for America's dependents', *Demography*, 21: 435–57.

Prout, A. and James, A. (1990) 'A new paradigm for the sociology of childhood? Provenance, promise and problems', in A. James and A. Prout (eds) *Constructing and Reconstruction Childhood. Contemporary Issues in the Sociological Study of Childhood*, London: Falmer Press.

Prout, A. and James, A. (1997) 'A new paradigm for the sociology of childhood? Provenance, promise and problems', in A. James and A. Prout (eds) *Constructing and Reconstruction Childhood. Contemporary Issues in the Sociological Study of Childhood*, London: Falmer Press

Qvortrup, Jens (1987) 'Introduction' *International Journal of Sociology*, 17 (3): 3–37.

Qvortrup, J. (1989) 'Comparative research and its problems', in K. Boh *et al.* (eds) *Changing Patterns of European Family Life. A Comparative Study of 14 European Countries*, London and New York: Routledge.

Qvortrup, J. (ed.) (1993) *Childhood as a Social Phenomenon: Lessons from an International Project*, Eurosocial Report 47. Vienna: European Centre.

Qvortrup, J. (1997) 'A voice for children in statistical and social accounting: A plea for children's right to be heard', in A. Jame and A. Prout (eds) *Constructing and Reconstruction Childhood. Contemporary Issues in the Sociological Study of Childhood*, London: Falmer Press.

Qvortrup, J., Bardy, M.G. and Wintersberger, H. (eds) (1994) *Childhood Matters. Social Theory, Practice and Politics.* Avebury: Aldershot.

Qvortrup, J. (2007) 'Childhood in the welfare state', in A. James and A.L. James (eds) *European Childhoods: Cultures, Politics and Childhoods in the European Union*, Basingstoke: Palgrave (forthcoming).

Rainwater, L. and Smeeding, T.M. (1995) *Doing Poorly: The Real Income of American Children in a Comparative Perspective*, Luxembourg Income Study, Working Paper No. 127.

Ringen, S. (1997) *Citizens, Families, and Reform*, Oxford: Clarendon Press.

Salmi, M. (1995a) *Depression och barn* [Depression and children]. Paper to 8th Nordic Seminar on Social Policy, Hässelby, Stockholm, 9–11 February, 1995.

Salmi, M. (1995b) *Barn i den ekonomiska depressionen* [Children in the economic depression]. Paper to 18th Nordic Congress of Sociology, Helsinki, 9–11 June, 1995.

Sgritta, G.B. (1997) 'Inconsistencies: childhood on the economic and political agenda', *Childhood*, 4 (4): 375–404.

Sgritta, G. and Saporiti, A. (1990) *Childhood as a Social Phenomenon. National Report Italy*, Eurosocial Report 36/2. Vienna: European Centre.

Skocpol, T. (1994) *Social Revolutions in the Modern World*, Cambridge University Press: Cambridge.

Smith, J.P. (1989) 'Children among the poor', *Demography*, 2: 235–48.

Spencer, H. (1911) *Essays on Education etc*, London: J.M. Dent & Sons Ltd. and New York: E.P. Dutton & Co. Inc.

Stephens, D. and Huber, E. (1995) *The Welfare State in Hard Times*. Paper for conference 'Politics and Political Economy of Contemporary Capitalism', Humbolt University and the Wissenschaftszentrum, Berlin, May 26–27, 1995.

Thomas, W.I. (1966) *On the Social Organization and Social Personality: Selected Papers*, Chicago/London: The University of Chicago Press.

Thomson, D. (1996) *Selfish Generations? How Welfare States Grow Old*. Cambridge: The White Horse Press.

UNICEF (2007) *The State of the World's Children*. UNICEF: Florence.

Vleminckx, K. and Smeeding, T.H. (eds) (2001) *Child Well-Being, Child Poverty and Child Policy in Modern Nations: What do we know?* Bristol: Policy Press.

Ward, C. (1994) 'Opportunities for childhoods in the late twentieth century Britain', in B. Mayall (ed.) *Children's Childhoods. Observed and Experienced*, London: Falmer Press.

Wintersberger, H. (1997) *Children and the Welfare Mix: Distributive Justice Between Generations in a Welfare Society*. Paper based on lecture given at the South Jutland University Centre on 9 January, 1997.

Wirth, L. (1945) 'The problem of minority groups', in R. Linton (ed.) *The Science of Man in the World Crisis*, New York: Columbia University Press.

Wolfenstein, M. (1955) 'Fun morality: An analysis of recent American childtraining literature', in M. Mead and M. Wolfenstein (eds) *Childhood in Contemporary Cultures*, Chicago and London: The University of Chicago Press.

Zeiher, H.J. and Zeiher, H. (1994) *Orte und Zeiten der Kinder. Soziales Leben im Alltag von Großstadtkindern*. Weinheim und München: Juventa Verlag.

Zinnecker, J. (1990) 'Vom Straßenkind zum verhäuslichten Kind. Kindheitsgeschichte im Prozeß der Zivilisation' I. Behnken (ed.) *Stadtgesellschaft und Kindheit im Prozeß der Zivilisation. Konfigurationen städischer Lebensweise zu Beginn des 20. Jahrhunderts*, Opladen: Leske & Budrich.

4 Children as Respondents

The Challenge for Quantitative Methods

Jacqueline Scott

Introduction

The sentiment that children should be seen and not heard could not be more inappropriate for the current era in which there is a growing demand for research that involves interviewing children. The construction of childhood that views children as incomplete adults is coming under attack and there is a new demand for research that focuses on children as actors in their own right. The French historian Philip Aries (1962) suggested that modern Western childhood is unique in the way that it quarantines children from the world of adults, so that childhood is associated with play and education rather than work and economic responsibility. The quarantine of childhood is represented in the exclusion of children from statistics and other social accounts (Qvortrup 1990) and there exists very little material that directly addresses the experience of childhood, at the societal level. (For a useful overview of quantitative data available on children in Britain, see Church and Summerfield 1997 and ONS 2000). In surveys of the general population, children have been usually regarded as out of scope and samples are usually drawn from the adult population, with a minimum age of 16 or 18. Interviews with children have long been central to the research of developmental psychologists, child psychiatrists and educational specialists, but until quite recently general purpose surveys have not included children as respondents (see Roberts, this volume).

In this chapter I reflect on why children are so often excluded from large-scale quantitative research. I argue that the social and economic questions that such research addresses are often framed in ways where the adultcentric bias is unacknowledged and inappropriate. I also elaborate on how, at least for research using the life course perspective (Elder et al. 1993; Elder 1995), the crucial concepts of choice and agency means that it is essential to collect information from children themselves concerning their present experiences and future aspirations. Until recently survey researchers, when investigating aspects of childhood, have preferred to ask adult respondents such as parents or teachers to report on children's lives, rather than to ask children themselves. In part, this has been because of concerns about the cognitive ability of children to process and respond to structured questions about behaviour, perceptions, opinions and beliefs. Drawing on research from cognitive psychology, I suggest ways that questionnaires and interview practice can be modified to make them more suitable for young respondents. I also reflect on ways that practical and ethical challenges posed by the inclusion of children in general surveys can be overcome. By including children in population surveys, especially longitudinal surveys, social scientists can improve the theoretical understanding and empirical knowledge of the dynamics of social inclusion and exclusion that are so evident in childhood experiences and life course trajectories.

The exclusion of children from social surveys

Survey practice has tended to follow the 'quarantine' approach with children being, at best, the subject of proxy information and, at worst, invisible. Moreover, much of the research that does take children into account is concerned with the impact of children on adult lives, rather than focusing on children as social actors in their own right. Panel studies of households, for example, are conducted as if children are auxiliary members, whose presence contributes to measures of household size, density, the labour market participation of mothers, household income and the like. Survey research that is interested in children *per se* is relatively rare. Yet, as any parent will attest, children do have voices, they express opinions, they observe and judge, and they exert a crucial influence on the way families and households function. Moreover, there is often a very large gulf between parental observations about their child and the child's own perceptions. For example, when asked about their children's subjective health, parents portray a much rosier picture of children's well-being than children do of themselves (Scott 1997a). Furthermore, adolescents may go out of their way to conceal risky behaviours that would invoke parental sanctions or concern. Of course there are topics where the responsible parent is better placed to provide information about the child than the child themselves, for example health diagnosis that relies on detailed knowledge of early childhood illness. Nevertheless, for questions tapping the child's own viewpoint, proxy information is clearly inadequate.

In this chapter I argue that the best people to provide information on the child's perspective, actions and attitudes are children themselves. Children provide reliable responses if questioned about events that are meaningful to their lives. For example, in investigations of latch-key children, researchers have found that accounts by parents and children often differ. Moreover, children have provided crucial insights into the diverse ways that young people appraise and respond to situations where they are left unsupervised (Solberg 1990; Belle et al. 1997). Similarly, research on children whose parents divorce has reached the point where children's views are crucial for examining the risk factors associated with the diverse ways in which marital disruption can affect children's development (Elliot and Richards 1991; Kiernan 1992). Previous studies have usually focused on aggregate associations (e.g. divorce and children's lower educational attainment) but, with children's own accounts and insights, it is possible to examine how some young people's aspirations and priorities prove resilient to the most disadvantaged family circumstances (Furstenberg and Hughes 1995).

The quantitative data we collect about society becomes far richer if our accounts include information that can be provided by children. Once children are viewed as competent social actors in their own right then it clearly makes sense to ask them about their own contributions and participation in social and economic life. The range of questions that it is appropriate to ask children is much wider than was previously believed. For example, it has been standard practice for definitions of work to be confined to adult activity that failed to include the child's own work contributions (Morrow 1994). Yet, children's ability to perform household chores and care for younger siblings can be crucial to the household economy, when both parents are out at work (Solberg 1990). Similarly, time budget studies often ignored the fact that children have their own time (for an exception, see Timmer et al. 1985). Even studies on the costs of children have tended to view children as items on the parents' budget, rather than as economic actors who exercise considerable clout in family expenditure on food and consumer durables. Including children as respondents can, therefore, improve our knowledge on a whole range of social and economic issues by providing a more accurate and complete account of social life.

Yet interviewing children does pose some particular practical and methodological problems and the current state of knowledge about conducting survey interviews with children is very fragmented. There are many problems to be solved when the respondents are children, including problems of language use, literacy and different stages of cognitive development. There is also a heightened concern about data quality, with some scepticism about whether an adult interviewer can obtain reliable and valid accounts from children, especially in areas where the information may be sensitive and subject to adult sanctions and control. In addition, issues of confidentiality and ethics become especially important when interviewing minors. Yet, as this chapter shows, there are solutions to such problems that deserve consideration, given the potential benefits of collecting data directly from children themselves.

In this chapter, I discuss some of the accumulated knowledge regarding the techniques for interviewing children in person in large-scale surveys and the strategies for optimizing the measures used and the quality of the resulting data. The chapter draws together practical knowledge from diverse sources and reflects on the lessons that can be learned for quantitative research concerning children. This practical knowledge comes from a very wide range of disciplines, including psychology, anthropology, education, criminology and sociology. In addition, in order to illustrate the constraints and practical challenges of including children in an ongoing large-scale, general purpose, survey, I describe, as a case study, the development and implementation of a

Young Person's questionnaire for children aged 11–15 in the British Household Panel Study. First, however, I consider why, in our supposedly child-oriented society, children are so often ignored by large-scale, general population, survey research.

The exclusion of children in surveys has at least four distinct causes. First, there is the inertia of practice. Most studies, even when their subject matter requires information about children, interview only adult respondents. Second, children may be omitted because of the tendency to accredit adults with greater knowledge, experience and power (Backett and Alexander 1991). Third, interviewing children is viewed as too problematic to be worth the possible pay-off. Interviewing minors poses both practical and ethical issues which researchers might wish to avoid. The fourth reason is ignorance or perhaps a half-truth. Children are commonly believed to lack the communication, cognitive and social skills that are the prerequisite of good respondents. Experimental research has clearly demonstrated, however, that even preschool children are able to appreciate someone else's point of view, can make social judgements and even identify false intentions and beliefs (Astington et al. 1988). Additionally, developmental and cognitive research on children's competency has led to innovative forensic interviewing techniques aimed at improving young children's testimony in criminal trials, including cases of child abuse (Lamb 2005a and 2005b). Nevertheless, children's cognitive capacity clearly does increase with age and the rudimentary levels of cognitive development remain relevant for understanding the question and answer process and for highlighting the ways in which children may differ from adult respondents.

Different methods for different age groups

Research methods that involve children as respondents have to take account of the wide range of cognitive and social development that depends primarily on age, but also on the gender, socio-economic background and ethnicity of the child. Standard questionnaire techniques are clearly inappropriate with preschool children. For example, very young children find it difficult to distinguish between what is said and what is meant and thus almost any hypothetical question becomes problematic (Robinson 1986). This implies that less structured methods of interviewing are more appropriate for younger children (see Mayall, this volume). However, once children have reached the age of 7, it is possible to use both individual and group semi-structured interviews with children. The classic study *The Lore and Language of Schoolchildren* involved interviews with more than 5,000 children (from 7 to early teens) and revealed a distinctive child-centred culture of customs and beliefs (Opie and Opie 1959). One problem is that while pre-teen children can and do tell us about themselves, they have also mastered the art of impression management and, like adults, will tend to edit their answers (Fine and Sandstrom 1988). Thus, the Opies found that if they asked about superstitions, children said (as they are expected to say) that all superstitions are silly. But probing the child's own perspective revealed a world of half-beliefs and superstitious practices that invest children with some degree of control over the unpredictability of everyday experiences.

Thus, once children have reached the age where they are able to process and respond to standard questions, they are also adept at controlling what they reveal. This is aptly illustrated by a study of children aged seven onwards to investigate the strategies used to persuade parents and other adults to buy them things (Middleton et al. 1994). Using group discussions in school, the researchers found that children reported using begging, repetition, direct action, bribery, part-payment, negotiation, threats and actions, each with varying degrees of success. The range of techniques reported by 7-8-year-olds was already large and not much was added to the persuasion repertoire, after the age of 11. The authors note that, if anything, the younger children were less reticent in discussion than teenagers. By adolescence, young people are wary of revealing their secrets to an adult.

For children under 11, visual stimuli can be especially useful in the questioning process, because pictures make the issue far more concrete than verbal representation alone (see O'Kane and Christensen and James, this volume). Aids to memory can also be used to good effect, as children tend to forget even a relatively limited set of response options. Often a simple modification of question format is sufficient. For example, the standard Likert type response (agree strongly, agree, neither agree nor disagree, disagree strongly) can easily be unfolded by first asking 'Do you agree or disagree?' and then probing for strength of feeling. Children's performance on memory tasks improves markedly with age and, by 11, children's ability to remember is not so different from adults (although the information content of memory is much more limited). Most children of 11 and older are fully able to articulate their perceptions, opinions and beliefs and, with relatively little adaptation, surveys designed for adults can be used with adolescents.

Although, by adolescence (aged 11 onwards), it is possible to use a standardized questionnaire instrument, problems of literacy, confidentiality and context have to be taken into account. Often the instruments are very similar to the ones used with adults and, with adult help, standardized instruments can be successfully used with even younger children. In order to identify problems with comprehension and ambiguities in question wording, to detect flippancy and boredom, and to discover discrepancies between the children's understanding and the researcher's intent, pretesting the survey instrument is crucial. A variety of pretest methods can be useful, including cognitive techniques such as asking the child to 'think aloud', coding of non-verbal behaviours, and even video analysis of the interview interactions. Certainly, most questionnaires developed for adults or older children will need some adaptation before they are suitable to use with younger children.

It is also sometimes necessary to adapt standard interview practice. For example, interviewers may need more leeway than is normal, as children tend to ask for more guidance than adults, especially when they are unsure what a question means. In such circumstances, it is preferable for interviewers to paraphrase the question, than give the standard response whatever it means to you. Standard interview practice might also have to be modified to protect children's privacy and confidentiality, especially in settings where children are likely to worry about their responses being reported to the adult authorities. Unfortunately, confidentiality issues can also become real ethical dilemmas if children reveal self-actions or adult behaviours that put them at risk (Stanley and Sieber 1992).

Table 4.1 presents, by way of illustration, summary information for seven large-scale social surveys that collect information from children using structured questionnaires, in Britain. The different surveys have different strengths and weaknesses, depending on the context and method used, as I discuss below. The table is confined to face-to-face and self-completion questionnaires. Other forms of data collection including time diaries and web-based surveys are discussed briefly further in this chapter.

The importance of context in interviewing children

Children's social worlds span many different settings but home and school are two of the most important (see Mayall, this volume). Context is especially important in interviewing children because the expression of the child's personality, in terms of behaviour and attitudinal preferences, is often so context dependent. The same child could be boisterous and outspoken at home, but shy and reserved at school. Thus where the interviews are carried out is quite likely to influence the way children respond. In addition, the interviewer setting is important because the social meaning children will attach to concepts such as work or honesty may differ depending on whether children are at home or at school. The mode of interview is also very important in terms of data quality. Whether the interview is face to face, by telephone or self-completion may enhance or reduce the likelihood of different response biases such as social desirability or response contamination. (These and other response biases are discussed more fully in the next section.)

Interviewing children in schools is, on the whole, more cost-effective than interviewing children in the home. One problem of classroom surveys is that they usually rely on self-completion schedules, which can encounter difficulties with literacy and motivation. Motivation is often less of a problem with younger children, who may even approach a survey questionnaire as if it were a test. This test-taking mentality, although likely to enhance what is perceived to be the correct response, may be beneficial in making children pay greater attention to the questions. A main drawback of school-based interviewing is that children of all ages are likely to be influenced by the proximity of class mates. Even if answers are supposedly confidential, children are likely to quiz one another on their responses and may be tempted to give answers that win favour with the peer-group.

Table 4.1 Surveys interviewing children in Britain

Study name and survey type	Country and year	Sample	Method of data collection	Context
British Household Panel Study	Britain 1994– annual	Children aged 11–15 in panel households N≈900	Walkman tape self-administered	Home interview
British Social Attitudes	Britain 1994	Children aged 12–19 N = 580	Face-to-face	Home interview
National Child Development Study Longitudinal Cohort	Britain 1965, 1969, 1974, 1981, 1991	Children born in one week of 1958 N≈16,000	Face-to-face	Home interview
Twenty-07 Longitudinal Cohort	West Scotland 1987/8	Youngest cohort aged 15 N≈1,000	Face-to-face and self-completion	Home interview
National Crime Survey	England and Wales 1992	Children aged 12–15 N≈1,000	Self-completion	Home interview
OPCS Smoking Survey	England 1994	School children N = 3,045	Self-completion and smoking diary	School interview
School Health Education Unit, University of Exeter	England 1984–annual	School children aged 11–16 N≈10,000	Self-completion	School interview

Interviewing children in the home is more time consuming and therefore more costly. One concern that is usual in contacting children at home is the need to deal with parents as gatekeepers. In my experience, with the British Household Panel Study (BHPS), this rarely caused a problem, but parents were already participating in the survey. On the whole, we found that children are very keen to participate and seem pleased to be treated as household members who have something useful to contribute in their own right. Interviewing children, if anything, improved our household response rates because their enthusiasm raised the interest of other household members. With household studies, there is the risk, however, that children's answers will be influenced by the presence of parents or siblings. Even if the interviewer is instructed to interview the child in private if possible, complete privacy is often impractical or elusive in the home. In a later section I discuss how we overcame the privacy and confidentiality issues in the BHPS Young Person's Survey.

Interviews with children at home are usually carried out in person and this has at least three advantages over the self-completion methods that are often used in schools. First, it is possible to include more complex routing so that particular questions are only asked in specific circumstances that have been elicited by earlier responses. Different questions, for example, might be appropriate, depending on whether the child lives with one parent or with two. Second, it is possible to make use of visual aids and show cards which allow for more elaborate response options. Third, if the questions do not elicit sufficiently clear or elaborate responses then the interviewer is able to prompt for further information. All three are particularly important when interviewing young adolescents. Routing is needed to ensure that children at different stages of social development are asked appropriate questions. Visual aids are useful when there are vocabulary problems and limited attention span. Interviewer prompts are essential when inadequate answers are given, because of lack of communication skills.

New interviewing techniques using Computer Assisted Personal Interviewing (CAPI) methods add further enhancements that could be used to good effect with younger respondents. Not only do they make complex routing relatively effortless for the interviewer, but also they provide the opportunity to incorporate videos and other visual and audio stimuli that reduce the need to rely so heavily on verbal questions and answers.

Telephone interviewing can be a far more economical alternative and, at least in the USA has proved effective with children aged 11 and older (Reich and Earls 1990). The success of interviewing young people by telephone is not surprising given the amount of time teenagers spend on the phone confiding in friends. But a major drawback with the telephone interview is the possible lack of privacy. This is particularly crucial when interviewing children and may limit the usefulness of telephone interviews as a means of collecting sensitive information.

One relatively novel method of collecting sensitive information from children is the diary method. Diaries are also good for collecting information that is too detailed for retrospective reports to be reliable. In principle, the method should be useful if the format can be made sufficiently simple and internal checks for accuracy can be devised. The Family Expenditure Survey, for example, has incorporated expenditure diaries that are used with children (Jarvis 1994) and the new panel study Home On-Line is using a time-use diary with children aged 9-15 (BHPS 1998).

The increasing prevalence of internet use in the home means that the Web offers new ways of contacting and interviewing children. Even so, such interviews remain problematic for at least two reasons. First, the population of internet users is still a highly select group, for example in the UK, in 2000, the ONS Time Use Survey shows that 54 per cent of primary school children and 65 per cent of secondary school children used the internet at home, with boys far more frequent users than girls (ONS 2002). Second, ethical issues remain, and when contacting children via e-mail or internet, it is good practice to ensure parental permission is obtained, when possible. Internet and e-mail based surveys are bound to become increasingly useful for both adults and children as broadband access becomes more widespread (see Selwyn and Robson 1998; Fox et al. 2003; and Couper et al. 2001). At present, however, the most persuasive uses of Web based social-research are when electronic surveys are used to complement conventional methods of administration. Internet survey are often used for exploratory research, for example on-line surveys of bullying allow the participating young people to express their views, but the quality of the resulting information in terms of both reliability and generalisability is hard to assess.

Are children any less reliable than adult respondents?

An old proverb says it is only children and fools who tell the truth. In contrast, Belloc's cautionary tales tell us of Matilda who told such dreadful lies it made us gasp and stretch our eyes. Social constructions include the contradictory portrayal of childhood as a time of wide-eyed innocence and wilful deceit. In this section, three questions will be considered. First, are children any more or less reliable than adult respondents? Second, how can we evaluate the quality of data from children? Third, how can we improve data quality?

There is a seeming reluctance to take children's responses at face value, perhaps because children's opinions are seen as especially pliable and susceptible to suggestion. This is an area that is coming under the glare of public scrutiny in recent times, as there is mounting concern about the reliability of children's testimonies in cases concerning child abuse and the like (Fincham et al. 1994; Ceci and Bruck 1994). There is little reason to discredit children as respondents, however, because in highly traumatic circumstances children, like adults, have been known to lie or display memory distortion. Moreover, modern psychological and medical evidence suggests that children are more reliable as witnesses than previously thought, and reliability can be increased by skilful interviewing (Spencer and Flin 1990). The interviewing advice is very familiar to survey researchers: give the child unambiguous and comprehensible instructions at the start of the interview; avoid leading questions; explicitly permit 'don't know' responses to avoid best guesses; and interview the child on home ground, if possible. There is growing evidence to suggest that the best source of information about issues pertinent to children is the children themselves. While parents and teachers can provide useful insights into child behaviour, the direct interviewing of children provides a far more complete account of the child's life. For example, in the health domain, young children often report depressed symptoms of which their parents appear to be unaware and school-age children report far more fears than their mothers' account reveal (Tizard 1986). Older children may be involved with alcohol and drugs without their parents' knowledge. Yet, when it comes to younger children's own behavioural problems, parents can be more forthcoming than the children (Reich and Earls 1990). For many areas of research, therefore, it is desirable to gather information from multiple sources, as any one account may be biased (Tein et al. 1994).

Improving data quality

The quality of data that results from interviewing children will depend on a number of different factors. First and most basic is the appropriateness of the research topic and measures used. In designing suitable measures for young children, researchers have to, at a minimum, ensure that the questions really do measure the desired concept; that the questions are unambiguous and that children interpret the questions in the way the researcher intended. Research concerning the question and answer process in surveys with children is extremely sparse. However, the research clearly suggests that the clarity of questions influence the quality of the data, especially for younger children and that complex questions are problematic regardless of the child's age (De Leeuw and Otter 1995).

We also know that both younger children and adolescents alike tend to respond to adult questioning, whether or not they know the answer, or have an attitude on the issue at hand (Parker 1984; Weber et al. 1994). Children are often called on by adults to give answers even when they do not have the information and responses of 'don't know' can be deemed as cheek, inattention or lack of cooperation. It is understandable then that children are likely to construct a response rather than refuse to answer, but this can make for low stability on issues where the children's knowledge is limited or their attitude are non-crystallized (Vaillancourt 1973). Thus, in order to achieve meaningful data, questions have to be pertinent and relevant to the children's own experience or knowledge. However, when this condition is met it is clear that even quite young children can make insightful respondents, as the following two studies illustrate.

In the USA, a specially adapted self-report instrument measuring and social behaviour was administered to boys as young as 7 (Loeber and Farrington 1989). In order to obtain independent measures of behaviour information was also collected from the primary parent or caretaker. When questioning the boys, interviewers first checked whether each item was clearly understood, by probing for examples. Only those items which the child could interpret were included in the subsequent inventory. Information was collected on whether the child had ever engaged in each kind of antisocial behaviour, and, if so, whether they had done so in the past six months. Bounded recall methods were used to establish the six month period, using Christmas, school terms and events from personal life.

Not surprisingly, there were marked differences between 7-year-olds and 10-year-olds in understanding the meaning of questions, with skipping school, for example, understood only by 75 per cent of American first-graders (aged 6-7) and almost 100 per cent of fourth-graders (aged 10–11). The most prevalent antisocial behaviour was hitting siblings (a concept well understood by all). The boys' estimates were fairly consistent with parental reports, but for most behaviours there was higher correlation between parental and child reports at age 7 than at age 10. One possible interpretation is that older children are less reliable. This, however, would be at odds with nearly all other empirical evidence, and a far more likely interpretation is that mothers know less about the behaviour of older children. Thus the different correlations reflect different states of parental knowledge.

In an Australian study of children in families, even primary school aged children (aged 8-9 years) were able to give articulate and informative responses to questions about objective family circumstances as long as the questions were about the here and now, or very recent past (Amato and Ochiltree 1987). However, this study provides clear evidence that questions that are outside the child's own experience, such as what parents do at work, are problematic if the interest is in adult job characteristics rather than children's perceptions. The objective quality of data, for this sort of question, improves markedly with older children (aged 15-16 years), who give answers that are more in line with the parental response.

Asking questions that are meaningful to the child's own experience is not, however, sufficient to guarantee that children will give meaningful answers. A second factor that is fundamental to improving data quality concerns the child's willingness and ability to answer the questions and articulate his or her subjective experience. This depends in part on the appropriateness, number and order of the response alternatives. One method of testing the effects of response alternatives is to use a split ballot whereby the sample is randomly split and a different version is given to each half. In a rare split ballot experiment with school children (aged 10 and over), evidence was found that children were prone to a primacy effect, being more likely to choose the option that appeared first when required to select among a list of five or more options (Hershey and Hill 1976). A similar problem occurred when using multi-item picture stimuli. Pictures are often considered useful because not only are they non-verbal but also they hold the limited attention of younger children.

However, pictures do not ease the basic decision-making process and, when interviewing children, responses are likely to be less prone to measurement error if the choices are kept simple. Children's responses will also be subject to the standard biases that have been relatively well researched in the question and answer process for adults – things like context effects, acquiescence bias, social desirability and the like. However, it is important not to simply assume that findings applicable to adults will generalize to children. For example, it has been claimed that children may be less susceptible than adults to social desirability bias. Nevertheless, the validity of this claim depends on the definition of social desirability. Social desirability is often defined in adult-centric terms. For example, good citizenship tends to be interpreted in terms of voting, community participation and the like. There are standard devices for over-coming adult reluctance to report behaviours that contravene what is perceived as socially desirable and to answer threatening questions whether they be about alcohol consumption, infidelity or the like (see Bradburn and Sudburn 1979). There is less consensus on what counts as a threatening question for children because what counts as appropriate behaviour is age dependent. In addition, children's own ideas about social desirability are heavily context dependent. For example, in one situation children might be tempted to downplay their reports of delinquent behaviour and cigarette or drug use, but in another situation they may be prone to exaggeration.

It is also the case that context effects and acquiescence bias may well take a different form, at different stages of the life course, depending on the subject matter at issue. For example, the norm of reciprocity which exerts a powerful influence on adults to answer contiguous questions in an even-handed way (Schuman and Presser 1981) may not have the same moral imperative for younger children. However, it has been claimed that young children are particularly suggestible and interviewers approbation or disapproval can have a marked effect. Nevertheless, experimental work found little evidence of acquiescence bias among older school-aged children (Hershey and Hill 1976). This is an area where clearly more research is needed but, until we have more evidence, it seems good practice to include internal consistency checks, where possible, when interviewing children.

A third set of issues concerns the children's motivation to give careful and truthful answers. In this regard, the interviewer and the rapport between interviewer and child are crucial. A good relationship can encourage more forthcoming responses, especially when children are convinced that their responses are truly confidential. However, the relationship between inter-viewer and child can also be a source of error. For instance, interviewers who are intimidating or impatient may inhibit children in a way that has damaging consequences for data quality. None of these factors are distinctive to children – they all apply to adult respondents as well – but achieving optimal conditions might require somewhat different solutions for children.

In the following section, I discuss the development of the BHPS Young Person's Survey, to illustrate one way in which a general purpose survey can be adapted to incorporate the different approach that is needed with children.

The BHPS young person's survey

The British Household Panel Study was launched in 1991, with the remit of monitoring micro-social change in Britain through the 1990s and beyond. The survey is carried out by National Opinion Polls (NOP) on behalf of the University of Essex. The BHPS involves an annual survey of each member of a nationally representative sample of at least 5,000 households, making a total of approximately 10,000 individuals. For the first time, in 1994 (for the fourth wave), children aged 11-15 years who were members of the panel households were interviewed in person. Almost 800 children were eligible and they were spread across some 600 households. These children automatically become adult sample members when they reach the age of 16 (Scott et al. 1995).

Interviewing children in their homes, as we have seen, is often ruled out as being too time consuming and expensive. For the BHPS this posed no problem as we were already interviewing the adult members of the households. Interviewing children at home, however, does pose special problems because it is not always possible to carry out the interview in private. Our main concern was to find a way of guaranteeing that the children's answers would be private and confidential. Not surprisingly, children may well find it difficult to be frank and honest, if their parents or siblings are present. But how can children be interviewed in such a way as to guarantee complete confidentiality, when their answers might well be overheard? Standard face-to-face interviews are not sufficiently private and self-completion methods were ruled out as unsuitable given some children's limited reading skills.

We turned, therefore, to a new and relatively untested interview method that involved pre-recording the Young Person's questionnaire on a personal Walkman. Listening to the questions on tape has two significant advantages. First, unlike in a standard interview, no one else can hear the questions. Moreover, because the answer booklet only contains response categories, the method ensures complete privacy. Second, unlike the standard self-administered questionnaire, the method overcomes the problem of literacy, which can be particularly acute when the respondents are children.

The Walkman interview method was first developed and tested in the USA for the Youth Risk Behaviour Surveillance System Questionnaire for the National Center for Health Statistics (Camburn et al. 1991). Early use of the Walkman technique demonstrated that it is possible to ask for sensitive information from children, while ensuring that the answers would be private and confidential. This feature is particularly important to the BHPS because the young person's component of the survey relates to health attitudes and behaviours within the family, including such highly sensitive material as drug use and mental health. It seems likely, however, that for almost any topic it is important to ensure privacy from other family members. Children from 11 onwards are particularly sensitive to privacy issues in the home, as is manifest by the common 'private, keep out' signs on bedroom doors.

Having decided on the appropriate mode of interview, it was still necessary to test the application of the Walkman method in the British context. There were many issues to be resolved. What was the preferred voice type and the optimal speed of reading, for the pre-recorded interview? What question formats were most appropriate for the method and could open-ended questions be used? Our pretest phase had two parts: first, we used qualitative group interviews with children to give feedback on the use of Walkmans, and second, we piloted the structured interview in the home setting.

Using focus groups to develop the survey instrument

The children's component of the BHPS has been commissioned by the Health Education Authority to focus specifically on the changing nature of health-related attitudes and behaviours of young people and their families. We had very little previous research to draw on for background information in formulating our questions. Given the lack of knowledge about this area, it made sense to use more qualitative methods to help inform the development of the structured survey instruments. Using focus groups was one method of eliciting information from children themselves that was undoubtedly preferable to guesswork (Morgan 1993).

Turning to the literature on focus groups, at the time, we found surprisingly little guidance about conducting focus groups of children. Most of the material to date had been produced by market researchers. Conventional wisdom regarding best practice for interviewing children in a group setting suggested that:

- children should be interviewed in restricted age groups as otherwise older children will dominate;
- boys and girls should be interviewed separately as they have such different communication styles;
- groups should be small, with no more than eight children at maximum.

Thus, in order to ensure group identity and cohesion we separated the groups by gender, age (11-13 years and 13-15 years) and socio-economic category. The groups were conducted in three different parts of England: the South, the Midlands and the North. The recruiting and conduct of the focus groups was carried out by the qualitative division of NOP, which used a combination of doorstep screening and snow-balling to fulfil the recruitment criteria.

Group sessions were conducted in the interviewer's home. The children's focus groups lasted approximately two hours, with a break for a fast food snack at half-time. The group leader followed a detailed discussion guide, which included topics such as freedom and rules in the house, family communication and sources of advice, health beliefs and practices, anxiety and depression and future aspirations and expectations. For some of the topics visual materials were used to stimulate discussion (for example a picture of Munch's 'The Scream' was used to probe feelings of anguish). In addition, some semi-structured questions were included that we hoped might prove suitable measures for this age group. For example, we showed a card with a range of smiley faces to see whether young people could identify their state of happiness with respect to different aspects of life. We feared that the smiley faces might be insulting to children of this age range, who are so sensitive to being treated as kids. However, to our surprise, the scale worked extremely well, prompting some very sophisticated discussion of mood states and changes. Even children as young as 11 have remarkable insight into impression management and self-presentation in everyday life and drew attention to the fact that answers might be different depending on whether the question wanted to know how you feel inside, how you are trying to appear to other people, or how other people perceive you to be (Scott et al. 1995).

A further use of the focus groups was to inform the development of the Walkman method of interviewing. At the end of the focus groups, Walkmans were handed out to each participant together with a short self-completion booklet in which they could record their answers. This short test interview was designed to provide feedback on the voice type, the speed of question delivery and the clearest design for the answer booklet. It was also important to test out the appropriate format of questions and, in particular, whether children could handle open as well as closed questions in the taped interviews. Group discussion then gave more general feedback on the Walkman method. Fortunately, young people were familiar with Walkman sets and were able to manage well without adult intervention. The only technical problems were caused by adult ineptitude with the machines!

Feedback from these groups indicated that young people were very sensitive to the quality of the voice rather than having a preference for a particular sex, age or accent. There was, however, less consensus about the optimal speed of question delivery and preferred interview pace. In order to give adequate time for the children to answer, we initially repeated both questions and answers on the pre-recorded questionnaires, but this caused considerable irritation to some children. Therefore, we subsequently recorded the question and response only once, but repeated the main thrust of the question. Children do vary considerably in the amount of time they need to respond. A taped interview, however, offers some advantages over the personal interview, in this respect. Children can pause and rewind the tape, whereas they might be embarrassed or reluctant to ask an interviewer to repeat the question or to allow them more time to think. Simple questions with numeric responses proved particularly suitable for these taped interviews, which rely on verbal memory. However, children as young as 11 are able to deal with open-ended questions, although the mean length of answer tends to increase with age, and younger children tend not to elaborate answers, unless specifically probed.

The focus groups showed beyond doubt that, given the right encouragement, young people are more than willing to say what they think. Thus the groups were both useful in their own right, providing a wealth of qualitative materials to analyse and they were also extremely useful in developing the quantitative research instruments and method. Nevertheless, focus groups are clearly no substitute for a structured pretest that replicates as closely as possible the real household interview setting.

Interviewing young people and parents at home

The structured household pilot survey was crucial in determining the appropriate length of interview, for children of this age group. The questionnaire had been pre-recorded with 83 questions in all, of which three were open-ended. The interview on average lasted 30 minutes. Surprisingly, interviewers reported no problems with this length of interview, even for our youngest respondents. For pretest purposes we had asked interviewers to be present when the children were doing their Walkman interview, so they could observe any difficulties. Interviewers were simultaneously conducting the parental interviews. This proved disastrous, as the children's presence inhibited the parent's responses. For our main survey, therefore, children are encouraged to do the Walkman interview in a different room, where possible.

Certain questions had to be modified as a result of our pretest experience. For example, we had followed standard advice and depersonalized possible threatening questions by asking children to respond in terms of people of my age. Some children, however, are very literal in their interpretation and tried to guess the age of the script reader (or interviewer). Children are all too used to having their opinions ignored by adults and not being consulted even on matters that directly concern them. Survey questions, therefore, have to be extremely explicit that it is the child's own views that are wanted. We also found that we had not taken sufficient account of the complexity of family life today and questions that refer to mother or father are often inherently ambiguous when children are living with step-parents or parent substitutes.

Vocabulary has not yet caught up with the reality of family situations and it is best to allow respondents to use their own terminology for relationships. The ethics that apply to interviewing children need, if anything, to be more stringent than with adults. Children are relatively powerless in society and, despite the attention given to children's rights, have relatively little recourse to official channels of complaint. It is therefore very important that researchers are particular conscious of their ethical responsibilities when interviewing children. In particular, special attention needs to be paid to explaining the research purpose in a comprehensible fashion and obtaining informed consent from the children themselves.

The BHPS children's questionnaire is preceded with the same statement of confidentiality and voluntary participation as we use with our adult respondents. Following our practice with adult respondents, young people are offered an incentive (a money voucher) to take part in the survey. It has been questioned whether bribing children with money is ethical. Our position is that the incentive is acknowledging that we attach the same worth to children as to our adult respondents. Unfortunately, monetary considerations hindered our ideological commitment and children are paid at a lower rate than adult participants. Thus, even as respondents, children experience life's inequities.

The children's survey has now become an established part of the British Household Panel but in the interests of reducing costs and decreasing completion time, the Walkman method of interview was replaced with a self-completion questionnaire from 2002 onwards. A systematic investigation of data quality has not been undertaken. Indeed, it would be hard to attribute change to mode of administration differences without designing a methodological experiment that would further reduce data comparability. Nevertheless, whatever the mode of collection, the children's survey data are unique because, each year, young people are interviewed about their family life and the way it has changed, their relations with parents, their school achievements, and their hopes and aspirations concerning family life, education and work. As part of the ESRC programme on Youth and Social Change, these prospective data have been used to examine teenagers at risk and how some young people are able to beat the odds to overcome family disadvantage and gain good educational qualifications (Scott 2004). More generally, we are interested in the life trajectories of young people who are regarded as vulnerable because they come from low-income families or disrupted households. Relevant to the study is the theorem of individuation (Beck 1992) which stresses that people have to construct their lives more actively than ever before (Giddens 1996: 243). The usual focus of such concepts is adults, but the idea is just as relevant to children. We shall also be using the concept of social capital, which was first introduced by James Coleman to refer to the mechanism by which the advantages and disadvantages associated with household structure, financial capital and human capital are transmitted to the next generation (Coleman 1988). However, in many studies, social capital is seen as part of the way parents and larger social forces irrevocably shape children's lives. Our interviews with children will enable us to counteract this overly deterministic view and show the importance of children's own experiences, attitudes, aspirations and achievements for shaping their own destinies. The active role young people play in coping with their family environment and forming their own life choices has often been overlooked. This perhaps is not surprising when so much quantitative data has relied solely on adult informants.

Conclusion

Interviewing children is no fad. Improved data about children are essential in a society where children's role as consumers and citizens is being taken increasingly seriously in the economy, in law and in social policy. In this chapter I have taken it as axiomatic that it is only by interviewing children directly that we can understand children's social worlds. Moreover, I have argued that general population surveys that omit accounts of children provide biased estimates of many important social variables. However, interviewing children does pose distinctive methodological problems that could impinge on the quality of the data.

I suggested that while structured questions are not appropriate for younger children because of cognitive and language limitations, by pre-adolescence, children are quite capable of providing meaningful and insightful information. However, children are also well versed in techniques of impression management and issues of privacy and confidentiality are especially important, if children are to give honest and complete answers. The setting of interviews is also important, in this respect, and it is crucial to find ways of avoiding response contamination both in the home and at school.

I have stressed the difficulties involved in ensuring that survey instruments take account of the wide range of developmental stages of childhood. Pretests are especially important as children's understanding of a question can be quite different from that which the researcher intended. It is also important that questions are not posed from an adult-centric perspective. One useful way of investigating the children's own understanding of an issue is to use qualitative, in-depth group discussions, prior to developing the structured questionnaire. Another way is to use cognitive pretest methods such as think aloud techniques, to probe how the question is understood and why a particular answer is given.

I described the development of the Young People's Survey of the British Household Panel Study to illustrate some of the challenges and possible solutions in interviewing children in a large-scale general household survey. Children's focus groups proved a very successful way of identifying appropriate questions for obtaining sensitive information. The groups also provided useful feedback on technical aspects of using a pre-recorded interview and self-completion answer booklet instead of the more standard face-to-face or self-completion methods. Although no longer part of the BHP survey, taped interviews have two main advantages for use with children: they overcome literacy problems and they ensure privacy and confidentiality, when interviewing in the home. The common wisdom that asking questions is a useful way of getting information as long as the respondent is able and willing to answer applies just as much, or perhaps even more strongly, when the respondent is a minor. Consternation about the reliability of children as witnesses in areas such as child abuse might stimulate further research in this area. However, the danger is that such research would highlight very specific problems, rather than providing a more general understanding of the question and answer process with children. Methodological research on conditions that enhance the ability of children to be good respondents is extremely sparse. Hopefully, it will expand rapidly as the practice of interviewing children in large-scale surveys becomes more widespread. Asking children is likely to be one of the best ways of learning how to improve the quality of our data. It is important, however, not to overemphasize data quality issues with respect to children. Data quality is always an issue, regardless of the age of the respondent.

There is an increasing concern to understand childhood experience in quantitative social research as the life course paradigm becomes more influential. What unites different life course studies is that they view human development over individual, social and historical time. Life course studies recognize that in order to understand the way people's lives unfold in a particular social setting two things are necessary. First, we need to understand how early events and influences persist and fade across the life course in a changing world. Second, we need to understand how an individual's actions and societal change are reciprocally linked.

In a fast-changing society, it is important to evaluate the effects of policies and the long-term effects of experiences on individuals. The imprint of circumstances on childhood, whether it is war, parental conflict, educational reform, or the pervasive influence of TV soaps, has lasting consequences. Yet often the stress on long-term outcomes tends to draw attention away from the importance of understanding present-day experiences. It is one thing to study childhood adversity because we want to investigate the long-term consequences for adult psychopathology. It is another to study children because we want to know how they are doing in the here and now. Both are important subjects for quantitative research. A better understanding of the adult outcomes of childhood experiences will give us new insights into many of the ongoing theoretical debates, for example the relative importance of social and genetic factors in the accumulation of advantage and disadvantage. However, it is also crucially important to understand what it is like for children growing up in an era of family upheaval and rapid social change. Quantitative research allows us to explore the diverse ways that children negotiate the transitions, turning points and humdrum realities of their everyday lives.

Acknowledgements

This chapter is a revised version of a paper that was presented at the American Statistical Association's International Conference on Survey Measurement and Process Quality, Bristol 1995 (see Scott 1997b). I wish to acknowledge the support of the Economic and Social Research Council (Grant LI 34251027) and the Health Education Authority who supported the development of the Young Person's Survey in the British Household Panel Study.

References

Amato, P. and Ochiltree, G. (1987) 'Interviewing children about their families: a note on data quality', *Journal of Marriage and Family* 49: 669–75.
Aries, P. (1962) *Centuries of Childhood*, Harmondsworth: Penguin.
Astington, J.W., Harris, P. and Olsen, D. (1988) *Developing Theories of Mind*, Cambridge: Cambridge University Press.

Backett, K. and Alexander, H. (1991) 'Talking to young children about health: methods and findings', *Health Education Journal* 50 (1): 34–8.

Beck, U. (1992) *Risk Society: Towards a New Modernity*, London: Sage.

Belle, D., Norell, S. and Lewis, A. (1997) 'Children's transitions in afterschool hours', in I. Gotlib and B. Wheaton (eds) *Stress and Adversity over the Life Course*, Cambridge: Cambridge University Press.

Bradburn, N. and Sudburn, S. (1979) *Improving Interviewing Methods and Questionnaire Design: Response Effects to Threatening Questions in Survey Research*, San Francisco, CA: Jossey-Bass.

British Household Panel Study (1998) *British Household Panel Study News issue 14*, Wivenhoe Park: University of Essex.

Camburn, D., Cynamon, M. and Harel, Y. (1991) 'The use of audio tapes and written questionnaires to ask sensitive questions during household interviews'. Paper to National Field Directors' Conference, San Diego, California, May.

Ceci, S.J. and Bruck, M. (1994) 'How reliable are children's statements? It depends', *Family Relations* 43 (3): 255–7.

Church, J. and Summerfied, C. (eds) (1997) *Social Focus on Children*, London: HMSO.

Coleman, J. (1988) 'Social capital in the creation of human capital', *American Journal of Sociology* 94 (suppl. 95): S95–S120.

Couper, M., Traugott, M. and Lamias, M. (2001) 'Web survey design and administration', *Public Opinion Quarterly*, 65 (2):230–53.

De Leeuw, E.D. and Otter, M.E. (1995), 'The reliability of children's responses to questionnaire items: question effects in children's questionnaire data', in J.J. Hox *et al.* (eds) *Advances in Family Research*, Amsterdam: Thesis.

Elder, G.H. Jr (1995) 'The life-course paradigm: social change and individual development', in P. Moen, G. Elder and K. Luscher (eds) *Examining Lives in Context: Perspectives on the Ecology of Human Development*, Washington, DC: American Psychological Association.

Elder, G.H. Jr, Modell, J. and Parke, R.D. (1993) *Children in Time and Place: Developmental and Historical Insights*, Cambridge; Cambridge University Press.

Elliot, J. and Richards, M. (1991) 'Children and divorce: educational performance and behaviour after and before parental separation', *International Journal of Law and the Family* 4: 258–76.

Fincham, F., Beach, S., Moore, T. and Diener, C. (1994) 'The professional response to child sexual abuse: whose interests are served?', *Family Relations* 43 (3): 244–54.

Fine, G. and Sandstrom, K. (1988) *Knowing Children: Participant Observation with Minors*, Sage Qualitative Research Methods Series, No. 15, Newbury Park, CA: Sage.

Fox, J., Murray., C. and Warm, A. (2003) 'Conducting research using web-based questionnaires: practical, methodological and ethical considerations', *International Journal of Social Research Methodology* 6 (2): 167–80.

Furstenberg, F. Jr and Hughes, M. (1995) 'Social capital and successful development among at-risk youth', *Journal of Marriage and Family* 57 (3): 580–92.

Giddens, A. (1996) *In Defence of Sociology: Essays, Interpretations and Rejoinders*, Cambridge: Polity.

Hershey, M. and Hill, D. (1976) 'Positional response set in pre-adult socialization surveys', *Social Science Quarterly* 56: 707–14.

Jarvis, L. (1994) 'The feasibility of children keeping FES expenditure diaries: a qualitative study', *Survey Methodological Bulletin* 35 (1): 1–2.

Kiernan, K. (1992), 'The impact of family disruption in childhood on transitions made in young adult life', *Population Studies* 46: 213–34.

Lamb, M.E. (2005a) 'Testimony, children's compentence in C.B. Fisher and R.M. Lerner (eds) *Encyclopedia of Applied Developmental Science*. (Vol 2:1085–86) Thousand Oaks, CA: Sage.

Lamb, M.E. (2005b) 'Forensic Interviewing', in C.B. Fisher and R.M. Lerner (eds) *Encyclopedia of Applied Developmental Science* (Vol 2:477–79) Thousand Oaks, CA: Sage.

Loeber, R. and Farrington, D. (1989) 'Development of a new measure of self-reported antisocial behavior for young children: prevalence and reliability', in M. Klein (ed.) *Cross-National Research in Self-Reported Crime and Delinquency*, Dordrecht: Kluwer Academic.

Middleton, S., Ashworth, K. and Walker, R. (eds) (1994) *Family Fortunes: Pressures on Parents and Children in the 1990s*, London: Child Poverty Action Group.

Morgan, D. (1993) 'Using qualitative methods in the development of surveys', *Social Psychology Newsletter* 19 (1): 1–2.

Morrow, V. (1994) 'Responsible children? Aspects of children's work and employment outside school in contemporary UK', in B. Mayall (ed.) *Children's Childhoods Observed and Experienced*, London: Falmer Press.

ONS (2002) *Office of National Statistics, 'Social Focus in Brief: Children'* http://www.statistics.gov.uk/downloads/theme_social/social_focus_in_brief/children/Social_Focus_in_Brief_Children_2002.pdf

Opie, I. and Opie, P. (1959) *The Lore and Language of Schoolchildren*, Oxford: Oxford University Press.

Parker, W. (1984) 'Interviewing children: problems and promise', *Journal of Negro Education*, 53 (1): 18–28.

Qvortrup, J. (1990) 'A voice for children in statistical and social accounting: a plea for children's right to be heard', in A. James and A. Prout (eds) *Constructing and Reconstructing Childhood*, London: Falmer Press.

Reich, W. and Earls, F. (1990) 'Interviewing adolescents by telephone: is it a useful methodological strategy?', *Comprehensive Psychiatry* 31 (3): 211–15.

Robinson, W.P. (1986) 'Children's understanding of the distinction between messages and meaning: emergence and implications', in M. Richards and P. Light (eds) *Children of Social Worlds*, Cambridge: Polity.

Schuman, H. and Presser, S. (1981) *Questions and Answers in Attitude Surveys*, New York: Academic Press.

Scott, J. (1997a) 'Children's well-being in changing British households'. *Paper to International Conference on Urban Childhood*, Trondheim, June.

Scott, J. (1997b) 'Children as respondents: methods for improving data quality', in L. Lyberg *et al.* (eds) *Survey Measurement and Process Quality*, New York: Wiley.

Scott, J. (2004) 'Family, gender and educational attainment in Britain: A longitudinal study', *Journal of Comparative Family Studies* 35 (4): 565–89.

Scott, J., Brynin, M. and Smith, R. (1995) 'Interviewing children in the British Household Panel Study', in J.J. Hox *et al.* (eds) *Advances in Family Research*, Amsterdam: Thesis.

Selwyn, N. and Robson, K. (1998) 'Using e-mail as a research tool', *Social Research Update*, Issue No. 2.1, http://www.soc.surrey.ac.uk/Sru/SRU21.html

Solberg, A. (1990) 'Negotiating childhood: changing constructions of age for Norwegian children', in A. James and A. Prout (eds) *Constructing and Reconstructing Childhood*, London: Palmer Press.

Spencer, J. and Flin, R. (1990) *The Evidence of Children*, London: Blackstone.

Stanley, B. and Sieber, J. (eds) (1992) *Social Research on Children and Adolescents: Ethical Issues*, Newbury Park, CA: Sage.

Tein, J-Y., Roosa, M. and Michaels, M. (1994) 'Agreement between parent and child reports on parental behaviours', *Journal of Marriage and the Family* 56 (2): 341–55.

Timmer, S., Eccles, J. and O'Brien, K. (1985) 'How children use time', in T. Juster and F. Stafford (eds) *Time, Goods and Well-Being*, Ann Arbor, MI: Institute of Social Research.

Tizard, B. (1986) 'The impact of the nuclear threat on children's development', in M. Richards and P. Light (eds) *Children of Social Worlds*, Cambridge: Polity.

Vaillancourt, P. (1973) 'Stability of children's survey responses', *Public Opinion Quarterly* 37: 373–87.

Weber, L., Miracle, A. and Skehan, T. (1994) 'Interviewing early adolescents: some methodological considerations', *Human Organizations* 53 (1): 42–7.

5 Conversations with Children

Working with Generational Issues

Berry Mayall

Introduction

This chapter is about how adult researchers can learn about children's knowledge. The basic assumption here is that we adults need to take account of children's knowledge in the work of trying to understand relationships between social groups. Children constitute a social group, a permanent feature of society, and thus their knowledge of what it means to be a child and what it means to children to engage with adult individuals and adult social groups is needed as part of the task of improving our understanding of how the social order works. Complementary to such proper understanding is the need to consider what, if anything, should be done to improve the social condition of childhood.

I use the word 'knowledge' rather than 'perspective' or 'opinion' because in this chapter I want to draw attention to the temporal features of understanding. The word 'knowledge' implies something derived from experiences in the past; people reflect on these, build on them and arrive at a body of understanding, commonly in process of revision; and an important means of refining and enlarging our knowledge is through verbal interactions with others. It is part of our new conceptualizations of children, therefore, that we credit them with knowledge, rather than with the relatively transient and flimsy 'perspective', 'view' or 'opinion'. I argue that through conversing with children we can learn about what they know, and, to some extent, how they learn.

In this chapter I focus specifically on the idea that generation is key for understanding childhood and children's lives. Children's daily lives and thus childhood as an institution are structured by adult views of how those lives should be lived and of what childhood is (see Qvortrup, this volume). Key relationships are with adults in homes, schools and public spaces. Adults have divided up the social order into two major groups – adults and children, with specific conditions surrounding the lives of each group: provisions, constraints and requirements, laws, rights, responsibilities and privileges. Thus, just as the concept of gender has been key to understanding women's relationships to the social order, so the concept of generation is key to understanding childhood. This means that the adult researcher who wishes to research with children must confront generational issues.

Generational issues underlie the linked goals and methods of research about children and childhood, but have not always been recognized and taken into account. Much research, notably within psychological paradigms, has been carried out on children, based on the assumption that children, compared to adults, are incompetent, unreliable and developmentally incomplete; so it is the goal of the researcher, on the basis of adult paradigms of child development, to improve knowledge of children's position and progress on the journey to adult maturity (see Woodhead, this volume). Commonly, the researcher's stance is that of detached observer. By contrast, researchers, broadly within anthropological traditions, seek to suspend notions of generational and status difference, in the attempt to reach understandings of children's take on social life. This method involves participant observation with children; it includes watching, listening, reflecting and also engaging with the children in conversation, as appropriate, to naturally occurring events and to the researcher's understandings during the process of fieldwork. For Mandell (1991) and Thorne (1993), participant observation of children has required trying to adopt the 'least-adult role', blending in to the social world of the children, not siding with adults, operating physically and metaphorically on the children's level in their social worlds. As Thorne wryly notes, this social positioning by the researcher is, however, very hard to sustain; she found herself exchanging complicit glances with the teacher, and the children too sometimes questioned her role and her purposes (see Davis, this volume).

The first approach to research accepts the generational order; it assumes the superiority of adult knowledge, and the relevance of documenting childhood in the light of that knowledge. The second approach questions the generational order; good information about childhood must start from children's experience. In order to get good data, children are to be taught by the researcher that power issues between children and adults can be diluted or defused to the point where children accept the adult as one of themselves. But, according to my information from children, they think otherwise: a central characteristic of adults is that they have power over children.

In writing these paragraphs I have deliberately chosen certain prepositions, linked to goals and agendas. In the traditional psychological paradigm, research is on children; it aims to study their development and they are to be observed, measured and judged. The second approach proposes working *with* children, in the sense that the adult tries to enter children's worlds of understanding, and her own understanding and thereby her agendas may be modified through the research experience; however her purposes are not necessarily made available to the children (see Woodhead, this volume).

In my own research programme over the last eight years, I have perhaps sited myself somewhere between these two approaches. Essentially, I am trying to work with generational issues, rather than to assume adult superiority or to downplay these issues. I am asking children, directly, to help me, an adult, to understand childhood. I want to investigate directly with children the knowledge they have of their social position, the status of being a child, and child-adult relations. I want to acquire from them their own unique knowledge and assessment of what it means to be a child, mainly in the major social contexts where their lives are spent, at home and at school. I present myself as a person who, since she is adult, does not have this knowledge; for though I can remember some things about being a child, I may have forgotten much, and childhoods may vary and have probably changed over the years since I was a child. I do not deal here with whether or how to work with children at the later stages of research, when one has to write papers such as this one. This chapter is about issues to do with processes of data collection.

My comments derive from my experiences of four studies exploring aspects of ordinary children's activities in daily life.[1] In this programme of work, I started from the assumption, gained from earlier work on mothers' health care of their pre-school children, that the character and quality of children's daily lives are best studied across contexts. That is, we need to look at the totality of the day, and at the impacts of one context on another. For instance, the activity of a 5-year-old and her mother at home is structured by the demands of the school. So in these studies I have tried to take account, in various ways, of children's daily lives across and between the arenas designated for them: home, school and the short times and small spaces between; and of the importance of adult belief and behaviour in those arenas. The experience of taking part in these four studies has been a developmental process of learning about goals and methods of research with children but here I draw, mainly on the first of these four studies, 'Child Health Care'.

Research conversations

In this study of child health care I aimed to explore social contexts as frames for children's experience, to ask how far children take part in the promotion, maintenance and restoration of their health at home, at school and anywhere else, who else takes part, and what factors or structures facilitate or inhibit child health care in the two settings. I spent two days a week in one school, over two terms (1990-1), first with a reception class (children aged 5/6 years) and then with a Class 5 (children aged 9/10 years). I worked as a general helper around the classroom, accompanied the children through the day, observed and recorded daily events, and chatted to the children about their activities.

In the first days, part of my aim was to become a familiar figure, for whom the children did not behave in special ways during their class-work and with whom children might confidently talk. I thought becoming familiar might take several weeks, but as the reception class teacher explained to me, the children were used to a range of adults being there—as helpers, listening to reading, teaching computing, taking part in trips, helping with swimming. As time went on, I engaged directly with the children in a range of activities. First, with the reception class children I held discussions in twos and threes, drew pictures and talked about them; made a book of them. With the 9-year-olds I started with a whole class discussion about the research, discussed issues with them in groups of three or four, in collaboration with the teacher set up a regular writing slot about health care at home and school, carried out a whole class brainstorm on where health care takes place, and worked with pairs of children on filling in and discussing a 24-hour diet sheet. At the same time, with the initial aim of getting adult views, I carried out informal interviews with teaching and non-teaching staff, and I then arranged to talk with parents at home.

Conversations at school

Methodologically, the school and the home pose very different challenges, and different again are children's own arenas. At school, the social circumstances of carrying out research with children differed as between the reception class and the older class.[2] The 5- and 6-year-olds were spending their day in a relaxed atmosphere, where they worked for short periods of intensive activity with the teacher or a helper on reading, writing or numbers; at other times the teacher encouraged them to engage with sand, water, building, painting and board-game activities; and at some points in the day they had even freer choice–to make up games, play in the home corner, run around and leaf through books. The children were new to school life, and mostly looked extremely enthusiastic about the opportunities it offered. They had plenty of time to construct their own social life in the classroom, as well as at playtimes. Under these circumstances, doing research with me was acceptable, even fun, but not a great release from classwork.

In order to explore children's knowledge, I aimed to engage with them in conversations, where an opening gambit could lead wherever children wished. The teacher and I agreed in thinking the children might enjoy the experience more if they remained in the familiar social context of their class-room. A possible downside of this, as I recognized, was that conversation, particularly about the pros and cons of school, might be somewhat inhibited. However, one way of helping the children feel confident was by asking them to talk with me in twos, and I asked for a child to choose a friend. This social context did seem to be supportive and enabling. At ease with each other, and thereby, perhaps, more confident with the third, adult participant, children could follow on each other's leads, pick up points and confirm, comment or move on. For example, in the following conversation Jane was readier to talk, but the topics she chose to focus on seemed to offer a context or trigger allowing Mary to contribute too.[3]

I: What do you like about school?
Jane: I like dinners. The desserts are nice. I like it at playtime. There's lots of time to play. I like it cos it's fun. You can do all kinds of things.
I: Is that at playtime?
Jane: And inside: pictures, playing and looking at books.
Mary: And apparatus. Drawing, games, painting and playing.

I: And do you like class-time and assembly and hall-time?
Jane: All of them.
Mary: And outings. You get fresh air.
Jane: It's a big building. There's lots of space.
Mary: I like the flowers [i.e. in school garden]. And I like painting.
Jane: Dippy painting.
I: Are there things you don't like about school?
Jane: I don't like about when I'm going to be in Class 6 [the top class], cos I've seen Miss X shouting at them.
Mary: And I don't like the dinners. I don't like reading time.

A somewhat different set of factors fed into decisions about working with the older children in Class 5. They had much more work to get through, and indeed some commented that it was never-ending. Some, especially boys, thought school was boring; and both boys and girls resented their teacher 'going on' at them about their behaviour. There was very little free time in class. The teacher and I agreed that, since an empty, quiet room nearby was available, this would be a good working environment. Under these circumstances, the children were eager to join in with the research. They were also very familiar with each other, and with the topics of the research: life at home and school, and health care issues. So they talked freely and at some length; they joked and chatted. It also seemed that they identified me as a non-official adult at school: a person to whom adverse comments about school could be made, twisted ankles and grazed elbows displayed and discussed (but, they said, not mentioned to staff). The following quick-fire snatch between four 9-year-olds is typical.

I: Whose job is it to keep you healthy?
Ann: Our Mum.
Joan: Our Dad.
Adam: It's mainly our job.
Peter: I think mainly our job.
Adam: Because we're the ones–
Peter: We're the ones that have to take care of ourselves. Like when we live by ourselves we will.
Adam: So we're like keeping ourselves healthy, by doing things ourselves.
Ann: It's my body, so it's my job.
Adam: So it's mainly us.
Ann: Because your Mum and Dad, they might nag you–take your vitamins, eat your greens or whatever, but we're the ones who do it anyway.
I: OK.
Peter: Our Mum and Dad do encourage us to eat things, like take vitamins and eat healthy food, so that's partly, they do it.
Adam: But us mainly. We do it. Sometimes!

I: Is that at home or in general?
Joan: Mainly at home.
Adam: Mainly.
Ann: Mainly.
Peter: Yes, because we eat there. Well, we do eat at restaurants, but we mainly eat at home.
I: Of course, you do eat at school.
Ann: Ugh.
Joan: Ugh.
Adam: I have my own food at school.
Peter: So do I.

Though these discussions were initiated by me, they were not very different in character (perhaps a bit more focused) from conversations I heard around the classroom and corridors. The children were working through points, elaborating, confirming, opposing and diverging, as in an Italian *discussione* (Corsaro, this volume). Talking with friends is an important way of acquiring knowledge; so for the researcher, listening to conversations can be one means of learning about this process.

Conversations across schools and homes

Understanding of what people say requires exploration of context. This was demonstrated to me by two 6-year-old girls whom I asked to talk about the merits of home. It was through their comparison of home with the social worlds of school that some important themes emerged.

I: What do you like best about being at home?
Sandra: Um, nothing much.
I: Nothing much? Do you prefer being at school?
Sandra: Yeah. I prefer being at school. Do you, Rita?
Rita: Well, not really.
Sandra: I do, because it's fun. It's not all fun, because sometimes we do boring work.
Rita: Sometimes we have to do really boring things and–
Sandra (shouting)–and sometimes we have to do really hard things that we can't even do!
Rita: And sometimes when we don't want to do something, the teachers won't let us not do it.
I: So you have to do things at school?
Rita: Yeah. Sometimes we don't have to.
I: Do you have to do things at home?
Sandra: No, not really.
Rita: Well, my Mum tells me to put my stuff away. I don't really.
Sandra: I don't really either.

In this extract, these girls compare the generational order of the home and the school. The commands and demands made by teachers and parents differ; there is more leeway for children at home. A second theme is the contrasting features of school: on the one hand it is fun, but on the other hand it can be boring or too difficult.

These two girls were friends and in their conversations with me they were confident and chatty. They were sufficiently at ease with each other that they could, at some points, set aside the generational order of my conversation with them. That is, they moved out of the adult question – child reply mode, and talked with each other. Yet in some circumstances, working with the generational order posed different challenges for me, the researcher, and demanded different routes to arrive at understanding. The case of Richard was one such challenge. In an attempt to explore children's school days as days that start and end at home, I asked them to talk with me about first thing in the morning, and coming to school. Richard was the only 5-year-old child who said he hated school.

Richard: What I do in the morning? I hate school. and I don't like coming. You silly, stupid school! ... I don't like staying at school. I like being with my Daddy and Mummy better. I love my Daddy and my Mummy. ... I stay asleep and then I don't have to come to school, and my Mummy woke me up and got me up. And I didn't wanna go to school. So she said, you have to. So I had breakfast and then I got to school.

Other conversations with Richard confirmed his dislike of school – he had experienced violence in the playground, and, he said, 'I don't like coming to school because everyone grunts.' His teacher had told me she was worried about him, for though he had been in her class for some time he had no clear friends or established companions and he seemed sad and subdued. Later I arranged to go to his home and talk with his mother. When I got there, she told me how pleased he was that I was coming, and he showed me round the flat, sat in on the conversation and drew me a picture to take away. Richard, his mother said, had established an important position in the family as the eldest of three. He made his own and his brothers' beds. He was highly competent. 'He washes up, makes beds, polishes – not very well. He'll tidy up my bedroom for me. He tries to be a teacher at home, teach the others.' But he was 'sometimes a bit moody when he gets home, he's got the hump.' In talking with me Richard had made negative comments about school, and comparison with his happy relations with his parents. But it was his mother's accounts, together with observation of the scene at home, that helped me understand better his knowledge of his own identity and his difficulties in adjusting to the world of the school.

Conversations at home

Collecting data in people's homes presents other challenges, compared to school. Initially I had assumed that I was going there to complement children's acounts with parental ones. But as a guest in the family home, the researcher's social position does not have clearly established parameters; it has to be negotiated. There is a triangle of conventions and negotiations. As an adult, and a guest, the researcher may feel obliged to accept what conditions are offered by the adult, the parent. But as a guest of the child too, the researcher must take account of what the child sees as appropriate. And third, the parent and child may negotiate between them how the social event is to be structured and who will take part. In the case of the Child Health Study, the children already knew me when I visited their home; and several welcomed me to the home and settled down with their mother to take part in the conversation. Mothers did not ask their child to go away, and nor did I. Since I had explained – usually on the phone, as well as by letter – that the interview concerned the child's daily life, it seemed to me, and I think to the mothers, that if the child wished it, she had every right to be there, and to take part.

In the event, children's contributions to the conversations provided me with data I had not expected. I learned about aspects of children's knowledge acquisition, and of child-parent relationships. Ron, for instance, welcomed me to his home and took me round, then settled down to listen and to contribute to the conversation. This extract shows the importance of his contribution.

I: Do you have any rules?
Mother: Oh dear, it's mainly: don't hurt each other. I do mind about that, but they do fight.
Ron: Not break the furniture up. Not break the windows.
Mother: Yes, I do say that. They're not allowed in my room when I'm working, and not working. What else, Ron?
Ron: Chocolate.
Mother: Yes, no chocolate unless they've eaten something decent beforehand.

When I raised the topics of rules, this mother replied in terms of child-to-child relationships. But Ron pointed out that his mother also had rules about physical destructiveness. Her appeal to him – 'What else, Ron?' – paid tribute to the relevance of his contributions, and he went on to remind her about a food rule. The interchange not only demonstrates that he has knowledge, it also shows that she knows he has knowledge. Later in the interview, she expressed concern about Ron not eating healthy food, and he then listed the healthy foods he did eat. By appealing to him in the context of the interview, she pointed out to the researcher that in this family people talked openly about rules, and, perhaps, that the researcher should remember to include Ron in the conversation.

Later in the same project, I similarly aimed to explore parents' accounts of 9-year-olds' daily lives at home and school. By now I knew that children might wish to take part, but I had not reflected enough on the implications of this. Only after I embarked on these conversations did I realize more fully that children's wish to participate should be overtly accepted. Later on, when I read through the transcripts, I remembered my difficulties about asking mothers to talk about a child in the latter's presence; I thought perhaps I should have asked the two of them to discuss the topics between themselves, or to have sought each person's view on each topic and on the other's contribution. But, as with Ron and his mother, children and mothers helped resolve this situation, by taking control of the conversation. The character of the child-adult relationship included respect for each other's knowledge and for each other's participation. In this next interchange, we learn that Kate (aged just 10 years) has knowledge of how and where her mother spent her childhood, and has reflected on her own childhood by comparison. The context of the conversation provides space and time for leisurely discussion and development of the points.

I: Are you happy with the division of responsibility between her and you. Do you wish she would do more, or less, or are you happy?

Mother: Certainly it's very different from when I was a child. I mean, when I was five I used to go on a bus to school that was five miles away.

I: In the country?

Mother: Yes. In some ways I think it's quite strange. I mean, when I think of myself at ten, I had much more responsibility.

I: What sorts of things did you do?

Mother: Well, I mean, we would regularly go off to the cinema on Saturday afternoons, which was a bus ride away.

Kate: The shops. You went shopping with your friends.

Mother: We went shopping.

I: Was that in London?

Mother: No, it wasn't in London, no.

Kate: That's probably why. We live in London, with lots of cars.

Mother: Yes, I, it was a different sort of world.

Kate: Where you go [that is, in the country of her mother's childhood] there is only about one car every half hour. You went across the moors.

Mother: Yes, well that's true. Well, I could walk home from school without meeting a car. Very different world. So in some ways I find it quite strange. It's a very sheltered sort of existence but on the other hand–

Kate: You do expect a bit more from me. You tell me off when I'm not being responsible enough. Otherwise you wouldn't tell me off.

Mother: Yes, this year I think, now. Yes.

The experience of taking part in these interviews showed that informal conversations with pairs or groups of children, and with children together with their mothers in the familiar social surroundings of home allowed access to children's knowledge and to accounts of daily life from both child and adult perspectives. In addition, some of the mothers were keenly interested in the research aims and this led me on to further refinement of the conversational method. In order to facilitate more detailed accounts of children's daily experiences, I arranged with some mothers for conversations to take place at home, with the mother as lead interviewer, having been briefed by me about the research purposes and topics. The child, comfortably ensconced in a favourite chair, surrounded by familiar objects, and able to leave the room if she wanted, discussed the school day with her mother, with me as prompter. Leading up to this example, Clare (aged 6 years) has been telling about her favourite thing – playing teachers. She and her mother discuss the daily routine in Miss Lane's class, and Clare's preference for Miss Hawes, who has now left the school. This gives Clare the opportunity to detail why she doesn't like Miss Lane.

Mother: What do you like about Miss Hawes?
Clare: She annoys me, Miss Lane.
Mother: Does she? Why?
Clare: Well, she doesn't let people get drinks when you're working.
    [Mother and Clare between them describe the complicated route to a drinking fountain.]
I: So can you go and get a drink when you want one?
Clare: Well, you have to ask the teacher first, and if she says, No, you can't, then if she says Yes, you can.
I: Sometimes she says, No?
Clare: Yeah, sometimes.
I: Do you know why that is?
Clare: Because she wants you to get your work done.
Mother: Oh.
Clare: Because she thinks if you go while you're doing your work, sometimes you stay there a long time and you don't want to finish your work, that's why you stay there.
I: Is that true?
Clare: Sometimes. Sometimes people don't finish their work, they stay at the drinking fountain and they come back when it's playtime.
    [All three participants moved on to the issue of children wanting to go to the lavatory in class-time. Clare says permission is sometimes withheld.]
I: Why does she sometimes not [let you go]?
Clare: [Pause]
I: Is it the same, about getting your work done?
Clare: [Pause]
Mother: Do you think sometimes if you've just come back from play or if you're going to be going to play in a few minutes?
Clare: No, if you've just come back from play and you want to get a drink, or you need to go to the toilet, she says, No because you've had all that time to get it in in the playground.
I: I see, so she says you should have done that at playtime. I mean, does anyone ever have an accident in the classroom because they weren't allowed to go to the lavatory?

Clare: Umm.

Mother: Do you remember one time you wet your trousers, didn't you, and was that because you didn't remember quick enough that you wanted to go. Or weren't you allowed to go?

Clare: I was allowed to go, but I didn't get there quick enough. And I didn't want to tell Miss Lane.

It is hard, through a snippet, to give the flavour and value of these long conversations. But the mother's knowledge about the geography of the school, her sympathetic engagement with the topics and her knowledge shared with the child of the child's history (the 'accident') provides an enabling context for Clare to make important points about the social order of the class-room and child-teacher relations.[4]

Another study, Children, Parents and Risk, revealed further aspects of conversing with children at home. The choice of the home as research setting accorded with the aim, to investigate the home as a place of safety or risk for children (aged 12, 9 and 3 years). Suzanne Hood and Peter Kelley, the researchers on the study, asked the older ones to say where they would like the discussion to take place. Age and generation were probably inter-locked factors in the decision. In some cases, a parent seemed to steer the children towards agreeing on a place where s/he could keep an eye on the interview – such as a sitting room next to the kitchen. A few 9- and 12-year-olds chose their own room – a relatively private place where, perhaps, they could speak openly. Yet in some of these cases, the researchers felt that their presence in a child's own room was itself an intrusion and therefore inhibiting.

We did not ask to talk with 3-year-olds on their own, but tried to arrange the conversation with a parent at a time when the child could be present. As we have described elsewhere (Kelley et al. 1997), interesting and difficult generational issues arise in this situation. In recognition of adult rights and power in the home, the researchers sometimes found themselves siding with the adult or ignoring the child's account; and parents sometimes over-rode children's contributions, or diverted the conversation if children made contributions that exposed aspects of family life which adults preferred to keep hidden. Both children and parents may wish to present a family front (the harmonious happy family) to the researcher. On the other hand, the presence of a parent can enable a very young child to make contributions to the conversation. Thus the familiarity of being at home was harnessed in another study, where the researcher asked the child (aged 4 years) to 'tell her day', by taking the researcher literally step by step from bedroom, to bathroom to kitchen and so on, in order that these familiar places could provide triggers for children's accounts.

Conversations in children's domains?

Within the time-scale and funding of the Child Health Care Study, I could not work with children in other settings where children spend time (apart from home and school). Yet as 9-year-olds told me, they highly valued spending time in places where they were not in the immediate view and power of adults (5-year-olds said much less about this.) From my point of view, explorations of children's knowledge of their social positioning within the generational order would be made more complete by tapping into these experiences. So, as a minimum, I aimed to encourage children to converse about these. In this next extract, I had picked up from earlier conversations their commonly uttered word of distaste, 'boring', and asked 9-year-olds to discuss it.

I: So what is boring?
Billy: School, because we have to work and it's all boring except PE. And break.
Don: Work is boring. I don't like it.
I: What do you like?
Billy: Being at home.
Don: Yeah. Going out.
Billy: Playing with friends because it's fun. You can do what you like. You aren't being told what to do.
          [After more discussion of their teacher who 'shouts at them all the time', I asked again, What do you like doing?']
Billy: Playing with my friends.
Don: Swimming. I go nearly every day after school. It's fun and it gives you exercise, more than at school where you don't get any exercise except in the playground. They make you sit down all the time.
Billy: I like playing tennis, being with friends.
I: Do you prefer being with friends to parents? [leading question!]
Don: Easily! You can do what you like, go where you like. Buy crisps. Where with parents, they go, No! It's true, isn't it?
I: Last week [half term holiday week], did you enjoy that?
Don: Yes, really good. I went out every day with my friends. My parents just picked me up at the end of the day.
I.   What about you, Billy?
Billy: I played short tennis, finished a game on my computer, went to the park with my friends.

Billy and Don here give a vivid account of the pressures they experience in the generational order, and the contrasting importance for them of time and space without the immediate impact of adult command. Excursions to children's homes vividly endorsed their comments about the adequacy of private space and free time. Children from wealthy homes had a room of their own, with books, computers, music, space; and they said their jobs at home were mainly self-care – tidying their room, organising clothes, making packed lunches. Children from poor homes lived in cramped spaces, shared rooms, and some told me they had many household tasks. Since the school was near to my own home, I also had some (adult) knowledge about local geography.

This meant that I could, somewhat, recognize and engage with their accounts of playing out, and of their route to school – for their parents allowed some the freedom of walking alone or with a friend. Being able to acknowledge reference points in children's accounts was an important means of facilitating easy conversation.

But to work with children in what Moore (1986) calls childhood domains might provide especially valuable contexts for data-collection, contexts which could lead to detailed accounts, and to revelations of knowledge not commonly known about by adults. Moore's study aimed to explore where children choose to spend time and what they value about these places but, as he explains, his research raised methodological problems. Though he got permission from parents to work with children at school, when he went a stage further and asked children if he could accompany them to their favourite play spaces, he was met with parental suspicion. Within UK society, with its adult fears of strangers, researchers can gain access to children only with parental consent; and increasingly one is required to specify exactly what methods and topics one plans to use.[5] It is indeed a marker of the control exercised over children's lives, knowledge and rights in the UK that children's own consent to research is not considered adequate.[6] However, researchers are learning how to work with children on use of space, in ways acceptable to adults. Current studies are harnessing the goodwill of both children and their parents to investigate children's use of space, in order both to develop theoretical understanding of childhoods and to consider policy implications for the development of physical environments fit for children.[7] One important issue in this, alluded to above, is the ethics of investigating time and space deemed by children as theirs and outside the immediate authority of adults.

Conclusion

In this chapter I have explored the research conversation as a means of data-collection with children and have suggested that it has some advantages. It enables one, somewhat, to hand over the agenda to children, so that they can control the pace and direction of the conversation, raising and exploring topics with relatively little researcher input. Through these means, researchers can arrive at good understanding about what matters to children. In the case of the research I have referred to, I feel confident that children do, as I initially thought, regard their lives as largely controlled by adults. Generational issues loom large in their accounts of life at home and at school. This experiential knowledge throws into sharp relief the value for children of arenas where adult power has less immediate impact, though of course, as children recognize, their own domains in time and space are structured by individual adults and by social policies.

A second major advantage of conversations with children is in helping adults tap into one of the means whereby, through talking with each other, children firm up knowledge, and learn more about aspects of their social worlds.

For instance, just as mothers learn about motherhood by talking with other mothers, so children learn what it means to be a child and about varieties of childhoods, by comparing experiences, discussing emotional responses to events, and debating values. And one way in which children learn how to enact childhoods acceptable to other children and to adults in specific settings is through talking with each other (compare James 1996).

A further point is worth noting here (though not explored in detail in this chapter): the conversation demonstrates children's social skills with each other (see Corsaro 1997 and this volume). Analysis of conversations with pairs or groups of children can show their cognitive abilities to listen, take note, reply, add in points. It can also show aspects of their affective relationships; children in group conversations are generally positive (rather than negative); they listen to each other, and often support and enable each other to speak. Furthermore, children help with the social presentation of other children by explaining to the researcher that their companion is shy, or not generally talkative, or always has a lot to say, or isn't feeling well. Children's conversations can be interpreted as offering the spectator a showcase of their collectivity. In many of the conversations I was present at, children were presenting a collective front, as children, in some cases in overt opposition to the power of adults. In other cases, they were sharing their understanding, as children, of their social worlds. Such presentations and sharings were given specific force and relevance in the social context of the conversation which included the researcher – a friendly person, but nonetheless a representative of the other main social group, adults. Children often had fun with this context, by testing out the acceptability to me of anti-adult comments.

Finally, conversations are one means of acquiring good enough data as a basis for policy-oriented work. Analysis of children's own understandings of the social conditions of childhood is an important pre-condition for considering what policies are appropriate to enable children to lead satisfying lives. Children's understandings both complement and reinforce macro-studies (e.g. Qvortrup 1994; Therborn 1996; Sgritta 1997) in indicating that their rights are poorly recognized, and that social policies should directly address children's interests, rather than, simply, adults' interests.[8]

Notes

1 Child Health Care (1990-2); funded by the Nuffield Foundation and the Institute of Education. Main publications: Mayall, 1994 and 1996; 'Health in Primary Schools (1993-5); funded by ESRC. Main publication: Mayall et al. 1996; 'Children, Parents and Risk' (1995-6); funded by ESRC. Main publication: Kelley, Mayall and Hood 1997; 'Negotiating Childhoods'(1997-9); funded by ESRC.

2 At this time, 1990-1, though the Conservative Government had introduced measures (1988) to tighten up children's days at school (the National Curriculum, testing at 7 and 11 years, and competition between schools), these measures had not yet bitten deep, or not at the school in question. Staff told me they were child-centred, and holistic in their approaches; the regime offered some resemblance to the 'progressive' ideals of the 1960s.

3 All the names used in excerpts have been changed to preserve anonymity. 'I' refers to the researcher.

4 See Tizard, B. and Hughes, M. (1984) for discussion of the enabling character of mother-child knowledge and relations in promoting children's discourse.
5 The problems this can raise in research with children include the point that children may, in conversation go far beyond the limits the researcher has outlined for access purposes.
6 By contrast, a Finnish research colleague, Leena Alanen, has had no difficulty in securing consent from parents to her walking home with children from school, and going with them to the places where they spend their time after school. This general consent allows her to follow the children's lead, wherever they choose to take her.
7 As part of the Economic and Social Research Council's Children 5–16 Programme, two projects are studying children's use of space: Childhood, Urban Space and Citizenship, and Exploring the Fourth Environment.
8 A comprehensive discussion of measures needed to recognise children's rights is given in a report by the Children's Rights Development Unit (1994 recognize).

References

Children's Rights Development Unit (1994) *A UK Agenda for Children*, London: CRDU.

Corsaro, W. (1997) *The Sociology of Childhood,* Thousand Oaks, CA, Pine Forge Press.

James, A. (1996) 'Learning to be friends', *Childhood* 3(3): 313-30.

Kelley, P., Mayall, B. and Hood, S. (1997) 'Children's accounts of risk', *Childhood*, 4(3): 305-24.

Mandell, N. (1991) 'The least-adult role in studying children', in F.C. Waksler (ed.) *Studying the Social Worlds of Children: Sociological Readings,* London: Falmer Press.

Mayall, B. (1994) *Negotiating Health: Children at Home and Primary School,* London: Cassell.

Mayall, B. (1996) *Children, Health and the Social Order*, Buckingham: Open University Press.

Mayall, B., Bendelow, G., Barker, S., Storey, P. and Veltman, M. (1996) *Children's Health in Primary Schools,* London: Falmer Press.

Moore. R.C. (1986) *Childhood's Domain: Play and Place in Childhood Development*, London: Croom Helm.

Qvortrup, J. (1994) 'Childhood matters: an introduction', in J. Qvortrup, M. Bardy, G. Sgritta and H. Wintersberger (eds) *Childhood Matters: Social theory, Practice and Politics,* Aldershot: Avebury Press.

Sgritta, G.B. (1997) 'Childhood on the economic and political agenda', *Childhood* 4(4): 375-404.

Therborn, G. (1996) 'Child politics', *Childhood* 3(1): 29-44.

Thorne, B. (1993) *Gender Play: Girls and Boys in School*. New Brunswick, NJ: Rutgers University Press.

Tizard, B. and Hughes, M. (1984) *Young Children Learning*, London: Fontana.

Postscript

Re-reading this chapter, I see that things have changed! Life at an English primary school has become more routinized and pressured; so it provides a different research context and access may be more difficult. Also, when I did the main study I report on here (1990-1), there were few written accounts of research interviews with children (but see Waksler 1991). This accounts for the tentative, exploratory character of the research process I describe.

Since then there has been an explosion of similar work, much of it driven by the 1989 United Nations Convention on the Rights of the Child, together with the interlinked concerns of the sociology of childhood. In complement we find increasing emphasis on ethical issues inherent in research with and for children. Thorough and challenging work on ethical issues has been carried out by my colleagues Priscilla Alderson (1995) and Virginia Morrow (2004) who together updated the work. My attempts to respect the children and their parents at the time might not now be considered adequate. However, during the data-collection process, I did include some relevant measures: respecting children's wishes about if, when and how to participate; feeding back initial findings for them to discuss further; providing them with a written account of the findings.

A point commonly put to me when discussing this and similar research with colleagues is that it would be helpful to give more attention to differences between children, by sex, ethnicity, age. This suggestion, I think, arises from the long tradition, established in psychological research, of seeking difference, as a basis for helping children, or to sort them for various purposes (e.g. education). I should like to stress here the point so clearly made by Qvortrup (this volume), that the sociological enterprise differs from the psychological. Sociological research is centrally concerned to find commonality between people; and it is on the basis of this commonality that one can argue that, for instance, children constitute a social group, in relation to the other major group, adults (e.g. Therborn 1996; Mayall 2002; Qvortrup 2005). Childhood is a status where its inhabitants have in common the specific ways in which large-scale socio-political and economic forces affect their lives.

In this connection, therefore, the concept of generation seems promising as a key variable in considering relations between children and adults. Discussions of ideas inherent in the concept, and nascent in my original chapter, have now been complemented by empirical studies (Alanen and Mayall 2001; Mayall and Zeiher 2003). Power relations between adults and children allow adults to influence children's lives, both through policies, laws and customs, and also at the level of personal relations. However, it is well to regard these not as fixed structuring influences; rather they are processes in which both sides engage and negotiate towards constantly changing patterns of generational relations.

References

Alanen, L. and Mayall, B. (eds) (2001) *Conceptualizing Child-adult Relations*, London: RoutledgeFalmer.

Alderson, P. (1995) *Listening to Children: Children, Ethics and Social Research*, Barkingside: Barnardo's.

Alderson, P. and Morrow, V. (2004) *Ethics, Social Research and Consulting with Children and Young People*, Barkingside: Barnardo's.

Therborn, G. (1996) 'Child politics: dimensions and perspectives', *Childhood* 3(1): 29-44.

Mayall, B. (2002) *Towards a Sociology for Childhood: Thinking from Children's Lives*, Buckingham: Open University Press.

Mayall, B. and Zeiher, H. (eds) (2003) *Childhood in Generational Perspective*, London: Institute of Education.

Qvortrup, J. (ed.) (2005) *Studies in Modern Childhood*: Society, Agency and Culture Basingstoke: Palgrave Macmillan.

Waksler, F.C. (ed.) (1991) *Studying the Social Worlds of Children: Sociological Readings*, London: Falmer Press.

6 The Development of Participatory Techniques

Facilitating Children's Views about Decisions Which Affect Them

Claire O'Kane

Introduction

Since the late 1980s there has been an increasing interest in listening to children's experiences and viewpoints, as separate to, and different from adults. Changes reflect an acknowledgment of children's rights to participate as promulgated by the United Nations Convention on the Rights of the Child (see O'Kane 2003; Theis and O'Kane 2005; Hart and Tyrer 2006). Such interest is also in line with the establishment of a new paradigm for the study of childhood, which seeks to explore childhood, children's relationships and cultures as areas of study in their own right (see James and Prout 1990, 1997). The emergence of the paradigm in part reflects a move away from seeing children as passive recipients of adult socialization, to a recognition that children are social actors in their own right. Alongside adults, children are active participants in the construction and determination of their experiences, other people's lives and the societies in which they live. Children can be viewed as a social group with specific relationships to other social groups, such as parents, social workers, teachers and community elders. However, it is also important to acknowledge the diversity of different childhoods. Childhood is only one variable of social analysis, alongside other variables, such as class, gender, culture or ethnicity (James and Prout 1990, 1997).

The growth of interpretive perspectives, such as symbolic interactionism and social phenomenology in the social sciences have given impetus to the new directions in the study of childhood (James and Prout 1990, 1997). 'Within the interpretive tradition aspects of everyday life which are taken for granted are examined by "bracketing them off"'. The aim is to render them culturally strange by a process of detailed and critical reflection, thus bringing them into the sphere of analysis' (James and Prout 1990: 15).

The methodological shift in research methods, from approaches which view children as 'objects of concern', to methods which engage children as 'active participants' has been charted elsewhere (see Butler and Shaw 1996; Hill et al. 1996; James and Prout 1990, 1997; Morrow and Richards 1996). Within the subdiscipline of the 'sociology of childhood' a pattern has been noted (Hill et al. 1996) which identifies that sociologists initially focused on adults' constructions of childhood (e.g. Dreitzel 1973; James and Prout 1990, 1997; Rogers 1993); then children's status as a distinct social group was explored (e.g. Qvortrup et al. 1994); before studies finally began to explore children's own perspectives (e.g. Mayall 1994).

Commitment to conducting research with children, rather than on them, about them, or without them, necessitates consideration of many theoretical, methodological and ethical issues. Consideration needs to be given as to whether existing research methodologies and ethical positions, largely designed for adults, are appropriate when the research participant is a child (Sinclair 1996; Punch 2002; see Scott, this volume).

Whilst many ethical issues are salient in doing research with participants of any age, some issues present themselves differently, or more sharply when the participants are children. In part, the difference is due to children's understanding and experience of the world being different from that of adults, and in part to the ways in which they communicate (Thomas and O'Kane 1998a). However, ultimately, the biggest challenge for researchers working with children are the disparities in power and status between adults and children (Morrow and Richards 1996; Hart and Tyrer 2006). Working within a historical and cultural context in which children's voices have been marginalized, researchers face great challenges in finding ways to break down the power imbalance between adults and children, and in creating space which enables children to speak up and be heard.

Questions concerning adult-child relationships must be carefully considered. How can we as adult researchers gather information about children's childhoods with children? If we are not children, how can we understand and convey children's experiences? What difficulties may arise? It has been suggested that qualitative work with children should be regarded as a process of narrative inquiry (Shaw 1996), as children are both living their stories in an experiential text but also telling their stories as they talk to their own selves and explain themselves to others. Furthermore, in trying to understand children's childhoods, it has also been suggested that inter-relations between agency and structure need to be addressed (Mayall 1996). As children's experiences are lived through childhoods constructed for them by adult understandings of childhood, of what children are and should be (Mayall 1996). Additionally, in considering childhood as structured, mediated and experienced by children and adults, we have to consider the linkages between generation and gender (Mayall 1996).

Furthermore, in undertaking research with groups of children it is also important to understand power relations amongst children, to ensure that the research work does not contribute to the creation of strengthening of hierarchies amongst children (Hart and Tyrer 2006). Factors of age, gender, birth order, educational attainment, caste/class, ethnicity, (dis)ability, as well as individual personality and physical stature all play a role in shaping the power relations in childhood (Hart and Tyrer 2006).

This chapter focuses on the use of participatory techniques as an approach which can enable children and young people to talk about the sorts of issues that affect them. With a commitment to gaining a clearer understanding of the perceptions and cultural constructions of young people, the use of participatory techniques fall within an interpretive tradition of research (Bulmer 1984; Hart and Tyrer 2006). An indication will be given as to how the use of participatory techniques can enable an exploration of the similarities, as well as the differences among children's experiences (e.g. with regards to age and gender) in a particular social-cultural context (see Christensen and James, this volume).

The chapter is based on the experience of using participatory techniques to engage with children in the middle age-group (8–12 years old), in a study exploring children's participation in decision-making when 'looked after' by local authorities in England and Wales. It also draws upon the experience of researchers using participatory techniques in other cultural and social contexts (Johnson et al. 1995; Kefyalew 1996; Boyden and Ennew 1997; Woodhead 1998; Punch 2002; O'Kane 2003; Christensen 2004; Veale 2005; Hart and Tyrer 2006, Tisdall et al. 2006). The use of participatory techniques by researchers in an international context indicates how these methods can be adapted in a variety of situations, enabling greater exploration of the cultural contexts which structure children's lives (Hart and Tyrer 2006).

An initial description of the 'Children and Decision-Making Study' is followed by a brief explanation of the context in which participatory techniques have been developed. Some of the reasons for selecting participatory techniques as a methodology for research with children will then be highlighted. The central part of the chapter goes on to focus on three of the main techniques used in our study, namely: *the decision-making pocket chart, the pots and beans activity* and *the diamond ranking.* The presentation of such examples provide illustrations of the ways in which participatory techniques help us to engage with children in individual and group settings. Additionally, reflections upon our experiences, enables an exploration of the strengths and weaknesses of such techniques, as well as some opportunities and threats which determine their usefulness (SWOT analysis). Throughout the chapter, linking our practical experience back to theory, dialogue concerning varied contemporary issues which arise when conducting research with children will be furthered.

The Children and Decision-Making Study

The Children and Decision-Making Study undertaken in 1996–1997 consisted of a three-stage project, which aimed to explore how children in their middle years who are 'looked after' by local authorities are enabled to participate in decisions about their care. The first stage involved a survey of 225 children aged 8–12 years who were looked after by seven local authorities. Information was gathered from social workers to supply data about children's participation in the most recent decision-making meeting. The second stage involved a detailed study of 47 children using interviews, group discussions and participatory activities to learn more about their perspectives on decision-making processes, together with interviews with adults, and observation of meetings. The third stage was concerned with the development of guidance and training resources to facilitate the inclusion of children in decision-making processes.[1]

Whilst this chapter focuses on the qualitative research with children, triangulation of varied approaches, accompanied by contextualization offered important opportunities for improving the validity of social research (Lucchini 1996). Furthermore, by reflecting upon the 'research process' and 'research relationship' as additional areas of insight, lessons were gained for wider practice (Connelly and Ennew 1996; Solberg 1996; Kay et al. 2003). Solberg (1996: 53) has highlighted that an *'exploration of the interaction between the researcher and the researched, and the special case of adult-child interaction, may throw light on adult-child interactions in general'*.

The context

A variety of terms are used to describe the range of participatory approaches, from which specific tools and techniques can be adapted (see Pretty et al. 1995; Steiner 1993; Cornwall et al. 1993). However, within the context of rural development work in which such approaches have been widely used, the term 'Participatory Rural Appraisal' (PRA) has become common. Whilst PRA may be seen as a set of techniques, it has been more widely identified as a methodology or philosophy.

Varied methodologies can be grouped according to their philosophical under-pinnings. In contrast to the contemporary research community which operates within a prevailing positivist paradigm, PRA falls within a 'post-positivist' or 'constructivist' paradigm. Whereas conventional positivist inquiry is linear and closed, seeking to measure, aggregate and model behaviour, constructivist methodology has been promoted for its qualitative exploratory power in providing 'depth, richness and realism of information and analysis' (Chambers, 1994: 14). Rather than only looking for statistically significant relationships, one key principle of PRA is that it seeks diversity (Holland and Blackburn 1998).

The roots of participatory methods and approaches can be traced to many sources and traditions; however five have been identified as particularly influential. These include: active participatory research inspired by Paulo Freire (1972); agro-system analysis (see Conway 1987); applied anthropology; field research on farming systems; and rapid rural appraisal (see Pretty et al. 1995; Cornwall et al. 1993; and Chambers 1992). Correspondingly, PRA approaches have been used in a variety of ways. However, a number of common principles underlie their use: support of local innovation, respect for diversity and complexity, enhancement of local capabilities, interactive analysis and dialogue, and support for further action (see Pretty et al. 1995). Furthermore, both researchers and researched are recognised as active participants in the production of data, necessitating recognition of the issues of power, control and authority in the research process.

PRA philosophy stresses key principles, behaviour and attitude for researchers, that enable them to become active listeners, as the use of participatory techniques are grounded in an understanding that each person's understandings of their situation may be as valid as any other. Hence, participatory approaches provide space for the research participants to establish their own analytical framework, and their own interpretation of reality.

Although participatory approaches remain more associated with development practice than with academic research, they have been recommended for both, as the use of participatory approaches involves continuous interaction between theory and practice, as we learn through experience, reflection and learning (Pretty et al. 1995). Bulmer (1984) argues that problems, theories and methods in social science are inter-related, and that 'theory and method intertwine at all stages of the research process' (Bulmer, 1984: 5).

In seeking to involve participants in the research project: 'participation does not simply imply the mechanical application of a "technique" or method, but is instead part of a process of dialogue, action, analysis and change' (Pretty et al. 1995: 54). The successful use of participatory techniques lies in the process, rather than simply the techniques used. Thus, a commitment to ongoing processes of information-sharing, dialogue, reflection and action greatly facilitate the genuine use of participatory techniques (see Theis 1996; Hart and Tyrer 2006). Participatory techniques have been most widely used in an overseas context with adults. They are particularly advantageous in communities where there are low levels of literacy, as the methods of information collection do not rely heavily on reading or writing skills, but place greater emphasis on the power of visual impressions, and active representation of ideas. Furthermore, with a focus on enabling dialogue about people's own reality, they assist in giving people greater power in defining their own situation and ideas.

The selection of participatory techniques as a research method

In taking account of children's views in research, a variety of methods such as: ethnography, participant observation, interviews, focus groups, participatory activities and surveys have been used. A range of factors influence the selection of research methods, including availability of time, access, resources, as well as the researcher's goals, training, and their perception of children.

In the particular context of this study, participatory techniques were selected for their power of communication, as well as for their suitability to research meetings which are structured in space and time. Naturalistic observation and ethnographic methods have enabled explorations of features of children's life worlds (Corsaro 1979; James 1993; Christensen 2004; see also Corsaro and Molinari; Davis, Watson and Cunningham-Burley; Gigengack, this volume), however, these methods can be time consuming. In research with children it can be difficult to gain access to children, as their adult caretakers seek to protect them from intrusive or negative experiences (Butler and Williamson 1994; Hood et al. 1996; Mauthner 1997; Shaw 1996).

This study involved listening to the views of over 45 children in their individual homes, as well as in groups in more public settings. Participatory techniques were selected as an alternative to ethnographic methods, as they can be less invasive and more transparent. In comparison to ethnography where the relationship between the researcher and the researched is less defined or bound, use of PRA requires a more formal relationship through participation in defined activities. The researcher can be identified as a facilitator of activities (Robinson-Pat 1996; Boyden and Ennew 1997; Hart and Tyrer 2006). Rather than imposing extensive periods of observation on children, use of participatory techniques in individual and group settings required that children (with their informed consent and permission from their carers) dedicated specific times to participate in the research process.

Reviewing the relative benefits of research methods such as observation, interviewing, checklists, matrices and literature, Kefyalew (1996) examined the reality of children's participation in research in Ethiopia. His findings indicated that participatory research methods were innovative, fun and suitable for children, as they enabled them to take a more active role and to talk about their needs. However, Kefyalew highlighted that participatory techniques were only effective when false expectations were not raised, when resources were properly used and stereotypical views (of both methodologies and children) were set aside (Kefyalew 1996).

Within the research meetings we aimed to provide a space which would allow the child participants greater control over the agenda, giving them the time and space to talk about the sorts of decisions that most affected them. An exploration of our own perceptions of childhood, and the differences between child and adult participants furthers an explanation as to why participatory techniques were selected as an appropriate research methodology for our goal (see James et al. 1998; Morrow and Richards 1996; Solberg 1996; Hart and Tyrer 2006).

Social anthropologists James et al. (1998) have provided a four-fold typology, illustrating how the way we 'see' children informs the selection of our methods and techniques. Four models: 'the developing child', 'the tribal child', 'the adult child' and 'the social child' are described (see James et al. 1998). The developing child is seen as incomplete, lacking in status and relatively incompetent (e.g. Piaget 1968). In contrast, the tribal child is viewed as competent, part of an independent culture which can be studied in its own right, but not as part of the same communicative world as the researcher (e.g. ethnographic work of the seventies). Thus, in both these constructions children are unable to have the same status as adults. In contrast, the adult child and social child do have this capacity. Whereas the adult child is seen as socially competent in ways comparable to an adult (e.g. Alderson 1993; Bluebond-Lagner 1978), the social child is seen as having different, though not necessarily inferior social competencies (e.g. Johnson et al. 1995).

With particular adherence to the 'social child' (whilst also exhibiting aspects of the 'adult child') we approached children in the study as social actors in a UK context in the 1990s. Whilst stressing the uniqueness of children, the 'social child' position seeks to encapsulate different dimensions of childhood.

James et al. (1998) suggests that the development of research techniques which enable us to engage more effectively with children would allow children to participate on their own terms. Thus enabling us to learn more about their experiences of the world. For example, it has been found that children, particularly younger children communicate through mediums other than verbal explanations or written form (e.g. James et al. 1998; Alderson 1995; Clarke and Moss 2001, see also Introduction, this volume). Furthermore, Waksler (1991) suggests that if children find they are not understood by adults, that their view of a situation is not allowed validity, or that their world is out of control, they may choose alternative strategies for communication, rather than communicating directly.

Therefore it makes sense to utilize alternative forms of communication, such as play, activities, songs, drawing and stories. Veale (2005), for example, describes how drawing is one 'method of creating a methodological frame that children could fill with their own meaning'. In enabling children to explain their drawings Punch (2002) suggests that rather than ask children 'what have you drawn' it would be more revealing to ask them to explain 'what their drawing meant to them and why they decided to draw those images'. James et al. (1998: 189) calls on us

> to make use of these different abilities rather than asking children to participate unpractised in interviews or unasked in surveilling gaze. Talking with children about the meanings they themselves attribute to their paintings or asking them to write a story .... allow children to engage more productively with our research questions using the talents which they possess. (see Christensen and James, this volume)

In recognising both the biological and structural conditions which structure children's lives, we need to develop communication strategies which engage children, build upon their own abilities and capabilities, and allow their agenda to take precedence. Research with children in a variety of contexts provides supportive evidence that participatory techniques provide one such communication strategy. The use of participatory activities draw upon a range of lessons regarding effective communication with children: they allow children and young people to shape the agenda; they focus upon real-life concrete events; and they involve 'handling things' rather than 'just talking' (Steiner 1993).

Methods that have worked well with children have included: drawings, mapping, flow diagrams, play, matrices, transect, drama, stories and songs (Johnson 1996; James et al. 1998; Nieuwenhuys 1996; Chawla and Kjrholt 1996; Alderson 1995; Sapkota and Sharma 1996; Boyden and Ennew 1997; Punch 2002; Veale 2005; Hart and Tyrer 2006). For example, in an action research project with street children, Nieuwenhuys (1996: 54–5) found the 'preferred activities of children such as games, story telling and drawing may be more effective in bringing out the complexities of their experience than methods and techniques used by/with adults'. Additionally, in an Action-Aid research project in Nepal, it was found that drawings allowed children 'the freedom to express views, imagination, and interpretation of the surrounding world in their own terms. Moreover the adult-child power imbalance was relatively reduced by giving full control to the child; this in turn enhanced their confidence' (Sapkota and Sharma 1996: 61).

In conceptualizing children as a minority group, the use of PRA techniques are particularly conducive to research with children. They assist in transforming the power relations between adults and children, enabling children to set the agenda and describe their own reality, rather than being limited by answering questions from the researcher's agenda, or trying to give 'correct' or 'best' answers. 'PRA techniques seek maximum involvement of the children, mutual trust and an open forum for debate' (Johnson 1996: 32).

With an emphasis on visual representation of ideas, they can be designed to work with children of different ages with varied literacy skills. Moving away from developmental theories which have constrained the methods of many researchers (Shaw 1996), the use of participatory techniques allows age as a construct of children's ability to participate to be minimized (Solberg 1996).

Within many societies, particularly in Southern nations, children often assume social and economic responsibilities at a young age. For example, children may look after their siblings, assist in household, agricultural or income generating activities to contribute to the family livelihood (see O'Kane 2003; Woodhead 1998; Hart and Tyrer 2006). Global research has shown that these responsibilities can actually result in pro-social behaviour and development of children's capacities (Woodhead 1998). Thus, in facilitating and supporting children's participation in research activities, researchers need to consider the appropriateness of different methods not only in relation to chronological age but also in relation to the lived experience and consequent competencies of individual children (Hart and Tyrer 2006). However, in general, methods that rely more on visual representation are more suited to younger children. Methods that involve a great deal of analysis, especially in relation to ideas of causation ('why?' questions) require particular skills that are more likely to be found amongst older children (Hart and Tyrer 2006).

Whilst participatory techniques were selected as an alternative to ethnographic methods for this study, they build upon and can be used within the context of individual interviews and focus group discussions. Indeed, for participatory techniques to become a research method, it has been suggested that they 'must be used in context and in continuous dialogue with the children concerned' (Nieuwenhuys 1996: 55). In particular, sensitive interviewing has been shown central to the successful use of participatory research techniques. Thus, it is useful to draw upon guidance from other researchers with regards to qualitative research interviews with children (e.g. Butler and

Williamson 1994; Mayall 1996; Mauthner et al. 1993; Morrow and Richards 1996; Solberg 1996).

For example, taking on Butler and Williamson's (1994) advice, the development of a range of participatory techniques and the creation of varied opportunities for communication enabled us to be more creative and flexible in our approach.

> Creativity in working with any particular research instrument is also important. We believe that any issue with children and young people must flow from their experiences. It is hard for them to think the unthinkable. One's framework of questions must be constructed around experiences, observations and aspirations. One's language, sensitivity (or toughness) and tolerance of tangents must tune in to the individual or group being spoken with.
> (Butler and Williamson 1994: 37)

In seeking to engage children as capable, social actors with creative abilities to communicate about their experiences of decision-making processes and events, participatory techniques were chosen as a creative methodology which would enable children to participate in interesting and meaningful ways. Whilst focused on 'concrete events' the participatory activities enable dialogue about complex and abstract issues, facilitating the child's own interpretation of the relationships, messages and negotiations that structure their lives. Thus, diminishing methodological problems surrounding interpretation of children's activities by adults (see Hazel 1996; Solberg 1996).

Use of participatory techniques in the study

The second stage of the Children and Decision-Making Study involved qualitative research interviews and activities with 45 children from the study population, as well as interviews with the children's social workers, carers, and some of the parents, in order to facilitate children and adults' perceptions of children's role in decision-making processes. The techniques used in our research interviews with children were developed from a range of sources in accordance with the particular aims of the study, as participatory techniques must be developed in accordance with setting, culture, language, ethnicity, ability, time and available resource factors (see also Hart and Tyrer 2006).

Some of our techniques were adapted from existing PRA approaches, others were adapted from activities used by 'Dynamix' a creative training company (with whom the author had worked). A few others built upon existing 'direct work' materials used by child care practitioners to facilitate communication with children (often in difficult circumstances) (e.g. Ryan and Walker 1993; Aldgate and Simmonds 1988); as well as practical tips designed by teachers for 'discussion exercises' with pupils.

All children received an information pack which outlined the nature of the research (in leaflet and tape form), and included two activity sheets, a self-addressed envelope, as well as information leaflets for the carers and parents. With children's choice to participate as a determining feature, the sample of children was consequently partially self-selected. However, particular efforts were made to include children across the age-span from diverse backgrounds (with regards to sex, legal status, type of placement and ethnicity), including children with disabilities.

All children were given opportunities to participate in (at least) two individual interviews, and the majority were offered the opportunity of attending an 'Activity Day' to share their views and ideas with other children. The individual and group meetings were shaped by the use of a range of participatory activities, which were designed to enable an exploration of children's views on three intertwining aspects of children's participation in decision-making processes: their understanding, their experiences of taking part and their perceptions of how they would like to take part (the ideal).

By focusing on one main technique that was commonly used in the first and second individual meeting with the child, and in the group activity day, brief insights to the context, and to the process and outcomes of using participatory techniques will be facilitated. The three respective techniques to be described are: *'The Decision-Making Pocket Chart'*, *'The Pots and Beans Activity'* and the *'Diamond Ranking Exercise'*.

The first meeting: The decision-making pocket chart

Most meetings took place in the child's current living place on a school night after school. In the first meeting the children were encouraged to set up their own *Decision-Making Pocket Chart*. This involved the child building their own decision-making chart on a big sheet of paper, with two axis: 'what sorts of decisions' (on separate cards along the top) and 'what people' (on separate cards down the side). Making a gridded chart, different colour stickers were then used as a gauge of how much say different people had in different decisions.[2]

The decision-making chart activity was useful as it enabled us to explore children's views of the decisions and the people that were more important to them, whilst also facilitating further discussion on concrete issues about decision-making processes from the child's point of reference. For example, the following extract of an individual interview with an 11-year-old girl, highlights the sorts of decisions and people that she found important in decision-making. The interviewer's question followed a brief explanation of how the decision-making chart is set up:

I: So what sorts of decisions are made about you?
g11:   Whether friends can sleep over here or not .... Having a tidy bedroom .... What time you have got to come in at night ... What friends you bother with ... you know whether they are trouble or not ... I can't think of anymore.
I: Is there anything else?

g11:   Not really.
I: Well what we will do, we will start with them, and if you think of any others you can add them on another card. Do you want to write them on the cards?
g11:   Yeh.
(*g11 writes them on the cards.*)
I: …. So what we need now for these cards is the people who you think help make decisions with you, for you or about you? Write each person on a separate card, as well as yourself.
g11:   There is X and Y (foster carers). I call them my Mum and Dad … Social workers.
I: Does anybody else help make decisions?
g11:   Sometimes my real mother and father.
I: Anybody else?
g11:   No.

On the rare occasion that a child found it hard to think about decisions, they were encouraged to look through some cards that other children had written, to see if any of those decisions were important to them. For example, in the following illustration an 8-year-old boy built up his chart through choosing cards from previous children:

I: So what sorts of decisions are made about you or your life?
b8:   I don't know.
I: Do you want me to show you what some of the others have done and see if you want to use any of these?
b8:   Yeh.
It was decided that the cards would be read through and different piles could be made of the ones he did and didn't want.
I: Shall I read through some of these and see which ones you want?

Where I go (yes); what sports I do (yes); where you live (no); friends (no); food (yes); clothes (no); haircuts (yes); homework (no); tele (yes); pocket money (no); school (no); houses (no); singing (no); tele (I've got it!)

b8:   I don't want to talk about food
I: Right so it is these ones is it? You have got: where I go, what sports I do, haircuts and television.
b8:   yeh.

Once the chart was completed there was a clear visual impression of who was having what say about different decisions in the child's life. Thus the chart acted as a useful focus to seek children's views about more general aspects of decision-making processes. For example, children's views were sought about: whether they were surprised by anything on the chart; the roles of different people; how much say they thought they should have; the age at which they should have a say; and the way their involvement changes as they get older. The creation of the chart created a natural space for discussion on more abstract aspects of decision-making processes and the roles different people play in their lives.

For example, in setting up his decision-making chart a 12-year-old boy in foster care explained how the decision is made about where he is allowed to go. Common to all children's discourses were their descriptions about the ways in which their lives are structured by boundaries which adults place around them:

I: So what sorts of decisions are made about where you go?

b11:   Well I go some places where I'm not supposed to go and some places I am, so I give myself yellow (*some say*) for that. My (foster) mother hates it when I go to places that I'm not allowed. She tells me only dare stay in the boundaries.

I: So how far do these boundaries go?

b11:   I'm not allowed out of this valley.

I: Do you think the boundaries ought to be the same or change as you get older?

b11:   They change a little bit now. I used to only be allowed out among these streets. Now I can go up the mountains, up the farm ... My (foster) father doesn't say much where I go, but he asks me where I am going. My brother says quite a bit on 'you shouldn't only go there' or 'shouldn't have gone there or you'll get into trouble', like trespassing, stuff like that.

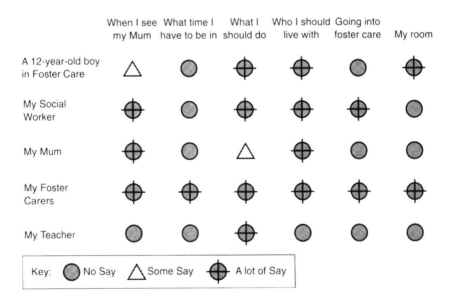

Figure 6.1: An example of a decision-making chart of a 12-year-old boy in foster care

The examples shown so far have illustrated how the use of the participatory techniques enable researchers to focus on the child's agenda, rather than the researcher's agenda. As children grasped the rudiments of the chart, they often directed the pace of the interview. For example, in the following illustration a 10-year-old boy had been talking about a decision about wanting to see his cousins, when he moved the discussion on to highlight the way decisions were being made about contact with his siblings:

b10:   When I see my cousins, I miss my cousins a lot that is why.

I: How often do you see them?

b10:   I saw them four years ago now ...

I: .... So how much say do you have about seeing them?

b10:   I've put a red *(no say)* ... the social workers have a say.

I: You've got a lot of say for the social worker and no say for you and the rest. So how do you think they made that decision or why?

b10:   Yeh, because they are the ones looking after me.

I: So why do you think they made that decision for you not to see your cousins?

b10:   Because they want to make sure nothing happens – something like that.

I: So what do you think about them making those decisions. Do you think it should be like that or do you think you should have more say?

b10:   Nothing – it is just like that. Next one now – when I see my brothers and sisters, coz I love my brothers and sisters and I really want to see them.

I: And do you see them?

b10:   Once in a while, but I haven't seen them for the past three years now.

Whilst the meaning and interpretation of individual decision-making charts had to be carried out with the individual children concerned, broader comparisons enabled us to build a picture of the sorts of decisions and experiences that were common to children in a shared social-cultural context. Through comparisons of children's decision-making charts we were able to determine similarities, as well as differences in children's discourse. In particular, some clear differences amongst groups of children, according to gender and age were identified.

In comparing children's decision-making charts, one construction of children's childhoods which became apparent is the importance of daily decision-making. Day-to-day decisions (such as where they go, who their friends are and what they do) can be as significant to children as more long-term decisions about their future. Our findings echoed the words of researchers from an earlier study about children's experiences of risk in their daily lives:

For parents, making the right decisions now was important for the child's futures. Although children endorsed this view, they placed equal emphasis on how these decisions affected the quality of their lives "now", as children in the present.

(Hood et al.1996: 319)

For example, the sorts of decisions that were mentioned most often by children in their decision-making charts were decisions about: where I go (80 per cent of children); what I do (73 per cent); school (47 per cent); play (47 per cent); contact with families (44 per cent); where I live (40 per cent); who my friends are (38 per cent); times to come in (38 per cent); clothes (33 per cent); food (33 per cent); times to go to bed (29 per cent); sports (27 per cent); TV (24 per cent); what activities (24 per cent); home/ house work (22 per cent) and sibling contact (20 per cent).

Furthermore, children's construction of their decision-making charts clearly illustrated that women are still more involved with children than men (Qvortrup et al. 1994). In each role of carer, parent, grandparent or social worker, it became apparent that women's involvement in decision-making about children's lives greatly outnumbered their male counterparts. For example, 60 per cent of the children had a card for their mothers, compared with 29 per cent for their fathers.

Comparing children's charts there were differences about the sorts of decisions that were mentioned according to gender, age, legal status and differences in placement (see Thomas and O'Kane 1998b). In terms of gender differences, boys focused more on activities, play, sports, and times to be in; girls on relationships, family contact, school, and why they are in care. Additionally, with regards to age older children were more likely to mention decisions about where they live, who their friends are, pocket money, times in and to bed, compared with younger children who were more likely to mention school, television, mothers and play.

The second meeting: The pots and beans activity

The second meeting usually focused on ascertaining children's views about their participation in review meetings,[3] as well as their participation in the study. *The Pots and Beans Activity* was useful for ascertaining children's views about the review process and in gaining a comparable quantifiable measure of varied aspects of their preparation and participation in a review meeting. In gathering this information in a quantifiable way it could be directly compared to the social workers' reports gathered in the first stage survey.

The pots and beans activity used a jar of beans and six different pots with different labels: preparation before the meeting, support, how much you speak, how much you are listened to, how much influence you have and how much you like meetings. For each pot the child was given three beans, and they were told that they had to decide how many beans each pot deserved.[4]

The example shown further of an 11-year-old boy talking about his experience of review meetings illustrates how the pots and beans activity provided a framework for children to express their views about both what had happened, and what would make it easier for them to participate. Additionally it enabled discussions on how much children spoke in meetings, how much they were listened to and how much influence they thought they had. As illustrated below, children were very thoughtful about how many beans they put in each pot. Thus, this proved a useful technique for gaining insight into varied aspects of the participation process:

I: So, what I've got is this one – preparation before the meeting. So if you feel you had a lot of preparation – like they told you who would be there or what sort of things you wanted to talk about – you put in three. If you felt you had some preparation put two, and if you feel you didn't have any you put one in.

b11: Right *(he puts in two beans)*

I: OK. Two. Do you want to say what preparation you had?

b11: Well, they asked me how do you feel about staying here, and is there anything wrong that you want to do something about.

I: What do you think would have made a difference about having this extra one?

b11: If they said what we were going to do and what their names were.

I: Support. So the next one is about how supported you felt by other people, to be able to go to that meeting to be able to say what you wanted.

b11: Well I'd say three, coz I had a lot of support. Because my foster mother was saying 'oh you need to say what you want – if you don't like it here just say and they can arrange something else for'. My father was saying the same thing as well. So I had a lot of support there.

I: Good. The next one is how much did you speak in the meetings?

b11: Well, I was a bit younger then and I was a bit shy – so I'll put in one, coz I didn't feel confident and let it all out.

I: So if you had a meeting now how much do you think you would speak?

b11: I'd say quite a lot because I've grown up now, and I can just say what I want to say.

The group activity days

Considering the widespread lack of consultation with groups of children and young people on matters that concern them in society (Treseder 1996), adult agendas often define the concerns which society deems to be important about children (Stainton-Rogers and Stainton-Rogers 1992). Therefore, group discussions with children and young people are important to ascertain children's perspectives.

Using participatory techniques with groups of children enabled focused opportunities to explore children's own definitions of the cultural norms which structure their lives, as well as opportunities to clarify similarities and differences between different children's experiences and beliefs. Use of a number of participatory techniques provided a series of frameworks for discussion, within which children's experiences and definitions could be explored.

The activity days drew upon literature concerning 'focus groups', which have been described as group discussions organised to explore a specific set of issues (Kitzinger 1994). Kitzinger (1994) has identified nine advantages of focus groups which rely on the interaction of participants. Such interaction highlights the respondents' attitudes, priorities, language and frames of reference; encourages a wide range of communication; helps to identify group norms; provides insight to social processes; and can encourage open conversation about embarrassing subjects. Furthermore, with attention to the interaction between participants, a researcher can explore differences; use conflict to clarify why people do what they do; explore arguments to see how people change their mind; and analyse how particular forms of speech facilitate or inhibit peer communication.

Additionally, information gathered in group settings may prove different to information collected in individual meetings, even when the same participants are involved (Hoijer 1990). In the triangulation of different methods, such differences are useful, as such differences are not to be classified in terms of 'honesty and dishonesty' or 'truth or falsehood', but rather as an acknowledgement of different types of discourse in the 'private' and 'public' arena (Kitzinger 1994). It has been noted that

> focus groups do not easily tap into individual biographies or the minutia of decision making during intimate moments, but they do examine how knowledge and, more importantly, ideas both develop, and operate, within a given cultural context.
>
> (Kitzinger 1994: 116).

As such, it was predicted that the activity days would be most useful in gaining insight into the cultural context regarding everyday life of children in the middle age-group who are looked after in the UK, and less useful in gaining further personal details. This proved to be the case. Discussion centred on a wider range of issues and people than had been discussed in the individual meetings, though in much less depth.

Bringing groups of children and young people who didn't know each other together demanded consideration of group dynamics and attention to literature concerning varied aspects of discussions within groups (e.g. focus group discussions, discussion techniques). Thus, alongside the endeavours to break down barriers which have been documented so far, a range of additional strategies to enable equal opportunities for participation in group activity days were utilized. The use of ice-breaker games, initial explanations, the establishment of agreed positive groundrules, and the occasional use of a listening ball, all assisted in creating an atmosphere in which children's voices should be equally valued and listened to.

The overall shape of the activity day programme which ran from 10.30am to 3pm and the range of activities used is shown in Figure 6.2. By focusing on just one of the activities used: *the Diamond Ranking Exercise*, an illustration as to how children negotiate and explain experiences and structures which affect their lives, will be given. Diamond-ranking activities are powerful tools for clarifying ideas and concepts, as they involve discussion, sorting and prioritizing of issues.

Activity Day: Outline of the programme

---

* Arrivals and Setting Up
* Games: Name Games (line in order of name; zombies); When the Wind Blows
* Explanations about the Day
* Hopes for the Day
* Positive Groundrules
* Graffitti Wall for Ongoing Feedback
* BREAK
* Activity 1:   Draw Around a Person: What Sorts of Decisions are Made about You?
* Activity 2:   'Children Should be Seen and Not Heard' Statement
                  In Line according to age/ At What Age Should You Have a Say
* Activity 3:   Diamond Ranking: What is most important for children to have a say
                  Split in 2 groups (with cards); agree on what = most important
* LUNCH, GAMES, GRAFFITI WALL, POSTER DESIGN GROUP
* Activity 4:   Jigsaw (splits them into two groups and gives instructions)
                  Draw hand (age) and agree 5 things that make a good social worker
* Activity 5:   Create an Alien Review Panel
                  Questions and Answers about Review Meetings.
* Activity 6:   Any other ideas/ Poster Making
* BREAK
* Activity 7:   'Good Ideas for the Future'; Poster Design Group; How to keep in touch
* Activity 8:   Evaluation: Move to Side of Room; Caption Sheet: 'Thoughts about Today'
* Activity 9:   Applause Chair, Thankyou and Cards.
ENDINGS, packing up, goodbyes and Minibus Route Home.

Figure 6.2: Outline programme of the children's activity day

Diamond ranking exercise: what is most important?

This activity aimed to explore children and young people's views on issues that were most important in taking part in decision-making. It also enabled us to observe the process of children making co-operative decisions. Prior to the activity day a list of nine statements about taking part in decision-making were carefully identified from the previous individual interviews with children. Nine statements on aspects of the decision-making process identified included: *to be given choices, for adults not to pressurize me, to let me have my say, to get what I want, to have time to think about things, for adults to make good decisions, to be supported, to be listened to, and to find out what is going on.* These statements were individually written on to square post-its. Two grids with nine squares in the shape of a diamond (see Figure 6.3) were also constructed, with 'most important' written by the top square, and 'least important' written by the bottom square.

Each group of children had to work together to decide which statement should go in the 'most important' square, the 'least important' square, and the ones in-between. Once the groups had reached a consensus on the placement of their cards, they were asked to feedback their grid to the other group, explaining the placement of their cards. Group dialogue highlighted similarities and differences between and within groups about broader aspects of the decision-making process.

The overall placement of the cards made by children is shown in Figure 6.3. The placement of cards presents a challenge to perceptions of children commonly held by adults, that children are out to 'get what they want'. An extract shown below focuses on dialogue between two groups of children as they share their diamond ranking placements. This section of dialogue provides a glimpse of a world-view shared by children that is more concerned with being included from a justice perspective, than with getting what they want:

b12: Well we have got one thing the same: 'to get what I want' is least important .... The top ones and bottom are almost the same.

I: Do you want to say why you have both put 'to get what I want' least important?

g12: Coz it is pointless isn't it. You don't talk to people to get what you want do you?

I: So what do you do it for?

b12: I think you do do it to get what you want, but it is not the most important thing. Getting a say is one of the most important things isn't it? Being listened to is one of the most important.

g12: It is like you don't come here to get what you want.

I: And why have you both agreed 'to be listened to' at the top?

g12: Because that is the most important thing.

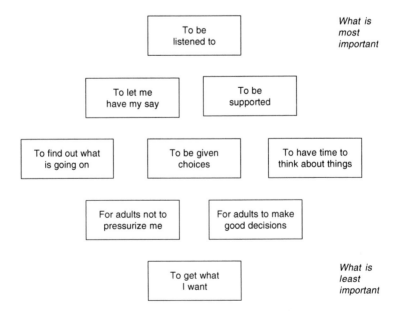

Figure 6.3: Diamond ranking: overall placement of statements by children

Methodological considerations for good practice

> When space is made for them, children's views express themselves clearly.
> (Mauthner 1997)

A range of myths about participatory methods exist, many of which have been challenged by Pretty et al. (1995, 68–70). For example, contrary to a common criticism of PRA as a quick way of doing things, the proper use of participatory approaches encourage dialogue, joint analysis and learning, processes which take time and may be complex. There is a danger that PRA is used as simple technique without recognition of the importance of additional skills needed by the facilitator, with regards to communication, facilitation and conflict negotiation skills.

It has been found that the successful use of participatory methods greatly depends on the individuals involved, on the quality of facilitation and the context in which they are applied (Dolphin Project 1993; Freeman et al. 1996; Pretty et al. 1995; Boyden and Ennew 1997; Hart and Tyrer 2006). A research methodology is concerned with more than the tools selected. Attention to personal style and facilitation skills are essential. Whilst the activities provide a source of data in themselves (e.g. decision-making charts, diamond ranking), dialogue around the activities provides the richer source of interpretation and meaning (see Christensen and James, this volume).

In determining whether a child or young person's account reflect their real thoughts or understanding of what is going on, Shaw (1996) suggests that a good account will bear some relation to our approximate understanding of real social conditions. It will be plausible and coherent, making sense of other available information. Through their initial focus on 'concrete' events, the use of participatory techniques enhances the gathering of information with children, which reflects their construction of reality.

With regards to facilitation, researchers need to find ways of engaging with the child or young person, to build a relationship where respect, openness and a genuine intent to listen is evident. A wide range of strategies to break down the power imbalance between the child participants and adult researcher should be used. For example, in our study, strategies used included: giving child-centred information; choice of participation, as well as choice of when, where, how and with whom the meetings takes place; maintaining confidentiality; placing the child in control of the tape player; use of participatory activities; humour; seeking children's views on how to improve the situation; as well as valuing their time, by thanks, as well as payment for their participation in the activity days. Furthermore, broader preparations which are essential for ethical practice must be ensured, including attention to informed consent and choice of participation; privacy and confidentiality; potential responses to child protection issues raised; and issues of payment or reward (see O'Kane 1998; Thomas and O'Kane 1998b).

The setting has a significant effect on the way techniques can be used. Private space with minimal disturbances in an environment where the child or young person feels comfortable, is likely to be most conducive for productive research meetings. Factors such as when and where interviews take place, who is present, who will be told, are all likely to have an effect on what the child will talk about. Whilst the presence of some adults may facilitate explanations and communication with a child, some adults have a tendency to regulate children's voices, by challenging or redefining what they say. Similarly, older or more confident siblings may dominate the direction of discussions. Furthermore, in group meetings venues which are accessible and provide enough space, light and privacy should be carefully sought.

Broader contextual factors relating to the socio-cultural and political context also need to be considered when developing and implementing research with children (see Hart and Tyrer 2006). Consideration of the local context may influence which issues can be explored, the ways in which questions are phrased, the composition of groups, and the timing and location of activities. Furthermore, each specific tool or method implies a particular mode of communication – visual, verbal, performative, etc. Hart and Tyrer (2006: 30) emphasize how *'our understanding of the appropriateness and nature of different modes of communication is strongly shaped by cultural factors'*. Certain forms of communication may be unfamiliar in particular settings and therefore challenging to employ for the purposes of research. For example, the use of drama and role play has worked well in a country like Sri Lanka where a strong tradition of performance exists and where children commonly perform songs, sketches and dances. However, in other settings such activities may be considered immodest or provocative, particularly for girls (Hart and Tyrer 2006).

Reflections upon the relative benefits of participatory techniques

> Ethical guidelines call on researchers to avoid undue intrusion, and using methods which are non-invasive, non-confrontational and participatory, and which encourage children to interpret their own data, might be one step forward in diminishing the ethical problems of imbalanced power relationships between researcher and researched at the point of data collection and interpretation.
>
> (Morrow and Richards 1996: 100)

It has been argued elsewhere that the use of participatory methods can help resolve a number of ethical problems in research with children, and can also enhance validity and reliability of research findings (see Thomas and O'Kane 1998a). Participatory techniques enable children to direct the content of the discussions, and rely on children explaining their interpretation of their reality to the interviewer. In such a way the use of participatory techniques as a research method are very conducive to social constructionist research.

The SWOT analysis shown below demonstrates a range of benefits (as well as some of the limitations) that result from using creative, innovative research methods with children. Participatory techniques are a powerful tool enabling children's voices, needs and interests to be articulated, and to take precedence over adults' research agenda. Rather than expecting children to answer the researcher's questions, the use of participatory techniques enable the creation of a more flexible environment in which participants are given more control over the agenda. Furthermore, by encouraging children, young people and adult participants to set the agenda we are more likely to encompass new and more relevant areas of questioning as we proceed.

In any exploratory study concerned with listening to children's experiences or views, the researcher cannot predict the content of the discussions. Whilst there may be a sense of wanting to charter a boat in an unknown territory, use of participatory techniques allow children to navigate and set the parameters. For example, at the outset of this study there was an inclination to focus the study on children's participation in formal decision-making meetings held by social services. However, in choosing to develop research techniques which allowed children to have more of a say in setting the research agenda, our study has ended up focusing more on the significance of day-to-day decision-making. Children's discourse on participation in decision-making was very much focused on the negotiations, rules and regulations that structure their lives, as well as adult-child relations, and the roles of multiple adults.

As a responsive research method, the use of participatory tools assist in transforming power relations between the adult researcher and the child participants. Other researchers have commented that the 'social event of the interview provides a means to challenge as well as reinforce models of childhood and adulthood' (Hood et al. 1996, Mayall and Alderson, this volume). At the end of one interview with one 12-year-old boy, he spontaneously commented:

b12:   I've gotta say this … two visits you have come to see me haven't you? It has got to be the most confident I have ever been about this stuff. I don't think I have ever been so confident talking about it.
         A comment at the end of another interview by a 10-year-old girl illustrates both the child's willingness to speak out, and her preference for creative communication:
g10:   Do you mind if I sing a song at the end?
I.:   No.
g10:   Coz I think if I sing a song it will help and if you show Nigel (other researcher) the tape he might like my singing or something, coz singing does come in handy sometimes don't it?

Other children who participated in the study compared the use of participatory techniques favourably to other methods of communication used by their social workers. It became clear that many children in the middle age-group preferred methods of active communication (doing or moving), rather than passive communication ('just talking'). For example, in talking about preparation for his review meeting during the pots and beans exercise, the following discussion took place between the interviewer and a 10-year-old boy:

I: So preparation – how many beans?

b10: This is about the meeting isn't it?

I: Yes, that's right.

b10: I'll have two.

I: So what would make it better? What would people have to do to get a three for preparation?

b10: If they bring us something for us to do – like this. So that'll be three out of three.

I: So that would really help – if you could do something like this instead of talking?

b10: Yeah.

I: .... Have you ever been asked to fill in consultation forms?

b10: Yeah

I: .... Was that good – did that help?

b10: ... Not as good as this one ... This is the best one I've had.

In our study we also found that the use of participatory techniques facilitated explanations about the purposes of the research and the form that it will take. The activities provided a greater degree of transparency, which distilled the degree of 'mysticism' about research, and lessened participants' fears about what may happen next. Transparency is critically important in attempting to conduct good practice in research with children, as it is one way to tackle the problematic area of 'expectations' with regards to participatory work with children.

> Participation may indeed be an empowering process, but the limits of this power need to be acknowledged in order to make the potential for real achievements clear.
>
> (Chawla and Kjrholt 1996: 45).

Such transparency also seemed to facilitate more genuine participation by children in the research process, as well as enhancing working relationships and trust from the adult caretakers. Children's 'socio-political positioning means that adults must give permission' (Hood et al.1996: 126). Therefore, in seeking to involve children in any participatory activity it will be important to make attempts to gain active support from children's adult caretakers. In gaining a degree of partnership and trust with a child's caretakers, they are more likely to trust you and to give the child or young person more space and autonomy in making choices about when and how they see you.

Being given the space to take part on their own terms, many children became greatly involved in the meetings, expressing a sense of ownership of their materials and ideas, whilst also becoming more motivated to take part in further aspects of the research process. For example, the illustration below shows how a 10-year-old was able to take ownership of the visual material that was one outcome of using participatory techniques:

g10:   ... Are you going to keep this grid? Can I keep this grid? Would it be OK if I took it to school tomorrow to show miss? Because I told her you were coming and I said I would tell her what happened.

I: Yeh, I have numbered these, so if you want to set it up again to show your teacher you can do.

g10:   Thanks, that would be nice.

I: If you keep it now. Then what would be useful, is if next time I come I could make a copy of it to show Nigel who I work with.

g10:   Yeh, because I told Miss D *(teacher)* you were coming and I said if we do anything I'll ask if I could show her.

In another example, in the first interview conducted with an 8-year-old girl she decided that she wanted to keep a lot of the completed activity sheets and pocket chart. However, mid-way through the second interview she said:

g8:   You know these sheets I kept from last time, when you said if you wanted you could take them and photocopy them – this week you can take them.

I: All right. I'll take them and photocopy them and then send them back to you. Thank you it will be nice to see them again.

However, participatory techniques also have their limitations. In choosing to use research techniques which are more responsive to the participants, rather than the researcher's agenda, you are forfeiting the opportunity to gather information in a uniform way. The research topic, plans and methods may be subject to re-negotiations. Such negotiations may create obstacles in terms of expectations established between the research funder and/or the employer (Hart and Tyrer 2006). Whilst the framework of an activity can be carefully designed to ensure that a broad area of interest will be discussed, participants are given more control over the focus and agenda. Thus, in being responsive to individual children, you are limiting the field of investigation to issues that they find significant, and/or are willing to discuss. Furthermore, the reasons that certain topics are excluded are often unknown, it may be that this topic has little significance, or it may be the topic is too sensitive to talk about.

However, an advantage of this method is that it aids sensitive interviewing with children. In approaching children as social actors in their own right it gives them more control over what they want to talk about. For example, one

Strengths	*Opportunities*
Transparency in explanation	Encompasses qualitative and quantitative methods
Children greater control over the agenda	Enables active listening and responsive questioning
Choice of participation	Easier to explain
Real consent through participation	Non-threatening
No right or wrong answers	Transparency – assists in gaining trust from adults
More interesting and fun	Fun
Innovative	Basis for dialogue and building of relationships
Breaks down power	Visual representation of children's views
Powerful visual representation of ideas	Adaptable for children with different abilities
Focus on real life events	Active partnership from adult caretakers
Enables responsive and sensitive questioning	Greater communication
Provides structure for concrete dialogue	Builds upon children's capabilities and interests
Flexibility and Adaptability	Allows for variety, ambiguity and conflicting replies
Does not rely on literacy or writing skills	Variety of expressive methods
Reaches children of a wide range of age and ability	Increases children's confidence
Movement and tactility - 'not just talking'	Further development work
Children's ownership	Opportunities to listen to each other
Children able to interpret their own data	Prioritization of issues
Materials can be cheaply developed or adapted	Confidentiality, privacy and space to speak
Weaknesses	Good facilitation skills
Lack of uniformity	Threats
	Adult redefining children's words and interpretations
Topics not mentioned for varied reasons	Questions about objectivity
Reasons for exclusion of topics unknown	More powerful speaks (e.g. older sibling, adult)
Requires a level of conceptual understanding	Lack of time and resources
Some activities are exclusive of children with severe learning difficulties	Lack of interest
Costs and transport of bringing children together	Adult pressurizing child to take part
Time	Unclear or too high expectations
	Lack of space and privacy
	Negative view of children's capabilities
	Children may raise sensitive issues which place them at risk
	Poor facilitation skills
	Subjects research plans, topics and methods to (re)negotiation which may cause difficulties with research funder or employer

Figure 6.4 SWOT analysis for participatory techniques with children

10-year-old girl commented on her preference for the building of her decision-making chart which allowed her to set the agenda, compared to other games that social worker's had used which forced the agenda:

g10: I'm happy to talk to you another time, because it is easier to talk to someone like you than it is to talk to social workers and that about problems.

I: So why is that then?

g10: Well, mostly because they are talking about choices in my life. And this chart – they don't do stuff like that. It is harder too, because they talk to someone else – normally they talk to our mother to see if they're getting on with it. They sometimes talk to the child, but it is much harder for me to talk to the social worker.

I: ... So what things would make it easier to talk directly to the social worker?

g10: It would make it easier if they would ask me a question and let me decide. I would make my own decision in my head – like we do on that chart. Then I could tell it to everyone I wanted to hear ...

I: So does the chart help to talk about things?

g10: Yeah – like I decided the question and I decided what people. Because the other games they are just set questions ... If there is a card and you pick a card - coz when you roll the dice you've got to do it. Once a card said 'have you left anyone?' That would make people upset – especially if they are fostered. So when you decide your own questions it is easier to consider, because then you won't get upset and start crying.

Furthermore, whilst the use of participatory techniques may be less time-consuming than ethnographic methods, a lot of time is required to give researchers the space to develop, use and analyse participatory techniques with children, individually and in groups. Processes of contacting, information-giving, negotiating, arrangement-making, travelling to and from, conducting interviews, analysis and feedback all require a large amount of time and resources.

With regards to the suitability of using participatory techniques with children of different ages and abilities, a range of participatory techniques can be adapted to suit children and young people of varying ages, with various levels of literacy or conceptual skills (see Davis, Watson and Cunningham-Burley, this volume). However, some techniques clearly require a certain level of conceptual or physical ability. For example, in our study two children with some learning difficulties were able to make their own decision-making chart, particularly when given more time. Yet, the researchers were less able to engage another two children who had more severe learning difficulties in this activity, as its conceptual nature proved too difficult. However, the use of pictures rather than words in all of the activities may assist in their appropriateness when literacy skills are an issue (see Rabiee et al. 2005).

A number of children commented on their preference for participatory techniques as they were more 'fun' and less 'boring'. Butler and Williamson (1994: 38) have commented on the use of humour in research with young people: 'we would reiterate that humour and self-effacement are useful personal attributes to take into the interview, though they are rarely mentioned in research methods textbooks'.

In both the 'movement evaluations,[5] and evaluation forms children in this middle-age group expressed the importance of 'fun' as a factor which describes how interesting a research meeting is. For example, the range of feedback from 'your thoughts about the day' evaluation forms from ten young people attending one activity day included the following descriptions:

> fun (7); enjoyable (5); funny (4); exciting (4); cool (4); good (2); excellent (2); ace (2); amazing (2); fantastic (2); terrific (2); great (2); made new friends (2); a laugh; smart; not how I expected – I thought it would be just talking; it was more activity than just talking; not bad; tiring; I liked the good communication; it was in blocks – not one load; discuss a lot; helped; educational; brilliant; playful; the games were good; fantasy; Claire is good; Nigel is funny; I liked it.

However, with the 'fun' element there is a danger that participatory techniques may be taken less seriously. Participatory techniques should not be labelled as 'childish' techniques.[6] Whilst other researchers have recommended the use of structured activities that have been used for younger children (McAuley 1996), I'd argue that participatory techniques are useful as a research method for young people and adults.

There is an ongoing debate amongst children and adults about the importance of age as the marker of status, privilege and competence (Hood et al. 1996). Within our study it was clear that increasing age is associated with being treated with more respect, dignity and independence (see Thomas and O'Kane 1999). However, if researchers wish to engage with children as social actors to learn more about the relationships, activities and structures which describe their 'childhood', I'd suggest that they approach all age groups with a fundamental sense of respect and a belief in their capacity to take part. Participatory techniques have primarily been developed through work with adults. It is fundamentally through the researcher's overall approach that they can demonstrate their respect for the research participants, whatever their age. Furthermore, children and young people can themselves be supported to conduct their own participatory research with their peers, and/or with adults.

Conclusion

Article 12 of the United Nations Convention on the Rights of the Child 1989 clearly ascertains that children and young people have a right to be involved in decisions which affect them. This right extends from decisions affecting them as individuals, to decisions which affect them collectively as children – an acknowledgement that they are social actors in their own lives. Social researchers can play an important role in embracing the challenge to create space for children and young people to be listened to and heard, and I would advocate that the use of participatory techniques would facilitate such a task.

> Understanding children and childhood, if one starts from the position of adulthood, requires listening attentively to their agendas, and participating with them in the research process.
>
> (Hood et al. 1996: 118)

Participatory techniques provide one framework which is responsive, with open-ended research goals and methods which allow children to set their own agenda. Furthermore, these methods can be adapted to suit work across a wide age-range of children and young people, and can be used in a wide range of settings.

Information gathered with children through the use of participatory techniques in our study has drawn attention to a wide range of matters which concern children (see Thomas and O'Kane 1998a), and has also highlighted a range of contemporary theoretical issues concerning the nature of childhood and adult-child relations (see Thomas and O'Kane 1999). Whilst reinforcing messages that children's lives are structured by boundaries regulated by adults, in discussions surrounding the participatory techniques the children provided clear illustrations of their active attempts to negotiate and push back the boundaries, thus demonstrating that they are social actors in their own right, with their own agenda.

The use of participatory techniques can enable researchers to conduct research with children which can form part of the emerging work:

> in qualitative research on 'voice' or 'voicing' the concerns of the silenced …. developing research methodologies on the basis of partnership, which in turn involves a new role in the power structure for the researcher – a move from the plunderer of information to facilitator which enables the child to be active part of voicing their concerns.
>
> (John 1996: 21)

Furthermore, I would advocate and support increasing efforts to strengthen partnerships and capacity building initiatives between researchers and child led groups and initiatives, enabling and supporting child-led research processes and participatory research facilitated directly by children and young people with their peers.

Acknowledgements

I acknowledge all children, young people and adults with whom I have had the privilege to work in participatory ways – I have learnt from you all. I am very grateful to Nigel Thomas for his comments on the original version of this chapter and for sharing publications which have informed the updated version. Feedback from Pia Christensen has also been helpful.

Notes

1 The research was conducted by Nigel Thomas and Claire O'Kane, with reference to an advisory group including academics, children's advocates, local authority staff and young people with experience of the care system. The study was funded by the Nuffield Foundation.

2 It was explained that the stickers were like traffic lights: the green sticker was like 'go' and meant 'a lot of say'; the orange sticker was like 'get ready' and meant 'some say'; and the red sticker was like 'stop' meaning 'no say'.

3 A 'review meeting' is a meeting held by social services when children are 'looked after' by the State. The concept of a review is a continuous process of planning and reconsideration of the plan for the child.

4 For example: 3 beans meant 'really good' (e.g. I had a lot of preparation from my social worker and carer); 2 beans meant 'quite good', 'OK' (e.g. OK I had some preparation, but I could have done with a bit more); and 1 bean meant 'not very good', 'not much' (e.g. I didn't have enough support). For each labelled pot the child had to put in 1–3 beans depending how good it was.

5 In 'movement evaluations' a line is set up in a room. One end of the line represents 'really brilliant' and the other 'really awful', midway represents 'OK'. Children are asked various questions (e.g. was today interesting?) and asked to stand on the line according to their evaluation.

6 Participatory techniques should not be labelled as a 'childish' technique in any derogatory sense of the word. If they were described as a child-centred method in terms of being more suitable to research work which engages children in describing their reality – this may be less demeaning.

References

Alderson, P. (1993) *Children's Consent to Surgery*. Buckingham: Open University Press.

Alderson, P. (1995) *Listening to Children: Children, Ethics and Social Research*, Barkingside, Barnardos.

Aldgate, J. and Simmonds, J. (1988) *Direct Work With Children*. London: BAAF/Batsford.

Article 31 Action Pack (1995) *Children's Rights and Children's Play*. Birmingham: Play-Train.

Bluebond-Lagner, M. (1978) *The Private Worlds of Dying Children*. Princetown: Princetown University Press.

Boyden, J. and Ennew, J. (eds) (1997) *Children in Focus – a manual for participatory research with children*. Stockholm: Rädda Barnen, Save the Children Sweden.

Bulmer, M. (ed.) (1984) *Sociological Research Methods*. London: Macmillan.

Butler, I. (1996) 'Children and the sociology of childhood', Ch. 1, in I. Butler and I. Shaw, (eds) *A Case of Neglect? Children's Experiences and the Sociology of Childhood*. Aldershot: Avebury.

Butler, I. and Willliamson, H. (1994) *Children Speak: Children, Trauma and Social Work*. Harlow: Longman.

Chambers, R. (1992) *Rural Appraisal: Rapid, Relaxed and Participatory.* IDS Discussion Paper 311, IDS, Brighton, UK.

Chambers, R. (1994) *Participatory Rural Appraisal: Challenges, Potentials and Paradigms.* IDS: University of Sussex.

Chawla, L. and Kjrholt, A.T. (1996) 'Children as special citizens', *PLA Notes*, Special Issue on Children's Participation, Number 25, London: IIED.

Children's Participation Pack (1996) *A Practical Guide for Playworkers.* London: Save the Children and Kirkless Metropolitan Council.

Christensen, P. (2004) 'Children's participation in ethnographic research: issues of power and representation', *Children and Society* 18: 165–76.

Clarke, A. and Moss, P. (2001) *Listening to Young Children. The Mosaic Approach.* London: The National Children's Bureau.

Connelly, M. and Ennew, J. (1996) 'Introduction: Children out of place', *Childhood* 3 (2):131–46.

Conway, G.R. (1987) 'The properties of agro-Ecosystems'. *Agricult. Systems* 24: 95–117.

Cornwall, A., Guijt, I. and Welbourn, A. (1993) 'Acknowledging process: Challenges for agriculttural research and extension methodology', in I. Scoones and J. Thompson (eds) (1994) *Beyond Farmer First.* London: IT Publications Ltd.

Corsaro, W.A. (1979) 'We're friends right? Children's use of access rituals in a nursery school', *Language in Society* 8: 315–36.

Dolphin Project (1993) *Answering Back: Report by Young people Being Looked After on the Children Act 1989:* University of Southampton.

Dreitzel, P. (1973) *Childhood and Socialisation*, New York: Macmillan.

Freeman, I., Morrison, A., Lockhart, F. and Swanson, M. (1996) 'Consulting service users: The views of young people', Ch. 16, in M. Hill and J. Aldgate (eds) *Child Welfare Services: Developments in Law, Policy, Practice and Research*, London: Jessica Kingsley Publishers.

Freire, P. (1972) *Pedagogy of the Oppressed*, California: Continuum.

Hart, J. and Tyrer, B. (2006) *Research with Children Living in Situations of Armed Conflict: Concept, Ethics and Methods.* Refugee Studies Centre, Working Paper Series (Working Paper 30), University of Oxford.

Hazel, N. (1996) 'Elicitation techniques with young people', *Social Research* 12, University of Surrey.

Hill, M., Laybourn, A., and Borland, M. (1996) 'Engaging with primary-aged children about their emotions and well-being', *Children and Society* 10 (2): 129–44.

Hoijer, B. (1990) 'Studying viewers. Reception of television programmes: theoretical and methodological considerations', *European Journal of Communication* 5: 39–56.

Holland, J. and Blackburn, J. (eds) (1998) *Whose Voice? Participatory Research and Policy Change.* London: IT Publications.

Hood, S., Kelley, P. and Mayall, B. (1996) 'Children as research subjects: A risky enterprise', *Children and Society* 10 (2): 117–28.

James, A. (1993) *Childhood Identities: Social Relationships and the Self in Children's Experiences.* Edinburgh: Edinburgh University Press.

James, A. (1996) 'Learning to be friends: Methodological lessons from participant observation among English schoolchildren', *Childhood* 3 (3): 313–29.

James, A. and Prout, A. (1990, 1997) *Constructing and Reconstructing Childhood: Contemporary Issues in the Sociological Study of Childhood*, London: Falmer Press.

James, A., Jenks, C. and Prout, A. (1998) *Theorizing Childhood.* Cambridge: Polity Press.

John, M. (1996) 'Introduction: Voicing', in M. Johns (eds) *Children in Charge: A Child's Right to a Fair Hearing.* London: Jessica Kingsley Publishers.

Johnson, V., Hill, J. and Ivan-Smith, E. (1995) *Listening to Smaller Voices: Children in an Environment of Change*. Somerset: Actionaid.

Johnson, V. (1996) 'Introduction: Starting a dialogue on children's participation', *PLA Notes*, Special Issue on Children's Participation, Number 25, London: IIED.

Kay, H., Cree, V., Tisdall, K. and Wallice, J. (2003) 'At the edge: Negotiating boundaries in research with children and young people', *Forum: Qualitative Social Research* 4 (2).

Kefyalew, F. (1996) 'The reality of child participation in research: Experience from a capacity-building programme', *Childhood* 3 (2): 203–14.

Kitzinger, J. (1994) 'The methodology of focus groups: the importance of interaction between research participants', *Sociology of Health* 16 (1): 103–21.

Lucchini, R. (1996) 'Theory, method and triangulation in the study of street children', *Childhood* 3(2): 167–70.

Mauthner, M. (1997) 'Methodological aspects of collecting data from children: Lessons from three research projects', *Children and Society* 11: 16–28.

Mauthner, M., Mayall, B. and Turner (1993) *Children and Food at Primary School*. London: SSRU/ Science Education, Institute of Education.

Mayall, B. (1994) *Children's Childhoods: Observed and Experienced*, London: Falmer Press.

Mayall, B. (1996) *Children, Health and The Social Order*. Buckingham: Open University Press.

McAuley. C. (1996) 'Children's perspectives on long-term foster care', Ch.12, in M. Hill and J. Aldgate (eds) *Child Welfare Services: Developments in Law, Policy, Practice and Research*, London: Jessica Kingsley Publishers.

Morrow, V. and Richards, M. (1996) 'The ethics of social research with children: An overview', *Children and Society* 10 (2): 90–105.

Nieuwenhuys, O. (1996) 'Action research with street children: A role for street educators', *PLA Notes*, Special Issue on Children's Participation, Number 25, London: IIED.

O'Kane, C. (1998) 'Children and decision-making: Ethical considerations', in V. Johnson, E. Ivan-Smith, G. Gordon, P. Pridmore and P. Scott (eds) *Stepping Forward: Children and Young People's Participation in the Development Process*. London: Intermediate Technology Publications.

O'Kane, C. (2003) *Children and Young People as Citizens: Partners for Social Change*. Save the Children South and Central Asia.

Piaget, J. (1968) *Six Psychological Studies*. New York: Vintage.

Pretty, J.N., Guijt, I., Thompson, J. and Scoones, I. (1995) *Participatory Learning and Action: A Trainers Guide*. London: IIED Participatory Methodology Series.

Punch, S. (2002) 'Research with children: The same or different from research with adults?' *Childhood* 9 (3): 321–41.

Qvortrup, J. *et al.* (1994) *Childhood Matters: Social Theory, Practice and Politics*. Vienna: European Centre.

Rabiee, P., Sloper, P. and Beresford, B. (2005) 'Doing research with children and young people who do not use speech for communication', *Children and Society* 9: 385–96.

Robinson-Pat, A. (1996) 'Using PRA in academic research: Reflections after fieldwork in Nepal', in *IDS PRA Topic Pack on Participatory Research*. Sussex: Institute of Development Studies.

Rogers, R.S. (1993) 'The social construction of child-rearing', in A. Beattie, Gott M, Jones L and Sidell M (eds) *Health and Well-being: A Reader*. Macmillan Basingstoke: MacMillan Open University.

Ryan, T. and Walker, R. (1993) *Life Story Work*. BAAF.

Sapkota, P. and Sharma, J. (1996) 'Participatory interactions with street children in Nepal'. *PLA Notes*, Special Issue on Children's Participation, Number 25, London: IIED.

Shaw, I. (1996) 'Unbroken voices: Children, young people and qualitative methods', Ch.2, in I. Butler and I. Shaw (eds) *A Case of Neglect? Children's Experiences and the Sociology of Childhood*. Aldershot: Avebury.

Sinclair, R. (1996) 'Editorial', *Children and Society* 10 (2):87–9.

Solberg, A. (1996) 'The challenge in child research: From 'being' to 'doing', Ch. 5, in M. Brannen and M. O'Brien (eds) *Children in Families: Research and Policy*, London: The Falmer Press.

Stainton-Rogers, R. and Stainton-Rogers, W. (1992) *Stories of Childhood: Shifting Agendas of Child Concern*, Hemel Hampstead: Harvester Wheatsheaf.

Steiner, M. (1993) *Learning from Experience: World Studies in the Primary Curriculum*, Staffordshire: Trentham Books.

Theis, J. (1996) 'Children and participatory appraisals: Experiences from Vietnam', *PLA Notes*, Special Issue on Children's Participation, Number 25, London: IIED.

Theis, J. and O'Kane, C. (2005) 'Children's participation, civil rights and power', in J. Ensor and P. Gready (eds) *Reinventing Development? Translating Rights Based-Approaches from Theory into Practice*. London: IIED.

Thomas, N. and O'Kane, C. (1998a) *Children and Decision-Making: A Summary Report*. International Centre for Childhood Studies: University of Wales Swansea.

Thomas, N. and O'Kane, C. (1998b) 'The ethics of participatory research with children', *Children and Society* 12 (5): 336–48.

Thomas, N. and O'Kane, C. (1999) 'Experiences of decision-making in middle childhood: The example of children "looked after" by local authorities', *Childhood* 6 (3): 369–87.

Tisdall, K., Davis, J.M. Hill, M., and Prout, A (2006) (eds) *Participation For What: Children Young People and Social Inclusion*. London: Policy Press.

Treseder, P. (1996) *Empowering Children and Young People: A Training Manual for Involving Children and Young People in Decision-Making*. London: Save the Children and Children's Rights Office.

Veale, A. (2005) 'Creative methodologies and their use in a participatory research project in Rwanda'. In Greene and Hogan (eds) *Researching Children's Experiences*. London: Sage.

Waksler, F.C. (1991) 'The hard times of childhood and children's strategies for dealing with them', in F. Waksler (ed) *Studying the Social Worlds of Children: Sociological Readings*. London: Falmer Press.

Woodhead, M. (1998) *Children's Perspectives on their Working Lives: A Participatory Study in Bangladesh, Ethiopia, the Philippines, Guatemala, El Salvador and Nicaragua*. Stockholm: Rädda Barnen/ Save the Children Sweden.

7 Childhood Diversity and Commonality

Some Methodological Insights

Pia Christensen and Allison James

Introduction

Though the concept of childhood may loosely describe the early part of the life course, the experience of those we deem children is now recognized to vary considerably, both across time and in social space (James et al. 1998). However, although such a perspective would seem to have toppled developmental psychology from its conceptual prominence in being able to provide an account of the progress of children towards adulthood, the extent to which 'the social' is itself regarded as offering an adequate account of childhood diversity varies. For some, the biological progression from birth through infancy to adolescence still signals a fundamental base upon which the social world simply inscribes its differentiating marks; for others, by contrast, it is the process of socialization or enculturation which is deemed the more important signifier of the diverse paths which children will take as they grow up (Woodhead 1999). But although they may be recast in a number of different contemporary idioms, such polarizations of opinion are, in essence, simply rehearsing a rather older debate about the balance to be struck between 'nature' and 'nurture' in understanding the differences which do exist between children. And, precisely because of the long history of this debate, this dualism can still represent an unhappy tension to be overcome when both designing and executing a piece of research with children.

An age/developmental based approach is, for example, often incorporated in the methodological design as if it were a 'natural' feature of childhood research. Mauthner (1997) for instance argues that the 'age' of a child necessarily determines the kinds of research techniques which can be used. Others more unquestioningly take 'age' for granted and design their methods to accord with the supposed developmental or cognitive abilities of their study population of children. Thus, as James, Jenks and Prout have questioned:

> How often do researchers choose an age group simply because they feel that the children will be 'old enough' to engage effectively with the researcher's project, rather than because at that particular age in that particular society children are sharing a particular social, rather than simply, developmental experience?
>
> (James et al. 1998: 174)

In light of these assumptions about the commonality which age brings to experience, this chapter seeks to explore the ways in which childhood diversity can be critically attended to in the research process. It does so by analysing a particular method used for a piece of research in which the topic of childhood diversity was itself under scrutiny through calling into question the significance for children of the common denominator of 'being 10 years old'.[1] Through a reflexive critique of our methods, we suggest that due attention to how children respond to and engage with the research is revealing of children's different social experiences and social competences. The chapter also shows how children develop a reflexive thinking, both about the research process and the differences in social experiences revealed whilst being involved in it (see Corsaro and Molinari; Alderson, this volume).

The study

The study was carried out with some 10-year-old children living in an urban and a rural location in the North of England and its focus was on various aspects of their time use and understanding in their everyday life at home and at school.[2] With a firm belief in the methodological and epistemological advances to be gained from adopting a perspective in which children are regarded as competent social actors who can inform research of their own views, the study set out to explore the extent to which 'age' is a useful concept for classifying and categorizing children's everyday experiences and practices. Thus it took as its starting point the suggestion that the child's position in the life course gives us significant insight into the experiential shape of children's everyday lives. At the same time it acknowledges that the generational experience of 'being a 10-year-old child' will vary not only across cultures but also, in quite subtle ways, within cultures. Indeed, it may change in and through different localities. These propositions were formulated into a set of broad research questions: Are there similarities in the daily lives of 10-year-old children and if so of what kind are they? Does the diversity of their social experiences at home and at school and in relation to geographical location – living in a rural and an urban location – elide any meaningful commonality of experience and social competence in relation to age?

To explore these wider issues of age and generation the research used the lens of 'time' itself and posed a series of particular questions to explore with the children: How do 10-year-old children spend their time? How is children's everyday time organised at home and at school and how much say do they have in decision making over time use in these different social contexts? How is children's everyday time use negotiated with their peers and with adults? What ideas and values do children attach to 'time' as time passing, to their past, present and future? What values do children attach to the idea of growing up? What meanings do children attribute to being at the brink of moving to secondary school? To what extent do children relate notions of 'competence' and 'maturity' to age?

Methodologically speaking, however, these questions are not immediately easy to ask or indeed talk about! 'Time', 'time passing', 'time values', 'growing up' and 'maturity' are rather abstract notions. Difficult to pin down, they are not the hottest of conversational topics and, we feared, might be a sure turn-off as an opening gambit for an interview! To explore the understandings and meanings that children attribute to such temporal concepts we devised, therefore, a series of graphic designs and vignettes to enable us to do so. The 'tools', as we came to call them, were inspired by those often used in participatory rural appraisal by development workers (Chambers 1992, 1994; see also O'Kane, this volume). PRA techniques were originally developed to help people with limited literacy or verbal skills to express their views about topics such as patterns of land use and inheritance or decision-making in a village community. Often involving very simple resources – for example, a stick with which to draw maps in the sand, or using piles of pebbles or stones to represent the distribution of power or control held by particular people. These techniques are generally regarded as empowering. Through their use people whose views rarely get heard are enabled to express them and are provided with a medium through which to 'speak'. This latter aspect was, from our point of view, the very attraction of adopting such techniques. As we shall show, in the study the tools acted as mediators in the communication between us, as researchers, and the children as informants. The specificity of these techniques provided a way to concretize what are often rather abstract or implicit ideas about time and in each case the tools gave us a firm starting point for our investigation of different aspects of time use.

The focus for our discussion here is the 'My Week' chart (Figure 7.1), which was designed and used early on in the research to produce a set of basic data about how children spend their time; another tool – the 'Time With My Family' chart – was designed to explore more qualitative aspects of time use, while the 'Who Decides' chart was used to gain ideas about the control and negotiation of time between children and their teachers, parents, siblings, at home and at school. In the following sections we describe in detail the use of the 'My Week' chart and show that both in the process of using it, as well as its outcomes, the interweaving of children's cognitive developmental, social competences and their social experiences are demonstrated. In this way the tool reveals both the similarities and the very real diversities which constitute the social experience of being a '10-year-old child' and thus calls into question the usefulness of 'age' as a static and fixed analytical category within the life course.

The 'My Week' chart aimed to facilitate children in their thinking about how they spend their time during a week. The children were asked to consider an 'average' or usual kind of week during the school term and to tell us what they did and how much time they spent doing different things. After explaining what the exercise involved the children were presented with a piece of paper, inscribed with a large circle, which was entitled 'My Week'. The children were asked to divide up the circle in such a way that it would represent their weekly activities and how much time they thought they used on each activity. They were then told that they could complete this task as

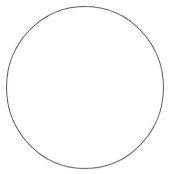

Figure 7.1 'My Week' tool

they saw fit and that they could do exactly what they wanted with the circle. In this way we aimed to deconstruct the very specificity of the 'tool' as a sole representational device; it was simply to be seen as one among many.[3]

Thus, the collection of data which resulted was extremely varied; it includes charts with no divisions and simply a summary of activities written down; geometrically divided charts; charts with wiggly lines; charts with pictorial illustrations; charts which list activities in order of importance; charts that have few subdivisions and charts with many; charts with hours calculated accurately; charts with simple guesstimates; charts left blank and charts shaded with an immense complexity of colour and patterns. In one school, the children completed the task in small groups with the researcher present and while the children completed the task, the tape recorder was left running. Not only did this mean that more information was gleaned about what children actually did during the week – because the researcher was able to talk to the children while they were deciding what to put on their charts – the recording also, very importantly, helped to capture the *process* of doing the activity. In the tape transcripts, discussions about the content of the charts are interspersed with other conversational snippets which reveal a great deal about the form and process of the method itself. At the other school the children in most cases took the task home, and then returned to school with the task completed to discuss their charts together in small groups. The children were asked to reflect on the way they had produced them; some had completed the chart with the help of a parent; others had called each other up to discuss how to do the task or had compared their notes at school and then chosen to copy or amend their own charts accordingly. The children then discussed the content of their individual charts in the group. Recordings were again made of these group discussions. Thus, it is both the 'form' and process of using the tool, as well as the data which it actually yielded that comprises our understanding of the similarities and diversities in the patterning of time use among 10-year-old children.

Visualising diversity and commonality in childhood

The use of visual media in social research is increasingly common (Prosser 1998) and, in work with children, is now a recognised way in which to engage effectively with children. Pictures, photographs and other visual images have all been used as ways in which to enrol children's enthusiasm and interest in a research topic – see for example, studies of children's friendships (Hallinan 1981), of their attitudes towards disability (Richardson et al. 1961) of their understanding of health education messages (Wetton and McWhirter 1998) and their views of hospital space (James et al. 2007, forthcoming). More recent studies have extended to work with children's own photographic views of primary school settings (Clarke and Moss 2001) and of their neighbourhoods and life in the city (Hubbard 1991, 1994; Christensen and O'Brien 2002; Rasmussen 2004). These studies have shown how when children themselves become active photographers, although such methods are complex, they also provide much insight into what is meaningful to children from their own perspectives.

The use of visual media can, as stand-alone techniques, be roundly critiqued – children's comments about photographs and pictures may simply be just that. However, when used alongside other methods, they also permit exploration of particular issues in more depth by encouraging a concentrated focus on the topic; they can also form part of a methodological triangulation through allowing the researcher to assess the extent to which a group of children share a particular attitude or opinion which has been randomly gleaned by the researcher from a casual comment made in passing or overheard.

The graphic tools which we developed can, we suggest, be added to this range of visual research methods and indeed extend the potential for research with children. What the 'tools' did was to enable children to participate in the research process by creating images for themselves, which were about themselves. This confirms that one of the most important features of these 'tools' is that they work to mediate the communication between the researcher and the children. First and very practically, as noted, the tools permitted the concretizing of the very abstract notions of time use. Second, the tools provided another medium of communication over and above that of talking. Rather than employing the more adult-centred frame of the interview or conversation, we utilized one unified form – the circle – and drew upon children's own competences and skills with pens and paper to express their experiences of being 10-years-old; of being a pupil at school; of living in families; and of residing in a village or an urban neighbourhood. As we will go on to show, it is out of this commonality of method that the diversities which exist between them was first revealed. Third, using the tools gave children the opportunity to offer a commentary on, not only the final image on the page as they might do about a photograph or a picture, but also the process of producing it. These visual tools provide, therefore, a rich, multilayered and mediated form of communication which is facilitated both by the image and by its very process of production.

It is the form and process of using the tools that we consider in the next section, taking account of the theoretical proposition offered by Rapport that

> individual contents and cultural forms constitute one social reality that cannot be properly or ideally described in the absence of the other ... it is their meeting in opposition which is socially constitutive.
>
> (1993: 164–5)

He suggests that culture can be described as a 'fund of behavioural forms' within which, nonetheless, can be seen 'complex and often diverse individual world-views' (1993: 165). Here we show how the children drew on two particular communal forms of representation to complete the 'My Week' task. One of these derives from their common experiences and competences of everyday school practice. The other has its basis in children's own cultural practices of drawing, doodling and copying. It is the commonality of these forms which, we suggest, enabled the children to offer to us their own subjective account of time use in their everyday life.

My Week: Being a schooled child

The 'My Week' tool was particularly revealing about the commonality which children share as 'school children'. More directly, it recalled in them a shared and common educational history. Most of the children immediately likened the circle to the familiar mathematical concept of a 'pie chart' which they had encountered in maths and geography lessons at school. As one boy confidently said when he was presented with the piece of paper: '[I've] done that before.' In this sense, then, this particular drawing activity highlighted a similarity of experience among the 10-year-old children: that of solving a problem through working with a pie chart.

However, in that this skill – doing a pie chart – had been developed in the context of schooling, it was one which, unlike more general drawing, carried with it aspects of the 'hidden curriculum' of the schooling process, a factor which, in turn, shaped the way in which the children carried out the task. For some children the task was viewed as being akin to a school task and thus suspiciously subject to the regulatory devices and regimes which control the production of work for children within school. When seen in this way, what was a shared and common experience threatened, from the children's point of view, to become one which potentially marked out their difference in skill from one another. Thus, negotiating their way around this potential point of divisiveness also became part of the process of completing 'My Week' and revealed, to the researchers, the diversities in terms of educational competences which arise for children through the daily, shared experience of schooling.

Some children, boys in particular, were very exacting in the execution of 'My Week', treating it as a geometrical exercise or a mathematical task: they used rulers to draw straight lines, asked for rubbers to remove the trace of lines drawn in error and checked with the researcher that they were doing it right. Despite every effort being made to reassure the children that there was not in fact a correct way in which to complete the task, many children nonetheless carried it out according to such an agenda. They continued to seek guidance, asking 'Can you ...?', 'Do you just ...?' As they set about completing the task. One girl asked, 'Shall I just put school?', enquiring, whether that large period of time identified as 'school time' needed to be subdivided into its different phases of 'play time' and 'work time'.

Such questioning and checking for reassurance, however, does not suggest that children were incompetent in carrying out the task – all the children were able to successfully complete it. Rather, such questioning draws upon the hierarchical relations that already exist between adults and children, and in particular between teachers and pupils at school. These position children as having only a relative competence and one which, moreover, is subject to teachers' continual judgement and assessment.

But the framing of the task by the children's communal experiences of the school curriculum and of being a 'schooled' and disciplined child is perhaps most clearly seen in the following question often asked by the children towards the end of the task: 'Do you put your name on it?'. It is through the naming of their work that children both claim their authorship of it at school and are made responsible for it. The naming of a piece of work permits the progress of an individual child to be assessed; as each piece of work is submitted to the teacher the log of marks, checked off against names, records the child's progress through the school year. Through this process are mapped the diversities in intellectual and academic achievement that exist between children.

My Week: Being a competent child

The shared discourse of schooling described above, which framed the completion of the 'My Week' task for some children had the potential to reveal differences between them with regard to their competence as school children. However, the task also made use of children's shared skills as children. This can be seen through the different ways in which the charts were created which represented almost an antidote to school work, through drawing on less legitimated practices of schooling – free drawing, doodling and copying.

It is significant, we suggest, that many of the children chose to complete 'My Week' using drawings rather than words. Drawing or doodling was seen by the children in the schools where the study was carried out as an ordinary, rather than specialized, activity – as something which they just do, as something with which children routinely fill up time on their own or in the company of others. Being able to draw does not necessarily mean having a particular skill in using a representational device. Neither does it always represent a mark of personal artistic achievement. As they draw, children happily chat with one another and in this sense drawing can be an accompaniment to socializing. As a cultural practice among children, unlike among adults, it is something which children expect to be able to do and also enjoy doing and it was clear that the children themselves considered 'all' children to be competent at it.

This understanding was rather poignantly brought home to one of the researchers during one wet playtime when the children had to stay in the classroom out of the rain. Being a time in the day marked out as non-lesson time, children were permitted to read comics or do other recreational activities. Common amongst these was to draw. A group of children engaged the researcher's attention as she sat with them at the table:

C: Would you like to do some drawing?
R: Yes
C: (busily drawing) What are you going to draw?

The researcher, pencil in hand, was suddenly nonplussed. She realized, rather belatedly, that she did not know 'how' to draw in the way that the children did. It was a skill which she no longer had. Trained in art, for her as for many adults, drawing had come to involve an act of interpretation, usually from material object to visual representation on a page rather than a 'free flowing' experiential activity.

Thus, although some children are, of course, recognized by their peers to be exceptionally 'good at drawing', drawing is generally regarded by them as a non-specialist skill. This means that a child's drawing, unlike their spelling or neat handwriting, is less open to be critiqued or judged by others, including other children. Drawing falls outside the educational framework of presentational skills, of 'success' and 'failure', of 'right' or 'wrong', the framework through which academic achievement is commonly experienced by children. In this sense then the insertion by children of pictures in the pie charts could be seen as a strategy to mask the different competences revealed in their writing (Figure 7.2)

Other potential differences between children were elided in another way. Some children, for example, chose to work in pairs, deciding together what should be included on the charts and how information should be displayed. Although such a collaborative effort clearly detracts therefore from the usefulness of the data as representing an account of each particular child's week, these ways of using the tool tell us something further about children's own views concerning difference and similarity, diversity and uniformity. As noted elsewhere (James 1993; Christensen 1998) a sense of sameness is important for children, providing for them a feeling of belonging, a way in which to smooth over the potential which any personal diversity or deviation might have to rupture the social relations which exist between one child and another. 'Copying' each other thus masks any potential differences among children, inducing a sense of sharing both in the process of making the chart and in the presentation of the final product. Whereas children 'working collaboratively together' is encouraged as a skill that children need to develop more generally within the classroom, it

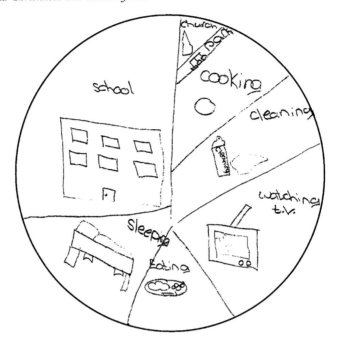

Figure 7.2 'My Week': girl aged 10

is a working practice that is nonetheless discouraged, and indeed disapproved of, in those lessons when tasks are meant to be completed by children independently (Christensen 1999).

That the children chose to copy each other when doing 'My Week' in the context of the school room – a space where such a practice is not usually permitted - may, in itself, register yet other aspects of childhood's diversities and similarities. It may, for example, reveal how the children are differentiating between the various temporal frameworks at work within the school - that which governs lessons and that in which the more recreational tasks are located. In this sense, participating in the research was perhaps defined by the children as 'not working'. In this time space, they judged 'copying' to be permitted. It received no sanction from the researcher as, indeed, neither did a refusal to do the task! In this sense, then, children's production of similarity by copying can be seen as children choosing to treat the space and time framed by the researcher as children's own time, allowing them to do things in the way they wished to. This was in opposition to the 'curriculum time' of the school day, where they would have to do what was required of them (Christensen et al. 2001). Thus, although clearly for some children the discursive practices of the educational setting of 'My Week' framed the way they completed it, leading as we have shown to the revelation of shared experiences between them, for most children completing the task became

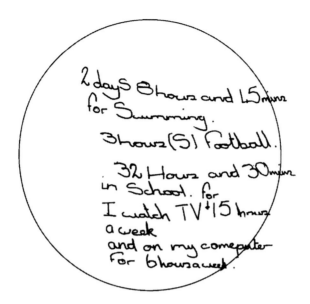

Figure 7.3 'My Week': boy aged 10 (a competitive swimmer)

something through which they expressed their idiosyncrasies, personal skills and their varied social experiences (Figure 7.3).

For example, perhaps affirming Walkerdine's (1985) observation that the structuring of girls' identities at school is largely as 'good girls', in contrast to the boisterous boys' identities as 'real boys', it was often the girls who asked for most reassurance from the researchers. One girl checked continually on her progress as she completed the task:

> Shall I just leave it like that?
>
> Shall I do it in pen?
>
> Can you put 'school'?

And, the final reassurance:

> Is it a double M in swimming?

Most boys, on the other hand, seemed less concerned with whether they were doing it right. Having decided it was a pie chart, they carried out the task with confidence. Their concern was directed at the product, the final image which they produced. Thus, many of the boys were keen to devise the chart with a scientific accuracy, to the extent in some cases of using a protractor to ensure that each segment was as an exact account of time spent as possible (Figure 7.4):

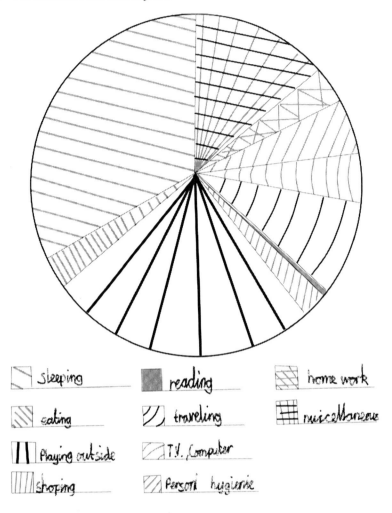

Figure 7.4 'My Week': boy aged 10

B: Er .... that's about right for eating, all of these are right 'cos I divided [it] up into twenty four things and then ...

R: Twenty four hours ?

B: And then, er, I say, so that's nine hours sleeping and then, er six, no eight hours outside and then like the other things ...

However, it is clear that other diversities, beyond those of gender, were revealed in the process of children putting pencil to paper. Although most children quickly took charge over and responsibility for structuring the task, they would continually keep an eye on how other children in the group undertook the task. This they did through a process of comparing their work with another's and remarking on the differences and similarities they could observe between them. For example, one boy looking at his neighbour's chart, enquired: 'Why are you colouring it in?' His own circle was simply left black and white, thus differing from the multi-coloured diagram of his neighbour. Another boy decided to make a key for his chart with which to unlock its content – 'I'm doing a key!', he announced proudly. In these ways the uniform task of making a pie chart revealed an array of diverse forms, expressive of children's individuality as children, of their personal and social experiences of an ordinary week. Sometimes, as we will go on to show in the next section, through this process the children themselves became aware that they had different experiences of being 10-year-old.

Children as reflexive interpreters

While introducing a science lesson a teacher involved in our research observed to the children: 'Every graph has a story to tell. It is not just a pretty pattern.' In this way, she wished to alert the children to the deeper layer of information that a graph represents. But she also wished to signal its difference from 'pictures' produced while doodling or drawing. This observation is pertinent to our understanding of the 'My Week' charts, which the children produced: while many were, indeed pretty patterns they all also had stories to tell. However, the teacher's dismissal of the aesthetic in favour of the rational account is unwarranted for, as we shall detail below, some of the charts spoke eloquently not only about the particularities of individual children's lives, but also helped to detail the experiences which children have in common with one another and those that make up childhood's diversity. Thus, we suggest that attention has to be paid to data as a compilation of content, form and the research process through which they have been produced. And as we discuss below an important part of this process was the children's reflexive critique about their own progressive understanding of the task they were completing. For example, while filling in her 'My Week' chart one girl kept up a continuous monitoring of her own progress: 'My pen's running out. I have to fit Monday all in there, Oh my god, Monday, Tuesday, Wednesday, Thursday, Friday. I can put Monday in there ...'

A boy, half way through, critically assessed his own chart, saying: 'I did that wrong'. He then redrew the segments so that the chart more accurately expressed that which he wished to say. Another boy justified his chart in the following way: 'That's divided into six 'cos we have six hours in school.' He then carefully divided the segment into units representing the different days of the week and wrote in each space what he did at school each day.

These observations underscore the importance of seeing children as competent interpretive social actors when participating in research (see Corsaro and Molinari, this volume), a point which can be exemplified further through an analysis of the content of the charts which reveal children's conceptions of time and their social experience of time use.

For example, most of the children did not put divisions such as 'sleep time' or 'meal time' on their charts. Indeed, for many, the representation of 'sleeping' seemed particularly problematic, for the children had already experienced 'sleeping' as a 'time' when one is not conscious of 'time' at all! As one boy observed: 'It feels like you're, just like that: you're going to sleep and you just woke up.' However, some of the children were, nonetheless, keen to explore this aspect of time use. One boy showed the researcher his chart as he was filling it in:

B: That (amount of) time in bed?
R: Um, it probably is that much time actually.
B: I've put the bed on that side?
R: Yes, you can do.
B: So if I go to bed at about, say about nine erm ...
R: You don't have to make it very, very accurate.
B: ... forty-eight hours.

A similar concern to explore in detail the quantities of time which particular kinds of activities take up was demonstrated by other children too and reveals the power of graphic techniques to permit the expression of children's growth in awareness of their time use:

R: So, how did you find out whether this was sort of about two hours
      maybe eating a week, no a day isn't it?
B: No, that would be about an hour!
R: An hour, OK.
B: Like, twenty minutes.
R: For each meal?
B: Yeah.
R: So, you sort of sat and thought, 'Well, how much time do I use?'
B: Yeah.
R: You didn't use a watch to time yourself?
B: No ... I sort of guessed.

Besides 'sleeping' and 'eating', most of the charts also did not include everyday routine activities such as washing oneself, going to the toilet, brushing one's hair, etc. These did, however, appear on one boy's chart but, significantly, he had taken his chart home and engaged his mother as a co-respondent:

R: Tim, how did you make yours, how was your mum involved in doing it?
T: Erm, she like figured out the percentages with me and she gave me
      the idea for that, she gave me some of the idea, for most of these, like
      personal hygiene.

However, that such everyday activities are excluded from most children's charts is highly suggestive. First it indicates that children's own awareness of time use was indeed prompted by the 'My Week' chart. Until his mother intervened it had not occurred to Tim that coping with 'personal hygiene' actually took up a particular amount of time in the week (Figure 7.4). Second, noting what the children omitted from their charts provides more general insight into the cultural meaning of time for children. Two boys were comparing their charts:

Joe: Well, I know sleeping was correct 'cos I figured it out on a calculator, and reading's right and so's travelling but all these lot are random but they're about right I reckon.

Michael decides to challenge his chart:

Michael: I think reading's wrong, I think that's wrong.

Joe retaliates, insisting that it is his view that is being asked for and that, in his opinion, his own assessment of the time he spent reading is correct:

Michael: Reading, yeah that's your opinion and playing outside.

However, the question which Michael then retreats with reveals both the reason for his initial challenge of Joe's estimation and, at the same time, illustrates that children may attach particular values to certain forms of time use. In effect, Michael is attempting to seek out an explanation, through his challenge, for why 'reading' featured such a lot on Joe's chart. Michael said:

Michael: Did you spend a lot of time on your own over half term or ...?

It is clear from Michael's incredulous query that, in his view, only someone who *had* to pass a lot of time alone could possibly have such a large segment set aside for reading. However, Joe quickly denied this:

Joe: Um, no not really. I was mainly outside most of the time and at my friend's house and everything.

In his reply Joe both defended the accuracy of his chart while nonetheless confirming the importance for children of presenting themselves as sociable, as someone with friends, rather than as someone who sits inside on his own reading.

Two final examples relate to children's experience of time as 'flow' punctuated by 'happenings' which, we suggest, largely emanate from children's contact with the institutional structures through which childhood is framed. A conversation between the researcher and Maria is revealing in this respect:

Maria: Can you put things that (pauses) I like to do when you sometimes ...

Unfortunately, Maria was at this point interrupted by the researcher who, at first, thought Maria meant: Can you put things down when you only do them sometimes? Later the conversation revealed, however, that drawing – the activity in question – was one that Maria liked to do 'all the time'. It was in this sense an habitual weekly activity which she spent much time doing. This misunderstanding is revealing. Seen in this new light Maria's question makes a quite subtle distinction between those things that she did regularly during the week – activities which emanate from social and institutional structures such as going to school, playing rugby, doing housework – and those regular activities that were less structured and not imposed upon her. These were the things she enjoyed doing and chose to do herself. In this sense then the distinction made by Maria was between activities so closely related to the experiential 'flow' of everyday time that only with difficulty could they be located within an exact time frame and those 'happenings' which are significantly bound to a temporal and spatial structure. Drawing represents for Maria an activity which she is likely to drift in and out of in between having to do other things; it is one which she is not obliged to do, but one she has some own control over.

Similarly revelatory moments occurred with respect to the experience of being 10 years old. Although sharing numerical age the very differences in respect to children's competence and maturity which 'My Week' revealed made two girls reflect on the ample differences of social experience between them. (The girls knew each other well from their shared everyday life at school.) After thinking for a short while about what her week consisted of one of the girls turned to the researcher and said: 'I've only put four things down!' The researcher explored with the girl whether she had indeed left out some things which she might want to add to her chart by asking the girl more exacting questions such as: 'Do you do any cooking at home?'. This prompted the girl to reflect further on her weekly activities and yielded a much longer list which showed that she was expected to make a large contribution to household work: on a regular basis she looked after the cat and dog, laid the table, washed the pots, cleaned her bedroom, made her bed and often did some cooking. Her friend, working next to her, and listening in on the conversation then revealed that she only had to look after her cat and rabbit, that her mum made her bed for her and that cooking was something she only occasionally helped with. In this way the two girls were suddenly made aware of their very different home lives and the contributions that were expected of them. In such concretization lies, then, the potential for increasing children's own awareness about the shared and the diverse aspects of children's social experiences which such 'tools' may facilitate.

Conclusion

This chapter has argued that although children may share in a common biology and follow a broadly similar developmental path, their social experiences and their relative competences as social actors must always be seen as contextualized, rather than determined, by the process of physiological and psychological change. Through exploring the use of a specific research technique we have exemplified the scope for achieving a better understanding of the diversities as well as commonalities of childhood and the importance of acknowledging the interrelationship between the form, content and process of research.

Thus, as we showed, providing a uniform and specific model – a blank circle – allowed children to work as individuals within the relative fixity of its conceptual form. Children designed visual images of their weekly time within two shared frames of reference – that of schooling and that of children's own practices and peer relations – and in this way drew on common social skills and competences to represent their own individual and everyday social experiences. This process, as we have also demonstrated, showed children as actively interpreting and reflecting on the research they take part in and thereby potentially gaining new insight into their own and other children's social experiences and practices.

In thus showing how commonality and diversity intersect we have seriously called into question the use of 'age' as a dominant signifier when accounting for and understanding the shape and experience of children's everyday lives. In this sense, then, the methodology of this piece of research will allow us to contribute to the debate about the sensitivity of global developmental paradigms in accounting for children's own experiences and the local conditions of childhood. Global paradigms, it is suggested, may over-standardize models of childhood as a particular segment of the life course by according priority to age and thus induce a determined and determining conformity which might underplay the impact of local social and environmental contexts on the everyday lives and experiences of children. The consequences of such global models may be, then, to privilege commonality above diversity, with such a privileging turning out to be potentially detrimental and socially excluding of some children.

Notes

1 This chapter draw on findings from 'Changing Times', a research project, which the two authors undertook together with Chris Jenks, Goldsmiths College in London. The study was funded under the ESRC Children 5–16 Programme: Growing into the 21st Century.

2 The tools were used alongside interviews and participant observation, which took place in primary and secondary schools in a rural and an urban area of Northern England. The 12 month fieldwork period covered the time of transition from primary to secondary school when, it was thought, children's experiences, use and organisation of time would change considerably. Towards the end of the project a large-scale quantitative survey was conducted in both these settings, drawing on the key findings of the qualitative study.

3 The choice of a circle to represent a week clearly has embedded with it notions of cyclical, repetitive time. However, though we acknowledge that such a representation therefore has the potential to shape children's thinking, it was apparent to us that by 10 years old children were already familiar with different cultural notions of time - for example, that time has a value and should not be wasted; that the life course can be figuratively represented in linear form with a unidirectional movement from birth to death. Through giving children

the circle as a prompt to their thinking about time we drew upon this cultural repertoire. However, that children also chose to disrupt or ignore the circular form suggests that it did not limit or restrict the expression of their ideas.

References

Chambers, R. (1992) *Rural Appraisal: Rapid, Relaxed and Participatory*, IDS Discussion Paper 311, Brighton, UK: IDS.

Chambers, R. (1994) *Participatory Rural Appraisal: Challenges, Potentials and Paradigms*, University of Sussex: IDS.

Christensen, P. (1998) 'Difference and similarity: how children's competence is constituted in illness and its treatment', in I. Hutchby and J. Moran-Ellis (eds) *Children and Social Competence: Arenas of Action*, London: Falmer Press.

Christensen, P. (1999) *Towards an Anthropology of Childhood Sickness: An Ethnographic Study of Danish School Children.* PhD Thesis, Hull University.

Christensen, P., James, A. and Jenks, C. (2001) 'All we needed to do was to blow the whistle': Children's embodiment of time', in S. Cunningham-Burley and K. Backett-Milburn (eds) *Exploring the Body*, London: Palgrave.

Christensen, P. and O'Brien, M. (eds) (2002) *Children in the City: Home, Neighbourhood and Community.* London: RoutledgeFalmer.

Clarke, A. and Moss, P. (2001) *Listening to Young Children: The Mosaic Approach*, London: National Children's Bureau.

Hallinan, M. (1981) 'Recent advances in sociometry', in S.R. Asher and J.M. Gottman (eds) *The Development of Children's Friendships*, Cambridge: Cambridge University Press.

Hubbard, J. (1991) *Shooting Back. A photographic View of Life by Homeless Children.* New York: The New Press.

Hubbard, J. (1994) *Shooting Back from the Reservation. A Photographic View of Life by Native American Youth* New York: The New Press.

James, A. (1993) *Childhood Identities: Self and Social Relationships in the Experience of the Child*, Edinburgh: Edinburgh University Press.

James, A., Jenks, C. and Prout, A. (1998) *Theorising Childhood*, Cambridge: Polity Press.

James, A., Curtis, P. and Birch, J. (2007, forthcoming) 'Care and control in the construction of children's citizenship', in A. Invernizzi and J. Williams (eds) *Children and Citizenship*, London: Sage.

Mauthner, M. (1997) 'Methodological aspects of collecting data from children: lessons from three research projects', *Children and Society* 11 (1): 16–29.

Prosser, J. (ed.) (1998) *Image-based Research*, London: Falmer Press.

Rapport, N. (1993) *Diverse World Views in an English Village*, Edinburgh: Edinburgh University Press.

Rasmussen, K. (2004) 'Places for children – children's places', *Childhood* 11 (2): 155–73.

Richardson, S.A., Goodman, N., Hastorf, A.H. and Dornbusch, S.M. (1961) 'Cultural uniformities in reaction to physical disabilities', *American Sociological Review* 26: 241–6.

Walkerdine, V. (1985) 'Child development and gender; the making of teachers and learners in the classroom', in Early *Childhood Education: History, Policy and Practice*, Bulmershe Research Publication No. 4.

Wetton, N.N. and McWhirter, J. (1998) 'Images and curriculum development in health education', in J. Prosser (ed.) *Image-based Research*, London: Falmer Press.

Woodhead, M. (1999) 'Reconstructing developmental psychology', *Children and Society* 13 (1): 3–19.

8   Race, Gender and Critical Reflexivity in Research with Young Children

Paul Connolly

Introduction

This chapter focuses on some of the ways in which race and gender can impact upon research with young children. It provides a critically reflexive account of a previous ethnographic study I conducted in a multi-ethnic, inner-city primary school in England that examined the peer cultures of 5–6-year-old children and the place of race and gender within these (see Connolly 1998). The arguments presented in this chapter are built upon three core premises. While each of these premises is well recognized and accepted, it will be shown in this chapter that, when they are drawn together, they offer a new and important way of understanding the power dynamics that underpin research with young children.

The first premise is that there is nothing natural or inevitable about the ways in which race, gender and childhood manifest themselves in young children's lives. All three of these social dimensions can be said to be socially constructed in that the particular nature and forms that each takes is context-specific and the product of particular times and places. There is thus no universal form that either race, gender or childhood takes but rather they tend to vary as they reflect the particular social, political and economic forces that are at play within any specific context. This is an approach captured well in relation to race and gender in terms of notions such as 'racial formations' (Omi and Winant 1994) and 'gender projects' (Connell 1995) and is also clearly an approach that underpins the diverse range of work within the sociology of childhood (James et al. 1998; Mayall 2002; Corsaro 2004; Jenks 2005).

Within this, poststructural perspectives have been important in developing our understanding of the non-essential and context-specific nature of discourses on race, gender and childhood and how they tend to construct particular subject positions and binary opposites – such as 'black'/'white', 'boys'/'girls' or 'adult'/'child' – that locate individuals in particular relations of power to one another (MacNaughton 2005; Robinson and Jones Diaz 2006). By definition, these subject positions are therefore highly contested as individuals and groups struggle to re-negotiate these identities in order either to challenge, maintain or to reinforce the relations and structures of power they are located within. As such, identities forged around race, gender and childhood are also not universal or fixed but are forever changing and evolving as they reflect the way in which power relations are reconfigured over time and across place.

The second key premise is that children are socially competent and actively involved in the negotiation of their social worlds (Hutchby and Moran-Ellis 1998). This is a particularly important assumption when conducting research with young children given the continued influence of traditional developmental models of childhood with their emphasis on children progressing through a fixed number of universal and invariant stages (Burman 1994; Morss 1996). Such models tend to locate 5–6-year-old children, for example, within Piaget's (1977) 'pre-operational stage' that constructs them as socially incompetent and thus lacking the basic skills to: appreciate the perspectives of others (egocentrism); look beyond the immediate to see the wider picture (centration); and think logically and rationally (lacking an appreciation of reversibility and conservation). It is not surprising that researchers who have this as their starting point would not only be working with a particular model of childhood but would also be led to see the children of this age as being passively socialized into the pre-existing racial and gender identities that have been set for them. In contrast, accepting young children's social competence and agency offers a very different way of understanding the impact of race and gender in their lives; one that focuses on the active role that the children themselves play in appropriating, re-working and reproducing particular racial and gender identities within the specific contexts that they find themselves (Skelton 2001; Connolly 1998, 2004; MacNaughton 2000, 2005; Van Ausdale and Feagin 2001).

The third and final core premise is that it is impossible to divorce the researcher from the research process itself, as if the latter can be undertaken in a clinical and objective manner. Rather, the research process is inevitably a product of the relationships forged between the researcher and the research participants, and will therefore ultimately reflect the decisions made and approaches taken by the researcher as well as the particular responses adopted by the participants to these. Essentially, this final premise can be seen as little more than a recognition of the need for researchers to be critically reflexive – in other words recognizing the role they have played in informing and shaping the research process and thus the data and findings that result (Hammersley and Atkinson 1995; Brewer 2000). It is something that is captured well by Bourdieu (1990) when he argues for the need for researchers to take 'two steps back' from the research process; the first step representing the traditional one taken by researchers in attempting to gain an overall impression of what is going on; and the second representing the researcher stepping back from themselves in order to understand how they are as much a part of and contribute to the unfolding social milieu as everyone else.

Clearly, none of these three premises is new or original and certainly none should come as a surprise to readers of a book such as this one. However, it is when these three assumptions are combined and applied to research with young children that they raise important issues and challenges. In this sense, bringing these three premises together requires researchers to acknowledge and reflect upon the power relations and struggles that are inherent in the research process between themselves and the young children. As Christensen (2004: 175) has argued: '[i]n the process of research, power moves between different actors and different social positions, it is produced and negotiated in the social interactions of child to adult, child to child and adult to adult in the local settings of the research' (see also Robinson and Kellett, 2004). Not only does this require a recognition of the active role that young children can play in resisting and challenging the relationships created between themselves and the (adult) researcher, but also an understanding of how this can be played out around the subject positions created through wider discourses on race, gender and childhood.

It is this sense of research with young children being a dynamic, context-specific and contested enterprise that provides the focus for this chapter. In particular, I examine how my identity as an adult white male researcher informed the particular nature and forms of relationships developed with the young children in the ethnographic study mentioned earlier and what the implications of all of this is for conducting future research in this area. The chapter begins with a brief outline of the study itself and the methodology used before then describing four critical incidents from the fieldwork that capture some of the struggles and tensions involved in the research. These incidents are then used as the basis from which to draw out a number of key points to be considered more broadly in relation to qualitative research with young children.

Methodology

As mentioned earlier, the main aim of my ethnographic study was to gain an understanding of the significance of race and gender in young children's social worlds. The research focused on 5–6-year-old children in three Reception/Year One classes at East Avenue Primary School,[1] located in an English multi-ethnic, inner-city area. I spent a year and a half at the school (between January 1992 and June 1993) attending for three days per week on average and following the classes around the school and observing the children in a variety of settings. Alongside this I facilitated a large number of group discussions with the children from the three sample classes (73 in total). These took place in a separate room in the school and would generally include three children. One child would be chosen from the class and asked to nominate two others to come with her or him for an interview. This usually ensured that the children were 'friends' with one another and thus had already developed a certain rapport among themselves.

During the discussions I would usually sit around a table with the children and ask them to continue working on whatever they had brought with them from their class (usually drawing and colouring). Once they had started their work I would facilitate a discussion among the children by asking them very general questions such as: 'What were you doing in the playground today?' or 'What do you like to do when you are at home?' This was usually enough for the conversation to begin to take on a logic of its own as the children would engage in discussions among themselves. This approach is similar to what Christensen (2004) has advocated elsewhere in relation to working with and respecting children's 'cultures of communication' which gives children the space to raise whatever themes and issues they wished to discuss but also to discuss it in their own ways. Moreover, and as Mayall (this volume) has also found, informal conversations like these provide important insights into children's knowledge and experiences.

My main interest was in the ways that the children appropriated and reproduced discourses on race within their social worlds. Because I wanted to understand where and when racism became significant in their lives, I never introduced the issue of race myself but allowed the children to raise the issue 'naturally' during their conversations. My only other involvement in the children's discussions took place when they did choose to raise and discuss issues of race and/or make racist statements. In not wishing to be seen to condone such ideas and behaviour, I would purposely ask the child(ren) to explain what they had said and would give the clear impression that I did not agree with them by asking them to justify what they had said and also asking questions such as: 'Do you think that is a nice thing to say?' or 'How would you feel if someone called you a name like that?' From an ethical point of view, alongside ensuring that the children were not left assuming that I condoned their views, the use of such questions was also important in encouraging the children to reflect upon the consequences of their attitudes and behaviour and thus to begin challenging these.

A more detailed discussion of some of the particular methodological and ethical issues associated with this approach are discussed in detail elsewhere (see Connolly 1996, 1997). For the purposes of this chapter, the key point to draw out regarding this use of largely unstructured group discussions with the children is the fact that it reflected an attempt to at least partly redress the imbalance of power between myself as an adult and the young children (see also Morrow and Richards 1996; Christensen 2004; Mayall, this volume). By participating with their friends and also being given the space to raise whatever concerns they wished to, such an approach certainly helped to give many of the children greater confidence. The relative freedom they were given in the discussions also provided the basis upon which a certain amount of trust and rapport developed between myself and the children. As one of the incidents to be discussed below will show, many of the children came to enjoy and look forward to the interviews.

Moreover, and of relevance to this chapter, adopting this approach meant that I found myself in a contradictory position in relation to the children (see also Mandell 1991; Christensen 2004; Mayall, this volume). On the one hand I was an adult who, simply because of my position, was expected to adopt a 'teacher' role while in the more formal spaces of the school and classroom. Among other things, this role required me to monitor the children's behaviour and to intervene in situations where children were deemed to be behaving inappropriately within the context of school (i.e. throwing objects or disrupting the work of other children in class; running or shouting in the school corridors; and/or swearing or fighting while in the playground). However, and on the other hand, I was also someone they could confide in, to a certain extent, within specific contexts (such as the interviews and in more private conversations in the corridors and playground). As such, and within these specific contexts, the children were able to engage in particular forms of behaviour that I would otherwise have had to censure in my 'teacher role' if it occurred elsewhere. This included the children being able to swear and, in the context of the interviews, 'mess about' and not have to continue with their school work. Perhaps most importantly, it also included the children having the space to introduce and talk about 'adult' topics that would normally be considered to be taboo in the presence of teachers and/or in the more public and formal spaces within school. It was partly because of this contradictory role that I adopted in school that the children were able to test and challenge the adult/child boundaries that were in place and, as will now be shown in the following section, it was from within such a context that the children also introduced discourses on race and gender.

Critical incidents

To give some sense of the type of dynamics involved in the research process as explained above, four critical incidents are reported below taken either from transcripts made of the group discussions or from my field notes. Following Tripp's (1993) use of the term, I refer to these as 'critical incidents' not because of the intrinsic nature of the incidents *per se* but because they provided a vantage point from which I was able to recognize and understand some of the underlying dynamics evident in my relationships with the children. This is certainly the case in terms of the four incidents to be recounted below. On the one hand they were actually notable in their own right, given the unexpected nature of the racialized and sexualized discourses that the children introduced. In this sense they demanded some form of explanation. However, and on the other hand, what made them *critical* incidents was the fact that the search for an explanation led to the realization that these incidents were indicative of more underlying relationships that existed between the children and myself as the researcher. The nature of these relationships and the social dynamics which informed them will be drawn out and discussed in the following section. For now, each incident will simply be reported in turn.

Incident one

The following transcript[2] is taken from an interview with three white 6-year-old girls. Part-way through the interview and without prompting,

Nicky began to 'complain' about the fact that all the boys keep saying that they 'go out' with her (i.e. that they are boyfriend/girlfriend):

Nicky: Everyone keeps saying they go out with me!
PC: Do they?
Nicky: Yeah
PC: Who says that?
Nicky: Don't know their names, but they know my name.
PC: Why do they keep saying that, do you think?
Nicky: Don't know.
PC: Do they just say it about you or do they say it about
            anybody else?
Nicky: About me!
PC: Jamie and Daniel from Mrs Scott's class – they play with you a bit,
            don't they?
Nicky: Yeah, he says he goes out with me.
PC: Which one?
Nicky: Daniel.
PC: There's also somebody from Mr Wallace's?
Nicky: No, that's Emma's boyfriend [...] Emma goes out with James and
            Michael [*both black*] ... I hate black boys!
PC: You hate black boys?
Nicky: Yeah.
PC: Which black boys do you hate?
Nicky: Kylie said to me that Michael and Devan go out with her!
Kylie: No, James goes out with me! [...]
PC: But why do you hate black boys, Nicky?
Kylie: Because they're always around us, ain't they, Nicky?
Nicky: Yeah! ... What? Kissing?
Kylie: [*laughs*] No, chasing!
Nicky: Well, Daniel's always chasing me!
PC: But Daniel's white, isn't he?
Nicky: Yeah.
PC: So it's not always black boys that are around you, is it?
Kylie: Yeah.
Nicky: No!

Incident two

This second incident took place during a discussion involving three 6-year-old boys. Their friend, Jordan, was not at school on that day and the transcript begins with me asking them if they knew where he was:

PC: Where's Jordan today?

Stephen:	He's at home boiling his head off!
Jamie:	No! Kissing his girlfriend!
PC:	Kissing his girlfriend? Who's his girlfriend?
Stephen:	He's waiting at his girlfriend's house.
PC:	Is he? Who's?
Jamie:	Yeah, waiting for her.
Stephen:	And when she comes in, he's hiding right, and when she comes in he's going to grab her and take her upstairs and then she's going to start screaming and he's going to kiss her ... and sex her!
PC:	And sex her? And why's she going to be screaming?
Stephen:	Because she hates it!
PC:	Because she hates it?
Stephen:	Yeah!
PC:	So if she hates it why does he do it?
Stephen:	I don't know!
Jamie:	Because he loves her!
Stephen:	He'll sing 'I want to sex you up!'

Incident three

This third incident arose in a discussion between three other boys who formed a close friendship group. Two of the boys (Clive and Mark) were white and the third (Amit) was South Asian:

Clive:	I don't like Pakis!
Amit:	You do like Pakis, stupid!
Clive:	No, I don't – I only like you!
PC:	Why don't you like them?
Mark:	'Cos they speak Gujarati!
	[...]
PC:	Clive, why don't you like them?
Mark:	Because they smell horrible.
Amit:	'Cos they smell like a clock!
Clive:	Yeah, like Amit does!
PC:	You like Amit, don't you Clive?
Clive:	Yeah.
PC:	You like Amit, and yet Amit's an Asian as well, isn't he?
Clive:	Yeah.
PC:	So, you said you don't like them—why not?
Clive:	'Cos he ain't a proper Paki!
PC:	Why isn't he a proper one?
Clive:	Because he doesn't smell right!

Incident four

This final incident occurred in the classroom where I sat with a group of 5- and 6-year-old children helping them with their work. It began with Daniel who was excited and rushed over to the table:

Daniel: Miss! Miss! Miss! [*referring to PC*] me and Annette we broke off Stephanie's peg! [*in the cloakroom*]. When we're upstairs [*i.e. for an interview*] we'll tell you!

PC: What peg?

Daniel: Annette saw it wobbling and Annette broke it off! [*Annette walks over to the table and remains standing*]. Annette, didn't me and you break off that peg?

Annette: [*nods and smiles before calmly putting her work on the table*]

Jamie: And me!

Annette: [*Shakes head*]

Jamie: Yeah! I did didn't I Daniel?

Daniel: [*no response*]

Jamie: Come and sit here Annette [*pulling back the chair next to him for her to sit on*]

Annette: [*walks over and sits next to Jamie*]

Daniel: [*to Jamie and Annette*] Are you two going to have sex? [...] He pinches your bum!

PC: Who pinches your bum?

Daniel: Jamie!

PC: You've just said they're going to have sex – who do you mean?

Daniel: Yeah them two are going to have sex! [*pointing to Jamie and Annette*]

Jamie: No! Them two! [*pointing to Annette and another boy sat at the table*]

Daniel: No! Her and him [*pointing to Annette and then PC*] are going to have sex!

Annette: Nnoooo!

Taking two steps back

The incidents recounted above were in no sense representative of the relationships I had developed with the children. While discussions about girlfriends and boyfriends were quite popular among many of the children (Renold 2005), discussions that directly implicated me and/or were explicitly racialized or sexualized were relatively rare. Rather, it is clear that these incidents were at least partly the products of my presence and involvement in the events that were taking place. What the children chose to say and do, and in particular the way they drew upon discourses on race and gender within this, would certainly suggest that they were partly directed towards me, as an adult white male.

In attempting to understand the underlying motivations and social dynamics that gave rise to these incidents, it is important to place them within the overall framework introduced at the beginning of this chapter. In this sense, I want to suggest that these incidents may at least partly reflect the social competence and agency of these children and, in particular, their attempts to draw upon discourses on race and gender to resist and challenge their subject positioning as children.

To understand this argument it is important to begin with a recognition that the primary school environment is probably one where the discursive positioning of adults and children is most explicit and pervasive. The very organization and structure of the school constructs what it means to be an adult/teacher and a child/pupil, and marks out the boundaries of what is and what is not regarded as acceptable behaviour. The power and authority of the teacher is inscribed in all aspects of school life from the organisation of the school day (Pollard 1985) right down to the organisation of desks and tables in classrooms (Giddens 1985). Moreover, it is also evident in the fact that, while there are clearly marked out areas where children can and cannot go within the school (i.e. the staff room, anywhere in the school building at playtimes and so on), adults/teachers are 'allowed' to intrude in all and every aspect of the children's social spaces. All of these social structures therefore underline the authority of teachers/adults and create the climate within which children are expected simply to conform and be obedient.

Given such an environment it is not surprising to find that children are actively involved in attempting to challenge and subvert these boundaries. From my own fieldwork observations such activity took on many forms and was testament to the ingenuity and social competence of the children. For example, the children would attempt to create space for themselves away from the teacher's gaze in more secluded parts of the playground or, in class time, at the back of the classroom and/or by escaping to the toilet. In addition, the children would also engage in a number of different practices aimed at subverting the teacher's authority either directly, through simple defiance, or more commonly and routinely indirectly through coughing, making other noises and/or completing tasks set at a slower rate than was expected of them (see Connolly 1998).

These discursive positions of adult and child and the routine struggles that took place over the boundaries that marked them out provides one of the principal contexts for understanding the children's behaviour in the four incidents recounted above. As already stated, I adopted a rather contradictory position in relation to the children. While I was an adult and would be forced to adopt the authority of the teacher in more public and formal settings within the school, I had also purposely created particular spaces within which the children were not subject to the same degree of authority and control. These spaces were most commonly found in the group discussions with the children but were also, as evident in incidents three and four above, to be found in the more private and informal interactions between the children and I in other settings within the school. Against the background of the general struggles that the children engaged in to subvert the authority that adults had over them within the school, this effective 'blurring' of boundaries in relation to my own position quite possibly provided the context within which some of the children would attempt to play upon and capitalize from the contradictions evident in my relationship with them (see also Christensen 2004).

The introduction of discourses on race and gender in their interactions with me can therefore possibly be seen as partly representing a more fundamental struggle that the children were engaged in: the aim of challenging my authority over them as an adult. In this sense, the children's introduction of explicitly adult ways of thinking and knowing could possibly be seen as a particularly effective challenge to the dominant discourses of what it means to be a child. A significant number of the interviews I conducted with the children, for example, included incidents where the children would swear, curse and/or be racist (see Connolly 1998). One way of understanding the tendency for the children to do this in my presence is that the children may have associated such behaviour with being an adult. It thus arguably reflected, at least in part, an attempt to challenge and re-negotiate their discursive position as children.

However, it is the introduction of specifically sexualized themes – as evident to varying degrees across all four incidents – that is arguably one of the most significant ways of attempting to undermine the boundaries that mark out the adult/child relationship. This is something that Walkerdine (1981) classically drew attention to over 25 years ago when she recounted an incident in which boys of nursery age were being disciplined by a female teacher. In their attempt to subvert her authority, they introduced sexualized discourses which attempted to shift the dominant relationship from one of adult/child to male/female and, consequently, re-position the female teacher into a more subservient role as an object of the boys' talk. Indeed, such attempts to appropriate and evoke differing discourses in attempts to gain power and status can be seen in Incident Four above. In this case, Annette was clearly afforded a significant degree of status among the boys for her behaviour. However, when she appeared to snub Daniel by sitting next to Jamie, Daniel attempted to re-position Annette within a gendered and sexualized discourse within which she was forced to assume a more subservient identity.

Clearly, the fact that I was an adult *male* meant that the introduction of such discourses on boyfriends/girlfriends, sex and violence as recounted in some of the incidents above would not have had the effect of re-positioning me in the same way as it did either for the female teacher in the account offered by Walkerdine (1981) or, to a differing extent, for Annette. However, it certainly had the potential to undermine the authority I had over the children as an adult. By engaging in the type of violent, misogynist discourse as evident in Incident Two, for example, the boys were challenging their subject position as children by encouraging me to recognize their 'adult' knowledge and status. Similarly, the suggestion that I might 'have sex' with Annette, as detailed in Incident Four, can be seen as another attempt to subvert the generational differences that exist and re-position me within the children's own sub-culture (albeit momentarily).

Beyond the possible use of explicitly racialized and sexualized discourses as a tactic to subvert adult authority, it would also seem from the four incidents recounted above that the knowledge and behaviour displayed by the children were also valued by them. It was certainly evident from my wider ethnographic study that the successful acquisition and reproduction of adult ways of being brought with it a significant degree of status among some of the children (Connolly 1998). The more that a child could successfully engage me as an adult, the more they could therefore successfully demonstrate their own adult competence to me and their peers. The key point arising from this is that some of the children's behaviour may well have represented what they felt I would positively value and respond to as a white male. As already touched upon above, for example, the boys in Incident Two could possibly be seen as attempting to undermine the boundaries between myself and them by engaging in a discourse that they felt would impress and/or appeal to me as an adult *male*. Similarly in relation to Incident One, Nicky and Kylie's trading of knowledge and experiences of boyfriends, and also the explicitly racialized manner in which this was done, could also be seen as an attempt to gain status among themselves and in front of me by demonstrating 'adult' competences. Incident Three can also be read, at least in part, as the white boys attempting to appeal to me as a *white* male through their claims that they do not like 'Pakis'. Indeed, this particular incident is also interesting in the way it illustrates the fluid and contested nature of children's social identities. In a similar vein to the way in which Annette was re-defined from being 'one of the boys' to being a girl, it can be seen here how Clive and Mark have attempted to de-signify Amit's identity as a South Asian and to claim him as white.

Implications for the interpretation of data

It has been argued that the four incidents recounted above can at least in part be understood in terms of the active role that young children are playing in resisting and attempting to subvert the existing discursive positions of 'adult' and 'child'. It is certainly clear that the data derived from these four incidents is, at least partially, a product of my own presence and influence as an adult white male. It would clearly be disingenuous to claim that the incidents recounted above, or the accounts of the children's lives offered in my research more generally, were 'true' and 'genuine' representations of the children's social worlds. The inevitable question that arises, therefore, is how can we interpret and analyze the data given these potential influences?

However, before discussing what claims we can reasonably make from the data, it is important to assess the status of the data. In particular, there will undoubtedly be some who would argue that my influence on the children's talk and behaviour has clearly rendered the data unreliable and/or invalid.

In this sense it would presumably be argued that the data presented offer a rather distorted and unrepresentative account of the children's lives and behaviour. However, such an argument is based upon the premise that there is a 'true' and 'accurate' representation to be identified and recounted. The problem with this is that there is no unitary, authentic account of children's lives to be found, only a diverse range of accounts (see Connolly 1997). As soon as we acknowledge the social competence of children then we have also to accept that they will approach and respond to particular social settings in differing ways. How a child talks to a teacher, for example, will be different from how they talk to their parent, which will also be different to how they talk to their friends. It is therefore meaningless to attempt to identify which of these represents that child's 'true' and 'authentic' voice. In a sense they are all equally authentic. Rather, the task is to understand the child's behaviour in the specific context within which it takes place (i.e. in front of a teacher, parent or friend).

The key argument from the foregoing discussion is that all data need to be fully contextualized. Ultimately, this means accepting that interviews and other forms of interactions with the children that researchers engage in also represent particular contexts that need to be taken into account (see also Christensen, 2004). Once we abandon the fruitless search for the true and authentic account of children's lives, we can dispense with the equally meaningless concern with avoiding the 'contamination' of data and, instead, begin understanding the interview or discussion as a particular social context that can help to provide additional insights into particular aspects of the children's lives (see Mayall, this volume).

With this in mind there are at least two key insights that can be reasonably drawn from the data illustrated in the four incidents recounted above. First, the data clearly demonstrate the social competence of these children and offers some insight into their levels of knowledge concerning gender, sexuality and race. This, in itself, is an important point that needs to be established within the broader context where dominant discourses on childhood continue to deny that issues of race and sexuality are even salient feature of young children's lives. Moreover, what the data suggest is that children of this age are actively engaging with and exploring knowledge and attitudes regarding race, gender and sexuality. While it clearly cannot be concluded that all, or even the majority of children. are doing this to the extent evident in the incidents above, what they do demonstrate is that children of this age are at least *capable* of doing so. More research along these lines with a diverse range of children in differing situations and contexts would certainly help to inform the development of diversity programmes that could be introduced in the early years and that are sensitive to and engage with the realities of children's lives. Second, the data offer some insight into the significance of this knowledge in the children's social worlds. While no claims can be made regarding how prominent or representative such discussions on race, sex and relationships were among the children, the above incidents do suggest that knowledge of such matters was valued and struggled over by these children. Within the context of the broader findings of the research study, it was clear that being and/or behaving like an adult provided one particular aspiration for some of the children (Connolly 1998). Arguably, the four incidents outlined above offer some indication of how the children have come to construct what it means to be an adult by drawing upon discourses on race and gender.

Conclusions

This chapter began by outlining three key premises regarding: the socially constructed nature of race, gender and childhood; the social competence and agency of young children; and the need for researchers to be critically reflexive. While all three of these premises are now largely recognized and accepted within social science research, it was argued that they do raise new and important issues when drawn together and applied to research with young children. In particular, and as illustrated through the four critical incidents that have been recounted above, they demand that researchers develop a much more critical appreciation of the power relations inherent within the research process; not only between the adult researcher and the children but also between the children themselves. In conclusion, there are three key issues worth drawing out from this.

The first is the active role that young children can play in challenging and re-negotiating their subject positions; not just as 'children' but also in relation to their gender and racial identities. This can be seen, for example, in the white boys' claims that their Asian friend, Amit, is not 'a proper Paki' (Incident Three). It is also evident in Annette's fluid gender identity (Incident Four) where she was accepted as 'one of the lads' for the most part but was always susceptible to being repositioned as a girl. As stressed at the beginning of this chapter, such examples remind us that there is nothing natural or inevitable about the ways in which gender and race impact upon children's lives. Rather, and as shown, children play an active role in determining the particular nature and forms that gender and race take in their lives. It is in recognition of this that researchers therefore need to avoid approaching their fieldwork with preconceived notions of how significant gender and race will be in children's lives. Rather, there is a need to begin with an acceptance that discourses on gender and race are context-specific and that they can only be understood within the context of particular sets of social relations that the children are actively involved in.

The second key issue to draw out is the need to understand how my position as an adult white male is likely to have played a role in influencing what the children chose to say and do in my presence. At one level, the introduction of explicitly sexualized and racialized discourses can be seen at least in part as a response to my identity as white and male. For example, it is unlikely that the boys in Incident Two would have introduced such violent and misogynist themes had I been a woman. It is certainly the case that my identity as a male was explicitly recognized in Incident Four when one of the boys claimed that Annette and I were 'going to have sex'. It would seem, therefore, that the particular discourses on gender that the children decided to introduce in conversations were at times influenced by my presence as a male. In a similar vein, it is difficult to believe that the children would have made so many racist comments during the many conversations they had with me during the course of the fieldwork if I had been black or Asian instead of white. It is in this sense, therefore, that there is always the possibility that a researcher's gender and race are likely to have some impact upon their relationships with the children and thus the particular ways in which the children choose to behave in their presence.

At another level, my position as an adult is also likely to have had some influence on the children's behaviour in my presence. While the particular nature of the racialized and sexualized discourses that the children chose to introduce in conversations with me may have partly been influenced by my identity as a white male, the fact that they chose to introduce such explicit adult knowledge at all is at least in part likely to reflect their recognition of my position as an adult. In this sense, and as argued above, the introduction of adult themes in conversations is a particularly effective way of undermining the dominant discursive positions of 'adult' and 'child' that tended to structure our relationships. Within this, it is impossible in retrospect to determine whether any specific incident was motivated by a desire explicitly to challenge and undermine my authority or simply reflected the fact that the children had come to trust me and to accept me as a confidant. Unfortunately, I only fully became aware of the potential influence that I could have had on the children long after the fieldwork had finished and have therefore not had the opportunity to explore the motivations underlying the children's conversations any further.

However, and as explained earlier, some of the children were routinely observed during my fieldwork to engage in activities aimed at avoiding and/or subverting the authority and control that adults exerted over them in school. Some of these activities were carefully planned and fairly sophisticated in nature. Given this, I would argue that it is therefore reasonable to conclude that at least some of the incidents involving children introducing such explicitly adult knowledge into conversations in my presence will have been similarly motivated by an explicit attempt to undermine their positioning as children; either by directly challenging the authority associated with my position as an adult or by attempting to appeal to me as a white male and thus move beyond the discursive boundaries that marked out our respective subject positions as adult and child. Perhaps the key point to draw out from the incidents recounted in this chapter is simply that adult researchers need to be aware of the possibility that what children say and do in their presence can sometimes reflect their attempts to challenge and undermine the authority and control that the researcher exerts over them as an adult.

The third and final issue raised by the recognition that research with young children is underpinned by power relations and struggles is that associated with how the data derived from research with the children can be interpreted. One of the main conclusions to arise from the arguments made in this chapter is that it is a fruitless task for ethnographic researchers to attempt to seek the authentic voices of young children. Rather, the agency of young children requires us to recognize that there are only multiple voices that reflect the very different contexts and sets of relations that young children find themselves in. In this sense the research process simply creates one more context within which young children are left to negotiate their attitudes and identities.

Notes

1 Pseudonyms are used for the local area, the school and the teachers and children to maintain their anonymity.
2 Key to transcripts:

/	Indicates interruption in speech
[...]	Extracts edited out of transcript to aid clarity
...	A natural pause in the conversation
[*italics*]	Descriptive text added to indicate the actions and behaviour of the children and/or to clarify the nature of the discussion

References

Bourdieu, P. (1990) *The Logic of Practice*, Cambridge: Cambridge University Press.

Brewer, J. (2000) *Ethnography*, Buckingham: Open University Press.

Burman, E. (1994) *Deconstructing Developmental Psychology*, London: Routledge.

Christensen, P.H. (2004) 'Children's participation in ethnographic research: issues of power and representation', *Children & Society* 18: 165–76.

Connell, R.W. (1995) *Masculinities*, Cambridge: Polity Press.

Connolly, P. (1996) 'Seen but never heard: rethinking approaches to researching racism and young children', *Discourse* 17: 171–85.

Connolly, P. (1997) 'In search of authenticity: researching young children's perspectives', in A. Pollard, D. Thiessen and A. Filer (eds) *Children and their Curriculum: The Perspectives of Primary and Elementary School Children*, London: Falmer Press.

Connolly, P. (1998) *Racism, Gender Identities and Young Children*, London: Routledge.

Connolly, P. (2004) *Boys and Schooling in the Early Years*, London: Routledge.

Corsaro, W. (2004) *The Sociology of Childhood*, (2nd edn), Thousand Oaks, CA: Pine Forge Press.

Giddens, A. (1985) 'Time, space and regionalisation', in D. Gregory and J. Urry (eds) *Social Relations and Spatial Structure*, London: Macmillan.

Hammersley, M. and Atkinson, P. (1995) *Ethnography: Principles in Practice* (2nd edn), London: Routledge.

Hutchby, I. and Moran-Ellis, J. (eds) (1998) *Children and Social Competence*, London: Falmer Press.

James A., Jenks, C. and Prout, A. (1998) *Theorising Childhood*, Cambridge: Polity Press.

Jenks, C. (2005) *Childhood*, (2nd edn), London: Routledge.

MacNaughton, G. (2000) *Rethinking Gender in Early Childhood Education*, St Leonards, NSW: Allen & Unwin.

MacNaughton, G. (2005) *Doing Foucault in Early Childhood Studies*, London: Routledge.

Mandell, N. (1991) 'The least adult role in studying children', in F. Waksler (ed.) *Studying the Social Worlds of Children*, London: Falmer Press.

Mayall, B. (2002) *Towards a Sociology for Childhood*, Buckingham: Open University Press.

Morrow, V. and Richards, M. (1996) 'The ethics of social research with children: an overview', *Children & Society*, 10: 90–105.

Morss, J. (1996) *Growing Critical: Alternatives to Developmental Psychology*, London: Routledge.

Omi, M. and Winant, H. (1994) *Racial Formation in the United States*, London: Routledge.

Piaget, J. (1977) *The Language and Thought of the Child*, London: Routledge & Kegan Paul.

Pollard, A. (1985) *The Social World of the Primary School*, London: Holt, Reinhart & Winston.

Renold, E. (2005) *Girls, Boys and Junior Sexualities*, London: RoutledgeFalmer.

Robinson, C. and Kellett, M. (2004) 'Power', in S. Fraser, V. Lewis, S. Ding, M. Kellett and C. Robinson (eds) *Doing Research with Children and Young People*, London: Sage.

Robinson, K. and Jones Diaz, C. (2006) *Diversity and Difference in Early Childhood Education*, Maidenhead: Open University Press.

Skelton, C. (2001) *Schooling the Boys: Masculinities and Primary Education*, Buckingham: Open University Press.

Tripp, D. (1993) *Critical Incidents in Teaching*, London: Routledge.

Van Ausdale, D. and Feagin, J. (2001) *The First R: How Children Learn Race and Racism*, Lanham Maryland: Rowman and Littlefield.

Walkerdine, V. (1981) 'Sex, power and pedagogy', *Screen Education* 38: 14–24.

9 Research with Children in War-Affected Areas

Mathijs Euwema, Donatien de Graaff,
Ans de Jager and Brechtje Kalksma-Van Lith

Introduction

There has been an interest in the psychological effects of war experiences on people ever since World War I, when British doctors discovered the *shell-shock* syndrome in soldiers who survived the horrors of the trenches in France. But it has not been until the past decades, especially since the 1992–1995 war in Bosnia Herzegovina and the 1994 genocide in Rwanda, that there has been an upsurge in psychosocial interventions for children in war-affected areas. More and more the base assumption was taking root that children who experience killings, fighting, and upheaval have to suffer from some form of psychological distress and are therefore in need of, not only physical rehabilitation (like food, medical aid, construction of houses, schools, etc), but also in need of forms of mental health care and psychosocial support.

Many International Non Governmental Organizations (INGOs) such as War Child Holland, Medicins Sans Frontières, CARE, Save the Children, World Vision and the UN's children's agency UNICEF, have become involved in designing and implementing psychosocial programmes for children in war-affected areas. Today there is hardly any war-torn region where no such interventions are taking place although the scale may still differ greatly per war-affected country or region.

Despite this increased interest for psychosocial interventions with children in war-affected areas, however, there has been little research into the actual (endangerment of) psychosocial development and well-being of these children, and even fewer research studies into the impact of interventions aimed at helping them. Because of demands made by donors, the larger public, and – not to forget – beneficiaries and other stakeholders in the field, there is now a growing recognition that research is needed into both the effects of war on the psychosocial development and well-being of children, and the impact that certain interventions may have on alleviating the problems of these children.

The following two topics therefore seem to be most relevant for research with children in war-affected areas: the effects of war on children's psychosocial development and well-being, and the impact of humanitarian interventions on the psychosocial development and well-being of war-affected children. Research into the effects of war on psychosocial development and well-being of children can include topics like: reactions to stress of war-affected children, their caregivers and communities; coping mechanisms of war-affected children, their caregivers and communities; identifying risk and protective factors in development of children in war-affected areas.

This chapter will mostly focus on research on the impact of humanitarian interventions on the psychosocial development and well-being of children in war-affected areas (the second topic). We take the position that this kind of research is the most interesting (and the most needed!), since it will not only almost automatically yield insight into the problems of war-affected children, and the ways these children, their parents and communities, are dealing with those problems, but also usually can lead to interventions that will improve the quality of life of war-affected children. In our view, when it comes to this subject, *action research* is the way to go.

Most research that is being done with children in war affected areas starts from certain theoretical perspectives on how researchers believe war *must be* affecting children. These perspectives are closely linked to distinctive approaches in psychosocial programmes for war-affected children. The first section of this chapter will describe the different approaches currently applied in the field; this is necessary to be able to understand the research issues involved. This section will also discuss some of the results from studies that have been conducted so far. The second part of the chapter will focus on some of the methodological and ethical constraints that have to be taken into account. In particular, we will emphasize the importance of research efforts to do no harm, something that is perhaps especially important when working in war-affected areas, albeit that it is often very difficult to anticipate unexpected negative effects in any kind of research intervention. In the final section we have formulated some suggestions for general guidelines for doing research with children in war-affected areas.

Approaches in psychosocial programmes with children in war-affected areas

Generally, two approaches to psychosocial interventions with regard to children in war-affected areas have emerged: the *curative* and the *preventative* approach. At one end of the spectrum we find interventions from a curative point of view, aiming at psychosocial and psychological treatment of war-affected children. The approach is strongly trauma-oriented, helping children deal with the stressful experiences they underwent. At the other end we find an approach that is more preventative in nature. Rather than focusing on past experiences, preventative interventions address the consequences of war and its present challenges. They aim to help children develop healthily within their social context in order to protect them from future mental and social disorders. It should be noted, though, that most programmes are not archetypes but moderate versions, to be found somewhere along a continuum. Many programmes combine elements of both approaches.

The curative approach

The curative approach is highly trauma oriented, focusing on the effects and symptoms of disproportionate stress situations on children. Response from a curative angle is based on psychotherapeutic approaches related to Western mental health concepts (Loughry 2001), such as Post Traumatic Stress Disorder or PTSD (Allwood et al. 2002), which single out individual or small groups of children and focus on the confrontation of experiences to help them overcome mental and social problems that are a result of war. The approach generally implies the involvement of mental health specialists, such as psychiatrists, psychologists and creative therapists.

As curative programmes focus on mental illness, they include a variety of methods such as psychotherapy, individual and small group counselling and creative therapy (Fazel and Stein 2002). The curative approach is treatment oriented and may operate from residential treatment centres, or aim towards capacity building local (mental health) service providers to deliver therapy to war-affected children. Therapists engage in 'longer' term targeted relationships with their clients to address problems. Curative programmes (usually as part of emergency and rehabilitation programmes) often have a clearly demarcated ending, although the 'long-term' nature of these interventions is sometimes difficult to match within such a concise time frame.

The preventative approach

The preventative approach towards psychosocial interventions with children in war-affected areas looks at children from a transactional, ecological perspective, as part of a wider social fabric of relationships and structures (Euwema 2006). The preventative approach moves beyond the traumatic experience towards understanding the daily problems of children and how the children cope with current stress situations. Crucial to this approach are children's resources to deal with such situations, which are regarded to be culture and context specific, as well as individually defined. Programmatic response is geared towards promoting psychosocial skills, such as life skills, continuity and normalization of structures. Family and community relations are regarded as key factors that enhance children's coping potential (Stichick 2001; Loughry and Eyber 2003). The approach also emphasizes children's agency and capacity to be involved in the design of programmes that are beneficial to them. Derived from concepts used in developmental psychology (such as system theory and the ecological model, Bronfenbrenner 1979), this approach seems to relate better to the often more collectivist culture societies of non-Western populations. With regard to children, it means that children's development (and their coping with crises) is shaped by transactional

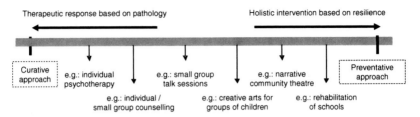

Figure 9.1 Curative versus preventative approach.

processes with the family and the environment. There is a constant interplay and exchange between the child's internal, psychological traits and its external, social environment.

Some preventative programmes focus on normalizing and restoring stable living conditions, e.g. rehabilitation of schools, community cultural traditions, etc. Other programmes are more specialized, helping groups of children deal with specific situations through various methods, which often include creative means such as drawing and play. Yet other programmes focus on children's social environment, supporting and informing parents and teachers to help them support the children. Preventative psychosocial programmes are future-oriented, aimed at structurally strengthening children's psychosocial development and well-being.

The continuum on which the two approaches take place can be visualized as shown in Figure 9.1.

Results from research studies with children in war-affected areas

As was explained in the introduction of this chapter, we will focus on research that is conducted to measure the effects and impact of psychosocial interventions on children in war-affected areas. In this section we therefore only briefly address research into the psychosocial effects of war experiences on children.

Studies into the effects of war on psychosocial development and well-being of children

Despite the challenges, a number of studies into the effects of war and complex humanitarian emergencies on children (and adults) have been conducted, many of those focusing on the prevalence of PTSD and related mental illnesses. Allwood et al. (2002) studied the relationship of violent and non-violent war experiences to children's trauma reactions and adjustment in a group of children from Bosnia. Bolton and Ndogoni (2000) made an assessment of trauma-related mental illness across cultures, finding prevalence of depression among Rwandan people, although not recognized locally as a distinct syndrome.

Epidemiological research is often coloured by the theoretical lens of the researchers, and may therefore yield very different results in different war-affected areas. Sometimes the prevalence of psychological distress (trauma, PTSD) is reported to be very high, whilst other studies show intense psychological distress amongst war-affected children to be relatively rare. Based on our own experience we think that *in general* most war-affected children will not develop severe psychopathology as a consequence of their conflict-related experiences. However, a certain percentage (usually no more than 5 to 10 per cent) of war-affected children can develop serious problems due to conflict-related experiences, problems that will negatively influence their healthy development. Of course, this is a generalization. A lot will depend on circumstantial factors, like the severity of the conflict, the impact the conflict has on children's lives (e.g. displacement, loss of caregivers), the way children are involved in the conflict (e.g. as victims or as perpetrators), the situation after the conflict (e.g. available adult support, possibilities for schooling) and the individual coping skills children may or may not possess.

In our view, epidemiological research into the psychosocial well-being of war-affected children has to be done with great cultural sensitivity (also in terms of the research instruments being used), a flexible theoretical approach by the researcher, huge involvement in all phases of the research project by children, their parents, and the community, and with a clear follow-up such as, for example, the research findings being integrated into appropriately designed interventions.

Studies into the impact of psychosocial interventions on war-affected children

Attempts are also made to study the effects of psychosocial interventions. The following paragraphs will elaborate on this search for evidence. As studies of a purely scientific nature are still limited, attention is also given to studies based on project evaluations and case studies. Evidence for success is categorized into the different types of interventions (curative and preventative), since the type of intervention is usually related to the type of effect-study that is conducted. In some cases, the studied intervention contains elements of both approaches.

As previously discussed, *curative* programmes generally address post-traumatic stress reactions and related mental health problems. They mostly target children directly, but may also use intermediaries (e.g. parents or caregivers) to help children deal with traumatic experiences of war. The belief that children and adolescents can be effectively treated with trauma-focused cognitive behaviour therapy is based on research (using randomized controlled trial (RCT)) in Western countries, which was subsequently applied to other settings. Although there are reservations towards the projection of findings to non-Western cultures, a number of authors have pointed at similarities, on the basis of research, such as a study into victims of violence in Los Angeles

(Stein et al. 2003). Another example is Goenjian et al.'s (2003) RCT into early adolescent survivors of the Armenian earthquake, from which it was concluded that standardized Cognitive Behavioral Therapy (CBT), including exposure techniques, can be effective for children in vulnerable populations from different cultures. Below, two examples of studies are presented of programmes with a predominantly curative approach.

Narrative exposure therapy, Somalia

The programme presented here is one of direct intervention with individual children. By means of a case study, evidence was gathered for the applicability of a specific therapy programme for successful treatment of traumatized children. Narrative Exposure Therapy (NET) is a standardized short-term approach for the treatment of survivors of war and torture, in which the participant constructs a detailed chronological account of his own biography into a coherent narrative. KIDNET is the adapted child-version of NET, with the assistance of play and visual aids to help children construct their story. A case study around the treatment of a Somali child (Schauer et al. 2004) shows a high frequency of the child's post-traumatic stress symptoms, using the Post-Traumatic Stress Diagnostic Scale (PTSDC). In a post-test the child's symptoms dropped to a degree below the diagnostic threshold for PTSD. With this outcome, KIDNET claimed to be a successful approach for the treatment of traumatized child survivors. Its short and pragmatic method is said to be particularly appropriate in war and disaster areas. However, a note of caution is made not to inflict further harm by exposing patients to traumatic memories and not allowing them enough time or treatment to deal with these memories. It is also acknowledged that better understanding is necessary of how parents, teachers and other significant adults can be involved in the recovery process of children, individually and at the community level.

Trauma healing in secondary schools, Rwanda

The intervention studied below (Olij 2005) promotes trauma awareness and healing within a school setting. Helping adolescents cope with the pain of the past, this programme is a classic example of an intervention with a curative approach.

In 2001, the African Centre for Rehabilitation of Torture Victims, a Rwandan association of trauma counsellors, launched the programme: Trauma Awareness, Healing and Group Counselling for secondary schools with severely trauma-affected adolescents. Before the intervention, many students indicated feeling lonely, isolated, experienced difficulties concentrating and suffered from PTSD, depression, fear and/or grief. These students were considered 'mad' and were referred to hospitals. But once back at school, the problems continued: large numbers of pupils were involved in outbreaks of rage and other crises. To address these problems, the intervention programme included: (1) training of school staff in 'helpful active listening'; (2) sensitization in the form of psycho-education for all students; (3) counselling, offered to staff, students, parents and guardians; and (4) youth clubs: anti-trauma clubs of students who sensitize others through various media (drama, poems, dancing, etc.). The programme was not scientifically studied but evaluated by means of interviews, observations, meetings and document study. The concluded achievements of the programme are multiple: students feel better 'listened to' by their teachers; they feel more accepted by others and have a better understanding of their own feelings; the general atmosphere as well as the school performance of students improved. The programme contributed to a reduction of trauma symptoms and no further crisis outbreaks occurred since the start of intervention. A generally felt problem, however, is that school staff lack time to offer sufficient services. Therefore professional trauma counsellors are still needed to provide counselling to the most-affected students.

Preventative interventions are based on the finding that the focus of children in many non-western cultures is rather 'community-centred' as opposed to 'ego-centred' (Refugee Studies Centre 2001), and, accordingly, that stressful experiences of war and its aftermath are dealt with at a collective level. People applying this approach find that most children are eventually able to deal with the atrocities of war without developing psychopathological problems on a large scale. Children's resilience is influenced by individual coping skills and social support. The preventative paradigm has resulted in programmes that work on children's strengths and agency, developing their cognitive, social and emotional capacities to actualize positive futures.

Here we will present two studies into preventative programmes and discuss the main results of these programmes.

Developmental trajectory for refugees, former Yugoslavia

The programme studied here (Tolfree 1996) takes as a starting point not that its beneficiaries are traumatized and 'affected' by war, but rather that they are capable and resourceful in dealing with problems themselves. The programme was built on the capacity of children for creative and imaginative play, through which issues can be explored and feelings expressed.

Acting upon the need for intervention with children seeking refuge in the Federal Republic of Yugoslavia (FRY), a group of developmental psychologists from the University of Belgrade developed the 'Hi Neighborhood' programme, which was later funded by UNHCR and Rädda Barnen. The central part of the programme consists of working groups in Collective Centres for refugees; groups for children, adolescents and adults operated concurrently. No attempt was made to advise the participants, but simply a platform was created for social interaction, and tools were provided with which they could build on their own resources. Individual and group expression was facilitated by a variety of media such as movement, human sculpting, performances and creative and expressive games. Workshops were very open, anyone could attend and leave as they liked. An important aim of the workshops was for participants to introduce whatever issues had relevance to them. The workshops improved social interaction among refugees, but they still had difficulties engaging with the local community outside the centres. Therefore, a range of activities was organized (meetings, outings, visits) to initiate interaction. Evaluation of the impact was conducted by means of a variety of methodologies: perusal of project documents, observation, interviews and discussion. Drawing exercises, rating scales and questionnaires with participants resulted in positive outcomes: at a basic level the programme provided friendship and recreational activities; at a deeper level it promoted the development of coping skills. Young participants developed cognitive, social and emotional competence and improved their self-esteem, which enhanced resilience. However, the open-ended nature of the programme and the need to deploy experienced professionals raised questions of sustainability.

Creative workshops, Kosovo

War Child Holland studied its creative workshop intervention, together with its partner organization World Child Kosovo (De Graaff 2006). The overall objective of World Child is to improve the psychosocial well-being of children and youth in Kosovo. In order to reach this goal, World Child organizes creative workshop cycles. In World Child's creative workshops art, music, drama, movement, and sports activities are being used. The studied creative workshop cycle took place in a school in Western Kosovo. The experimental group consisted of 90 children who were involved in the 8-week creative workshop intervention. Four workshop groups participated in this study, consisting of 18 to 30 boys and girls, between the ages of 9 to 15 years. The control group consisted of 114 children who were not involved in any intervention. Pre- and post-test data were collected from the children themselves and from their parents and teachers. Social and behavioural problems were measured by means of the Child Behaviour Check List (CBCL). Children completed the Youth Self-Report (CBCL-YSR), parents the CBCL and teachers the Teacher's Report Form (CBCL-TRF). Self-esteem was measured using the Culture Free Self-Esteem inventory (CFSEi) and hyperactivity, attention and impulsive behaviour by means of the AVL (ADHD questionnaire). The results showed some tentative positive effects of the creative workshop intervention on the social behavioural problems, thought problems and attention problems of the children involved. Also, it was found that children, parents and teachers were highly appreciative of the creative workshop intervention. Overall, the children indicated that participation was a very positive experience for them. In line with the children, parents and teachers reported that the children benefited from the creative workshops. This study shows that even within a population that is showing relatively healthy psychosocial well-being, improvements in terms of social and cognitive skills can still be achieved through a preventative programme.

Curative vs. preventative

The examples described above illustrate some positive results from both curative and preventative psychosocial interventions with children in war-affected areas, which may indicate evidence of success. It should be noted, however, that the field of research is still immature: the number of studies is limited, it remains difficult to draw conclusions across studies, and outcomes of programmes cannot automatically be generalized to the wider area of the interventions they belong to.

Reservations should also be made about the validity of some of the outcomes as sample sizes are relatively small and long-term effects have not been studied. To obtain a stronger base of evidence, additional research with larger numbers of children would be needed and more attention should be paid to the way children cope in the longer run.

An additional point of discussion is the methods of research being used. In fact, very few studies use strict scientific methods. This can be due to practical reasons, but also methodological reasons. Generally, research into curative programmes has a stronger scientific basis (in terms of the use of recognized psychological test instruments) than studies of preventative programmes have. This may be due to the fact that curative programmes are more suitable for structured measurement as they can make use of instruments developed in the mental health field, such as treatment-protocols and validated questionnaires measuring psychopathology. Concepts of individualized distress are more easily made operational than some of the concepts of general psychosocial development, such as 'resilience'. This also explains why scientific studies into preventative interventions still tend to express programme results in terms of a reduction of trauma-related symptoms, rather than a change in factors of positive psychosocial development.

From the current base of evidence, therefore, it cannot be concluded that one type of intervention is generally more successful than the other. The studies that have been conducted are difficult to compare, given the variety in approach and instruments being used.

Deciding which specific type of intervention to be used has to be based on what best fits the needs of the children and this may include a combination of methods. Children have diverse responses to crises, regardless of the severity of events they have witnessed. Because childhood is to a large extent socially constructed, children in different social settings experience different kinds of childhoods, leading to discrepancies in their safety and resilience during times of external stress. For example, in some societies resilience learning is part of the formal rites of passage (Boyden 2001). Differences do not only occur between children from various cultural backgrounds, but also appear in relation to other aspects of diversity, such as gender. It has therefore become of growing importance to understand the many different reactions of children to war experiences in order to be able to help them (Macksoud 2000).

Curative programmes may be useful in situations where children need special attention or are severely traumatized. It should be realized, however, that programmes addressing individual deficits generally need long-term attention, which was illustrated by the study into trauma healing at Rwandan secondary schools, where professional trauma counselling appeared to be a continuous need. Curative programmes also risk bringing out negative experiences that are not appropriately dealt with, as was concluded from research into KIDNET. Based on the same study it was argued that, within the context of curative programmes, there is a need to involve significant adults in the recovery of children.

Although the success of preventative psychosocial programmes for children in war-affected areas seems even more difficult to demonstrate scientifically than the effects of curative programmes, it is now widely regarded among humanitarian organizations focusing on psychosocial support for war-affected children as the most appropriate generic approach. Preventative programmes are both valued for their transactional, ecological approach, as well as for the practical solutions they offer to the challenge of improving the (psychosocial) situation of large numbers of children and families exposed to the stresses of armed conflict. As a result, attention is paid to the role of protective factors, including coping strategies, which mediate reactions to stress; they help children and communities restore normalcy and build on future development. To be able to assess the impact of programmes that aim to strengthen children's resiliency, research has shifted recently from describing psychopathology to investigating the means by which children cope with difficult circumstances. Some studies now focus on gaining better understanding of the protective factors that moderate the impact of traumatic experiences (Stichick 2001).

Methodological and ethical constraints in research with children in war-affected areas

While it is recognized that research knowledge is necessary to guide interventions designed to address the effects of war and violence on children, a scientific perspective is often difficult to maintain in the midst or soon after a conflict (Jensen 1996). There are both methodological and ethical constraints.

Methodological constraints

Quite a few challenges can be identified with regard to scientific research in the field of psychosocial interventions. First, there is relatively limited knowledge with regard to the impact of war on children's lives, particularly in the longer term, and how the effects of war are dealt with in different cultures.

Second, there is a lack of both systematic approaches and terminology, and especially a lack of cross-culturally valid instruments to measure locally described aspects of psychosocial well-being and the psychosocial development of children. Third, there are methodological constraints when measuring the effects of psychosocial programmes which are preventative in nature. Preventative interventions are focused on preventing children from developing psychosocial problems and are aimed at strengthening capacities and increasing their resilience to help them deal with future difficulties. It is difficult, therefore, to show effects of interventions in terms of a decline of problems, since the effects aimed for are to prevent children from future distress.

In pure scientific research, the use of a Randomized Controlled Trial (RCT), a prospective experimental study, is regarded as the most reliable way to attribute changes (or other results) to a specific intervention, by showing a statistical relationship. However, to date, the majority of research on children and war has come from the fields of medicine, psychiatry and psychology where, with a heavy emphasis on 'trauma' and psychopathology, the type of instruments used have been mostly developed and validated in Western countries. In practice, therefore, few studies into the effects of psychosocial programmes for children living in war-affected areas have been done according to RCT standards. Some organizations strive towards RCT studies but do not manage to meet the full requirements. Others, such as the Psychosocial Working Group (PWG 2002), argue that experimental designs such as RCT are often unfeasible to measure programmes that aim at achieving an urgent response, and they may also be unethical.

Furthermore, these kinds of tests mostly measure individual well-being, as opposed to measures at the social or community level and their reliance on questionnaires is questionable. Since large populations in the poorer countries of the world are illiterate (and these are the countries where most conflicts take place), or are not well trained in analytical cognitive skills (e.g. cannot easily choose an answer on a 5-point scale), the appropriateness of using quantitative questionnaires in these contexts is limited. Clearly, there is a need to search for other types of qualitative measures of well-being that can be used for effect-studies.

As described by Hart and Tyrer (2006), the question of how to use a research tool is equally important as deciding which tool to use. In this case, the research tool must be used in a way that complements the approach of the psychosocial project and must be aimed at helping the child participants to address and raise issues that matter to them, rather than simply for the purpose of the collection of information about them for and by outsiders. In line with this reasoning, one could argue that the type of research tools used must, preferably, accord with the type of intervention (e.g. a creative play intervention should be evaluated by means of creative research tools). When thinking about qualitative measures, one could think of systematic observations, focus group discussions or a participatory exercise such as a 'line debate' resulting in scoring on a Likert-scale or the Most Significant Change scale.

Other considerations regarding how to use research tools are related to the level and type of participation and to social dynamics. It is known that in developing countries, the way children are encouraged or trained to express ideas or knowledge is very much focused on replication, rather than on the free expression of thoughts. This might endanger the quality of all measurements. Furthermore, children do not always feel free to express themselves, and in certain social settings this might not even be culturally appropriate – for example, when adults are used to silencing the children, or in mixed gender groups where girls might feel uncomfortable sharing their feelings in the presence of boys. In some settings it might also be inappropriate to bring different ethnic groups together. All these dynamics will influence the relevance of data collected and researchers should be aware of this when designing their studies.

Ethical dilemmas and constraints

The first, most important ethical dilemma that can be raised when discussing research with children in war-affected areas is: why would you want to do any research with these children when it is so clear that they grow up in horrible circumstances, and are in need of support, not research?

The question this dilemma raises is of course very valid. Why would one want to put valuable resources and time into *research* with these children, when money and energy might be spent on simply helping them? In our view, research should indeed never be the most important feature of any kind of intervention with children in war-affected areas. Instead research should always be an 'add-on', which is the primary goal of the evaluation, and later improvement, of an intervention. However, if this argument were applicable, it would apply to all research that is done with children facing problems – it would also apply to research with street children in Sao Paulo, or underprivileged children in the United States. There is, therefore, a flipside to this ethical coin: if we do not do research into the needs and problems of children in war-affected areas, how can we be sure that our interventions will be suitable and effective? As was mentioned earlier, there has been an upsurge in psychosocial interventions for children in war-affected areas, but this has all been done from the assumption that these children need such help. As long as this assumption is not firmly based on knowledge of the needs, problems and infringed rights of the children in question, how can we be sure that interventions are useful? Both research into the nature of reactions and problems of children affected by war, and research into the effects of programmes for these children are necessary. But perhaps more than in other contexts, research with children in war-affected areas should never be done just for the betterment of science. The practical usefulness of the information that is gathered is of the utmost importance and this should therefore always play a leading role in deciding where, how and with whom research takes place.

Another important ethical dilemma relates to the use of control groups in research with children in war-affected areas. As mentioned above, the use of such control groups is deemed necessary as a prerequisite for scientifically valid research studies into the effects of interventions. However, the ethical question is clear: can you withhold support to a control group of children to examine the effects of such support? This will depend partly on the kind of support that seems to be needed. If it is a curative intervention aimed at children who are clearly suffering from severe psychological stress, stress that is so intense that it may endanger the children – for example, children expressing suicidal thoughts – one cannot and should not put the need for scientifically valid research first. On the other hand, if it is a research study conducted with children taking part in a preventative intervention, the immediate threats to children's health are probably more limited. In such cases a control group can be used, but children belonging to the control group should be given the possibility to participate in the intervention later on if indeed beneficial effects of the intervention are found. This was, for example, done in the War Child study in Kosovo described earlier in this chapter.

Researchers should also be aware of raising unrealistic expectations amongst participants. For example, when researchers ask questions about education – for example, are you going to school? – in a location where school enrolment and the quality of education is poor, the research may raise children's expectations about the improvement of their education. We recommend therefore that, when working with war-affected children, researchers should make sure to formulate questions about painful or ordinary everyday experiences carefully, so that the children understand the implications, especially if there is not the capacity to provide adequate support.

Ethical considerations should also play a role when selecting participants for intervention enrolment. All kinds of selections, especially those related to severity of war-affectedness, might easily lead to the stigmatization of the children who are selected. In the screening and involvement of the subjects of study, ethical questions have to be raised. Permission, and understanding of what is given permission for, is a prerequisite for any kind of sociological, psychological or anthropological research done in Western settings. This should also be the case for such research in non-Western countries, but experience teaches us that this sometimes may be difficult to obtain. And even if parents or children give permission to participate, it is not always clear whether they realize what they are giving permission for. Furthermore, the results of research are, in many instances, not shared with the participants or relevant others afterwards. This may be due to practical limitations, but very often this is simply not even considered. Sharing study results with all stakeholders might be beneficial later on, because it may convince beneficiaries of the importance of an intervention. For example, a mother who is complaining about lack of income because her child is going to school and cannot work full time at the market anymore, can be convinced of the benefits of the child's education for their future when research study results are shared and explained.

Guidelines for conducting research with children in war-affected areas

Research should be well planned and guided, since results of research studies might easily be misinterpreted, especially when they are in a negative direction, resulting in those involved - children, parents, NGO staff, etc. – becoming de-motivated as they feel the interventions are not useful. This eventually leads to donors losing interest. Efforts should be made, therefore, to clearly explain research results to all involved, and the implications these results can and should have for improving the lives of children in war-affected areas.

In the professional field of humanitarian aid there is of late an increased interest in the so called *rights based approach* (RBA). It is more and more acknowledged that assistance to people who find themselves in humanitarian crises like conflict should be based on internationally recognized human rights treaties. This has led to a change of approach: beneficiaries are no longer seen as 'recipients who are in need of charity', but as 'rights holders whose rights need to be respected or restored'. In the case of children this means that the United Nations Convention on the Rights of the Child (UNCRC), one of the most ratified treaties in the world, (only Somalia and the USA have not ratified so far) should be the guiding tool when designing and implementing humanitarian interventions. We think that the UNCRC should also be the framework on which any kind of research conducted with children in war-affected areas is based. Some of the key principles defined in the UNCRC include 'the best interests of the child' and 'child participation' principles that we have discussed earlier in this chapter. Whilst children for a long time were just seen as the victims of conflict, this is now more and more recognized as a too narrow view on their (possible) role (see also Gigengack, this volume). James and Prout (1997) argue that children must be seen as active in the construction and determination of their own social lives, the lives of those around them and of the societies in which they live. Children are not just the passive subjects of social structures and processes. The ability to exercise agency (the ability to shape one's own life and to influence the lives of others) may be limited or diminished for children in war-affected countries, but it still exists. Some children may actually find ways to benefit from the situation they are in – for example, learning new skills through cooperating with an aid agency – and thereby enhance their own personal development and contribution to the wider society. It is paramount, therefore, that children affected by war are actively involved in the planning, design, implementation and evaluation of research programmes. Only by letting the children speak their minds, and listening to their voices, can we hope to make a contribution to what ultimately should be the goal of most activities in war-affected areas: the prevention of future conflict.

We want to conclude by suggesting some general guidelines for doing research with children in war affected areas:

- Research done with children in war-affected areas should never infringe on the rights and needs of the children involved or, in other words, should always be in the best interests of the child. Practically speaking, this means that researchers always need to make sure that research does not interfere with children's possibilities to obtain necessary care (e.g. food, education, adult support, etc.), but this also implies that the research questions studied should be clearly linked to the daily practice of humanitarian assistance for children in war-affected areas (e.g. research should be practice-driven and not theory-driven).

- Research done with children in war-affected areas should always ensure children's participation in the design, implementation and sharing of results *to the highest degree* possible, since child participation in the design and implementation of research can contribute to children's empowerment. In addition, the participation of children also ensures the appropriateness of the research instrument, in terms of difficulty level, cultural appropriateness and so on, thereby increasing the reliability of the study.

- Research done with children in war-affected areas should always ensure the children's caregivers and the community's (parents, teachers, childcare professionals, community leaders, etc.) participation in the design, implementation and sharing of results *to the highest degree* possible. Sharing results with all stakeholders involved ensures an understanding of the practical implications of the study and increases the chance that the next steps will be taken to improve children's well-being.

- When conducting evaluations, or the effect of impact studies on psychosocial programmes for war-affected children, we feel that qualitative techniques are to be preferred over quantitative techniques. They are better suited for a war situation, culturally more valid, easier to administer, and give more insight into practical ways of improving interventions.

- Research done with children in war-affected areas should always be done with practical usefulness in mind. Results that are expected and obtained have to lead to outcomes and measures that will benefit the children in some way or another.

This list is by no means exhaustive, but we hope these guidelines will give researchers some 'food for thought', and will help them in designing and implementing valid and valuable research with children affected by war.

References

Allwood, M.A., Bell-Dolan, D. and Husain, S.A. (2002) 'Children's trauma and adjustment reactions to violent and nonviolent war experiences'. *Journal of the American Academy of Child and Adolescent Psychiatry* 41(4): 450–57.

Bolton, P. and Ndogoni, L. (2000) *Cross-Cultural Assessment of Trauma-Related Mental Illness.* CERTI Publications.

Boyden, J. (2001) *Social Healing in War-affected and Displaced Children.* Refugee Studies Centre, University of Oxford.

Bronfenbrenner, U. (1979) *The Ecology of Human.* Cambridge, MA: Harvard University Press.

De Graaff, D.C. (2006) *Effect-study Creative Workshop Cycle World Child Kosovo.* War Child Research Paper, War Child Holland, Amsterdam.

Euwema, M. (2006) *Child Development, a Reference Paper for War Child.* War Child Holland, Amsterdam.

Fazel, M. and Stein, A. (2002) 'The mental health of refugee children'. *Archives in Disease of Childhood* 87: 366–70.

Goenjian, A.K., Pynoos, R.S., Steinberg, A.M., Endres, D., Abraham, K., Geffner, M.E. and Fairbanks, L.A. (2003) 'Hypothalamic-pituitary-adrenal activity among Armenian adolescents with PTSD symptoms'. *Journal of Traumatic Stress* 16: 319–23.

Hart, J. and Tyrer, B. (2006) *Research with Children Living in Situations of Armed Conflict: Concepts, Ethics and Methods.* Working Paper Series, Refugee Studies Centre, University of Oxford.

Jensen, P. (1996) 'Practical approaches to research with children in violent settings', in R. Apfel and B. Simon (eds) *Minefields in Their Hearts: The Mental Health of Children in War and Communal Violence.* New Haven: Yale University Press.

Kalksma-Van Lith, B. (2005) *State of the Art in Psychosocial Interventions with Children: in War-affected Areas.* War Child State of the Art Paper, War Child Holland, Amsterdam.

Loughry, M. (2001) 'Dominant psychological paradigms in refugee literature and humanitarian interventions', in M. Loughry and A. Ager (eds) *Refugee Experience, Psychosocial Training Module.* Refugees Studies Centre, Oxford.

Loughry, M. and Eyber, C. (2003) *Psychosocial Concepts in Humanitarian Work with Children: a Review of the Concepts and Related Literature,* Washington: National Academies Press.

Macksoud, M. (2000) *Helping Children Cope with the Stresses of War: a Manual for Parents and Teachers.* New York: UNICEF.

Olij, J. (2005) 'Trauma awareness, healing, and group counseling in secondary schools', *Intervention* 3(1): 51–6.

James, A. and Prout, A. (eds) (1997) *Constructing and Reconstructing Childhood: Contemporary Issues in the Sociological Study of Childhood* (2nd edn). London: Falmer Press.

Psychosocial Working Group, PWG (2002) *Research Agenda.*

Refugee Studies Centre (2001) *Children and Adolescents in Palestinian Households: Living with the Effects of Prolonged Conflict and Forced Migration,* University of Oxford.

Schauer, E., Neuner, F., Elbert, T., Ertl, V., Onyut, L.P., Odenwald, M. and Schauer, M. (2004) 'Narrative exposure therapy in children: a case study', *Intervention* 2(1): 18–32.

Stichick Betancourt, T. (2001) *The Psychosocial Impact of Armed Conflict on Children. Rethinking Traditional Paradigms in Research Intervention.* Child and Adolescent Clinics of North America.

Stein, B.D., Jaycot, L.H., Kataoka, S.H., Wong, M., Tu, W., Elliott, M.N. and Fink, A. (2003) 'A mental health intervention for schoolchildren exposed to violence: A randomized control trial'. *Journal of the American Medical Association* 290: 603–11.

Tolfree, D. (1996) *Restoring Playfulness: Different Approaches to Assisting Children Who are Psychologically Affected by War or Displacement.* Save the Children Sweden.

10 Critical Omissions

How Street Children Studies Can Address Self-Destructive Agency

Roy Gigengack

Introduction

This chapter makes a plea for researching street children with ethnographic depth and vision. With the former I refer to the detailed and longitudinal fieldwork of street ethnography, and with the latter I mean a vision of how street children relate to society. There is room for the street-ethnographic vision, I argue, if it is seen in contradistinction to the two main discourses current in the literature. These two types of discourse, the institutional and the critical/activist, are discussed, and through a series of five statements I suggest how street ethnography can offer a different perspective. My central argument is that research on street children must pay attention to the paradoxes of self-destructive agency inherent in street children's lives. This critical issue has often been omitted in the literature whereas, during my own research in Mexico City, the young street people organized their daily survival around the acquisition and consumption of glues and solvents. These substances also marked their symbolic and olfactory boundaries (Gigengack 2006a: 185–99). Time and again the young street people expressed consciousness of the self-destruction that was going on, and they often acknowledged that they themselves took an active part in it (ibid.: 337–67). The longitudinal time frame of my research enabled me to see that most street youths do not die spectacularly. They rather perish, and die as young adults from inhalant-related sudden sniffing deaths.

Here then the term street ethnography refers to the detailed examination of the lives and deaths of young and older street people. It seeks to reconstruct the perspectives of the people under study through integrating description, interpretation, and diagnosis. On the one hand it illuminates what the young street people see as their world, how they experience their position in society and react upon it, and on the other, it clarifies how these meanings and experiences are structured through the power relations of the political economy.

The term street ethnography also refers to an established research tradition (Weppner 1977; Gigengack and van Gelder 2000). The fact that I put street ethnography so central in research with street children suggests a willingness to build upon the insights developed in that research tradition, as well as a sensibility to be cautioned by its shortcomings. This chapter therefore stands in contrast to much other street children research, which rarely takes inspiration from this literature. Most recent street children research typically remains within the limits of the sociology of childhood so that, as I go on to show, it seems to be an unwritten rule that the 'deconstruction of childhood' comes to precede analysis of street children's lives. It can be speculated, in line with the argument of this chapter, that this intellectual one-sidedness trivializes street children's lives in respect of behaviours such as inhalant use.

The argument presented below springs from my fieldwork experiences with young street people carried out in Mexico City between 1990 and 1997, amounting to more than 30 months, and several follow-up visits. My own early work, too, failed to take into account the self-destruction that was occurring under my nose. It took me years of fieldwork and writing to understand that the young street people's inhalant use was a form of self-destruction and not a survival strategy. It was only when I began to dream about the sniffing youngsters that I realized that in their inhalant use a larger issue was at stake. This chapter is thus also an admission that I, too, was able to misinterpret, and even overlook, what should have been obvious to me.

Street children in institutional discourse

The first type of discourse in relation to which street ethnography must position itself is the institutional. In its most pronounced form, the institutional discourse is produced through the bureaucracies of child care, such as UNICEF, the ILO, and the many state and non-governmental organisations that target street children. Institutional language, however, is not the privilege of institutes; journalists and scholars may use it as well. Key terms often reveal the institutional character of the discourse. A text may state, for example, that it is 'policy oriented' or in search of 'solutions' for 'the problem of street children.'

Institutional categories are widely accepted within street children research and while well-known distinctions, such as children 'on' and 'of' the street, can be practical in research, they are only valuable if the tenuous relations between child care and social science are acknowledged. In the hands of social workers, policy makers and other experts, the categorization of some children as 'street children' become a way to segregate particular young people for purposes of interventions and/or the distribution of funds. Following Bauman (1998: 106-7), the use of these professional categories are meant to reduce the variance of persons and cases, and therefore permits disregard for social diversity. Instead, typification replaces the documentation of individual qualities and personal circumstances. In other words, the categories of expertise are, and indeed need to be, estranged from the reality of the streets.

In fact, 'the street child' is a good example of a concept that is not well informed by street children's everyday lives. Institutional sources have abundantly documented that 'the street child' is usually a male; that he comes from poor and often female-headed households; that he runs away from child abuse in the home to drug abuse in the street; and that he lives under the most abhorrent circumstances. As Whyte (1993 [1943]: xv) pointed out decades ago, there is nothing wrong with this sort of generalising statements, except that there are no human beings in it.

The street child experts working in institutional care settings imagine for themselves a singular street child and take his miserable, meaningless existence as representative of all street children. Thus, each institution holds its own defining characteristics of the 'street child'. The United Nations' official definition of 'the street child or street youth' is, for example, 'any minor for whom the street (in the widest sense of the word, including unoccupied dwellings, wasteland, etc.) has become his or her habitual abode and who is without adequate protection' (cited in Agnelli 1986: 32). This definition is not designed for the interpretation of street children's lives and deaths. It is rather an institutional tool designed to help street children's helpers in their work. Social scientists must therefore interrogate concepts such as 'the street child', and interpret them as part of an institutional, rather than a social-scientific, vernacular.

Institutional discourses are, for example, underpinned by an inherently bureaucratic logic. The unspecified misery of 'the street child' prescribes what in institutional jargon is called 'action', and 'action' is what the bureaucracies of child care undertake. Thus, the singularity in the conceptualization of 'the street child' fits the agenda of institutional survival, since taking 'action' in the life of an individual is technically more feasible than intervention in a group.

From a street-ethnographic perspective, however, the notion of 'the street child' is problematic. One reason for this is its underlying essentialism. As in the UN definition, 'the street child' is usually depicted as homeless and without a family, and while these troubles are certainly relevant for a number of street children, they are not for all of them. A related problem is that definitions that spell out what street children do *not* have inevitably lump them together with other categories of people. Being homeless or living without a family may, after all, be as characteristic for non-street children as they are for street children.

A further recurrent element of institutional discourse is what Ennew and Milne (1989) characterize as the 'Number Game' – the rhetoric about millions of street children. Big numbers were especially popular during the 1980s and 1990s, when street children were still high on the policy agenda. For example, in that period the Dutch Minister of Development Co-operation believed that

> some eight million children are estimated to live on the streets of Brazil, attempting to scrape a living by doing odd jobs, and by begging, stealing and prostitution. The total number of street children in the whole of Latin America is estimated to be in the region of eighty to hundred million.
>
> (Pronk 1992: 8)

In the Minister's discourse, as in others, such high numbers had a function, since they added weight to the necessity of intervention. The Minister proclaimed that there should be more aid for the children of the poor, and the millions of street children served as a vehicle to express such commitment. The Pronk quote was also typical in that the source of the estimation was not mentioned. It is unclear to whom the term 'street children' actually refers, however, and it is in any case unlikely that the same criteria had been used to calculate the number for Brazil and the total number for Latin America. Later sources reproduced the cliché of the millions further by uncritically referring to the Minister's estimations (e.g. Schrijvers 1993: 20).

This focus on large numbers is detrimental as it renders the existence of young street people incomprehensible – with such dimensions it becomes practically impossible to obtain detailed knowledge of concrete situations and stories. And indeed, this lack of knowledge is reflected in the other clichés operating in institutional discourse. Particular phrases come back time and again in the institutional texts – 'the street child has no identity' or 'the street child sleeps wherever the night catches him'. As a first statement, then, I would argue that *street ethnography cannot be based on institutional discourse*. The fieldworker's prime task is to avoid thinking institutionally – and that is particularly difficult in the case of street children, for their needs and suffering are so obvious that, in thinking about them, one easily reverts to clichés.

The point is, of course, that the clichés and the other thought categories of institutional discourse tell more about the professionals involved with street children than about the street children themselves. Spradley's (1970: 68) labelling theory comes to mind here. Institutional discourse enables the average professional person to account for what appears to be strange and irrational. Young people living in groups, staying in wastelands and sniffing solvents a good deal are difficult to comprehend. Defining such kids as 'abandoned children' or 'children of the street' enables the expert to relate to them: he or she knows that these youngsters must be pitied, saved, and on occasion ignored. To paraphrase Bauman (1998: 106–7), the estrangement expressed through such categories is the core function of professional distance.

The activist critique

The second type of discourse against which street ethnography positions itself is the activist critique. This discourse is as well closely related to the institutions for street children, since its primary target is institutional praxis. Patently, the value of activist critique lies in scandalizing certain practices of intervention and condemning the omission of other practices. But the street children's activists often shift the target of their critique to the institutional *discourse*. Their underlying idea seems to be that just being critical helps the cause of street children.[1]

Typically, critical street children discourse consists of both scholastic and activist components. It enjoys a scientific overlay that the institutional discourse lacks and, on occasions, the activist critique is theoretical. The language often includes particular buzz words such as 'deconstruction' and 'social construct' – indeed deconstructionism is a common call raised in the activist critique offered by street children researchers. Thus, just as I argued above that street ethnography must challenge the institutional discourse so too must it engage in debate with the activist critique, for the danger of radical deconstructionism is that it may signify, and legitimize, an intellectual retreat from the destruction taking place on the margins (Bourgois 1996: 15).

Writers within the activist/ critical discourse often assume that they understand a priori what transformations are needed to ameliorate street children's lives (Guba and Lincoln 1994: 113). Nieuwenhuys, for example, is convinced that the poor are helped by 'critical distance', and she believes that 'the best way of helping the children of the urban poor to gain a sense of worth is by exposing the representations that negate what is valuable in their lives' (1999: 35). Advocates of street children such as, for example, Ennew (1986, 1994a: 175) and Aptekar (1988), argue for the need to separate 'fact' from 'fiction', and while there is nothing wrong with that, critical scholars may unmask the myths about street children at the same time as new myths start to lead their own life. And in the substitution of new myths for old ones, the activist critique can overshoot its mark. Examples of the flaws of the critical toolkit are concepts such as 'survival' and 'coping strategies' being used to describe children engaging in inhalant use and self-mutilation; 'pseudo-families' and 'supportive networks' to depict gangs in which distrust and even rape are known to occur; and 'meaningful relationships' and 'capabilities' being held to characterize street children's life-worlds, which are often also marked by indifference and idleness.

The romanticism inherent in much activist critique touches upon multiple and very complex dimensions, and here I can only trace some of its intellectual history. The influential volume edited by James and Prout (1997 [1990]) merits special attention, since it provided the activist critique with an intellectual underpinning stemming from the sociology of childhood. At the time, James and Prout presented the 'emergent paradigm' as a set of 'dissenting voices' and a 'challenge of orthodoxy', and although by now it has become the dominant, if not orthodox, approach in the study of childhood, in street children studies, these new conceptualizations gave rise to a radical deconstructionism (e.g. the volume edited by Connelly and Ennew (1996a)).

The new paradigm stipulated that 'children must be seen as actively involved in the construction of their own social lives' and suggested that childhood be analysed by a focus on 'the present, ongoing social lives of children rather than their past or future' as had hitherto been most often the case (James and Prout 1997: 4–5). Applied to street children studies, however, these prescriptions lead to approaches in which the successful, rather than the flawed, day-to-day survival becomes central. What is problematic is not that street children are seen as actors; rather that in such studies the underlying idea of agency is an unreflexively positive one. The retreat into the present further facilitates overlooking the self-destructive aspects of street children's agency: only through a shrunken time frame can persistent inhalant use be interpreted as a coping mechanism, and its consequences be ignored.

Another problem of applying the paradigm of constructing and reconstructing childhood to the study of street children lies precisely in the priority it gives to the understanding of childhood as a social construction. Significantly, James and Prout understand ethnography as a methodology to study childhood and not children (James and Prout 1997: 8-9). The priority of social constructionism, over ethnography, however, lead to approaches that seek to study how street children are represented. That is certainly a vital subject, about which a lot more is still to be found out, but it should not be confused with the study of street children proper. An ethnography of street children would tell us how these young people themselves see the world, what *they* do, and how *they* feel.[2]

Let me elaborate the shortcomings of the critical street children studies by dissecting the ontological assumptions of writings such as Glauser (1997[1990]), Boyden (1991, [1990] 1997), Ennew (1994a and b), Aptekar and Behailu (1997), Schepers-Hughes and Hoffman (1994, 1998), Nieuwenhuys (1999), and myself (Gigengack 1994). All these authors begin from a deconstructionist perspective, in which childhood is seen as a model, an invention, and even an export article. Childhood is thus not thought of as primarily what children live through or what happens to them. The kernel of their critique is that the very idea of street children is a construct of dominant society – a 'wrong image' – and that therefore it ought to be rejected. While that argument is certainly a first step in recognising complexity, it nonetheless comprises a series of beliefs about the reality of street children, which do not withstand scrutiny.

A first ontological assumption upon which this critical discourse rests is that the boundaries between street children and other urban poor children are irrelevant. Critical authors thus note that distinctions such as that between the children 'on' and 'of' the street function as conceptual containers and that they serve institutional interests. Typically, the deconstruction exercise is limited to discursively erasing the boundaries between the two categories but in doing so it tends to trivialize the objective differences between street and working children in terms of family situation, economic behaviour, and cultural characteristics such as appearance, speech and drug use. Connelly and Ennew (1996b), for example, propose the term 'children out of place'. Not only do they thus reduce street and working children to a metaphorical dimension of moral space, they also insist in lumping together widely divergent lifestyles. Schepers-Hughes and Hoffman (1998: 358) radicalize the same idea even further - 'street children are simply poor children in the wrong place' - practically invalidating any consciousness of difference within street children and other urban poor.

Such deconstruction exercises are doomed to fail. The label street children cannot be dodged simply because hitherto the term has been monopolized by the users of institutional discourse. That position would treat institutional discourse merely as a language game, or a group of signs, and not 'as practices that systematically form the object of which they speak' (Foucault 1972: 49). Along with the activist critique, one can take street children as a 'fiction' – but if everyone believes in it, a fiction can become a self-fulfilling prophecy (Merton 1996). If institutions such as schools, shelters, reformatories, and hospitals separate 'street children' from the rest, if ordinary citizens such as neighbourhood residents treat 'street children' as such, and if even the 'street children' talk about themselves as if they were 'street children', it becomes very difficult to separate the fiction and the real street children.

The second ontological assumption is that of hegemony. If street children are but a fiction, then it follows that representations of street children are the products of a dominant ideology. Some texts depart from an implicit notion of false consciousness, as can be seen in their use of key terms such as 'myths', 'stereotypes' and 'wrong images' (see, for example, Ennew 1994a: 13, 123, 175; 1994b: 409). Freire (1988) and Glauser (1997) have been more explicit. These authors resort to what Scott (1990: 72) would call respectively a 'thick' and a 'thin' theory of hegemony. Freire holds that working children may behave towards street children 'exactly like certain segments of the bourgeoisie', even though there are 'no substantial differences' between working and street children, and, he argues, it is through false consciousness that working children 'reproduce bourgeois ideology' (1988: 15). Glauser is more cautious. He subscribes to a thesis of hegemony, according to which 'those with social power ... define the reality of others by shaping and constraining the ways in which it is possible to talk and think [about street children]' (Glauser 1997: 151).

If the powerful determine how the others talk and think, they do so in a limited number of ways: a third ontological assumption of activist critique is that the representations of street children are not only false, but also univocal. A distinction between deviant and romantic stereotypes is common, but some authors assume that the dominant, Western model of childhood generates one monolithic 'popular opinion' about street and working children (Aptekar and Behailu 1997: 478). However, although such wrong images and stereotypes are the object of critique, the condemned representations of street children are seldom localized in a context.[3]

These three assumptions are highly problematic. If critical discourse assumes that the boundaries between street children and other urban poor are irrelevant, it is badly equipped to describe and interpret the formation and the management of these boundaries. The assumption of hegemony limits taking the popular representations of street children as an ambivalent and contradictory space and, depending upon the context, the other urban poor may identify as well as disidentify with street children, sometimes even simultaneously. Such complexities do not fit, however, with univocal representations unbound to context. An even bigger problem is the possibility that the young street people in fact see themselves as street children, a possibility which the activist critique can only interpret through an inherently circular argument of internalization.[4]

A main difficulty for critical activists is how to problematize the ongoing destruction of street children. My own work, for example, was initially in line with the critical street children discourse. I could thus 'deconstruct' street children by discussing for whom and why these young people constituted a problem. The list was long and I concluded that 'while the problem for the children is survival, the [street] children themselves are the difficulty for the adults' (Gigengack 1994: 382). That conclusion overlooked the fact that self-destructive behaviour was as much of a problem for street children as was their survival. Moreover, I also failed to address the question of whether street children were actually enough of a problem (see also De Swaan 1992). Had I asked when and for whom street children did *not* form a problem, my attention would have focused on social indifference, the sort of social exclusion that is not named as such. It would also have guided my attention to street children's destructiveness, their feelings of alienation, and ultimately their own indifference to survival. Had I inverted the central question of my article, I would certainly have concluded that it is a problem when street children are not defined as a problem.

Against those who believe that, due to a methodological suspension of judgement combined with the posturing of cultural relativism, street people have tended to be romanticized (Kamiya 1995), I would argue the opposite: romanticism is only possible through the lack of fieldwork. The problem of most critical discourse about street children is not its ethnographic approach but rather its often shallow empirical foundation. My 1994 article posed the one question and not the other because it was based on only 18 months or so of fieldwork. In retrospect, then, I was able to overlook street children's devastating, self-destructive capacities because of two reasons: first, the paradigmatic dominance of the activist critique in the literature, and second, my own relatively brief exposure to street children.

In this section, I have argued that the aims and assumptions of critical discourse may be at odds with the ethnographic project, and as a second statement I would suggest that *street ethnography should be cautious in formulating an activist critique.*

Street ethnography versus 'street childrenism'

I have reduced the proliferation of discourses on street children to two types: that of the institutional experts and that of the critical activists. Very roughly, it can be said that the former engage in the pitification of street children and the latter in their prettification. Both do so for the sake of helping street children, by either promoting some intervention programme or shattering some stereotype. From a street-ethnographic perspective, however, the institutional and activist discourses are part and parcel of the practices under study, and as such they should be documented and studied.

In this respect I find the term 'street childrenism' instructive to understand the dynamics of thinking about street children. The neologism indicates that in the institutional and the activist discourses the idea of street children is primarily used as a tool to bring about change. The institutional experts and the critical activists share 'street childrenism' in that both accept the idea of street children as a rhetorical means for action. Their discourses should not, however, be confused with ethnography. From the perspective of the latter, the idea of street children is basically an end in itself, serving purposes of description, interpretation, and diagnosis.

The term 'street childrenism' should not be taken as a negative value judgement. On the contrary, it rehabilitates the experts and activists. Experts and activists do not compete in social science arenas, as they have better things to do, and measuring their discourses solely against the yardstick of social science would be not only unfair, but also senseless, since ethnography does not make a truth claim. Institutional expertise and critical activism may appear problematic to social scientists, but they accord with the experiences and expectations of those who make these discourses and believe in them.

The discovery of street childrenism clears the way, then, for street ethnography. In both the institutional and the activist discourses, there is little room for the exploration of how young street people live and what they find meaningful since, in both discourses, street children are perceived primarily through the categories of their beholders. More adequate representations of the reality of street children's lives are therefore urgently needed and, as a third statement, I would suggest then that *street ethnography tells true-to-life stories based on intensive and longitudinal fieldwork.* With 'true-to-life' ethnography I mean that it strives for congruence with the reality of street children's everyday experiences. A first prerequisite for this is a 'feel' for what that reality consists of, an implicit knowledge of what it is that street children do, how they live and die. That knowledge can only be obtained through intensive work with young street people on a long-term basis. Detailed empirical descriptions are another requirement for reality congruence. Street ethnography is based on evidence. By contrast, in street childrenism, detailed descriptions of street children's lives and deaths are often hard to find.

Descriptions alone are not enough, however. Street ethnography is social science; it should have a vision. Even if the distinction between science and non-science is notorious, I would suggest that street ethnography meet criteria for social science, such as those formulated by the Dutch sociologist Goudsblom (1977). My fourth statement is then: *street ethnography must fulfil the requirements of precision, systematics, scope and relevance.* These criteria help further clarify the differences between street childrenism and street ethnography.

Both institutional expertise and critical activism are typically imprecise and unsystematic. For example, institutional sources mostly agree that '[a]s a way to describe these children, 'the street' is perhaps as woolly as its stones are hard' (Agnelli 1986: 32), without taking into account the implications of it. As a result, the meanings of their categories of street children may shift in arbitrary and often implicit ways (and hence the confusion about the number of street children). While critical authors such as Ennew (1994a) and (1994b), Nieuwenhuys (1999), and Panter-Brick (2002) acknowledge this problem there has been no systematic attempt to formulate an alternative.

Scope, or diagnostic potential, is, however, the biggest problem of street childrenism. The pitification inherent in institutional expertise and the prettification characteristic of the activist critique mystify the relational dimensions of street children's lives. It is, after all, through the social dynamics of inclusion and exclusion that the young street people are, and remain, the street children that they are. The underlying problem is that in both types of discourse the essentialism and the schematic generalisations run counter to thinking of street children as engaged in ongoing social relations.

Let me illustrate this difference in approach by briefly addressing what is probably the most recurrent issue in the street children studies, namely the definition of the term. Institutional authors usually attempt to define and refine the term 'street children', and critical scholars typically try to debunk its use value. Both of these formulas are not processual, however, in that they do not seek to determine who defines street children, in which context, and why. In street ethnography this becomes core: the definition of street children is at stake within the object itself (cf. Bourdieu 1992: 244).

Meeting the requirement of relevance may seem to be less of a problem for a field of study so characterized by human suffering. The fact that institutional and activist texts tend to shift gears quickly to ask how the 'problem' of street children can be solved or street children can be 'empowered' certainly adds to the appearance of it. But relevance cannot be assumed to be clear and unequivocal. Indeed, I would argue that essentialist generalisations may reduce relevance as much as they restrict scope due to two fallacies. The first, the fallacy of misplaced concreteness (Whitehead 1997 [1925]: 51), leads to such ideas that 'the street child' is 'contaminated' by a pathogenic entity called 'the street', or conversely that there are context-free 'wrong images' causing a good deal of harm. It is through such reification or 'the attribution of concreteness' (Bateson 1958: 263) that the institutional and activist habits of thought restrict their scope. The relevance of these same discourses, however, is reduced by the opposite error: the 'fallacy of misplaced abstractness' (Peacock 2001: xv, 24). As already pointed out, the institutional rhetoric of the very large numbers makes the individual stories of concrete street children obsolete, and the same can be said about the abstract factors that 'cause' the phenomenon – for example, the so-called marginalization cycle that explains how poor children degenerate into street children. Critical activists commit the same mistake whenever they conceptualize street children merely as an abstract 'social construct'. While the label for street children is an abstraction, for the young street people themselves it is a concrete reality.

Thus, if street ethnography is to make a difference, if it is to be relevant, it must concretize the reality of young street people by paying attention to the conditions under which these young people live and die.

Street ethnography is political

'Ethnographic presentations of social marginalization are almost guaranteed to be misread by the general public through a conservative, unforgiving lens', Philippe Bourgois (1996: 15) observes in his study of Puerto-Rican drug dealers in New York. He argues that the politics of representation has seriously limited the ability of intellectuals to debate issues of poverty and alienation. The parallels with the study of street children are striking. Documenting self-destructive agency and analyzing it as a central feature of street children's lives and deaths evokes resistance, as I have learned. One reader, for example, agreed that most street children research had avoided discussing self-destruction but, nevertheless, suggested that emphasizing it would bring an ethical dilemma. She could have argued the opposite as well, since evading a social problem potentially fosters indifference.

From an ethnographic point of view, it is also unacceptable only to latch on to positive representations of street children that the street children themselves know to be completely unrealistic. Elsewhere I argue that the trivialization of the destruction in street children's lives constitutes a symbolic assault on their world (Gigengack 2006a: 344–56). The deeper reason for this lies in what Bauman (1992: 115–19) so aptly terms 'legislative reason'. The role of intellectuals as legislators is one of 'desperately seeking structure'; their quest is for beauty, purity and order – and these are not precisely the graces of the world of young street people (ibid.: xi). The latter know, of course, that their world is ugly, impure and disorderly, and so do the other urban poor around them. But their lay interpretations of reality are not authoritative. Legislative reason presumes to invalidate common sense (ibid.: 120), and, in the end, it may even deny what the world of young street people is all about.

It has also been suggested to me that criticizing activist/critical discourse would imply a regression to apolitical positivism. I don't think so. Good research with street children *is* a political project, first of all because it exposes the wretched conditions in which the young street people live and die. One implication of this is that ethnography with street children is sensorial – for, especially in the context of street life, the senses are concrete and political. If they come to their senses – and don't lose their heads in discourses – street children researchers will be able to perceive the materiality of their subjects, as expressed in, for example, street children's bodily appearances and body odours (Gigengack 2006b).

Street ethnography is political also in the sense that stories about young street people and their self-destruction may motivate people somewhere in the world to improve the living conditions of those whom they see as

street children. It must as well be pointed out that street ethnography is political in the field, too. Working with young street people unavoidably involves
intervention and activism. That is notably so for humanitarian reasons, but it
also has a methodological rationale (Gigengack 2006a). Street children exist
in relation to institutional intervention and street child activism, and these
practices can only be known through participant observation.

In sum, street ethnography is political because it studies social suffering.
That characteristic further differentiates the street-ethnographic vision from
the activist critique, and also of course from the apolitical stance typically
adopted in institutional discourse. Street ethnography is not about the political
games that street educators, non-governmental charities, and Children's
Rights activists like to play. While street children researchers must recognize
that they do not work within a political vacuum – that their writings may
have intended as well as unanticipated political consequences, and that they
themselves may engage in activism – this does not mean confusing the
discourse of street child activism with that of ethnography. In the politics of
representation, the commitment of street ethnography lies with the key
objectives of description, interpretation, and diagnosis. These reflections
bring me to the fifth and last statement: *the street-ethnographic vision is thoroughly
but indirectly political.*

Conclusion: agency fused with victimhood

Institutional experts, critical activists, and social scientists have done a lot of
work. Yet they have fallen prey, like initially I have done myself, to the two
main types of discourses on street children: the institutional and the
activist/critical. These two discourses block our view on how young street
people live and die in specific places at specific times.

In particular, the literature consistently overlooks the paradoxes of young
street people's self-destructive agency. The institutional writings typically
assume that street children are passive victims of miserable circumstances and
therefore 'fall into drugs'. The critical/activist writings, in contrast, portray
strong and sturdy street children who do not engage at all in the self-destruction
that is common among street children. These omissions are critical, because
the street children themselves may see their self-destructive agency as
fundamental to their world and to the problems they encounter. If it is based
on intensive and longitudinal fieldwork, good street ethnography will be able
to show that, beyond all the coping with poverty, being a street child involves
self-destruction. The young street people's victimhood and their agency will
thus appear to be two sides of the same coin.

Acknowledgement

Jojada Verrips scrutinized the text innumerable times, and always urged me
to clarify my thoughts. I coined the concept 'street childrenism' together

with Raquel Alonso. I also wish to thank the editors for their thoughtful comments.

Notes

1 The discursive logic of the activist critique is thus actually a bureaucratic derivative too, for in order to be 'critical' the activist thinkers need the institutional discourse of the experts.
2 Thomas (1989: 47–8) makes a similar argument with regards to the history of childhood versus the history of children.
3 Catchy phrases such as the following are unclear about who stereotypes street children and why: 'Street children are *often* referred to as "vagrant", a term implying a random, purposeless wandering, attributed to individual failure' (Felsman 1989: 67, italics mine). 'For *many people* the street child is the embodiment of the untamed feral child; an outcast whose very existence threatens social chaos and decline' (Boyden 1997: 196, italics mine). '*Most people* see [tunnel kids] as simply another gang of doped-up, violent, homeless children' (Taylor and Hickey 2001: xvi, italics mine).
4 Critical street children discourse is often also underpinned by an epistemological assumption regarding the observed and the observer. Glauser's influential article ([1990] 1997) provides again a good example, all the more so since its retrospective postscript acknowledges 'a confident, almost omnipotent attitude' driven by 'an urge to contribute to concrete action' (ibid.: 163). Thus, a key passage in the article claims that 'those with social power ... define the reality of others', whereas 'deconstruction ... is necessary as a liberation from the influence and reach of unwanted power' (ibid.: 151). The ultimate implication of this claim is that the others are the passive recipients of the hegemonic construct of street children, whilst their liberation lies in the article itself: the epistemological assumption is that deconstructing street children is the privilege of intellectuals and not of the others.

References

Agnelli, S. (1986) *Street Children: A Growing Urban Tragedy*. London: Widenfeld & Nicolson.
Aptekar, L. (1988) *Street Children of Cali*. Durham and London: Duke University Press.
Aptekar, L. and Behailu A. (1997) 'Conflict in the neighborhood: Street and working children in the public space', *Childhood* 4 (4): 477–90.
Bateson, G. (1958) *Naven* (2nd edn), Stanford: Stanford University Press.
Bauman, Z. (1998) *Globalization. The Human Consequences*. New York: Columbia University Press.
Bauman, Z. (1992) *Intimations of Postmodernity*. London: Routledge.
Bourdieu, P. (1992) *Invitation to Reflexive Sociology*. Cambridge: Polity Press.
Bourgois, P. (1996) *In Search of Respect: Selling Crack in el Barrio*. Cambridge: University of Cambridge Press.
Boyden, J. (1991) *Children of the Cities*. London: Zed Books Ltd.
Boyden, J. (1997) [1990] 'Childhood and the policy makers: A comparative perspective on the globalization of childhood', in A. James and A. Prout (eds) *Construction and Reconstructing Childhood: Contemporary Issues in the Sociological Study of Childhood* (2nd edn), London: The Falmer Press.
Connelly, M. and Ennew, J. (1996a) 'Children out of place. Special Issue on Working and Street Children', *Childhood* 3 (2): 131–45.
Connelly, M. and Ennew, J. (1996b) 'Introduction: Children out of place', *Childhood* 3 (2): 131–45.
De Swaan, A. (1992) 'Are poor children enough of a nuisance? Reflections on the spread and stagnation of collective arrangements for child care', in *Two Pieces*. Amsterdam: Het Spinhuis.

Ennew, J. (1994a) *Street and Working Children,* London: Save the Children.

Ennew, J. (1994b) 'Parentless friends: A cross-cultural examination of networks among street children and street youths', in S. Nestman and K. Hurrelman (eds) *Social Networks and Social Support in Childhood and Adolescence,* London: De Gruyter.

Ennew, J. (1986) 'Children of the street', *The New Internationalist,* pp. 3–4.

Ennew, J. and Milne, B. (1989) *The Next Generation,* London: Zed Books.

Felsman, J.K. (1989) 'Risk and resiliency in childhood: The lives of street children', in T.F. Dugan and R. Coles (eds) *The Child in Our Times: Studies in the Development of Resiliency,* New York: Bruno/ Mazel, Inc.

Freire, P. (1988) *Paulo Freire y los Educadores de la Calle. Una Aproximación Crítica.* Serie Metodológica No.1. Programa Regional Menores en Circunstancias Especialmente Difíciles. Bogotá: UNICEF.

Foucault, M. (1972) *The Archaeology of Knowledge and the Discourse on Language,* New York: Pantheon Books.

Gigengack, R. (1994) 'Social practices of juvenile survival and mortality: Child care arrangements in Mexico City', *Community Development Journal* 29 (4): 380–93.

Gigengack, R. (2006a) *Young, Damned and Banda. The World of Young Street People in Mexico City, 1990–1997.* PhD thesis. Amsterdam: ASSR, University of Amsterdam.

Gigengack, R. (2006b) *The Olfactory Reality of Street Culture.* On street children, sensitive nostrils and the politics of smell. Paper presented at CEDLA, Amsterdam, 03-11-2006. http://www.cedla.uva.nl/20_events/PDF_files_news/abstract/Olfactory%20Reality%20-%20Roy%20Gigengack.pdf.

Gigengack, R. and van Gelder, P. (2000) 'Contemporary street ethnography: Different experiences, perspectives, and methods', in *Focaal.* Special Issue on Contemporary Street Ethnography, R. Gigengack (ed.), 36: 7–14.

Glauser, B. (1997) [1990] 'Street children: Deconstructing a construct', in A. James and A. Prout (eds) *Constructing and Reconstructing Childhood: Contemporary Issues in the Sociological Study of Childhood.* (2nd edn), London: The Falmer Press.

Goudsblom, J. (1977) *Sociology in the Balance. A Critical Essay.* Oxford: Basil Blackwell.

Guba, E.C. and Lincoln, Y.S. (1994) 'Competing paradigms in qualitative research', in N.K. Denzin and Y.S. Lincoln (eds) *Handbook of Qualitative Research.* Thousand Oaks, CA: Sage.

James, A. and Prout, A. (eds) 1997 [1990] 'Introduction', in *Constructing and Reconstructing Childhood. Contemporary Issues in the Sociological Study of Childhood* (2nd edn), London: The Falmer Press.

Kamiya, G. (1995) *Heart of Darkness.* http://www.salonmagazine.com/02dec1995/features/bourgois3.html Accessed April, 2007.

Merton, R.K. (1996) 'The self-fulfilling prophecy', in P. Sztompka (ed.) *On Social Structure and Science,* Chicago: The University of Chicago Press.

Nieuwenhuys, O. (1999) 'The paradox of the competent child and the global childhood agenda', in W. Fardon, W. van Binsbergen and R. van Dijk (eds) *Modernity on a Shoestring. Dimensions of Globalization, Consumption and Development in Africa and Beyond,* Leiden and London: EIDOS.

Panter-Brick, C. (2002) 'Street children, human rights, and public health: A critique and future directions, *Annual Review of Anthropology* 31: 147–71.

Peacock, J.L. (2001) *The Anthropological Lens. Harsh Light, Soft Focus* (2nd edn), Cambridge: Cambridge University Press.

Pronk, J.P. (1992) 'Children's rights', in M. Droogleever Fortuyn and M. De Langen (eds) *Towards the Realization of Human Rights of Children.* Amsterdam: Children's Ombudswork Foundation/ Defence for Children International-Netherlands.

Prout, A. and James, A. (1997) [1990] 'A new paradigm for the sociology of childhood? Provenance, promise and problems', in A. James and A. Prout (eds). *Constructing and Reconstructing Childhood. Contemporary Issues in the Sociological Study of Childhood* (2nd edn), London: The Falmer Press.

Schepers-Hughes, N. and Hoffman, D. (1998) 'Brazilian apartheid: Street kids and the struggle for urban space', in N. Schepers-Hughes and C. Sargent (eds) *Small Wars. The Cultural Politics of Childhood*. Berkeley: University of California Press.

Schepers-Hughes, N. and Hoffman, D (1994) 'Kids out of place', in *NACLA Report on the Americas*. (May/June 1994).

Schrijvers, J. (1993) *The Violence of 'Development': A Choice for Intellectuals*. Utrecht: International Books.

Scott, J.C. (1990) *Domination and the Arts of Resistance: Hidden Transcripts*. New Haven and London: Yale University Press.

Spradley, J.P. (1970) *You Owe Yourself a Drunk: An Ethnography of Urban Nomads*: Boston: Little, Brown and Company.

Taylor, L. and Hickey, M. (2001) *Tunnel Kids,* Tucson, Arizona: the University of Arizona Press.

Thomas, K. (1989) 'Children in early modern England' in G. Avery and J. Briggs (eds) *Children and Their Books: A Celebration of the Work of Iona and Peter Opie*, Oxford: Clarendon Press.

Whitehead, A.N. (1997) [1925] *Science and the Modern World*. New York: The Free Press.

Whyte, W. (1993) [1943] *Street Corner Society: The Social Structure of an Italian Slum* (4th edn), Chicago/London: The University of Chicago Press.

Weppner, R.S. (ed.) (1977) *Street Ethnography. Selected Studies of Crime and Drug Use in Natural Settings*. London: Sage.

11   Disabled Children, Ethnography and Unspoken Understandings

The Collaborative Construction of Diverse Identities

John Davis, Nick Watson and Sarah Cunningham-Burley

Introduction

This chapter discusses research that has been carried out in a special school for children with multiple impairments in Scotland. It describes the gradual process through which disabled children (who employed a variety of forms of verbal and non-verbal communication) enabled us to construct a complex understanding of their lives and identities.[1] The chapter discusses how this process was supported by techniques of reflexive enquiry and enabled the development of complex theoretical positions within both the paradigms of childhood and disability studies. Specifically, we consider how the ethnographic processes enabled us to: learn the children's (verbal and non-verbal) languages, develop a variety of research roles and question our own and other academic understandings of childhood and disability.

Entry into the field

This chapter demonstrates the need for researchers working with disabled children to be innovative within and sensitive to research settings that are full of contradictory expectations and pressures. We argue (as Davis 1998 and 1996 have argued), that the diversity of children's lives can be explored by ethnographers being reflexive about how different children respond to issues of access, the ethnographer's role and the research tools they employ.

At the beginning of the project it was imagined that John, the ethnographer, would spend 6 to 8 weeks in the special school prior to visiting some of the children in their home locations. However, despite his previous experience of working with children, the initial entry into the school was extremely difficult:

> After a very friendly meeting with the head teacher, I was thrown in at the deep end. I was introduced to the staff in the classroom and left to explain to them what I was doing there. The senior teacher and speech therapist introduced me to the children who were practising their parts in the forthcoming school play. Unfortunately, I could neither understand the

words of the children who spoke to me nor communicate with those children who did not employ the spoken word as a means of communication. This resulted in me relying on the staff to explain what the children said or signed. I found my admission into the school a quite frightening experience. On a personal basis, I didn't have a clue how I was expected to behave by staff and children and I found it extremely difficult to understand if the children were happy with my presence in their class. This led to a lot of standing around, getting in the way of children and staff, until my role in the class developed. This uncomfortable experience was compounded by my academic related fear that I would be unable to fulfil the requirements of my post—to develop interactions with disabled children in order to understand their social worlds.

(S1–15/5/97)

The outcome of this situation was that we were, at first, only able to tap into adult versions of the reality of life in the school. The most prominent message coming from the staff was contained in this comment:

These children don't think like us, it's impossible to know what they are thinking. Our children have severe difficulties communicating and if our children's machines break down then, unlike us, they can't see the cause and effect. They don't understand why it has happened and that until it is fixed it won't work again. They have no concept of the continuum ...

(S1–15/5/97)

Some children were dependent on machines to communicate (e.g. speech board), others employed them to move round the school (e.g. power chair) or as a means of entertainment (e.g. power scooter). This teacher believed that the children did not understand how their machines worked and therefore, that they lacked certain cognitive abilities.

One of our aims, on entering the school, was to discuss issues of informed consent, confidentiality and so forth with the staff and children (Alderson 1995; Morrow and Richards 1996; Alderson and Morrow 2004). We explained these issues to the staff. However, they appeared to reject the premise that the children would know what was going on. They seemed concerned that we understood that the children's impairments made them 'not like us'. The staff appeared to challenge our idea that we should explain the research to the children; we were reminded of Wax's (1971) comments that people will often try to re-socialize the researcher. It seemed clear that the staff were attempting to influence John's views and have him believe that these children were incapable of thinking for themselves.

John felt immense pressure to conform to their view that communication with these children would be troublesome due to their cognitive difficulties. This made us very aware that children's lives do not occur in a sociological void (Qvortrup 1994; James et al. 1998). John's experience helped us to understand the structural influences on children's everyday lives and chimed with Bourdieu's idea of habitus:

> It is in the relationship between the two capacities which define the habitus, the capacity to produce classifiable practices and words, and the capacity to differentiate and appreciate those practices and products (taste), that the represented social world i.e., the space of life styles, is constituted.
>
> (1986: 17)

Bourdieu suggested that social identity is defined and asserted through difference and that individuals and groups recognize how they are different from other individuals and groups. He indicated that the perception of difference involves a dialectic between conditions of existence (based on the distribution of capital) and habitus (the capacity to produce and appreciate practices). He argued that not only is it possible to differentiate people on a structural level in terms of economic capital but that different groups attribute cultural capital to certain behaviour and that they vie to impose their definition of which social phenomena constitute legitimate behaviour (see Davis 1996 for an explanation of this concept in relation to children's participation in sport and PE, and Connolly, this volume).

A homogeneous view of disability and childhood

We were conscious that there were similarities between the way that the adults appeared to label the children and Piagetian notions of the naturally developing child prominent within literature that was concerned with the medicalization of childhood (see Alderson 2000; Watson and Shakespeare 1998; Davis and Watson 2002 for further discussion of this link). Both notions (medical and psychological) pathologize children who do not achieve universally standardized developmental targets, seeing disability as the consequence of impairment. They show little awareness of the possibility that disability and a lack of ability to meet targets associated with developmental stages may have social and cultural roots. There appears to be a preoccupation with differentiating children on the basis of their impairments, 'measuring children's bodies and minds against physical and cognitive norms' (Priestley 1998: 208–9).

Prior to our study in the late 1990s images of disabled children had tended to emerge in studies that were preoccupied with issues of care and that involve narratives of dependence, vulnerability and exclusion (Watson and Shakespeare 1998; Priestley 1998). Such studies tended to describe disabled children as a homogenous group, over emphasize the structural context of childhood disability, make much of the link between disability and poverty, and yet only rarely discuss issues such as gender (Humphries and Gordon 1992; Lewis 1995; Middleton 1996; Norwich 1997; Priestley 1998). Our use of the social model of disability, by contrast, enabled us to move beyond notions of disabled children as medically defined unchanging individuals.

In keeping with this work, therefore, it would have been easy to paint a picture of the special school as simply creating structures of oppression. For example, the staff explained that the children came to the school from different local authority areas and had to travel distances. Each of these authorities had its own policy and practice concerning when and how the children were 'dropped off' in the morning and 'picked up' from school in the afternoon. The school policy was that each child should be toiletted before leaving for home. This meant that the staff had to organize the children to go to the toilet prior to the end of the school day. This process took not only half an hour out of the school day, it also meant the children were rarely given a choice about when they went to the toilet in the afternoon and how they governed their own bodily practice (see also Mayall 1994 in relation to children in general).

Indeed, we were aware that the staff's view of the children conflicted with our own social model perspective. It appeared to us that some staff had a 'them' and 'us' discourse concerning the children which could often be employed to justify practices that limited their opportunities (Davis and Watson 2002).

Many writers have suggested that disabled children are prevented from developing social skills and self-confidence because their lives are controlled by other people (Morris 1997; Norwich 1997; Alderson and Goodey 1998). Though there is much evidence to support these perspectives, they are generalizations of children's lives that do not investigate disabled-children's capacities to develop complex and multiple identities and to take action to confront the stereo-typical views that professionals hold about them (Davis and Watson 2002; Priestly 1998).

Indeed traditional social model perspectives which have characterized the social world as structurally and materially determined tend not to incorporate an understanding that disabled children may be capable of affecting the structures surrounding their lives and re-negotiating the structures they encountered (see Connolly this volume). It is possible to conclude that there was little awareness in both the medical and social models of disability of the fluid and diverse nature of children's lives (Davis and Watson 2002, Watson and Shakespeare 1998).

During the ethnography we were encouraged by the comments of one member of staff (Laura, a senior teacher) to consider whether different adults and children behaved in different ways:

> Like you wonder if someone like Jordan says a phrase that he's been taught or if he means it or if he is reproducing a set response, or Bobby he has his box with buttons to press for replies but if he's trying to tell you about home he may press the button for his address and rather than say 'I know where you live' you have to ask 'What is it about home?' The problem is that some of the less travelled staff don't look for the signs, they don't realise that the child is complaining about something or saying No. Like Scott when he shakes his fist they think he's being aggressive and he's not.
>
> (S1–20/8/97)

This account differentiated between the children on the grounds of their impairment related cognitive and communication abilities and between the staff on the grounds of their interpretation skills. Laura's views concerning 'less travelled staff' suggested that how the adults interpreted the children's behaviour depended on their cultural background which related to their prior experience and preconceptions. It appeared that adults who were not reflexive about their interpretations missed the significance of the children's behaviour, and thus denied their ability to initiate meaningful communication.

What is reflexivity?

Callaway (1992) tells us that reflexivity opens the way to a more radical consciousness of self, that it is a mode of self-analysis and political awareness. Hertz, in agreement, suggests that reflexivity is achieved 'through detachment, internal dialogue and constant (and intensive) scrutiny' of the process through which the researcher constructs and questions his/her interpretations of field experiences (Hertz 1997: vii).

This approach requires ethnographers to put their preconceptions and prejudices to fruitful use (Okely 1975; Campbell 1995). How people respond to the ethnographer's presence is examined in order that ethnographers can learn about the differences between their cultures and the cultures of those they study (Okely 1975; Wax 1971; Agar 1980). That is, ethnographers learn about others by comparing their own values to those of the people they interact with (Campbell 1995; Marcus and Fischer 1986; Geertz 1973).

In sociology it has been argued that the engagement of researcher and subject is a meeting of two languages (the meta-language of the sociologist and the everyday language of those he/she studies) and that this requires the sociologist to question how their academic knowledge influences their interpretations of others (Giddens 1976). However, this position does not take account of the personal culture of the researcher. That is, it does not emphasize the fact that the way the research communicates with people and reacts to the everyday occurrences of the research setting is in some way dependent on the values they have acquired, which may have little to do with academia, during their life course.

In the 1990s we believed there to be at least two languages at work in the head of the ethnographer. The first was the language/culture of his/her academic paradigm, the second the everyday language/culture based on the ethnographer's personal history. We defined the ethnographer's role as questioning the influence of both their academic and personal preconceptions on the processes of interpretation. Since that time our views have become more complex and we now see people's identities as a complex fusion of a range of social, biological, political, cultural and personal factors (Davis and Watson 2002). We believe that ethnographers should explain the relationship between the knowledge they develop within their final texts and their own identity. This explanation should include a discussion of their own relationship to events they portray (Crapanzano 1986; Prat 1986). This approach is neither 'navel gazing' nor 'narcissism'; rather it enables the reader to understand the ethnographer's experiences within the context of an ever-changing and fluid research setting (Okely 1992).

In this project the reflexive process took place both in the field, as John interacted with people in a variety of situations, and in the office when we, as a team discussed John's experiences. This occurred on a daily basis over the phone and during our weekly meetings where we considered his field notes. Team work reinforced the rigorous nature of the ethnographic process – not only did the ethnographer have to question his own interpretations but he had to take account of the interpretations of the research team.

As we have demonstrated, part of this process involved our prior academic preconceptions becoming evident and we were forced consistently to reconsider our own beliefs. This subsequently led us to write a number of papers that challenged disability studies to demonstrate more awareness of the complex identities included within 'disabled childhood' (Davis and Watson 2002; Davis and Corker 2001) and to critique notions of social inclusion within childhood studies (see for example Davis 2007; Tisdall et al. 2006).

Moving beyond boxes to diverse identities

We had, at first, homogenized the behaviour of the adults who worked in the school. But by analysing what staff said about specific children and the meanings that they attributed to children's behaviour, we were able to differentiate between the staff and build up a complex picture of the relationships between children and staff as well as between staff and between children. Therefore, the very process of gaining access was employed as a research tool (Wax 1971) and the impact of the researcher on the research setting was analysed as a source of cultural meaning (Okely 1975). By analysing the effect of John's presence on the research setting, as recommended by Campbell (1995), we discovered a great deal about his and our own cultural assumptions.

At first we found ourselves differentiating between the children on the basis of their communication techniques. Moreover, John found himself spending more time with those children who could (verbally or through signs) answer yes and no to questions. He began to set up in his mind a hierarchy based on his perception of the abilities of the children. The process of gaining access to the school and learning to communicate with the children meant that he himself was attributing more status to those children, who were easier to talk to (verbally or non-verbally).

This lesson was crucial in the case of the relationship between the researcher and Scott, one of the boys at the school. At first John had been unable to understand the meaning of his interactions with Scott. However, he was able to employ the everyday situations created by the structure of the school day to learn how to communicate with him. John began to get to know Scott, for example, by asking him questions about his home life during breaks in the class. Scott responded to his questions by shaking his fist or nodding his head. John attended a signs and symbols class where he worked with Scott gluing pictures onto A4 paper to make a picture story and during this class Scott spoke about his family. John realized that Scott had chosen not to speak to him and that he had previously mistakenly interpreted Scott's behaviour as meaning Scott could not communicate. This realisation came about because John attended the school on a daily basis which enabled him to interact with the children in a number of different educational settings.

Making mistakes, as Agar (1980) observes, can be fruitful in terms of creating opportunities for ethnographers to learn about the people they are studying. Agar (1980) also suggests that ethnographers should realise that when a person withholds their opinion it does not necessarily mean they do not have an opinion. By spending more time with Scott John was able to overcome his initial misunderstanding. It was clear from the work with Scott that he understood the rules of social behaviour and that he was in fact a mature competent person capable of offering the researcher his views (Mackay 1991; Alderson 1995).

It is important that this perspective is not set aside by those who work with disabled children and that they recognise children's ability to withhold access to their world (Mandell 1991). Even those writers from developmental psychology who show some awareness of debates concerning social aspects of disability tend to make a simplistic distinction between social and medical causes and ignore the agency of children when discussing, for example, 'developmental language delay'. Lewis and Kellet argue, for example, that it is important 'that as researchers we think carefully about how we talk about disabled children' (2004: 191). They make reference to the difference between (big) **D** deaf people who are born into Deaf culture and (small) **d** people who are not. Yet they show no awareness of the political context of oralism and the decades of discrimination that Deaf people have faced from oralists within educational systems. This becomes important when they argue, for instance, that we should consider behaviours that are primary and secondary 'to the disability' when looking for causes of developmental language delay, arguing that such delay may be linked to a child living away from their family (presumably in hospitals, respite settings or residential schools). Whilst this may be a reasonable assumption, Lewis and Kellet (2004: 191) somewhat underplay the possibility that some disabled children and adults may not view a lack of oral language as a 'problem' and that they may choose not to speak by way of symbols and signs for social, cultural or political reasons. Lewis and Kellet's lack of acknowledgement of the political context of disability is not surprising as they do not come from academic paradigms where issues of emancipation and reflexivity are at the core of discussions (e.g. disability studies or anthropology).

Indeed, although many writers promote the need for researchers to understand the diverse identities of disabled children, they do not move beyond the rhetoric to put this discourse into practice. In the main, simplistic medical or social categories are still used to differentiate between children and children's own categories of difference are ignored.

Norwich (1997) points out that disabled children are able to both ignore the negative influences on their lives and to challenge negative stereotypes of themselves. Writers such as Thomas (1978); Lewis (1995); Middleton (1996); Morris (1997); Norwich (1997) and Alderson and Goodey (1998) do make attempts to differentiate between disabled children/childhoods by way of social structural categories such as race, class and gender rather than by impairment. However, these studies tend to create new homogenized sub-groupings. That is, they define children by adults' rather than children's indicators of difference and they fail to recognize the fluidity of differences within groups of children of the same, class, gender or race.

Christensen and Prout argue that when doing research with children we should suspend our 'taken for granted notions about the differences and similarities between children and adults' (2005: 56). Similarly, our findings highlight the need to suspend taken-for-granted notions from developmental psychology concerning the competency of disabled children, often made from short one-off assessments (Davis and Watson 2000; Davis 2006). In our case we had originally intended to carry out participant observation in the school over eight weeks starting in mid May. In the end, despite starting on time, we worked in the school for over six months until mid December and carried out home observations and interviews into the New Year. Our observations took longer because there was a need to investigate the process of disabled children's lives, to investigate whether children who have experience of the same institutions, impairment, regime of care, therapy, etc. subscribe to different values or react, on a daily basis, in different ways to the same situations. Simply seeing them for a day or a week was not long enough to understand the politics of their world.

Despite our general agreement with social model perspectives we had not wanted to begin with pre-set sociological categories such as disabled–non-disabled; rather, we aimed to differentiate between children in terms of their own everyday experiences. This aim was strengthened by the work of a small number of authors during the 1990s who had been able to illustrate a variety of different childhoods from children's own perspectives (e.g. Levin 1994; Glauser 1990 and Ritala-Koskinen 1994).

Our initial aim was to study the experience of disabled children, taking seriously their role as social actors negotiating their own social worlds. Over time this broadened to include an understanding of how these negotiations were influenced by the variety of adults in the school. This process involved comparing the teachers' initial assertions that the children 'do not think like us' with the more nuanced view of Laura, cited above, which differentiated between groups of staff and children.

This experience reminded us of Agar's (1980) advice that researchers should be aware that what respondents tell them at first may be a generalization of their beliefs which contrasts with their actual behaviour and that it is usual, at times, for some informants' views to be incompatible with the interpretations of other informants and the ethnographer.

Learning languages

We realised that the process of learning how to communicate with the children would take time and that, as the ethnography unfolded, this task would require the adoption of imaginative fieldwork roles and constant reflexivity. That John had to learn a number of unwritten, rarely verbal, languages could have been a galling task; however, we drew strength from Campbell's (1995) work with the Wayapi people of the Brazilian rain forest. Campbell taught us that it is possible to learn an unwritten language:

> No dictionaries, no grammars; and no training in how to go about this most mysterious of all learning procedures. I had no idea what I was up against, what to look for, whether it would even be possible to 'learn the language' at all. Could there be such a thing in the world as a language that was impossible to penetrate? No there isn't. The bafflement of Babel is accompanied by the miracle of translation. Wherever languages find each other, time and again the astonishing processes of translation begin to grow. It didn't come easy for me though.
>
> (Campbell 1995: 34)

Campbell was aided in his task by Waiwai, the non-authoritarian head of the group he lived with. Whilst travelling, Waiwai taught Campbell the language:

> Three days just ambling back the way the four of us had come. I'd walk behind Waiwai . . . Waiwai would cut leaf after leaf and get me to shout its name. I'd try to write as we walked along and try to think up some way of remembering what the leaf looked like. This was his way of teaching me the language: learn the words for all the leaves . . . As a botanical lesson it was hopeless for me, but it was as good a way into the language as any, getting a feel for the phonemes and the word structure.
>
> (Campbell 1995: 21)

John's most helpful teacher was Rose, the speech therapist. She taught him that most of the children understood his language and where they did not – for example, children with hearing impairments – she taught him a form of sign language. The main task, therefore, became to learn how the children communicated their responses. This process was easiest with children who used some speech and had similar interests to John. For example, two boys, Douglas and Bobby, enjoyed football: discussions about different teams and various players enabled John to learn, very quickly, their way of communicating. In contrast, Lucy appeared not to employ recognizable signs. She had nipped John quite viciously on several occasions when he was sitting next to her. He thought this might be of significance until a teacher said that Lucy's behaviour was a reflex action. However, on a later occasion he was discussing Lucy with Rose and she said: 'The way into Lucy is to comment on her appearance, she takes that very seriously'. John realised that his gender had been affecting his inter-actions with the children; as a man he had guessed which subjects interested Bobby and Douglas, yet he had failed to identify what Lucy's interests might be.

Over the next few weeks John commented on Lucy's appearances, the way she looked each day, her make-up, nail varnish and clothing. At first Lucy never seemed to respond with a recognizable sign when John talked to her, yet she stopped nipping him. John was encouraged by this change. Eventually, Lucy started responding to his questions with a grimace for no and a smile for yes. This enabled John to discover what food she wanted for lunch, which staff she liked and what activities she enjoyed.

When we discussed this as a team we realised that this confirmed the anthro-pological view that access to a culture is contingent on negotiating the meaning of everyday cultural artefacts – in this example nail polish/clothing, in Campbell's example, leaves. Central to this negotiation was John's role of 'fashion commentator' which changed the nature of John's interaction with Lucy. Thus, John adopted a number of research roles within the school which had complementary and contrasting meanings. Rose's suggestion enabled John to temporarily bridge the gender divide and begin a long process that eventually led to Lucy leading the research interaction.

Bourdieu's idea of habitus has been interpreted as a process of socialization and cultural reproduction (James et al. 1998). However, if we accept the position of James et al. (1998) that children are capable of transforming cultural and social relations, then Bourdieu's notion of habitus becomes less rigid, allowing the possibility that children's social worlds are characterized by constant cultural and social negotiation.

We drew an understanding from this interaction that the social world of the school was fluid and that this fluidity, in part, could relate to the manner in which different groups interacted. Here, we built on the belief that, at the heart, childhood culture is 'a form of social action contextualized by the many different ways in which children choose to engage with the social institutions and structures that shape the form and process of their everyday lives' (James et al. 1998: 88). This fluidity was very evident in the different ways the children enabled John to take up different research roles.

Research roles: Friend/mediator/entertainer

A number of authors have discussed the role an adult should employ when researching young people. Roles such as: non-authoritarian adults (Mandell 1991; Fine 1987; Corsaro 1985); 'friends' (Fine and Sandstrom 1988); 'least adults' (Mandell 1991); and detached observers (Coenen 1986; Damon 1977), are recommended on the basis that they provide the researcher with the opportunity to interact with children.

Similarly, other authors have stressed the need to employ different research tools when working with children. Though we were interested in developing new research tools to aid the process of communication, in the end, we did not employ any pre-prepared 'child centred' or structured activities (Mauthner 1997). In keeping with James (1995), we recognized that the children we worked with had different competencies and experiences. In this setting this meant John was unable to employ techniques such as 'draw and write' (Pridmore and Bendelow 1995) or structured focus groups (Alderson 1995; Hoppe et al. 1995) or ask the children to make tape recordings (Mahon et al. 1996).

Core to this work is a concern to alter the power relations between adults and children in order that the researcher can gain access to children's worlds (Morrow and Richards 1996; Mayall 1994) and that researchers should help children to self empower (Alderson 1995; Morrow and Richards 1996; Ross and Ross 1984), whilst understanding their emotions (Levin 1994) and recognising their fears (Beresford 1997). However, as work by Davis (2000); Hill et al. (2004); Davis and Hogan (2004) indicate 'participation' has many meanings and children can participate in different ways during processes when projects are planned, carried out, evaluated, written up and disseminated.

Through our previous research we were aware of the ethical considerations, the variety of research roles and the plethora of research tools which might be employed to work with children and enable their voices to become evident. However, we believed that these techniques could not be applied universally to all children and therefore, that they should be questioned reflexively during the research process (see Davis 1998). Indeed, the fluid nature of the research process made this more explicit when a variety of adults and children invited John to carry out contrasting roles such as Friend/Mediator/Entertainer and Authoritarian/Non-Authoritarian/Helper.

Friend/Mediator/Entertainer

The staff encouraged John to take part in play activities such as ball throwing, card games of snap, dressing up, parachute games and relay races which enabled him to adopt a playful friend role. However, it should be noted that this process often involved other adults and positioned John as playing for, rather than with, the children.

John developed a particularly fruitful relationship with a boy called Bobby. Bobby would respond to questions by saying 'aye' and no and using signs. John learnt that Bobby employed various ways of saying 'no' and 'aye' which had different meanings. He also learnt that some staff had difficulty communicating with Bobby, that this led them to fail to comprehend the meaning of Bobby's actions and that, in some way, this was due to their tendency to undervalue (not attribute capital to) his behaviour (Bourdieu 1986). Over time Bobby began to ask John to translate when he wanted to speak to certain members of staff. However, John was concerned about the power relations involved in this process and therefore usually encouraged Bobby to speak or sign for himself. Towards the end of the project we came to understand how problems with the interpretative process led to conflict between Bobby and some members of staff (in this example, concerning the discussion of the result of a football match, the member of staff is Sharon):

John: *{Bobby and I are crossing the room, Sharon, an assistant and Rangers supporter, starts speaking to us}.*

Sharon: Well John, did you see the game last night? *{Rangers had played Celtic the previous evening}*

John: Aye, a wis there. Av almost lost ma voice shouting so much.

Sharon: Bobby, did you watch the game last night?

Bobby: Aye.

Sharon: *{looking at me as if to say, 'I don't believe him, watch this, I'll catch him out'}* Who won then?

Bobby: *{Puts his hands in the air and gets frustrated}* uh, uh, uh, *{like he's trying to spit something out but he just can't}*.

Sharon: See he doesn't know. *{Said in a triumphal way to me, then whispers, even though Bobby still can hear her}* A don't think he really knows what's going on, A really don't think he understands.

John: *{Bobby is really 'pissed off' with this and shakes his hands and head. I'm sure he watched the game because he spoke to me in signs earlier. Also I think he's finding it difficult to answer her question because the game was a draw and he can't say that word. He looks like he's going to give up, that he doesn't think he can make Sharon understand. I've had enough of Sharon so I decide to intervene.}*

John: Na na. I don't agree Sharon, a think he knows.

Bobby: Aye, aye.

Sharon: So what was the score? [still with disbelief]

John: Look a know that he doesn't usually watch the football but am sure he seen this game. Ay Bobby, now you tell me with signs, how many did Rangers score?

Bobby: *{Puts one finger up}*.

John: *{Without confirming he's right}* and how many did we *{Celtic}* get?

Bobby: *{Puts up one finger.}*

John: So the score was one one?

Bobby: Aye *{said with triumph and gestures at Sharon with his hand as if to say so there}*.

John: And which team were lucky?

Bobby: *{Really laughing at the assistant because she's a Rangers supporter, he uses a word I've rarely heard him speak}* Isss *{us}*.

Sharon: *{With a Damascus type conversion tone in her voice}* That's really good Bobby, a nivir realized that.

(S1–25/11/97)

This incident demonstrates the importance of closely attending to the children's ways of communicating and also the everyday politics of ethnographic observation. Some writers in developmental psychology write about observation as if it is a politically neutral activity (e.g. Tudge and Hogan 2005: 108).

This position has been criticized within disability studies because of the way that developmental psychologists and others in the medical professions have exploited disabled adults and children for their own career ends (see Davis 2000 for further discussion). In the case above, John takes a political stance and attempts to contribute to the circumstances through which Bobby can empower himself. John employs his knowledge of Bobby's communication methods to ask questions structured in a form which Bobby preferred and could respond to. He helps Bobby to get his message across, a role which could potentially have brought John into conflict with Sharon. However, his reward for taking this chance was to make Bobby happy. His friendship role with Bobby and his politics of disability forced him to question the legitimacy of Sharon's interpretation. In this way, John's relationship with Bobby contrasted with the authoritarian role which was expected of him by some staff and children in other situations.

Authoritarian/non-authoritarian adult/helper role

Particularly in a school setting an additional adult is often expected to help with supervision and surveillance of the children. John's reluctance to play this role stemmed from our perspective that it might alienate him from some of the children. However, John was placed in a very difficult position by the music teacher Margaret during a class which involved three boys called Scott, Douglas and Jordan:

John:	*{Douglas Jordan and Scott are in the music class. Scott is banging the drum when it's not his turn}*.
Margaret:	No! Scott! *{shouting}*.
Douglas:	That's not funny Scott.
Scott:	*{Shakes his fist at Douglas in disagreement but also laughs}*.
John:	*{Scott continues to bang the drum when Margaret doesn't want him to}*.
Margaret:	[*To me*] Would you hold Scott's hand until it's his turn to do it?
John:	*{I'm horrified. I don't just grab his hand}* Scott, shall I hold your hand? [I put my hand out and he doesn't stop me holding his left hand]
Margaret:	[*Insistently*] No! The other hand.
John:	I'm getting there, I rather thought I'd let Scott get used to me before putting the cuffs on.
Scott:	[*Laughs and lets me lightly hold the hand with the beater*].
John:	[*I decide not to hold his hand all class. I let his hand go, after which Scott only occasional tries to hit the symbol when it's not his turn. On these occasions I say,* 'Is it your turn?' *and he stops*].

Later Margaret talked to John about the boys:

Margaret:	Jordan, sometimes you want to just give him a boot, Scott just won't behave but Douglas's good at picking the different sounds higher and lower, not that that's what I'm teaching.

(S1–3/9/97)

In this example, the teacher demands that John take an authoritarian role by controlling Scott's hands. John voices his concern and waits to see if Scott will consent to him holding his hands. His decision was based on our ethical perspective that children should be able to choose whether or not to interact with ethnographers. The teacher becomes very impatient with this approach and chastises John for not acting quicker. Although John controls Scott's actions, Scott does not appear to mind. During this occurrence John's role changes from controller to that of coercer when he keeps saying 'Is it your turn?'. That is, he stops controlling Scott's body and tries to encourage him to follow the teacher's rules. John is put in a very difficult situation. Refusing to help the teacher might compromise his position in the school with the staff, but carrying out her wishes might alienate him from Scott. His decision was to ask Scott's permission but it is difficult to know if, in doing so, he was really giving Scott a choice.

Interestingly in the above example, Douglas sided with the teacher and in a later music class he asked John to hold Jordan's hands when he was beating a drum out of time. This experience enabled John to differentiate between the children who conformed to the staff's wishes and those who did not. Moreover, it demonstrated that this member of staff, the music teacher, did not employ empowering techniques to encourage Scott to participate in the class.

We learned from these events that John, by playing close attention to the requests made of him by children and staff, could identify individual children's and adults' perceptions of him and therefore, contrast their everyday values and expectations with his own. This enabled us roughly to group the adults and children on the basis of how they interacted with John. Again, by discussing this occurrence in our weekly meeting, we were able to allow these events to guide the next stages of the research process. A number of questions were identified for John to follow up; for example, why did a specific child ask John to do the same things as other adults in a classroom setting? Did Scott recognize John as different to the music teacher or had this incident led to Scott viewing John as possessing an authoritarian role?

An opportunity arose to clarify this later question a week after the music class incident. Scott and a number of other boys had just finished their lunch. One boy, Jason, suggested John put Bobby's splints on. John, realising the situation provided an opportunity to gain an insight into how the children viewed him, asked the children if they thought he should do this. Scott, through the use of signs, indicated that this was not John's role but the role of the occupational therapist, a teacher and an auxiliary who were all standing towards the far end of the room. Scott clearly did not associate John's role with that of other adults in the school. His view contrasted with the perception of Jason who believed John should put on Bobby's splints and Douglas in the music class above who asked John to hold Steven's hands. This suggested to John that some children were happy to accept the authoritarian role of adults whereas others were not. Importantly, it exposed the myth that in this school these children could not make choices with regard to their everyday lives.

Our research aim, to be reflexive about John's research roles, required him and us to question why certain roles made him feel happy, uncomfortable, nervous, etc. This process was especially important in a research setting where there were a number of different adult and child expectations concerning the researcher's role. Indeed, John's experience was comparable to that of Mandel (1991) who was forced into a variable role which juggled the expectations of adults and children. John needed to be flexible and he was forced to become aware that associating himself too closely with one cultural grouping might alienate himself from children and adults who possessed a different idea of what constituted acceptable behaviour. In keeping with the ideas of Wax (1971) and Agar (1980) the flexible negotiation of John's roles became a tool for understanding the cultures of those he interacted with.

In Bourdieu's (1986) terms John became acutely aware of how different social actors attributed cultural capital to different social practices, how they made judgements about their own and other people's behaviour. This led us to criticize Bearison's (1991) expectation that the researcher's role should be to represent children's voices but not to judge children's words. The ethnographic process involved John constantly making judgements and interpretations. What was important was that we questioned John's role in this process and that this inquisitorial stance also enabled us to understand the processes through which different children and adults judged each other's capabilities within the school. We would argue that at different times the ethnographic process is negotiated in different ways by the children and, therefore, that it is extremely fluid.

Conclusion

As is evident from the examples given in this chapter different adult cultures had, in contrasting ways, a structuring effect on the children's lives. The children were well aware of the need to adapt their behaviour to certain adults and to the different settings of their everyday lives. They were aware (just as we researchers discovered) that adults can close off or open up opportunities for children to make their own choices and yet, that in some way they construct their own childhoods.

Thus, neither adults nor children are homogeneous groups, and both actively create their own cultures within a set of pronounced cultural and structural constraints. In the 1990s a great deal of time was spent discussing the relationship between agency and structure. However, in recent years we have come to view the social world as a fusion of biological, cultural, individual and social influences. The structure versus agency divide is now viewed as simplistic and a number of authors have sought to replace it with metaphors from the vegetable patch including roots and onions (see Prout 2005 and Davis 2007):

> This root metaphor appears to view the world as one large mess of fibre optic cable where messages are transmitted and received along old and new pathways. An alternative way to view the social world is as a soft yet organically complex onion (personal correspondence Stephen Farrier 2006).

This enables us to value the organic aspect of the root metaphor but also to consider the potential for unintended leakages, openings and exchanges between the different layers, locations and communication pathways within the social world that we inhabit (In the science field some of these leakages might relate to the concept of 'osmosis').

(Davis 2007)

In this chapter, we have highlighted the benefits of employing ethnographic fieldwork as a means of researching children because it enables this more organic story to emerge. Ethnography provides researchers with an opportunity to carry out participant observation with children which allows for the emergence of detailed understandings of their everyday interactions and cultural meanings (Davis 1998; James and Prout 1990). The ethnographic process results in the ethnographer being confronted by conflicting ethical issues on a daily basis. We have also described how our project involved the children making their own decisions about whether to participate in the research process. We have described how we as researchers became sensitized to this decision-making.

We have told a partial story about how one ethnographer, through being reflexive, learned about different children's lives. Central to this approach was our ability to analyse the meaning of the roles, tools and ethical stances employed during the project. This has enabled us to conclude that children's researchers do not always have to use techniques like draw and write (indeed we have a feeling that these can often be used unreflexively). There is much to be gained from utilizing the everyday cultural artefacts and structural processes of children's social worlds.

The use of such an approach has enabled us to challenge the perception that disabled children are not capable of social action, and to argue that the social worlds of disabled children are as fluid as that of other social actors. By following Okely's (1975) assertion that ethnography does not involve a separation of fieldwork and analysis and Prout's (2005) belief that we must not create a false dichotomy between the social, cultural and biological – we are able to conclude that when certain authors represent the structural and material aspects of childhood (for example Qvortrup 1994), they should be asked to explain how these factors are negotiated, resisted and reformed by different individuals and groups (whether they be children or adults) on a daily basis.

Acknowledgements

In the earlier version of this chapter we thanked Mairian Corker, and the editors for their comments on earlier drafts of the paper. Sadly, Mairian Corker died on 22 January 2004 aged 51 – she is much missed.

Note

1 This chapter draws on the Life as a Disabled Child project which was part of the Economic and Social Research Council's (ESRC) Research Programme: Children 5–16 Growing Into the 21st Century Program. The project was carried out at the Universities of Edinburgh and Leeds.

References

Agar, M.H. (1980) *The Professional Stranger*, New York: Academic Press.

Alderson, P. (1993) *Children's Consent to Surgery*, Buckingham: Open University Press.

Alderson, P. (1995) *Listening to Children: Children Ethics and Social Research*, London: Barnardo's.

Alderson, P. (2000) *Young Children's Rights: Exploring Beliefs, Principles and Practice*. London: Save the Children/Jessica Kingsley.

Alderson, P. and Goodey, C. (1998) *Enabling Education: Experiences in Special and Ordinary Schools*, London: Tufnell Press.

Alderson, P. and Morrow, V. (2004) *Ethics, Social Research and Consulting with Children and Young People*. Ilford, Essex: Barnardo's.

Bearison, D.J. (1991) *They Never Want to Tell You: Children Talk about Cancer*, Cambridge: Harvard University Press.

Beresford, B. (1997) *Personal Accounts: Involving Disabled Children in Research*, Norwich: Social Policy Research Unit.

Booth, T. and Booth, W. (1996) 'Sound of silence: Narrative research with inarticulate subjects', *Disability and Society* 11: 55–69.

Bourdieu, P. (1986) *Distinction*, London: Routledge.

Callaway, H. (1992) 'Ethnography and experience: Gender implications in fieldwork and texts', in J. Okley and H. Callaway (eds) *Anthropology and Autobiography*, London: Routledge.

Campbell, A.T. (1995) *Getting to Know Waiwai: An Amazonian Ethnography*, London: Routledge.

Christensen, P. and Prout, A. (2005) 'Anthropological and sociological, perspectives on the study of children', in S. Green and D. Hogan (eds) *Researching Children's Experience. Approaches and Methods*. London: Sage.

Crapanzano, V. (1986) 'Hermes' dilemma: The masking of subversion in ethnographic description', in J. Clifford and G.E. Marcus (eds) *Writing Culture: The Poetics and Politics of Ethnography*, Berkeley: University of California Press.

Coenen, H. (1986) 'A silent world of movements: Interactional processes among deaf children', in Cook-Gumperez *et al.* (ed.) (1986) *Childhood Research*.

Connolly, P. (1998) *Racism, Gender Identities and Young Children*, London: Routledge.

Corsaro, W. (1985) *Friendship and Peer Culture in the Early Years*, Norwood, N.J: Ablex.

Damon, W. (1977) *The Social World of the Child*, San Francisco: Jossey-Bass.

Davis, J.M. (1996) *Sport for All?* PhD.: University of Edinburgh.

Davis, J.M. (1998) 'Understanding the meanings of children: A reflexive process', *Children & Society* 12 (5).

Davis, J.M. (2000) 'Disability studies as ethnographic research & text: Can we represent cultural diversity whilst promoting social change?', *Disability and Society* 15 (2): 191–206.

Davis, J.M., (2006) 'Childhood studies and the construction of medical discourses: Questioning attention deficit hyperactivity disorder; A theoretical perspective', in G. Lloyd, J. Stead and D. Cohen (eds) *Critical New Perspectives on ADHD*, London: Taylor & Francis Publishing.

Davis, J.M. (2007) 'Analysing participation and social exclusion with children and young people. Lessons from practice', *The International Journal of Children's Rights* 15.

Davis, J.M., Watson, N., Cunningham-Burley, S. (2000) 'Learning the lives of disabled children: Developing a reflexive approach', in P. Christensen and A. James (eds) *Research With Children*, London: Falmer.

Davis, J.M. and Watson, N. (2000) 'Disabled children's rights in every day life: Problematising notions of competency and promoting self-empowerment, *International Journal of Children's Rights* 8: 211–28.

Davis, J.M. and Corker, M. (2001) 'Disability studies and anthropology: Difference troubles in academic paradigms', *Anthropology in Action* 8 (2): 18–27.

Davis, J.M. and Watson, N. (2002) 'Countering stereotypes of disability: Disabled children and resistance', in M. Corker and T. Shakespeare (eds) *Disability and Postmodernity*, London: Continuum.

Davis, J.M. and Hogan, J. (2004) 'Research with children: ethnography, participation, disability, self empowerment', in C. Barnes and G. Mercer (eds) *Implementing the Social Model of Disability: Theory and Research*, Leeds: The Disability Press.

Fine, G.A. (1987) *With the Boys*, Chicago: University of Chicago Press.

Fine, G.A. and Sandstrom, K.L. (1988) *Knowing Children: Participant Observation with Minors*, California: Sage.

Geertz, C. (1973) *The Interpretation of Cultures*, New York: Basic Books.

Giddens, A. (1976) *New Rules of Sociological Methods*, London: Hutchinson.

Glauser, B. (1990) 'Street children: Deconstructing a construction', in A. James and A. Prout (eds) *Constructing and Reconstructing Childhood*, London: Falmer.

Hertz, R. (1997) 'Introduction', to Hertz R (ed.) *Reflexivity and Voice*, London: Sage.

Hoppe, M.J., Wolls, E., Morrison, D., Gillmore, M. and Wilson, A. (1995) 'Using focus groups to discuss sensitive topics with children', *Evaluation Review*, 19, 102–14.

Hogan, D. (2005) 'Researching the child in developmental psychology', in S. Green and D. Hogan (eds) *Researching Children's Experience*, London: Sage.

Hill, M., Davis, J., Prout, A. and Tisdall, K. (2004) 'Moving the participation agenda forward', *Children & Society* 18 (2): 77–96.

Humphries, S. and Gordon, P. (1992) *Out of Sight: The Experience of Disability 1900-1950*, Plymouth: Northcote House.

James, A. (1995) 'Methodologies of competence for competent methodology?', *Youth 2000 Conference*, Guildford.

James, A. and Prout, A. 'Contemporary issues in the sociological study of childhood', in A. James and A. Prout (eds) (1990) *Constructing and Reconstructing Childhood*, London: Falmer.

James, A. Jenks, C. and Prout, A. (1998) *Theorising Childhood*, Cambridge: Polity Press.

Levin, I (1994) 'Children's perceptions of their families', in J. Brannen and M. O'Brien (eds) *Childhood and Parenthood: Proceedings of the International Sociological Association Committee for Family Research Conference*, London: Institute of Education University of London.

Lewis, A. (1995) *Children's Understandings of Disability*, London: Routledge.

Lewis, V. and Kellet, M. (2004) 'Disability', in S. Fraser, V. Lewis, S. Ding, M. Kellet and C. Robinson (eds) *Doing Research With Children and Young People*, London: The Open University/Sage.

Lewis, A. and Lindsay, G. (eds) (2000) *Researching Children's Perspectives*, Buckingham: Open University Press.

Mackay, R.W. (1991) 'Conceptions of children and models of socialisation', in F.C. Waksler (ed.) *Studying the Social Worlds of Children: Sociological Readings*, London: Falmer.

Mahon, A., Glendewams, C., Clarke, K. and Crais, G. (1996) 'Researching children: Methods and ethics', *Children & Society*, 10: 145–54.

Mandell, N. (1991) 'The least adult role in studying children', in F.C. Waksler (ed.) *Studying the Social Worlds of Children: Sociological Readings*, London: Falmer.

Marcus, G.E. and Fischer, M.J. (1986) *Anthropology as Cultural Critique*, Chicago: University of Chicago Press.

Mauthner, M. (1997) 'Methodological aspects of collecting data from children', *Children & Society* 11: 16–28.

Mayall, B (1994) 'Children in action at home and school', in B. Mayall (ed.) *Children's Childhoods Observed and Experienced*, London: Falmer.

Middleton, L. (1996) *Making a Difference: Social Work With Disabled Children*, Birmingham: Venture Press.

Morris, J. (1991) *Pride Against Prejudice: Transforming Attitudes to Disability*, London: Women's Press.

Morris, J. (1997) 'Gone Missing? Disabled children living away from their families', *Disability & Society* 12 (2): 241–58.

Morrow, V. and Richards, M. (1996) 'The ethics of social research with children: An overview', *Children and Society* 10: 28–40.

Norwich, B. (1997) 'Exploring the perspectives of adolescents with moderate learning difficulties on their special schooling and themselves: Stigma and Self-perceptions', *European Journal of Special Needs Education* 12 (1): 38–53.

Okely, J. (1975) 'The self and scientism', *Journal of the Anthropology Society of Oxford*, 6: 171.

Okely, J. (1992) 'Anthropology and autobiography: Participatory experience and embodied knowledge', in J. Okely and H. Callaway (eds) *Anthropology and Autobiography*, London: Routledge.

Okely, J. (1994) 'Thinking through fieldwork', in A. Bryman and R.G. Burgess (eds) *Analysing Qualitative Data*. London: Routledge.

Priestley, M. (1998) 'Childhood disability and disabled childhoods: Agendas for research', *Childhood* 5 (2): 207–23.

Prat, M. (1986) 'Fieldwork in common places', in G.E. Marcus and J. Clifford (ed). *Writing Culture: The Poetics and Politics of Ethnography*, Berkeley: University of California Press.

Pridmore, P. and Bendelow, G. (1995) 'Images of health: Exploring beliefs of children using the 'draw-and-write technique', *Health Education Journal*, 54: 473–88.

Prout, A. (2005) *The Future of Childhood: Towards the Interdisciplinary Study of Children*, London: Falmer Press.

Qvortrup, J. (1994) 'Childhood Matters: An Introduction', in J. Qvortrup *et al.* (eds) *Childhood Matters: Social Theory, Politics and Practice*, Aldershot: Avebury.

Ritala-Koskinen, A. (1994) 'Children and the construction of close relationships: How to find out the children's point of view', in J. Brannen and M. O'Brien (eds) *Childhood and Parenthood*, London: Institute of Education, University of London.

Ross, D. and Ross, S. (1984) 'The importance of the type of question', *Pain*, 19: 71–9.

Thomas, D. (1978) *The Social Psychology of Childhood Disability*, London: Methuen.

Tisdall, E.K.M., Davis, J., Hill, M. and Prout, A. (2006) (eds) *Children, Young People and Social Inclusion: Participation for What?* Bristol: Policy Press.

Tudge, J. and Hogan, D. (2005) 'An ecological approach to observations of children's every day lives', in S. Green and D. Hogan (eds) *Researching Children's Experience*, London: Sage.

UPAIS/Disability Alliance (1976) *Fundamental Principles of Disability*. London: Methuen.

Watson, N. and Shakespeare, T. (1998) 'Theoretical perspectives on disabled childhood', in C. Robinson and K. Stalker (eds) *Growing Up With Disability*, London: Jessica Kingsley.

Wax, R.H (1971) *Doing Fieldwork: Warnings and Advice*, Chicago: University of Chicago Press.

Woodhead, M. and Faulkner, D. (2000) 'Subjects, objects or participants? Dilemmas of psychological research with children', in P. Christensen and A. James (eds) *Research With Children*, London: Falmer.

12 Entering and Observing in Children's Worlds

A Reflection on a Longitudinal Ethnography of Early Education in Italy

William A. Corsaro and Luisa Molinari

Introduction

In this chapter we evaluate theoretical and methodological issues in conducting longitudinal ethnographies of young children. We do this by reflecting on and examining field entry and data collection in the initial phase of our joint study of children's transition from preschool to elementary school in Modena, Italy. The following vignette based on field notes from the first author's (Corsaro's) earlier research in Bologna, Italy, serves to introduce the goals of our discussion in this chapter.

> Several years ago I returned to a preschool in Bologna, Italy, several months after completing a year-long ethnographic study of peer culture there. The anticipation of my return had been peaked by an exchange of letters with the children and teachers. Upon my arrival I was greeted by the children and teachers who presented me with a large poster upon which they had drawn my image and printed: 'Ben Tornato, Bill!' (Welcome back, Bill!). After handing me the poster the children swarmed around me, pulled me down to my knees and each child took a turn embracing and kissing me. In the midst of the jubilation I noticed a few new faces – 3-year-olds who had entered the school during my absence. One or two of these little ones shyly came up to touch me or to receive a kiss.
>
> Later in the day after the commotion had settled, I was sitting at a table with several children who were playing a board game. I noticed a small boy, who I later learned was named Alberto, eyeing me from a distance. He finally came over and asked: 'Sei Bill, veramente?' ('Are you really Bill?'). 'Yes, I'm really Bill,' I responded in Italian. Alberto, smiling, looked me over for a few seconds and then ran off to play with some other children.

One important aspect of the vignette for our discussion is the nature of Bill's relation to the preschool children and his participant status in the local peer and school cultures. The children's jubilant marking of Bill's return to the school was certainly related to the length of his absence – absence does indeed make the heart grow fonder. However, the closeness of Bill's relationship with the children went well beyond the joy accompanying the return of an old friend. Several ethnographers of children have pointed to the importance of developing a participant status as an atypical, less powerful adult in research with young children (Corsaro 1985, 1996, 2005; Fine and Sandstrom 1988; Mandell 1988; Mayall and Davis, Watson and Cunningham-Burley, this volume). As we shall go on to show, in this case Bill's very 'foreignness' was central to his participant status. His limited competencies in the Italian language and his lack of knowledge of the workings of the school led the children to see him as an 'incompetent adult' who they could take under their wings to show the ropes. They also saw his initial communicative difficulties with the teachers, and discovered that they were better at educating him about things than their teachers were. Thus, the children claimed him as one of their own, telling their parents: 'We can talk to Bill and the teachers can't!' Word of this *'famoso Bill,'* as one parent referred to him, quickly spread to the children's families.

A second important aspect of the story, which we draw out from this is its capturing of the importance of longitudinal ethnography for theory generation in the sociology of childhood. Recent theoretical work in this area is critical of traditional theories of socialization and child development for their marginalization of children. Traditional views focus on individual development and see the child as incomplete – as in the process of movement from immaturity to adult competence. The new approaches eschew the individualistic bias of traditional theories and stress the importance of collective action and social structure. In line with these new theoretical views, we have offered the notion of interpretive reproduction (Corsaro 1992, 1993, 2003, 2005). From this perspective we argue that the whole time children are developing individually, the collective processes that they are a part of are also changing. These processes are collectively produced by children and adults in the many interwoven local cultures making up children's lives. Sociologists need to address these collective processes developmentally or longitudinally and to document the nature of children's membership in these local cultures and their changing degrees or intensities of membership and participation over time and across social institutions. Longitudinal ethnography is an ideal method for such a theoretical approach, particularly when it aims to both document children's evolving membership in their culture (Lave and Wenger 1991) and when focused on key transition periods in children's lives. Bill's return to the school was his first attempt to extend the longitudinal design of our research toward this ideal.

Let's return to our story to consider the richness of longitudinal ethnography. Bill did not simply return to his field site and renew his research. Traces of his continued presence were sketched by the children and teachers in their reflective talk about their past experiences with him. The memories and emotions evoked by these informally occasioned discourses were deepened and intensified by a series of more focused activities: their reading and discussing of letters and cards sent by the researcher; their construction and enjoyment of a gift from him (a Halloween mobile of swaying jack-o-lanterns, witches, spiders, and ghosts along with a description of the wondrous but foreign children's holiday symbolized in the mobile); their composition of letters and art work to send to Bill; their discussion and anticipation of his return; and their construction of the poster to commemorate the 'homecoming'. A version of these discourses and activities was also produced in Bill's world – in his discussions in his family, with his colleagues, with his students, and in his research reports.

We argue that the homecoming did not mark the beginning of a new phase of a longitudinal study, but rather a continuing evolution of the researcher's membership in this group. In turn, the documentation of and reflection on this evolution is of central theoretical importance for grasping both cognitively and emotionally the nature of the children's evolving membership in the local peer and school cultures of this educational institution. Thus, we see the inextricable connection of theory and method in ethnographic research.

Finally, there is the ending of our story and the young boy, Alberto. In his interactions with his peers and teachers over the course of his first year, this mysterious Bill had become somewhat of a legend to Alberto. Thus, Alberto, being somewhat of a doubting Thomas, desired direct confirmation of his status. Alberto's interest in and fascination with Bill illustrates how the participant status of the ethnographer becomes embedded in the network of personal relations of those he or she studies over time in longitudinal research. Although Alberto needed to confirm the reality of Bill's existence, he was very much influenced by what he had learned about him from the other children. For example, he quickly seized on and relished in Bill's status as an incompetent adult. A few days after Bill's return several children were telling him about something that had occurred during his absence. The story had to be halted and repeated several times because Bill had trouble understanding. During the last retelling, Alberto joined the group and threw up his hands laughing: '*Ma uffa! Bill. Lui non capisce niente!*' ('Oh brother! Bill. He doesn't understand anything'). It becomes somewhat easier to empathize with the lower status of children in society when, as an adult, one finds oneself the butt of successful teasing at the hands of a 3-year-old.

The following sections of this chapter parallel the three main points of our introductory story: (1) entering the field and developing a participant status with the children and teachers in the preschool; (2) documenting our evolving membership in the local cultures in this setting; and (3) identifying and participating in the priming events which prepare the children for their coming transition to elementary school.

Field entry, acceptance, and participant status

Field entry is crucial in ethnography because one of its central goals as an interpretive method is the establishment of membership status and an insider's perspective (Corsaro 1996, 2003; Rizzo et al. 1992). In research in educational settings with young children these goals depend on dealing with and developing the trust of a range of adult gatekeepers; acquiring working knowledge of the social structure, nature of interpersonal relations, and daily routines in the setting; and gaining the acceptance of the teachers and children.

Dealing with gatekeepers

Our research in the *scuola dell'Ìnfanzia* was based on what Schatzman and Strauss have called 'mutually voluntary and negotiated entrÈe' in that our hosts (the director, teachers, and parents) held 'options not only to prevent entrée but to terminate relations with' us at almost any point thereafter (1973: 22). Because these adults had varying degrees of control over our access to the research site and the activities of the children, we refer to them as gatekeepers (Corsaro 1985).

The collaborative nature of our research was of clear importance in negotiations with gatekeepers. We had worked together on several earlier studies and pooled our data on observations in the Italian *asilo nido* (for 1 to 3-year-olds, Luisa Molinari) and the *scuola dell'Ìnfanzia* (Bill Corsaro) to study the emergence and extension of peer culture among Italian preschool children (Corsaro and Molinari 1990; Molinari and Corsaro 1994). In the present study, Luisa negotiated field entry with the director of the preschool, the first grade principal, and the preschool and first grade teachers. Together we presented our research aims and described the study to parents and later presented interim reports of initial findings to the teachers, parents, and interested members of the community. Luisa's knowledge of the preschool and elementary school systems in Modena (she is the mother of three young children who are at various points in these systems) was essential in developing initial rapport with the gatekeepers and in navigating through the bureaucracy of early education in Italy.[1]

An obvious question arises here: why didn't Luisa, who was native to the culture and this region of Italy, conduct the ethnographic research? Aside from the fact that Bill had a great deal more experience as an ethnographer of young children, there is another (perhaps more important) reason for our collaboration in this way. The ethnographer's acceptance into the world of children is especially difficult because of obvious differences between adults and children in terms of cognitive and communicative maturity, power, and physical size. As noted earlier, however, Bill's 'adult incompetence' helped in overcoming many of these obstacles to becoming accepted and drawn into children's everyday lives in his earlier work in Bologna. In fact, we would argue that one of the strengths of cross-cultural ethnographies of children is that the foreign ethnographer is often seen as a less threatening adult by children and youth (see also Berentzen 1995; Wulff 1988).[2]

Acceptance and participant status in the peer culture

Bill's initial days in the *scuola dell'Ìnfanzia* in Modena were a new challenge for him. For the first time he entered a preschool setting where he was the only true novice. In past research he had entered schools at the start of the term and at least some (if not all) of the children were, like him, new to the setting. Furthermore, in this instance he was not only entering the group at the midpoint of the school year, but almost all of the children and teachers had already been together for two and a half years. This fact coupled with his 'foreignness' led many of the children and adults to be very curious about him during his first days at the school.

Bill was introduced to the children by the teachers as someone from America who was going to come to the school often until the end of the year in June. As he had done in past research Bill's main strategy of entering the children's culture was to move into play areas, sit down and let the children react to him (see Corsaro 1985, 2003). Several of the older and more active children in the group (Luciano, Elisa, and Marina) often told Bill what was happening and generally took charge of him during the first few weeks. They escorted him to the music and English classes, and Bill overheard them making references to his presence to children in the other 5-year-old and the 4-year-old classes and reporting that: 'Bill would be a part of their class'.

Over the first week at the school Bill also got to know all the other children as he participated in a number of activities. For example, during his second day at the school he was seated next to a girl, Sandra, during morning snack. After they finished a snack of sliced apples, Valerio began handing out candy that he had brought as a treat to the other children. Bill was a bit disappointed that Valerio did not offer him a piece of candy, rather passing him by and handing one to Sandra and then moving on to the other children. Sandra said she did not like the kind that Valerio gave her and Bill suggested she ask him to exchange it. When Valerio had finished passing out the candy, Sandra called him over and asked for a chocolate candy and Valerio gave it to her and took back the fruit candy. Sandra smiled at Bill, clearly happy with this outcome. Bill smiled back even though he still had not received any candy.

This incident captures the complexity of field entry. Even though Bill had been trying hard to escape the usual form of adult/child relationship at the school, in this instance he was clearly put in his place as an adult. Bill's failure to be included in the sharing of the sweets was no doubt related to Valerio's perception of the uncertainty of his participant status in the routine (i.e., the sweets were usually only shared with other children). However, Bill's support of Sandra's attempt to get a particular flavour of candy did send the message that he was not a typical adult and that he was aware of subtle negotiations among peers in the routine.

Before long Bill was drawn more fully into peer activities. Later in his first week at the school he joined a group of boys who were playing with building materials. Consider the following example drawn from field notes.

Example 1
February 13, 1996

Renato, Angelo, Mario, and Dario are playing with plastic, grooved building materials. They hand me some of the materials and ask if I can get them apart. I accept this task willingly, but soon realize that the pieces are stuck together much tighter than I realized. In fact, I first push with all my might with no success. One of the teachers, Giovanna, now walks by, laughs, and says the children have found a practical use for me. I now realize that many of the pieces have probably been stuck together for a long time. Just about the time I am about ready to give up, I try holding one piece on the edge of the table with the other hanging over the edge. I push hard and the pieces pop apart. Angelo and Renato yell: 'Bravo Bill!', and then immediately hand me several more pieces. I easily separate the first two with my inventive method, but then I run into trouble again as several pieces will just not budge. Meanwhile the boys are copying my method with some success, so I keep at it. I then notice that Angelo and Mario are gathering up all the separated pieces and are putting them back in the box. They tell several other children that Bill got them apart, but they are not to play with them. I wonder about this. Are they afraid that they will just get stuck back together again? In any case I continue working on what has become an unpleasant task until to my relief I hear Giovanna say it is time to clean up the room.

Over the course of Bill's first month in the classroom the children drew him more and more into their activities. One day in early March as the children were finishing the morning snack in the hallway outside the classroom Valerio asks, *'Bill dì rosa'* ('Bill say pink'). Bill says pink and Valerio says, *'Cacca rosa!'* ('Poo-poo rosa!'). All of the children laugh uproariously at this 'poo-poo' joke. Carlotta now quickly repeats the routine asking Bill to say a different colour with the same resulting laughter and although Bill laughs along with the children, he is also a bit uncomfortable because several teachers are nearby.

We have discussed in earlier work how the mere mention of 'poo-poo' and 'pee-pee' is part of the humour of preschool children (Corsaro 1985). In this case, the children were not only trying to be funny, but also testing Bill to see how he would react. A few days after this incident, Bill was sitting at a worktable with several children and Renato suddenly jumped up and said, 'Watch Bill'. He then did a little dance and sang his personal version of a famous Italian song: *'Italia sì! Italia no! Italia cacca!'* ('Italy, yes! Italy no! Italy poo-poo!'). This time Bill was laughing as hard as the other children who witnessed this hilarious performance for in this instance, Renato's performance was funny well beyond the reference to poo-poo.

Bill's experience with the sweets, his helping of the children with the building materials, and his later inclusion in the 'poo-poo' jokes captures a period in which he was part of a range of transitory rituals that adults often must go through to be accepted into the peer world of young children. In the example of the sweets Bill's status as something other than a typical adult was still unclear to the children. Later the children grew accustomed to Bill entering into their play, coming down to their physical level by sitting on the floor with them, and by not directing their activities and intervening in disputes. In the example with the building materials Bill was accepted into the play as a peer, but his adult skill in being able to break apart the tightly wedged blocks was appropriated by the children. The last example of the poo-poo jokes was a test of Bill by the children because adults would often disapprove of such talk as silly and inappropriate. Bill's initial discomfort and then genuinely positive reaction to Renato's creative performance helped him to develop a sense of trust and acceptance in the children's peer culture.

A review of field notes over the first months reveals many other instances where Bill was gradually drawn into the children's activities. On one occasion, Valerio had brought some sunglasses to school and several of the children commented on and asked to wear them. Bill also asked to try them on and when he removed his own glasses to do so, Valerio took them from his hand, put them on and shouted, 'Look I'm wearing Bill's glasses!' Angelo, quickly grabbed them from Valerio, put them on, and began stumbling around the room to show that everything now looked blurry through the lenses. Several other children wanted a turn and Bill cautioned them to be careful with the glasses. Eventually Bill got his glasses back and began cleaning away the children's fingerprints with a special cloth he had to polish the plastic lenses. Valerio then asked to use the cloth to clean his sun glasses, embellishing the process by first spitting on the lenses. Although Bill preferred the dry cleaning method, he did not protest and Valerio asked to use the cloth several other times that day. Later in the day Luciano asked if he could use the cloth to clean his real glasses. Bill said fine but told him there was no need for spit.

In this example we again see how adult researchers can find themselves uneasy in their participation in children's peer culture. Bill had some fear that his glasses could be damaged in the play, and therefore cautioned the children to be careful. Also because the cloth for the glasses was for dry (not wet) cleaning, Bill restricted the use of the spit cleaning method, a restriction which also demonstrates the adult researcher's different view of body excretions compared to that of children.

After his first month at the school Bill noticed in a review of his field notes that most of the children had actively taken notice of him, included him in their play, and even teased him about his poor Italian. Reflecting on the notes he realized, however, that a few children seemed a bit shy around him and one girl in particular, Irene, had not yet spoken to him. This situation was about to change, however, as captured in the following excerpt from field notes taken a few days after his own review.

Example 2
March 7, 1996

This morning we are taking a field trip to see an art exhibit at a museum in the centre of the city. As we leave to go out to the bus I have Valerio's hand. Renato also asks to take my hand, but he then notices that Irene is alone and asks for her hand. Irene refuses, backing away from Renato and the group. As we walk toward the bus, Irene comes up and takes my other hand, Renato than takes Valerio's. Valerio lets go of my hand and Irene and I are left as a pair. When we reach the bus door I let go of Irene's hand as she moves onto the bus and I stand at the door with the teachers as all the children enter. When I get on the bus I see that Irene has saved me a seat next to her and I take it. I am a bit surprised by Irene's interest in me this morning because she is one of a few children who have acted a bit shy of me or at least uninterested in being around me. Now today she seems to have made up her mind to be my partner on the trip. On the bus ride Irene says little, but does tell me about other field trips the group has taken this year when I ask her about them. Throughout our entire time at the museum Irene stays close to me and again sits next to me on the bus ride back to the school. As we enter the school she seems very happy.

A few days after the field trip Bill had to alter his normal observational schedule at the school and spend a Monday at the University in Bologna. When he arrived at the preschool the next Tuesday morning several children ran up to him yelling, 'Hi Bill!' and called out to the others that he had arrived. A few minutes later at snack, Irene was sitting next to Bill and she asked what he did in Bologna. Bill was surprised at this, but then remembered he had told the teachers that he was going to Bologna. From Irene's question Bill took it that she or one of the other children had asked where he was. As Bill was thinking about all this, Irene asked why he went to Bologna and he responded that he had to go and talk to his friends at the university. It was clear that his missing one day of his normal schedule had been noticed by the children, and they had come to see him as part of the everyday routines in their class.[3]

As described earlier, the children quickly picked up on Bill's limited competence in Italian. They laughed at his accent and mispronunciations and took great joy in correcting him. One morning after Bill had been observing in the school for around five weeks the teacher, Giovanna, was reading a chapter of the *Wizard of Oz* to the children. After about ten minutes of reading and discussion, Giovanna was called away to answer a phone call and so she handed Bill the book suggesting that he continue reading the story. Aware that it would be a difficult task for Bill, the children yelled and clapped thinking this was a great idea. Bill immediately ran into trouble trying to pronounce the word for 'scarecrow' which in Italian is '*spaventapasseri*'. The children laughed and hooted at his stumbling over this and other words. Some children even fell from their seats in pretend hysterics at his predicament and his problems were made even worse given that there seemed to be a 'scarecrow' in every other sentence. To Bill's relief Giovanna returned and, when asked how he did, the children laughed and said he could not read well. Sandra yelled out, 'We didn't understand anything!' Giovanna then took the book back from Bill, but the children shouted: 'No, we want Bill to read more!' Taking the book back, he struggled through another page amidst animated laughter before handing the book back to Giovanna saying, 'Basta così, adesso' ('That's enough for now').

There are two aspects of the children's response to Bill's problems with the language that were different from his earlier experiences in Bologna. First, in Bologna he observed a large mixed age group where there was wide diversity in the children's literacy skills and although the Bolognese children were introduced to reading and writing, it was not a central part of the curriculum. In this group of 5-year-olds in Modena, lessons and activities related to reading and writing were now everyday occurrences in these last months of their last year in the preschool. Although they laughed at his errors, they realized Bill could read and they identified with his problems to some degree. Second, the children in Modena were also studying English and they realized that Bill was competent in this foreign language which was very difficult for them. In short, it was reassuring to them that this new adult in their midst shared some of their same experiences and challenges.

Acceptance and participant status with teachers

Giovanna and Carla, the two main teachers in the classroom we studied, had been working together for over ten years. They were interested in our transition project and expressed an eagerness to participate when we talked with them and the director before Bill began his observations. They were, as any teachers would be in such a situation, sensitive to Bill's presence in their classroom over the first weeks of observation, but were put at ease somewhat by his quick acceptance by the children, his frequent presence, and his commitment to experience life in the school from the children's perspective. The teachers noted in interviews at the end of the study that an adult male researcher who sings and dances with the children and gets down on the floor to play with them is not seen as threatening for long. Yet they did wonder what Bill was writing in his notebook and often found his descriptions of what he thought about the activities in their classroom to be a bit vague. In a later interview Giovanna noted she hesitated at times in raising her voice with the children (a not uncommon occurrence in most Italian classrooms) in Bill's presence. However, she also said that after a few weeks Bill became like a piece of furniture, a taken for granted participant in the setting.

Several events that occurred during Bill's first six weeks in the school capture his gradual acceptance as an everyday member of the local culture. The first was his acceptance of the role of '*Mago dei boschi*' ('The wizard of the woods') in a play the teachers performed for the children on February 20 which was Fat Tuesday, the celebration of Carnivale. Bill was aware of the play, *The Lambs and the Wolf*, because he had heard the teachers talking about it and observed them practising for the performance on several occasions. On the day before the scheduled performance Giovanna and Carla had left the classroom for a dress rehearsal while Bill remained in the room with the children during their English lesson. A few minutes later, one of the teachers from the 3-year-old class came in and motioned for Bill to come out to the hallway. She and another teacher from the 4-year-old group asked Bill to be the wizard noting that the only male in the school (an assistant teacher in the other 5-year-old group) was playing the part of the wolf. Bill saw Giovanna and Carla standing to the side smiling and surmised that they had volunteered him for the role. He was assured he would have no lines to speak and only had to tap the dead wolf (who was slain for his misdeeds by the lambs' mother) with a magic wand. Bill quickly accepted and a few minutes later successfully carried out his limited role in the rehearsal, receiving a loud ovation from all the teachers.

On several occasions the teachers delighted in testing and teasing Bill about his problems with Italian. This testing sometimes occurred when the children included Bill in various learning activities. In one instance the children were shown several objects. The objects were then put in a bag and the children were asked to reach in without looking, select an object and identify it. The children enjoyed this task and after every child had had a turn, Carla asked Bill to reach in the bag. She knew of course that he could easily identify the objects, but she also knew that he may not know the Italian word for many of them. Bill got hold of a can opener and immediately realized he was in trouble. He stuttered a little and then said in Italian, 'It's a thing to open things.' Carla and Giovanna laughed loudly and one child, Sandra, who was always quick to pass judgement shouted: '*Ma Bill È un apriscatole!*' ('But Bill it's a can opener!').

In a final example the children were having a English lesson in which they were attempting to learn the song 'Twinkle, Twinkle Little Star' in English. The English teacher first had the whole group of children sing the song in Italian and then went through it line by line with them in English. He then divided the children into groups of four and asked them to sing the song in English, assigning a grade from 1 to 10 for their performance. Although Bill thought the children did pretty well, the English teacher, Joseph, was a tough grader and no group scored above a 4. After each group had had a turn, Giovanna suggested Bill sing the song in English. He did so perfectly and Joseph gave him a ten. 'Now sing it in Italian', requested Giovanna. Bill pleaded to have the children sing it again so he could listen closely and they did so. Bill started out pretty well in his Italian rendition, but stumbled over several words, stopping after two lines. Giovanna and the children laughed loudly and Joseph shouted out Bill's grade: '*Sotto zero!*' ('Below zero!').

Overall, these examples involving the teachers, like earlier ones when the children teased and tested Bill, capture the subtle ways in which the ethnographer and participants collectively define and produce the ethnographer's participant status in the local cultures of the research setting. Language is often a particular arena for this collective process, with the lack of full linguistic competence working against the frequently perceived higher status of the ethnographer in a positive way such that it enables informants and participants to test, to reflect on, and to develop more fully their cross-cultural relationship with the ethnographer.

Becoming an active member of the group

After field entry and acceptance into the 5-year-old group, Bill became a regular participant in everyday and special activities and in this section we reflect on Bill's evolving membership in the group.

Participating in everyday routines

After several weeks in the school Bill found that he was often invited into play activities by the children. Consider Example 3.

Example 3
March 4 Free Play Outside

After meeting time the children start free play inside the school, but it is a nice day and Giovanna says they can go outside if they like. Some children go to get their coats as an assistant teacher, Patriza, is going outside with them. Renato asks me to come out, so I go to get my coat. When I get outside I see that it is mainly boys who have come out. They are climbing in the bars and running around. At one point Dario, Renato, and Valerio gather some sticks and place them on the ground under the climbing bars. They protect their sticks from the others. There is then some discussion of fire, and I suggest that Indians start fires by rubbing sticks together. Renato and Valerio decide to try this, but Dario says I do not know what I am talking about and it won't work. Several other boys join us and they all now begin to gather grass and leaves and place them with the sticks. They start to stir the leaves with the sticks and Dario says they are making salad. Shortly after this we are called back inside by Giovanna.

In this example Bill is invited into the play and at one point suggests an activity relevant to the ongoing activity. He is by no means given any special status in the play and, in fact, Dario rejects Bill's claim about being able to start fire with the sticks. Another example captures the children drawing Bill into their artistic activities.

Example 4
March 5 Painting

Giovanna and Carla were working on an art activity with seven children. The work was in line with a long-term project involving the children's thinking about light and dark, and it involved each child selecting a picture of a sunrise or sunset which had been clipped from a magazine. They then pasted the picture onto a larger sheet of art paper. The next step was to mix the colours and paint the blank page so that it blended with the magazine picture in the middle. Giovanna and Carla joked with each other encouraging the children who were working with the opposite teacher to select the more demanding magazine pictures. I was very impressed with the teachers' patience in their instructing the children on how to match the colours and the children's paintings. Despite the complex subtleties of many of the purple, pink, and violet hues of the sunrises and sunsets, it was very difficult to even discern the embedded magazine pictures in many of the children's paintings. Having little artistic ability, I felt very inadequate watching this activity. I was also envious of the children, begrudging the limited exposure I had had to art as a child. Later I moved over to another part of the room where Luciano and Sandra were painting with water colours. This was 'disegno libero' ('free painting') and was less complex than the project work. Yet the pictures the children were painting were very impressive. They had drawn houses, trees, flowers, grass, etc. in outline with a pencil and now were painting them in. They also used Kleenex to blot the paint on in some instances, creating a nice effect. They had surely been shown this trick by the teachers. I tell the children I am not so good at painting and did not go to preschool. Luciano says, 'But Bill it's easy!' He hands me a brush and instructs me to paint a small section of grass at the bottom of his picture. I accept this offer willingly and do a good job. But it is only a bit of grass – I could not produce a painting like Luciano's or Sandra's even with a good deal of practice.

We can see from this example the easy acceptance of Bill by the teachers and children – the teachers joking with one another demonstrated their high degree of comfort in going about their work in his presence. It was also apparent that Luciano and Sandra did not see Bill's admission of incompetence in painting as remarkable. Rather comfortable in their own everyday artistic work of this type, they easily included him into the activity.

Certification as a member of group 5b

As we discussed earlier, the group Bill observed in the *scuola dell'Infanzia* was one of two 5-year-old groups and there was also a group of 4- and 3-year-olds. Given that the 5-year-olds had been at the school for nearly three years, these children and their parents where very well known by all the teachers and many of the younger children. Thus, Bill was part of one of the most high status and visible groups in the school.

Bill's group was known as the '5bs'. After only a few days at the school, he noticed that both the teachers and the children in the other groups came to see him as a member of the 5bs. The 5b children certainly helped with this association. In situations when children from the various groups came together for joint activities children from the 5b group would often call out: 'Bill belongs to us!'. The children were also very sensitive to the correct pronunciation of Bill's first name. There was some tendency on the part of children from the other groups and other teachers to refer to Bill as 'Billy', thus transforming his name to fit the common Italian pattern of names ending in a vowel sound. The children especially relished correcting the music teacher and a substitute teacher in the 5b class who frequently made this error with the admonishment: 'Non Billy, Bill!'

The following example of the 'grass war' captures a dramatic confirmation of Bill's membership as one of the 5bs.

Example 5
April 18 La Guerra Dell'Erba (The Grass War)

The outside yard has been freshly mowed with cut grass laying all around. Some of the girls (Elisa, Carlotta, and Michela) begin gathering the grass and take it to an area under the climbing structure where they make a bed. At one point, Michela and then others lay down on the bed and say: 'Che morbido!' ('How soft it is!'). Several other girls enter the play, but Elisa, Carlotta, and Michela control the activity. The new recruits are allowed to bring grass, but not place it on the bed.

Later, Carlotta returns to say that one of the boys from the other 5-year-old group at the school hit her while she was gathering grass. The other girls become upset and decide to go get the boy. The girls march over carrying grass, come up behind the boy, and pummel him with the grass. The girls then run back to the climbing structure and celebrate their revenge – especially Carlotta who is all smiles. Eventually the boy gets a few of his friends and they come by and throw grass at the girls. The girls chase after the boys who are outnumbered and take the worst of it in another exchange of grass throwing.

The grass war now escalates with girls and boys on both sides becoming involved. In fact, all but a few of the 5-year-old group (5b) I am observing are now in the grass war. The war continues for some time until Marina suggests to the children in our group that they make peace. Marina with several children behind her marches up to the boy who hit Carlotta and offers her hand in peace. The boy responds by throwing grass in Marina's face. Marina returns to the group, and Carlotta says: 'They don't want peace!' But Marina says she will try again. The second time she offers her hand the boy throws grass again, but over the objections of another boy who is in his group. Marina stands her ground after being hit with the grass. The second boy pulls his friend aside and suggests they make peace. The other boy is against the proposal, but eventually agrees and the two then shake hands with Marina. Marina then returns to our group and declares: 'Peace has been established!' The two groups now meet for a round of handshaking. I also exchange handshakes with the kids from the other 5-year-old group who identify me as part of the opposing group.

In this episode the children from 5b appropriate objects from the adult world and use them to create an innovative pretend play routine, a creative activity which gives the children a shared sense of control over their social environment. The intergroup conflict between the two 5-year-old groups is both related to, and further develops, the strong solidarity within the 5b group and later the peace negotiation, symbolically marked by handshakes, demonstrates the children's awareness of a sense of community in the school. Bill's inclusion in the handshakes confirmed his place in this community.[4]

Participating in special events

Bill's participation extended to joining in the preparations for activities during grandparents' day and the two visits to the elementary school, both of which occurred in May, and culminated in the end-of-the-year school party in late June, an event which was always eagerly anticipated by the children and parents. However, this year's party was even more special because it would mark the end of the children's and their families' time at the school. Preparations occurred on two fronts. A small group of the most active parents encouraged all the children's parents, siblings, and grandparents to attend, enlisted volunteers to order and serve pizza and other refreshments, and collected funds to purchase gifts for the teachers. In the school the teachers and children were also busy. The teachers constructed small diplomas for the children and worked with the children on a group portrait. The last project involved the children drawing individual self-portraits which were then pasted onto a large group picture. The teachers then made a photocopy of the group picture and had it printed on Tee shirts for the children, teachers, and Bill who were all to wear these shirts at the end of the year party.

The children also practised several dances that they were to perform at the party and in these Bill had a key role because one of the songs danced to was a favourite of many American children, 'The Hokey Pokey'. Because the words were in English it was Bill's job to repeat the words while demonstrating the appropriate movements in the dance. The children and teachers loved this. Not only is it very funny to hear someone say and see someone 'Put their backside (and many other body parts) in and shake them all around', to the children it was especially funny to see Bill doing this. Additionally, one of the teachers, Carla, continually made an error in pronouncing 'Hokey Pokey' as 'Honky Tonky'. Bill corrected her trying to explain as best he could in Italian that Honky Tonky was a particular genre of music. Carla on the other hand thought he was just correcting her pronunciation. This incident is interesting because it was a reversal of roles – the teachers often had to correct Bill's Italian. He realized now that some of their corrections no doubt also went beyond mere pronunciation.

The big night of the party arrived. The children, teachers, and Bill showed off their Tee shirts, the parents loved the dancing (especially the Hokey Pokey), the children received their diplomas, and the pizza was great. The parents presented the teachers with very elegant wrist watches and they generously gave Bill a beautiful beach towel. After the ceremonies, gifts, and pizza we all played games. The first thing the parents wanted to try was the Hokey Pokey!

Identifying and participating in priming events

Earlier we discussed the concept of interpretive reproduction. We argued that this perspective stresses the importance of children's participation in collective processes with adults and peers in the local cultures which signify that one is part of a group. In these, certain cultural practices and routines prepare or prime members for future changes. Priming events – as we propose to call them – involve collective activities in which children, by their very participation, attend prospectively to ongoing or anticipated changes in their lives. Priming events are crucial to children's social construction of representations of temporal aspects of their lives (including important life transitions) because children's social representations do not arise from simply thinking about social life, but rather through their collective, practical activities with others (Corsaro 1990, 2005). In the *scuola dell'infanzia* we documented both formal priming events in which the children were clearly conscious of how the activities were related to their coming transitions to first grade and subtle priming events where awareness was less apparent as the activities were embedded in recurrent routines in the preschool (Corsaro and Molinari 2000, 2005; Molinari et al. 1998). Here we briefly consider some direct and other more subtle priming events in both the school and peer culture and their importance when conducting research with children.

Priming in the preschool curriculum

The most obvious priming events in the school curriculum for the children's transition to elementary school were the planned group visits in May to the nearby elementary school. Bill accompanied the children and teacher on two visits to the school. The first visit involved inspecting the art, science and music labs, the playground area, the gymnasium, and the cafeteria. In the second visit the fifth grade teachers took the children to their classrooms. In September the children would join one of four new first grade groups that would be taught by the fifth grade teachers. In this way they got to meet their teachers and see their future classrooms. However, what was most interesting about visiting the fifth grade classrooms was how excited the fifth graders were. The big kids took the preschoolers under their wings and took them to their desks, showed them their work, and told them all about their class and their teachers. The preschoolers loved all this attention from the older kids and, in turn, the older kids experienced these visits as a priming event preparing them for leaving school and the teachers with whom they had been working for the last five years.

One point we want to stress here is that the school visits served as priming events not only for the children, but for the researchers as well. Although arrangements had been made for our future research in the elementary school by Luisa in a prior meeting with the principal, we had not yet met the teachers or visited their classrooms. Thus, in these visits Bill, together with the children, met the school principal, the children's future first grade teachers, and became familiar with the classrooms and activities. During the visits he shared with the children a glimpse of their future schooling and the next phase of our longitudinal ethnography.

Priming in the peer culture

Although adults and children are often consciously aware of their participation in priming events, as we saw in our earlier discussion of the school culture, some priming activities have more subtle effects. In the peer culture these are often embedded in recurrent routines in which the focus is on peer concerns and values. In the following example we see how priming occurs in peer discussion and debate and the involvement of the researcher in these routines.

Example 6
April 2 The Hair Debate

A debate develops between Marina and Sandra. Sandra insists a doll with little hair (an infant) must be a boy because it has short hair. Marina disagrees and says when children are babies sometimes both boys and girls have short hair. But Sandra disputes this claim, and some children side with Marina and some with Sandra. Marina then points to the shelf where the children's personal books (which document the children's time in the school) are stored and asks me to reach up and get hers down. She says 'Grazie Bill', as I hand her the book. She then turns to a page where there is a picture of her when she was about one year old and she does not have much hair. 'See', she says to Sandra, 'this is me and I had short hair then'. Sandra now says, 'Hai ragione' ('You are right'), and the issue is settled.

Marina's use of Bill in this episode is interesting because she relies only on his size which enabled him to get the book down. She did not ask Bill for support for her position and did not assume he knew anymore than the children about the disputed topic. Theoretically, the episode is very interesting in several respects. It shows how the children take an element of the adult school culture – the existence of these books that they have created about their experiences in the school over the three years and use it to address an issue in the peer culture.

Subtle priming events also occur within peer culture when children spontaneously practise and evaluate literacy skills introduced in school projects (like those related to the *Wizard of Oz* we discussed earlier) in everyday peer activities. For example, in the last several weeks of school, the children would frequently print words (most especially their names and names of friends) into their drawings during *disegno libero*. They would also evaluate each other's skills (especially pointing out errors) and, on occasion, challenge each other to come up with new words or to write in cursive.

About this same time, however, the children also began to ask Bill to print things into the notebook he used to record field observations. The children were very aware of this book and in the first weeks often asked to see it and sometimes draw pictures in it. In the last six weeks or so, they frequently printed their names or certain words with their drawings. Consider Example 7.

Example 7
June 6 Printing Names

I am sitting at a table with Renato, Luciano, and Dario who are drawing pictures. Marina comes and joins us. She colours my hand with a purple marker and then she prints my first and last name in my notebook: BILL (in blue) CORSARO (in green) ... Carlotta now joins the group and prints my name in my notebook. Stefania then comes over and prints my name under where Carlotta has printed it and then she prints her first and last name. Valerio then joins us and prints the number 20 and his first name and his companion Angelo prints 21 and his first name. It looks like the following:
BILL
CORSARO
BILL
STEFANIA
DANATO
20 VALERIO
21
ANGELO

In a final example the children go beyond printing their names to composing a short letter.

Example 8
June 14 A Letter for Luciano's Little Sister

I am sitting at a work table with Luciano, Stefania and several other children. Luciano is printing a letter to his sister. Stefania tells me to write what Luciano is doing in my notebook. So I do so in Italian and show it to her:
Luciano scrive una lettera per la sua sorellina. ('Luciano is writing a letter for his little sister').
Luciano then suggest that Stefania also writes a letter to his sister which she does with Luciano's help. It reads:
CARA LUISA,
TANTI BACIONI DA STEFANIA LUCIANO E DA BILL. ('Many big kisses from Stefania Luciano and from Bill')

These examples nicely capture how literacy activities first presented in teacher directed tasks are appropriated and used by the children in their peer culture. Furthermore, the children document these priming activities *directly into Bill's notebook*. We see here an excellent example of research *with* rather than *on* children which is similar to research by Alderson and Mayall reported on in other chapters in this volume. Finally, this documentation by children of data directly relevant to our research interests demonstrates the value of longitudinal ethnography. It is the result of our acceptance, participation, and evolving membership in the school and peer cultures.

Conclusion

In this chapter we have discussed our use of longitudinal ethnography in further developing our theoretical perspective of interpretive reproduction. In a seminal set of articles on qualitative methods the sociologist, Howard Becker (1970), discussed the theoretical and methodological importance of formally documenting the history of the research process in ethnographic studies. Such documentation importantly integrates doing, rendering, and interpreting ethnographic research. All too often methodological discussions are separated from practice as discussions of data collection and analysis strategies including reliability, validity, and more recently the writing (or narrative rendering) of ethnography are abstracted away from the actual doing of ethnographic research (Clifford and Marcus 1986; Denzin and Lincoln 1994; Hammersley 1992) including the ethnographic study of children and youth (Fine and Sandstrom 1988; Waksler 1991). We have stayed very close to the practice of our longitudinal, comparative ethnographic research with young children to demonstrate how this practice was directly related to the development and extension of our theoretical perspective of interpretive reproduction.

From the perspective of interpretive reproduction, socialization is not something that happens to children; it is a process in which children, in interaction with others, produce their own peer culture and eventually come to reproduce, to extend, and to join the adult world (Corsaro 1992: 175). Interpretive reproduction is made up of three types of collective action: (1) children's creative appropriation of information and knowledge from the adult world; (2) children's production and participation in a series of peer cultures; and (3) children's contribution to the reproduction and extension of the adult culture. These activities follow a certain progression in that appropriation enables cultural production, which contributes to reproduction and change. The activities are, however, not historically partitioned. Instead these collective actions occur both within the moment and over time (Corsaro 2005: 41).

Thus, it is crucial to study interpretive reproduction longitudinally, as a process of children's evolving membership in their culture in the manner described in this chapter. We have shown how in a group of Italian preschool children, we were accepted and defined by them, and then with the children participated in events, which prepared or primed them for their coming transition to elementary school. These priming events involved activities that were both iterative (embedded in ongoing routines in the school and peer cultures) and projective (creative, often semiconscious glimpses into the future). In such priming events social actors are 'immersed in a temporal flow' during which 'they move 'beyond themselves' into the future and construct changing images of where they think they are going, where they want to go, and how they can get there from where they are at present' (Emirbayer and Mische 1998: 984).

As ethnographers, we not only experienced and documented these priming events, but also in some cases how we were appropriated by the children and teachers to take on active roles in the collective production of the events themselves. Finally, in some cases we were instructed by the children on which priming events to record in our notes (e.g., by Stefania to record Luciano's writing of a letter to his sister), and in other instances had the notebook and pen taken from our hands as the children recorded the priming events themselves. Thus, we actively entered (or were appropriated into) the temporal flow of interpretive reproduction and were primed with the children to move from the preschool to first grade. And that is exactly what we did. But a reflection and discussion of that transition is another story (Corsaro and Molinari 2005).

Notes

1 Dealing with gatekeepers also involved negotiations with an internal review board for human subjects at Bill Corsaro's university. Although the main element of attaining informed consent from the parents of children for observations and interviews was straightforward, one challenge we faced was the longitudinal nature of our study. The internal review board would not approve a one-time informed consent permission for observations and interviews over a number of years. As a result, the project had to be divided into a number of individual phases for the seven-year study. This accommodation resulted in a number of problems as the internal review board also demanded certain changes in the human consent forms in different phases. Consequently we had to ask parents' permission in somewhat different ways over the course of the study. The parents were confused with these multiple requests, but accepted our explanation of the nature of human subjects procedures.

   While human subjects permission was much less complicated in Italy, it was necessary that Bill Corsaro, who observed in the preschool on a daily basis, was required to have certain medical tests prior to beginning observations. These tests are mandatory for all individuals who work with children on an everyday basis in preschools. In Corsaro's case the taking and obtaining results of the tests was a complex process given the Italian bureaucracy for administering and certifying such tests to a non-citizen.

2 During the research we met twice a week to reflect on and discuss the ongoing research, in addition to the joint accomplishment of more practical research tasks. These twice a week meetings provided opportunities for evaluating Bill's reactions to events he observed in the field, discussing ideas about data collection strategies, analyzing observational and interview data, and generating and discussing initial interpretations. Our collaboration on this longitudinal, comparative ethnography continues. Overall, we found that our different cultural backgrounds and research experience enriched the quality of this collaborative ethnography.

3 Although Irene's behaviour can be interpreted in a number of ways, given our knowledge of her, which has developed over the course of this study, we believe that she was shy and used

the field trip as a means for acting on her growing interest in Bill. Having established a closer bond with Bill, she was then curious (and perhaps somewhat disappointed) about the change in his schedule.

4   Although Bill's inclusion in the peace-making phase of this example clearly demonstrates his membership in the 5b group, his actual participation in the activity fit his general status as a peripheral participant in the children's activities (Corsaro 1985, 2003). While his actual level of participation varied over time and across events, Bill refrained from: (1) initiating or terminating episodes; (2) repairing disrupted activity; or (3) settling disputes. What he did do was try to play (or take part in the school culture more generally) without dramatically affecting the nature or flow of activities. In this instance given his adult status (even though he was seen as an atypical adult), Bill could not actively enter into the grass war (e.g., 'throw grass', 'shout at and run after children') without dramatically affecting the play. On the other hand, given his participant status Bill did not attempt to stop the grass war and may have faced some serious choices if the play became overly physical. In such a case Bill's relationship with the teachers and children would have allowed him to signal for help if needed and he would, of course, have actively intervened in the play to protect a child from injury.

References

Becker, H. (1970) *Sociological Work: Method and Substance*, New Brunswick, NJ: Transaction Books.

Berentzen, S. (1995) 'Boyfriend-girlfriend relationship in social organization: A study of the growth and decline of 'go-with' relationship in a Black ghetto'. Unpublished Paper.

Clifford, J. and Marcus, G. (1986) *Writing Culture: The Poetics and Politics of Ethnography*, Berkeley, CA: University of California Press.

Corsaro, W. (1985) *Friendship and Peer Culture in the Early Years*, Norwood, NJ: Ablex.

Corsaro, W. (1992) 'Interpretive reproduction in children's peer cultures', *Social Psychology Quarterly* 55: 160–77.

Corsaro, W. (1993) 'Interpretive reproduction in children's role play', *Childhood* 1: 64–74.

Corsaro, W. (1996) 'Transitions in early childhood: The promise of comparative, longitudinal ethnography', in R. Jessor, A. Colby, and R. Shweder (eds), *Ethnography and Human Development*, Chicago: University of Chicago Press.

Corsaro, W. (2003) *We're Friends, Right?: Inside Kid's Culture*, Washington, DC: Joseph Henry Press.

Corsaro, W. (2005) *The Sociology of Childhood* (2nd edn), Thousand Oaks, CA: Pine Forge Press.

Corsaro, W. and Molinari, L. (1990) 'From seggiolini to discussione: The generation and extension of peer culture among Italian preschool children', *International Journal of Qualitative Studies in Education* 3: 213–30.

Corsaro, W. and Molinari, L. (2000) 'Priming events and Italian children's children's transition from preschool to elementary school: Representations and action', *Social Psychology Quarterly* 63: 16–38.

Corsaro, W. and Molinari, L. (2005) *I Compagni: Understanding Children's Transition from Preschool to Elementary School*, New York: Teachers College Press.

Denzin, N. and Lincoln, Y. (1994) *Handbook of Qualitative Research*. Thousand Oaks, CA: Sage.

Edwards, C., Gandini, L. and Forman, G. (eds) (1993) *The Hundred Languages of Children*, Norwood, NJ: Ablex.

Emirbayer, M. and Mische, A. (1998) 'What is agency?', *American Journal of Sociology* 103: 962–1023.

Fine, G. and Sandstrom, K. (1988) *Knowing Children: Participant Observation with Minors*, Newbury Park, CA: Sage.

Gandini, L. (1993) 'Fundamentals of the Reggio Emilia approach to early childhood education', *Young Children* 49: 73–7.

Hammersley, M. (1992) *What's Wrong with Ethnography?* London: Routledge.

Lave, J. and Wenger, E. (1991) *Situated Learning: Legitimate Peripheral Participation*. New York: Cambridge University Press.

Mandell, N. (1988) 'The least-adult role in studying children', *Journal of Contemporary Ethnography* 16: 433–67.

Molinari, L. and Corsaro, W. (1994) 'La genesi e l'evoluzione della cultura dei bambini', *Bambini*, X, 5: 38,45.

Molinari, L., Corsaro, W. and Zetti, S. (1998) 'Processi collettivi e conoscenza sociale: Uno studio etnografico nei contesti scolastici', *Rassegna di Psicologia* XV, 59–86.

Rizzo, T., Corsaro, W. and Bates, J. (1992) 'Ethnographic methods and interpretive analysis: Expanding the methodological options of psychologists', *Development Review* 12: 101–23.

Schatzman, L. and Strauss, A. (1973) *Field Research: Strategies for a Natural Sociology*. Englewood Cliffs, NJ: Prentice-Hall.

Waksler, F. (ed.) (1991) *Studying the Social Worlds of Children: Sociological Readings*. New York: Falmer Press.

Wulff, H. (1988) *Twenty girls: Growing Up: Ethnicity and Excitement in a South London Microculture*. Stockholm, Sweden: University of Stockholm.

13 Listening to Children: and Hearing Them

Helen Roberts

Introduction

In 1875, Andrew Doyle reported to the local government board at Whitehall on the emigration of pauper children to Canada. He spoke to many children, some of whom had happy experiences, some not. 'We all sicked over each other', was one description of the sea voyage, while a child patiently explained: 'Doption sir, is when folks gets a girl to work without wages' (Doyle 1875). Listening to children thus has a longer history than those of us currently interviewing children are inclined to acknowledge. Moreover, we are still not good enough at hearing them, in the sense of taking full account of what they tell us. As researchers, we are still learning ways of involving children fully in every stage of the research process from identifying meaningful research questions, to collaborating with researchers and disseminating good practice. And we are still learning that there may be occasions when such involvement may itself be exploitative or inappropriate, just as in other cases, not to involve children and young people represents poor practice.

Increasingly local authorities and voluntary organizations are looking at ways of consulting children and young people. In March 2005, the first Children's Commissioner was appointed in England with an express remit to give children and young people a voice in public life, a say, and to pay particular attention to gathering and putting forward the views of the most vulnerable children. His appointment followed the publication of *Every Child Matters; Change for Children* (DfES 2004), setting out the national framework for building local services around the needs of children in England – a document which itself followed extensive consultation with children and young people. It remains to be seen, of course, the extent to which young voices will be heard, and whose voices these will be, but there is no doubt that there has been a gradual change, bringing listening to children from the margins to the mainstream. At the same time, children are of growing interest to market researchers. A number of market research organisations have panels of children whom they can access, run school-based surveys, and are adept at running children's focus groups. It is thus not only researchers with an interest in childhood who have an interest in children. The media, business people, politicians, policymakers all have an interest in the views, the voice or the perspective of the child.

This should, of course, be good news for those concerned with listening to children and enabling them to speak out. But given this burgeoning interest what is there to stop children becoming merely a tool in the adult armoury, with no opportunity for genuine participation? And an awareness that there is not one set of views, one 'voice', one perspective, can be even more problematic when working with a powerless group, such as those children who are socially excluded, and in greatest need, than when researching or working with adults.

Child research in theory and practice

The majority of contributions to this book are from scholars. The perspective from which this chapter was originally written in 1999 was based on my experience as Head of R&D in a large UK childcare organisation, Barnardo's. After a decade in Barnardos, I returned to academic life in 2001, while continuing close links with policy and practice, in particular with Barnardo's.

Founded in the late nineteenth century by Dr Thomas Barnardo, the charity has always worked with the issues facing children and young people in greatest need. While this approach changed from one of child rescue to one which attempts to enable children and young people to thrive in their families and their communities, the issues with which Barnardo's now works are shockingly similar to those faced by Dr Barnardo and his colleagues. Children and young people on the streets, children facing poverty, children disadvantaged through racism or disability are those with whom Barnardo's works now, and worked then. Services are currently provided by the organisation to some 120,000 children and young people throughout the UK.

Research and development in Barnardo's is based in the organisation's Policy and Research Unit, with R&D staff working closely with policy and practice and parliamentary colleagues. The R&D work involves providing a resource for the evaluation of the organisation's practice, looking at the best available evidence of 'what works' for children experiencing difficulties working to transfer this into practice, and providing a service for the organisation which treats children and young people as a reservoir of expertise on their own lives, and provides opportunities to consult with them in a meaningful way.

Over the last decade and a half, the Economic and Social Research Council (ESRC) programme on Children 6–16, the Nuffield Foundation and initiatives from the Joseph Rowntree Foundation and the Carnegie Trust, among others, have ensured a place for those who research children in the research enterprise. The contribution of scholarship to our understanding of children's lives is crucial for those whose work is in policy and practice. One of Barnardo's charitable objects is to influence social welfare policy as it affects children and, in this, the knowledge generated by scholars and others can form a vital building block in lobbying, campaigning, or in negotiations with the local or national bodies.

However, research reports are only one source of knowledge. A real strength for all those who deliver direct services is that there is an opportunity for work which draws not only on sound secondary data, but also on the direct experiences of children and young people. For example, although the question of what counts as poverty may be contested in academic and political debates, the experience of a child living in poverty, vividly described, cannot so easily be dismissed. In order to generate sound work specifically aimed to advocate for the needs of children, relationships with those on the receiving end of services are crucial. Water metering (McNeish 1993), school exclusions, (Cohen et al. 1994) and the numbers of children and young people affected by their parents' HIV status for example (Imrie and Coombes 1995), were all identified through service users and practitioners in Barnardo's well before they became big policy issues, and gave the organisation the chance to set the agenda as well as responding to it. The ways in which an organisation like Barnardo's can advocate for the needs of children, young people and their families will range from quiet diplomacy to more robust campaigning and lobbying at central or local level. Good advocacy depends crucially on a clear and detailed understanding of the situation on the ground. Thus, work initiated by a project in Bradford, for example, working with young women under the age of consent who are sexually exploited (sometimes referred to as child prostitutes) resulted in a series of recommendations to the Home Office and the Department of Health, constructive meetings with the Association of Chief Police Officers and the Magistrates' Association among others (Barnardo's 1998). Barnardo's was clear that the full force of existing legislation needed to be targeted at adults who abuse and exploit children. Meanwhile, with funding from the Department of Health's Section 64 funding earmarked for child protection services, schemes were set up in various areas to provide direct services, to work with a police pilot in Wolverhampton set up to prosecute the men who abuse, rather than the girls involved, and to make contact with missing young women in Yorkshire.

More recent research reports from the organization have looked at the needs of young people at risk of sexual exploitation in London (Harper and Scott 2005) and the use of secure accommodation and alternative provisions for sexually exploited young people in Scotland (Creegan et al. 2005).

Sometimes, Barnardo's works as a single agency in its advocacy work, sometimes, in conjunction with other agencies such as the other children's charities, or, in the case of water metering, the British Medical Association. It is important that the R&D underlying this advocacy is robust - (certainly robust enough to withstand a grilling on the early morning Today programme), and the combination of practice, research, policy and its charitable objects make it both appropriate and possible for an organization like Barnardo's to be involved in advocacy in a way which might be less appropriate for scholarly researchers.

British industry, it is claimed, spends too much on dividends, and too little on R&D and investment. If this is so in industry (or the 'real world', as we in the parallel 'unreal' universe are urged to call it), how are we doing in child welfare? Are children in need getting sufficient dividends from our work? And how can we ensure that R&D works in their interests?

The following examples demonstrate some of the problems and dilemmas of listening to children, and the way in which it may be (or be perceived as) intrusive or inappropriate. Taking on board the views and feelings of children is one thing, parading them is quite another. Young children (and indeed many adults) may not always have the judgement to know what the consequences may be of exposing their feelings on television. For instance, a Panorama programme raised the issue of the distress children may feel during or after divorce. A tearful boy is televised during a therapy session. In the *Radio Times*, a viewer wrote: 'Little [x] was clearly too young to have consented to the filming ... The sequence was not necessary to establish the facts, simply public voyeurism of a small child's emotional exposure'. The editor replied: `We took every care to portray [his] therapy session sensitively. Filming took place with the consent of both parents and the therapists ... [Name] himself was keen to tell his story.'

Within social research too, there are examples of children participating in research where they may suffer distress (Grodin and Glantz 1994). One example from psychological research is the classic 'fear of strangers' experiment, where young babies are briefly separated from their mothers, and their response to the entry of a stranger and their mother's return are used as a test for the strength and quality of their emotional attachment (see Woodhead this volume). The babies' distress is usually short-lived, but often quite intense. What or whom does this experiment serve? Do we learn anything from it, and if we do, is it sufficiently worthwhile to counterbalance the short-term distress?

Nor is the history of social care without examples of children harmed by interventions intended for their good; the denial of information about their family of origin to adopted children was a case in point. It was frequently felt that children needed a fresh start in a new family, and that contact with the past would be counter-productive. There now appears to be good evidence that maintaining a link with the past is in many cases positive (Sellick and Thoburn 1996). Children in institutional care have been particularly prone to well-meaning experimentation in which their voices, even if listened to, go unheard. The Doyle report, referred to at the start of this chapter, is one example. It was not until the 1960s that the programmes sending children overseas from the UK terminated. Moreover, we know from the litany of enquiries into child abuse in residential care that in many cases, children had signalled their distress but had not been taken sufficiently seriously. This enabled brutality to continue, and half-baked theories on working with damaged children to flourish unchallenged.

This chapter explores the possibilities and problems of listening to children from the perspective of a researcher who has worked in a large voluntary childcare organization. It describes three specific initiatives in Barnardo's, aimed at listening to children with a view to affecting policy and practice.

Listening to children: children, ethics and social research

Since research questions and research agendas are still largely the province of adults, children's narratives tend to be edited, re-formulated or truncated to fit our agendas in much the same way as Graham (1983, 1984) elegantly describes in her account of the way in which women's lives are poorly served by some of social science's traditional research methods. Graham suggests that the narrative tradition is one way of addressing the problem of the fracturing of experiences which may occur through methods such as questionnaires and surveys.

Similarly, listening to children is central to recognizing and respecting their worth as human beings. Children are not simply objects of concern, of research, or of a media story. But while in medicine, ethics committees have offered some (albeit imperfect) protection for some time, it is both more recent, and more controversial for formal systems of research governance to cover ethical issues in relation to children and young people asked to take part in social interventions, or social research. For this reason, Barnardo's commissioned work which would enable the organisation to consider, and share with others in the child welfare community, ethical issues arising from research with children, including an element part-funded by the Calouste Gulbenkian Foundation on the training of young interviewers (Alderson 1995). Barnardo's was aware then, as it continues to be, that researching children and trying to involve them in decisions touching on their lives does not necessarily place researchers or others on the high moral ground, above those who in the bad old days would research children or intervene in their lives without so much as a focus group. It cannot be taken for granted that more listening means more hearing, or that the opportunity costs to children of participating in research on questions in which they may or may not have a stake is worth the candle.

Thus although ethical guidelines cannot give definititive answers, they can lead us to ask the right kinds of questions. Alderson (1995) in her work for Barnardo's, suggests ten topics raising such questions:

1   **The purpose of the research:** If the research findings are meant to benefit certain children, who are they, and how might they benefit ?
2   **Researching with children – costs and hoped for benefits:** Might there be risks or costs such as time, inconvenience, embarrassment, intrusion of privacy, sense of failure or coercion, fear of admitting anxiety?
3   **Privacy and confidentiality:** When significant extracts from interviews are quoted in reports, should researchers first check the quotation and commentary with the child (or parent) concerned?

4 **Selection, inclusion and exclusion:** Have some children been excluded because, for instance, they have speech or learning difficulties? Can the exclusion be justified?

5 **Funding:** Should the research funds be raised only from agencies which avoid activities that harm children?

6 **Review and revision of the research aims and methods:** Have children or their carers helped to plan or commented on the research?

7 **Information for children, parents and other carers:** Are the children and adults concerned given details about the purpose and nature of the research, the methods and timing, and the possible benefits, harms and outcomes?

8 **Consent:** Do children know that if they refuse or withdraw from the research, this will not be held against them in any way? How do the researchers help children to know these things?

9 **Dissemination:** Will the children and adults involved be sent short reports of the main findings?

10 **Impact on children:** Besides the effects of the research on the children involved, how might the conclusions affect larger groups of children?

In addition to these guidelines, Alderson (1995) suggests as good practice, and provides an example of, the production of explanatory leaflets for children and young people involved in research, helping them to understand what a project is about, ask the salient questions, and become part of the process rather than simply its objects of study.

What have the consequences of this work been within and beyond Barnardo's? It is frequently the case in scholarly life that the work of researchers, even the best researchers, languishes in journals with small readerships, or is presented at academic conferences but only peripherally touches the policy and practice domains. This is sometimes for the very good reason that the work is not intended for immediate 'use'. It may, for instance, be highly theoretical, and in that sense, academic in the best sense of the term. Sometimes, though, scholars intend their work to be used, and are unpleasantly surprised when, even after efforts to influence users, their work is not taken up. This will frequently be because 'user organisations' have their own knowledge, agendas, cadences and timetables. They are more likely to be influenced by a piece of research if they have been involved from the planning stage onwards. Alderson's work provided an example of ways in which academics and user groups, such as Barnardo's, can work well together. It was commissioned by a user organisation on the basis of a fairly tight specification of what were perceived as gaps in the ways in which both child welfare organisations and the academy approached research with children. Dissemination plans were made from the outset. Barnardo's was clear who needed to be influenced and why, and what the avenues open to us might be. Our first step was to set up an advisory group comprising policy, research and practice and parliamentary perspectives from Barnardo's, and externally a representative from a government department, a senior journalist writing on children's issues, and a number of researchers from other academic and children's sector organisations.

The project was carried out to a tight timetable, with a dissemination conference planned for the launch, to which practitioners, researchers, market researchers and representatives from the Department of Health were invited. The conference itself was a sell-out (only a proxy measure of success, to be sure, but a good early sign).

The immediate feedback, including from colleagues in the Department of Health, was very positive. But for those of us who work on the effectiveness of interventions, the acid test was whether it would have a wider influence, and more importantly, be used. In this sense, *Listening to Children: Children, Ethics and Social Research* (Alderson 1995) was an output, not an outcome. What might the longer term results be? Would a single child be better off as a result?

From this point of view, it has been heartening to find the publication widely cited in applications for research funding and influential in the genesis of two publications from the Joseph Rowntree Foundation, one on working with disabled children (Ward 1997) and the other on working with children and young people in groups (Hurley 1998). Again, in terms of a direct result for children, this can only be a proxy for success, but the development of guidelines suggesting respectful and inclusive ways of involving children in the research process is a step forward. By 2006, the Alderson guidelines, and the updated and revised version (Alderson and Morrow 2004) were being used and reproduced in research internationally, and were required reading for courses on children and ethics.

Everybody in? Involving young people in the research process

A consequence of the work described above was the inclusion of some of the young people with whom Barnardo's were working in a piece of research which Barnardo's was about to begin (see Alderson this volume). This resulted in a study conducted and co-authored by two of our professional researchers in collaboration with three young disabled men, involved in research for the first time (Ash et al. 1996, 1997). Lee Richardson, Marc Davies and Julian Bellew had been pupils at Barnardo's Princess Margaret School in the west of England, and were recruited to help us carry out a piece of work designed to explore the views of disabled and non-disabled students on inclusive policies in further education. Their personal experience of separate education brought an invaluable perspective to the study. After training and discussion, they not only conducted first-rate interviews with both able-bodied and disabled students, but, in much the same way as Ann Oakley had found in her study of motherhood (Oakley 1981), they faced questions from their interviewees. As Oakley points out: '... personal involvement is more than dangerous bias – it is the condition under which people come to know each other and to admit others into their lives'

(1981: 58). Just as Oakley (1981) was asked by her respondents whether it hurts to have a baby, and whether an epidural ever paralysed women, the limited opportunity, which many young people have to discuss the experience of being disabled was illustrated by questions to our researchers such as: 'Have you two [researchers] ever felt that you've been prevented from doing things that you'd like to have a go at?' The interviewers, like Oakley, eschewed the traditional research manual approach, which suggests that the interviewer parries, avoids or otherwise discourages questions:

> Never provide the interviewee with any formal indication of the interviewer's beliefs and values.
>
> (Sjoberg and Nett 1968: 212)

> If he [the interviewer] should be asked for his views, he should laugh off the request with the remark that his job at the moment is to get opinions, not to have them.
>
> (Selltiz et al. 1965: 576)

Our colleagues chose to answer: 'Yes, I think a parent with a disabled child is far more protective', and,

> Yes ... In fact it makes me want to go ahead even stronger, and do it because you're being held back and held back. You go to special school, and at the time, we both actually loved it, but now I regret it so much because it's so wrong. You should all be able to go to the same school, to be with local people of the same background. I didn't know anyone where I lived – it's so wrong. It's even harder when you've got communication problems. It's such a barrier, people talk for you, and you don't get a chance to say anything. You're told you will do this, or you will do that, you know 'you will have a cup of tea', or whatever.

Each response led to a new question:

> How do you get round that problem then, of people making decisions for you?

> Be a bit pig ignorant really. A bit rude sometimes.

> This might sound like a stupid question, but do you feel that you fit in with everyone else now, or do you still feel that you're separate.

> It depends really. You've really got to go out and compete. If you sit back in a corner then people won't talk to you. They'll just see you as an object. You've got to show that you can compete. It's not what you can't do. It's what you can do.

Our young interviewers, in this case, felt that it was right to share something of their lives with those they were researching. While it is unlikely that they would see their responses in terms of an educational intervention, it seems all too likely that the young people being interviewed were given a rare chance to learn something about the experience of disabled young people, and the disabling consequences of impairment. The questions, the methods and the composition of the research team serve to illustrate the importance of turning an abstract commitment to inclusion into something meaningful in day-to-day R&D practice as well as service delivery, an experience which has encouraged Barnardo's to do further work on the training of young interviewers, and experimenting with different forms of involvement of children and young people.

Young people's social attitudes

A further piece of work involved a large survey of social attitudes. When the first volume in Social and Community Planning Research's British Social Attitudes series was published (Jowell and Airey 1984), Sir Claus Moser, former head of the Government Statistical Service, welcomed an initiative which would enable civil servants, academics, journalists and others to explore how we think and feel as a nation. That first survey, and those which have followed, have tracked social attitudes via representative samples of adults living in Great Britain, and have provided one means by which we can begin to understand the way our beliefs, attitudes and values change over time. From the start, the survey has tracked the views of adults aged 18 or over. But what do we know of the attitudes of younger adults and children?

In 1993, Barnardo's approached Social and Community Planning Research with a proposal for a 'daughter' survey, based on young people in the households of adult respondents, to explore the social attitudes of a group of children and young people, which would be comparable to the adult survey in terms of both quality and substantive subject matter. We had until then lacked the foundations for a regular, authoritative survey of the views and attitudes of young people, charting the direction of change in their social attitudes. We know quite a lot about what adults think of young people and how that has changed over time. But how do they think adults are doing? What are their views of right and wrong? What basic political knowledge do they have? What are their views on education, on the relationship between different ethnic groups or on gender inequalities? As others have pointed out, if we want to know about what people think, there is no substitute for asking them (Turner and Martin 1981).

Barnardo's interest in this stemmed from our commitment to listening to young people and speaking out on their behalf or enabling them to speak out for themselves. While Barnardo's works with those in greatest need, in order to understand the lives and values of those at the margins of society, access to the wider picture is needed. The 'youth question' has long been a source of turbulent imagery, and youthful deviance seen as a portent of intergenerational conflict. This conception is somewhat belied by sound studies indicating mass adolescent conformity to core values and beliefs (e.g. Downes and Rock 1990). The Barnardo's/SCPR survey which resulted in the publication *Young People's Social Attitudes* (YPSA) provided an opportunity to look over time at these core attitudes and beliefs, and to compare these to the attitudes and beliefs of adults surveyed in British Social Attitudes (BSA).

The YPSA questions were subject to piloting, and we had useful feedback from the interviewers involved. This provided both reassurance on the issue of whether young people would be willing, able or interested in taking part in the work, and positive feedback from a group of interviewers who normally interviewed other adults. 'It's the easiest pilot I've done - they wanted to take part', 'It's good that children are being asked', and 'I couldn't believe the way they responded. It was brilliant'. One series of questions on the age at which children and young people should be expected to carry out household tasks such as washing up, or making their own beds resulted in interesting comments. Interviewers discerned from the pilots a tendency of children to give an age one year older than they actually were. Other responses included (for washing up) "when you can reach the sink". One interviewer reported a child saying that the age at which children should be expected to help with these tasks was "when I grow up". The interviewer said 'I gave her a look to see if she was taking the mick, and she said, "No, I mean it. I'm a child. I'm going to have to do it for the rest of my life".'

The feedback from the pilot made it clear not just that children and young people could answer the questions, but that they enjoyed being asked their opinions. Our findings did not present a picture of disaffected and rebellious youth. While the notion that 'young people like things pretty much the way that they are' would be unlikely to produce a successful newspaper headline (Newman 1996), the overall picture of young people portrayed by these data did not suggest that children and young people are storming the bastions of adult power. They wanted parents to have a bigger say than them in the educational curriculum, they felt that drug use at school should be punished, they didn't believe people should get married while very young, or leave school too early, and almost a third supported current film censorship laws. At the same time, they expressed strong opinions on racial prejudice, crime prevention, justice and poverty. Young people were clearer about what they thought of God and religion than what they thought about politics. While a quarter of young people replied that they did not know how they would vote if a general election were held tomorrow, they were more decisive on 'belonging' to a religion, or belief in God.

No survey finding, of course, can be taken as a precise statement about young people's social attitudes in Britain. As Jowell writes: 'Every finding is an approximation, part of a body of evidence which needs to be examined in the context of other evidence' (Jowell 1984: 7). A major aim of this work was to find another powerful way of giving young people a voice. While YPSA, unlike British Social Attitudes, is not an annual survey, it took place again in 1998, and in 2003. The datasets for all of these surveys can be obtained from http://www.data-archive.ac.uk/findingData/ypsaTitles.asp

While market researchers and pollsters were quick off the mark in understanding the importance of listening to children, academic researchers were slower to take up opportunities to work directly with young people - a caution which may have a basis in important methodological, ethical and other concerns. The issue of whether children can be reliable respondents sits alongside the question of whether they should be. Alderson's (1993, 1995) work suggests that they are able to participate in an informed way in research, and that we as adults, practitioners, researchers and policy makers have a great deal to learn from them. We know rather less about their views on participation.

Thus, in terms of these ethical and practical issues, those of us setting up YPSA were relieved to find that this first survey (Roberts and Sachdev 1996) demonstrated that children and young people were both willing and able to respond in a thoughtful way to a relatively sophisticated attitude survey. If they are willing to give their views on subjects on which they are, in a sense, 'experts', such as family life and education, we (that is 'we' in the broadest sense, including politicians, government departments, service providers and others) should be willing to listen to what they have to say, and incorporate their views into our understandings. Without asking children and young people for their views directly, it is all too easy to fall into imputing views to them, and stereotyping 'youth' on the basis of small samples or anecdote.

Childhood and youth are not simply a preparation for adulthood and much of the strength of the data collected rest on the picture they help us construct of the social attitudes of young people who are frequently judged on the basis of sketch and stereotype. Furnham and Gunter's (1989) *Anatomy of Adolescence*, based on a sample of National Association of Youth Club members interviewed during 1985 as part of International Youth Year, is a classic, and is referred to by a number of contributors to the YPSA report. We also linked the survey to a campaign Barnardo's was running: Give us a Break, which aimed to give young people from Barnardo's projects across the UK the opportunity to speak out on issues which affect them. Issues such as the rehabilitation of young offenders, the importance of promoting safe lifestyles, youth homelessness and the lack of opportunities for school leavers were highlighted at the launch of the report at *Planet Hollywood*. The report, and the lack of a voice for young people, was further raised in a variety of fora, including the All Party Parliamentary Group on Children. It was part of a climate of change, in which children and young people are more frequently being asked their views.

Children without a voice

There are some groups of children literally or metaphorically without a voice. In the case of our Young People's Social Attitudes survey for instance, since it was based on households, children on the street and children in residential schools were excluded, and it almost certainly under-represented those children and young people who spend an absolute minimum of time in the parental home. Some school surveys exclude those children who have problems completing a questionnaire, and very profoundly disabled children are excluded as participants from almost all research. Other children and young people, such as those who are roofless, though they may be excluded from household surveys, are so frequently asked by researchers or journalists to account for themselves and give their stories that this has become a trade for the young people as well as for the professionals. This means that we may have an abundance of information from disabled children on what is means to be disabled, and from homeless young people on living on the street, but we know far less about their views on issues which affect all young people. 'Inclusion' for them, ironically enough, can mean inclusion on the basis of their participating in research entirely focused on precisely those issues which exclude them. Disabled children and young people know about issues other than their impairment, just as homeless young people have views on issues other than homelessness. Work has been progressing in this area.

On the inclusion side, Jenny Morris's work for the Joseph Rowntree Foundation has included disabled children, sometimes with severe communication skills, including those with no speech. Specialist interviewers were used, and lessons learned (Morris 1998a), some of which were used for a policy think piece for Barnardo's on the rights of disabled children to the kinds of services which all children should be able to expect (Morris 1998b). Further work on including children from different groups has been produced, including children with autistic spectrum disorders (Beresford et al. 2004) and ventilator dependent children (Noyes 2000).

There are, of course, considerable theoretical, practical and ethical problems involved in including children and young people who have systematically been excluded from the domains where they might otherwise have a voice, and we need to be clear when it is appropriate for us to ask young people to donate time – one of their few resources – to researchers, and when it is not. In relation to researching roofless young people on their needs, a Barnardo's researcher persuaded a local authority that wanted to commission interviews of young people on the streets about what would make their lives better, that given the sound work already done in this area, with the needs of this group amply demonstrated time after time, resources would be better spent in using what we already know to provide services and resources for young people rather than deferring action until more knowledge could be created. The development of systematic review techniques to include qualitative work (Dixon-Woods et al. 2005; Petticrew and Roberts 2006) give further opportunities for high quality qualitative work with children (among others) being used more than once, rather than there being constant reiterations of small studies.

Child protection

A particular issue which needs a good deal of further thought by all who interact with children, as researchers, practitioners, or as citizens is the question of child protection. In Jenny Morris's research, referred to above, the reference group of young disabled people advising the project, all of whom had had experience of residential care, said that unless the researchers guaranteed confidentiality, people would not tell them about abuse. The research interviewers however, some of whom had experience of child protection work, felt they could not give such a guarantee, particularly if the abuse was still taking place, or the abuser was in a position to abuse other children. It was agreed that near the beginning of each interview, the researcher would say something like: 'Sometimes a person might talk about a situation where they have been harmed by someone. If this happens, I may need to talk to someone else, especially if it is something awful which is still happening to you, or if the person who harmed you may still be hurting someone else. I would want to be able to agree with you what should be done, and who should be told'. The response of one young man to this was, 'Well, that's one part of my life I'm not going to be able to talk to you about then, isn't it? I'm not having you deciding who to go and talk to about me' (Morris, 1998a: 55). While child protection protocols in research may sometimes be seen to be as much in the interests of risk-averse organizations as in the interests of children, who may feel silenced by them, it would be a careless researcher who did not consider such questions in advance of starting a study.

Evidence-informed research

In the late 1990s, when the original version of this chapter was written, there was something of a (albeit phony) paradigm war around those methods most appropriate to design, develop and implement services for children more likely to do good than harm (Oakley and Roberts 1996). Those who advocated trials as an appropriate method for exploring the effectiveness of interventions could be (and sometimes were) depicted as technocrats, more concerned with what works than with what matters – despite the fact that some of the proponents of well-designed trials were also distinguished qualitative researchers (Oakley et al. 2005). It has now been more widely acknowledged that listening to children is a key part of the evidence (Petticrew and Roberts 2003; Joughin and Law 2005), and that robust methods to test the effectiveness of interventions form part of the children's rights agenda.

Conclusion

On the basis of a number of examples, this chapter draws attention to some of the ways in which children and young people can be, and have been, involved in the research process. Encouraging children's participation in research is in some quarters now seen as a *sine qua non* of a pro-child stance. But the reasons why a child or young person should choose to participate in research are clearer in some studies than others. While it is likely that research on children which includes children and young people will considerably strengthen some aspects of the research, we cannot take it for granted that participation in research and the development of increasingly sophisticated research methods to facilitate children's participation are always in their interests. What serves a research agenda does not always fulfil a policy or practice agenda, or further a participant's interests. We cannot assume that those issues which we as researchers, or practitioners, or policy makers find compelling will hold quite the same interest for children and young people. However careful we are about informed consent, there are aspects of the adult/child relationship or practical issues concerning research in schools or youth settings, which may make non-participation difficult for a child or young person. For this reason, I believe that there is an onus on us to make participation in research, at whatever level, an experience, which is at best positive, and at worst, does no harm, to young people. The time that they devote to our research agendas is a gift, and one, which we should be prepared to reciprocate. In considering the inclusion of children in research, we need to be thoughtful in terms of, which particular research horse is appropriate for which particular policy course. There are some policy or practice related research questions for which the child's voice is entirely appropriate; others, for instance those relating to fiscal policies as they affect children, where it is likely that the child's voice would be no more than illustrative.

Whatever methods are used in consulting children, some of the questions of ethics go beyond the social relationships of social research. These include whether the questions asked are serious ones, are capable of being answered with the kind of research method proposed, whether the researchers have been appropriately trained for doing good research work with children and young people, and whether the research takes place in a context where consent can be freely given (or withheld). Other considerations, increasingly recognized by funders, include building into the study design and costed time appropriate methods for three-way knowledge transfer between research, policy and practice. A good example of an ethics protocol for a specific study can be found in Appendix 1 to Creegan et al.'s report on sexual exploitation (Creegan et al. 2005, available through a weblink in the references below).

It is clear that listening to children, hearing children, and acting on what they say are three very different activities, although they are frequently elided as if this were not the case. The (re) discovery of children in the academy is akin in some respects to the re-discovery of poverty, of women, or of the working class in the 1960s and 1970s. Children have always been with us (Zelizer 1986). There have always been people who have listened, sometimes been people who have heard, and perhaps less often, those who have acted wisely on what children have had to say.

References

Alderson, P. (1993) *Children's Consent to Surgery*, Buckingham: Open University Press.

Alderson, P. (1995) *Listening to Children: Children, Ethics and Social Research*, Barkingside: Barnardo's.

Alderson, P. and Morrow, V. (2004) *Ethics, Social Research and Consulting with Children and Young People*, Barkingside: Barnardo's.

Ash, A., Bellew, J., Davies, M., Newman, T. and Richardson, L. (1996) *Everybody In*, Barkingside: Barnardo's.

Ash, A., Bellew, J., Davies, M., Newman, T. and Richardson, L. (1997) 'Everybody In? The experience of disabled students in colleges of further education', *Disability and Society* 12 (4): 605–21.

Barnardo's (1998) *Whose Daughter Next? Children Abused through Prostitution*, Barkingside: Barnardo's.

Beresford, B., Tozer, R., Rabiee, P. and Sloper, P. (2004) 'Developing an approach to involving children with autistic spectrum disorders in a social care research project', *British Journal of Learning Disabilities* 32 (4): 180–85.

Cohen, R., Hughes, M. with Ashworth, L. and Blair, M. (1994) *School's Out: The Family Perspective on School Exclusion*, Barkingside: Barnardo's.

Creegan, Scott, S. and Smith, R. (2005) *The Use of Secure Accommodation and Alternative Provisions for Sexually Exploited Young People in Scotland*, Barkingside: Barnardo's Policy and Research Unit. http://www.barnardos.org.uk/secure_accommodation_and_alternative_provisions_for_sexually_exploited_young_people_in_scotland_2005.pdf.

DfES (2004) *Every Child Matters: Change for Children*, Nottingham: DfES publications.

Dixon-Woods, M., Agarwal, S., Jones, D.R., Young, B. and Sutton, A.J. (2005) 'Synthesising qualitative and quantitative evidence: a review of methods', *Journal of Health Services Research and Policy* 10: 45–53.

Downes, D. and Rock, P. (1990) Preface to J. Davis, *Youth and the Condition of Britain, Images of Adolescent Conflict*, London: The Athlone Press.

Doyle, A. (1875) *Pauper Children (Canada)*. Return to an Order of the Honourable, The House of Commons dated 8 February 1875.

Furnham, A. and Gunter, B. (1989) *Young People's Social Attitudes in Britain, The Anatomy of Adolescence*, London: Routledge.

Graham, H. (1983) 'Do her answers fit his questions?: Women and the survey method', in E. Gamarnikow, D. Morgan, J. Purvis and D. Taylorson (eds), *The Public and the Private*, London: Heinemann.

Graham, H. (1984) 'Surveying through stories', in C. Bell and H. Roberts (eds) *Social Researching: Politics, Problems, Practice*, London, Routledge & Kegan Paul.

Grodin, M. and Glantz, L. (1994) *Children and Research Subjects: Science, Ethics and Law*, Oxford: Oxford University Press.

Harper, Z. and Scott, S. (2005) *Meeting the Needs of Sexually Exploited Young People in London*, Barkingside: Barnardo's.

Hurley, N. (1998) *Straight talk: Working with Children and Young People in Groups*, York, YPS: Joseph Rowntree Foundation.

Imrie, J. and Coombes, Y. (1995) *No Time to Waste: The Scale and Dimensions of the Problem of Children Affected by HIV/AIDs in the United Kingdom*, Barkingside: Barnardo's.

Joughin, C. and Law, C. (eds) (2005) *Evidence to Inform the National Service Framework for Children, Young People and Maternity Services*, London, DH http://www.dh.gov.uk/assetRoot/04/11/24/04/04112404.pdf.

Jowell, R. (1984) 'Introducing the Survey', in R. Jowell and C. Airey *British Social Attitudes, the 1984 Report*, Aldershot: Gower.

Jowell, R. and Airey, C. (1984) *British Social Attitudes, the 1984 Report*, Aldershot: Gower.

McNeish, D. (1993) *Liquid Gold: The Cost of Water in the 90s*, Barkingside: Barnardo's.

Morris J. (1998a) *Still Missing? Volume 1, The Experience of Disabled Children Living apart from their Families*, London: Who Cares Trust.

Morris, J. (1998b) *The Children Act and Disabled Children's Human Rights*, Barkingside: Barnardos.

Newman, T. (1996) 'Rights, rites and responsibilities: The age of transition to the adult world', in H. Roberts and D. Sachdev (eds) *Young People's Social Attitudes*, Barkingside, Barnardo's.

Noyes, J. (2000) 'Enabling young "ventilator-dependent" people to express their views and experiences of their care in hospital', *Journal of Advanced Nursing*, 31 (5): 1206–15.

Oakley Ann (1981) 'Interviewing women: a contradiction in terms', in H. Roberts (ed.) *Doing Feminist Research*, London: Routledge & Kegan Paul, pp. 30–61.

Oakley, A. and Roberts, H. (1996) *Evaluating Social Interventions: A Report of Two workshops Funded by the Economic and Social Research Council*, Barkingside: Barnardo's.

Oakley, A., Gough, D., Oliver, S., and Thomas, J. (2005) 'The politics of evidence and methodology: lessons from the EPPI-Centre', *Evidence & Policy* 1 (1): 5–31.

Petticrew, M. and Roberts, H. (2003) 'Evidence, hierarchies and typologies: Horses for courses', *Journal of Epidemiology and Community Health*, 57: 527–29.

Petticrew, M. and Roberts, H. (2006) *Systematic Reviews in the Social Sciences: A Practical Guide*, Oxford: Blackwells.

Roberts, H. and Sachdev, D. (1996) *Young People's Social Attitudes*, Barkingside: Barnardo's.

Sellick, C. and Thoburn, J. (1996) *What Works in Family Placement?*, Barkingside: Barnardo's.

Selltiz, C., Jahoda, M., Deutsch, M. and Cook, S.W. (1965) *Research Methods in Social Relations*, London: Methuen.

Sjoberg, G. and Nett, R. (1968) *A Methodology for Social Research*, New York: Harper & Row.

Turner, C.F. and Martin, E. (eds) (1981) *Surveys of Subjective Phenomena: A Summary Report*, National Academy Press: Washington, DC.

Ward, L. (1997) *Seen and Heard: Involving Disabled Children and Young People in Research Projects*, York, YPS: Joseph Rowntree Foundation.

Zelizer V.A. (1986) *Pricing the Priceless Child*, New York: Basic Books.

14 Children as Researchers

Participation Rights and Research Methods

Priscilla Alderson

Introduction

Increasingly across the world, children are working as researchers and evaluators (UNICEF 2006). In Britain, for example, every government department is committed to involving children in the planning, delivery and evaluation of policies and services. This chapter considers matters raised by child researchers, illustrated through a review of an international literature. Three main areas will be discussed: the stages of the research process, the levels of participation, and the types of research methods in which young researchers are involved. The idea of seeing the 'researched' adult as a co-researcher and co-producer of data, equally involved in the analysis, is already widely acknowledged. This idea is usually argued for in terms of respect and shared control, and of addressing power imbalances in the research relationship. It can also be justified in terms of efficiency, as opening the way to a broader range of collection methods and a fuller understanding of the data. The same advantages can occur when children conduct research with more or less help from adults.

An explicit and implicit theme within this type of co-research is respect for the researched group and for their own views and abilities. Respect links closely to rights, and international treaties such as the UN Convention on Rights of the Child (UNCRC 1989) offer principled yet flexible means of justifying and extending respectful practices. With its near-universal support and quasi-legal status, the UNCRC formally justifies ethical standards of respect for rights within research. Growing awareness of the rights of children, and other 'minority' groups including women, has paved the way for involving children as researchers.

Until recently, research about children has concentrated on adults' efforts to protect children and provide for them, mainly by measuring the effects of health, education or welfare interventions in their lives, or their needs as assessed by adults, or by investigating their gradual development and socialization towards adult competence. However, the newer dimension of children's participation rights, enshrined in the UNCRC, involves moderate versions of adult autonomy rights. These concern children taking part in activities and decisions that affect them. Participation rights include especially three of the UNCRC's 54 articles. State parties should assure:

> To the child who is capable of forming his or her own views the right to express those views freely in all matters affecting the child, the views of the child being given due weight in accordance with the age and maturity of the child (12); (figures in brackets refer to relevant article of the UNCRC)

> the right to freedom of expression [including] freedom to seek, review and impart information and ideas of all kind ... through any other media of the child's choice (13);

> the right of the child to rest and leisure, to engage in play and ... cultural life and the arts (31).

The rights are qualified in several ways. Some, for example, are aspirational, not yet fully realizable, but only 'to the maximum extent of [each nation's] available resources' (4). The rights are also not absolute but conditional, affected by the 'evolving capacities of the child', the 'responsibilities, rights and duties of parents' (5) and the national law. 'The best interests of the child must be the primary consideration' (1, 21). Children's rights cannot be exercised in ways which would harm the child or other people. They must 'respect the rights and reputations of others', as well as 'national security and public order, health and morals' (13). The rights are not about selfish individualism but about solidarity, social justice and fair distribution. To claim a right is to acknowledge that everyone else has an equal claim to it. The claim affirms the worth and dignity of every person. Respect for children's rights promotes 'social progress and better standards of life in larger freedom' (UNCRC Preamble). Every government except the United States and Somalia has ratified the UNCRC, undertaking to publicize it 'to adults and children alike', to bring state laws and services to accord with it, and to report regularly to the UN on progress in doing so. Yet children's rights are still frequently challenged, for example, in how participation rights can complement yet also conflict with provision and protection rights.

Other influences, which have raised the status of children in research and as researchers, include the aftermath of the Gillick ruling in 1985 that children aged under 16 can give valid consent (for a review see Alderson and Montgomery 1996); new respect in the sociology of childhood for children as competent social actors, who are no longer seen as simply subsumed under the adult-dominated headings of 'family' or 'school' (Qvortrup et al. 1994; James and Prout 1997); and the well-publicized eloquence of young children, for example, on television. Central to this chapter, there is also research by children themselves, initially largely sponsored by non-governmental organisations (NGOs) in accordance with the UNCRC.

Child researchers and their rights

Children's participation involves changing emphasis in research methods and topics. Recognizing children as subjects rather than objects of research entails accepting that children can 'speak' in their own right and report valid views and experiences. Such 'speaking' may involve sign language when children cannot hear or talk, and other expressive body language and sounds, such as those made by children with autism and severe learning difficulties (Alderson and Goodey 1998), or children on mechanical ventilation (Noyes 1999; Davis et al. this volume). To involve all children more directly in research can therefore rescue them from silence and exclusion, and from being represented, by default, as passive objects, while respect for their informed and voluntary consent helps to protect them from covert, invasive, exploitative or abusive research.

This latter point relates to a major obstacle in conducting research with children: infantilizing them, perceiving and treating them as immature and, in so doing, producing evidence to reinforce notions of their incompetence. This can include 'talking down' to children by using over-simple words and concepts, restricting them into making only superficial responses, and involving only inexperienced children and not those with intense relevant experience who could give much more informed responses. When the views are collected of children aged 3, 4 and 5 years about long-term illness or disability they have deeply experienced, they are seen to have far more mature understanding and moral responsibility than is usually thought possible at these ages (Alderson et al. 2006). Alternatively, researchers' over-complicated or poorly explained terms, topics and methods can also misleadingly make children (and many adults) appear to be ignorant or incapable. Children may, however, help adult researchers to set more appropriate levels of talk (O'Kane, this volume).

Another obstacle for children is the common assumption by adults that the permission of parents or teachers will suffice, and that children need not or cannot express their own consent or refusal to take part in research. Social research can inform debates about young children's consent by providing evidence of their competence in their daily life and in research (Alderson 2000; Alderson and Morrow 2004), confirming the now commonplace assertion that children are social actors who influence their own lives, their societies and environments. Two related questions therefore arise. First, if children's social relations and culture are worthy of study in their own right, then who is better qualified to research some aspects of their lives than children themselves? Second, if children can be active participants, as this chapter considers, can they also be active researchers?

Children as researchers

Children begin to be researchers in their everyday school projects. In schools that I have visited, for example, Adam aged 5 made a graph about pets owned by children in his class, and Helen aged 16 tape-recorded interviews with her friends about their parents' divorce for her A level psychology project. Tariq's geography GCSE project was about the local allotments threatened with closure and involved him in checking local authority records and observing a council meeting. Classes of 9- to 11-year-olds watched a video about ponds, then had a brain-storming circle time and small group discussions to plan and draw a pond for their school playground. They worked to a budget and with adults' help created and stocked the pond.

In these examples, learning, the main occupation for everyone at school, overlaps with research, but this wealth of research in schools is almost entirely unpublished, and tends to be seen as 'practising' rather than as worthwhile in its own right. In contrast, comparable activities may be highly valued in other societies, as shown in the next example. Through Child-to-Child peer education, 600 Ugandan children at a village school became concerned that animals used the main well-pond. The children spoke with the village leader who called a meeting at which the children presented poems and dramas about the value of clean water. As a result, children and adults worked together on cleaning the well-pond and building a fence to keep out the animals (ISCA 1995: 236).

The second most usual way in which children are involved in research is in projects designed and conducted by adults (see O'Kane; Davis et al., Roberts, and Christensen and James, this volume). However, besides providing data in their traditional role as research subjects, increasingly, children help to plan questions, and collect, analyse and report evidence, and publicize the findings, as this chapter will review. Children are possibly more likely than adults to be interested in every stage of research. Many of them are used to enquiring, scrutinizing, accepting unexpected results, revising their ideas, and assuming that their knowledge is incomplete and provisional. Children may have less to lose, and more to gain, by asking radical questions, such as: Why do we have school assembly? Adults, by contrast, can feel threatened by research, which might critically question their own expertise, authority or convenience.

The third and less common, but expanding, area is research mainly initiated and directed by children and young people. Methods of involving unschooled adults as researchers, such as through participatory rural appraisal (Pratt and Loizos 1992), are also used effectively with and by children (O'Kane and Christensen and James, this volume). The following sections review the stages, levels and methods through which children are involved as researchers.

Stages of research when children are involved

Research in schools and universities, which mainly aims to add to knowledge, tends to concentrate on the middle stages of projects: collecting and analysing data and writing reports. In contrast, young researchers are usually keen to produce findings that will achieve changes in, for example, provision of services, and respect for their rights. They therefore often emphasize the follow-up stages of disseminating and implementing the findings. 'We want to show this to the social workers/Department for Education/Mayor of London', may be explicit initial aims. One main barrier is how rarely the initial and follow-up stages of research are funded, although they are so important in children's research (Wellard et al. 1997). The earliest stages may also be crucial: selecting and setting up the research team and sample groups, avoiding tokenism, working out team and power relationships and ways of resolving problems as they arise, jointly deciding the agenda, aims, methods and payments in cash or in kind (for example, Cockburn et al. 1997). Some of these important initial decisions may be taken for granted in hierarchical professional research teams. The following examples illustrate ways in which young people work through various stages of research.

Louise Hill planned research with children aged 8–12 years who had relevant experience about parents/carers being problem drinkers. They advised her on planning the research questions and methods, wording and posters. Given the potentially embarrassing and distressing nature of the research, she met small groups of children three times. They were in a Barnardo's support programme. She already knew some of them, and could count on the programme offering extra support to any child in need. The sessions were carefully planned, with fun and 'warm up' sessions, ending with 'cool down' activity (personal communication, 2007).

Natascha Klocker (2006) trained three former child domestic workers aged 14–18 in Tanzania in research skills. As a team they designed the research and conducted interviews and questionnaires with other child domestic workers, consulting them on ideas for improving regulation and law and introducing employment contracts. Working with legal experts, the research team is liaising with the Municipal Council to introduce a new bye-law, besides helping to set up an NGO 'Listen to the Child' to promote child workers' rights, and a weekly radio programme, which will employ young researchers.

Camille Warrington (2006) trained six young Gypsies and Travellers, aged 11–15 years, to interview their peers and families. While encouraging them to have as big a 'steer' as possible of the project, and regarding them as 'a key part of solutions to some of the problems they report', Camille felt that, given more time, the young people could have been more fully involved, although they actively disseminated their findings and presented them at the House of Lords.

Sort It Out! (OCRCL 2001), a survey of the views of 3,000 Londoners aged 3–17 years on their priorities for life in their city, was planned, designed and conducted by young people with adults' help. The 1998 Greater London Authority (GLA) Act established eight initial Strategies for the new London Mayor, which did not mention children. The Office of the Children's Rights Commissioner for London (OCRCL) opened in 2000 and was run for, by and with children and young people, and the friendly welcoming office with full-time staff was an ideal workplace for child researchers. A major aim was to persuade the Mayor to adopt a Strategy for Children and Young People and this was achieved. The survey, including thousands of postcards sent to Ken (the Mayor), informed the Strategy by identifying children's eight priorities: poverty, health, education, play, transport, family and care, housing with neighbourhoods and environment, crime and justice. These priorities have since influenced numerous GLA policies, and laid the foundations for the *State of London's Children* reports (Hood 2002; 2004), which set a model for all capital cities by extrapolating from national and local (borough/ward) records to produce regional citywide statistics. The reports have opened up understanding about young Londoners' lives, including their very high levels of poverty. The reports also act as tools for review and change, when they are updated about every two years. The original survey promoted numerous local projects around London, such as the videos made by youth clubs of their very poor local facilities, which they presented to shocked and impressed members of the House of Lords (personal observation). OCRCL research methods combined play and work with equal opportunity methods and assertion training (for example, Treseder 1997).

Khan (1997) reported a project conducted by 11 Bangladeshi street girls and boys aged 10–15 years. They interviewed 51 other street children aged 7–15 years in Dhaka. The research team held 18 meetings to choose the topics and questions, the methods and the interviewees. They conducted one or two interviews each morning and, as they were unschooled, they dictated all they could remember to adult scribes in the afternoon. The team then listened to every transcript and argued about the priorities they wanted to report. After much debate, comparing and synthesizing many matters, they identified 11 priorities. These included torture by police and muscle men (theft, being forced, for example, into smuggling arms, dealing drugs and sex work); misbehaving adults (name calling, never using the child's own name, chasing children, accusing them of being bad); dislike of present job; inability to get work without a guardian-advocate; street girls being hated and despised, their inability to find a husband and anxiety about the future when they could no longer stay on the street; low income (cheating by adult traders, having to find dirty rotten food); inability to protest against injustice without support from adult relatives; lack of vocational education. The young researchers dictated, and then had read back to them, three reports in Bangla and English. They were very keen to publish their views for specific international agencies, and they made radio and television broadcasts. They questioned the emphasis in international aid policies on providing health and education services; only two of their points referred to material or economic needs. They clearly wanted social change, justice and adults to respect and listen to them without violence or abuse, with policy makers rethinking the world from the viewpoints of children.

In a community project in England, children aged 3 to 8 years used cameras and conducted surveys and interviews about children's views on improving their housing estate. They published an illustrated report, which six of them presented and discussed with local authority officers at a 'proper' meeting around a table. Some of their recommendations were used, such as having the playground in the centre of the estate, not on the edge and beyond busy peripheral roads as the adults had planned (Miller 1997).

Young people also help to disseminate research memorably. I have attended conferences where they have read poems, created dramas and used playful audience role play, which have clearly impressed the practitioners and policy makers present. *Youth Policy and Social Inclusion* (Barry 2005) includes critical commentaries after each of the 13 chapters, written by young people in their teens and early twenties, explaining the relevance of the research reports to their own and their friends' experiences. Keogh and Whyte (2005) conducted emancipatory research on student councils, analysing and checking their findings with a young focus group, who also made posters which ranked action for school councils and listed challenges and possible solutions. Their colleague Ruth Emond worked with young authors who produced two reports on their experiences of residential care and school (Michael et al. 2002; Gerard et al. 2002).

Levels of children's involvement

The term 'child-centred research' loosely covers methods, stages or levels of children's involvement. Although methods involving games may appear child-friendly, a crucial aspect is the level at which adults share or hold back knowledge and control from children. This can be evaluated using the well-known participation ladder (Hart 1992), starting with the pretence of shared work (manipulation, decoration and tokenism), moving to children being assigned to tasks although being informed and consulted, with the top levels of projects more fully initiated and directed by children. Lansdown (2005) reviews how 200 Ugandan children were involved in investigating, hearing and handling child abuse cases within their community, and she offers a matrix for measuring participation, ethics, voluntariness, inclusion and the impact of projects from 'none' to 'considerable' impact. Drawing on her work with young researchers on war-affected populations, Marie Smyth (2004: 156) lists questions to check when 'do the researchers' good intentions slide into colonial smothering?

Levels of their participation are also affected by children's capacity to understand the relevant matters. Can young children, for example, understand critical analysis, or the politics of racism? A report by a teacher suggests that the 7-year-olds she taught could do so (Butler 1998). She describes how black children in downtown Chicago became conscious of racial, economic and political oppressions, as they discussed their own experiences intensely in class. They analyzed contradictions between the rhetoric and reality in their lives, the social pressures that restrict individual agency, and how they can work for social justice, power, unity and community change. Hart (2002) investigated poor housing with very disadvantaged children. Through looking beyond local conditions at the history and politics of housing, the children came to question how they had blamed themselves and their families for their condition. Hart considers that, 'the resulting consciousness [may be] more important than the research itself or any direct action it may lead to' (2002: 23).

However, young researchers may be more likely to experience anger, frustration, disillusionment and cynicism. After they have been highly involved throughout their projects, their findings tend to be ignored or forgotten instead of being implemented (Willow 2002). Many reports emphasize how young researchers have learned and benefited from their involvement, but say little about how adults too might have learned, and gained, and implemented young researchers' recommendations to benefit many other people. Kirby and Bryson (2002: 7) warn against such token involvement, and ask 'how systems can change to accommodate young people's participation rather than expecting young people to participate in predefined ways'. Kirby et al. (2003) review how genuine sustainable participation depends on change to many levels and attitudes within organisations to promote respect for children's rights and actions. Working with ten advisers/researchers aged 14–19 years, who attended a residential course on methods, they selected 29 participatory projects, from among an initial 150, aiming to inform and 'move on' future work

Methods used by young researchers

Children's real involvement relates more to their own informed choosing and using of methods and not to any specific method (Punch 2002; Ennew and Plateau 2004; Nairne et al. in press). Child researchers use many methods, singly or in groups, with or without adults. They select research topics, general questions and methods, specific survey questions or interview topics, and the respondent samples and observation sites. Some conduct pilots and revise their plans for data collection, collation and analysis. After the analysis by hand or computer, they write reports and disseminate the findings, and discuss them with policy makers. Research reports by young groups range from long, printed reports to a poster or wall newspaper, an internet message, a video or photographic exhibition, with reports and drawings by the whole team or from smaller groups. School projects have included producing a video and exhibition on a town's facilities for disabled people, and surveying and proposing new road safety measures which were built. Children have also been involved in projects ranging from improving architectural designs for a new children's hospital in Derby, to working on anti-poverty measures in Greenwich (all in Willow 1997). One group reviewed multi-cultural policies in their school, designed and presented a policy to the student council, and planned in-service training sessions for school governors and staff with a local race relations group (CCSE, nd). Young people are also involved in an ethics committee (NICCY 2007) and in doing evaluations (Save the Children 2007). During school lunch time training sessions with academic researchers, 10-year-olds soon become skilled in conducting small projects on topics that matter to them, such as the effect on families when mothers do paid work.

They reflexively end their reports with a section on 'if I did this project again I would ...' (Kellett 2005).

Some children seem to be able to understand complex methods. For example, Emily Rosa, aged 9, designed an elegant randomized trial of 21 therapeutic touch healers who took part in 280 tests. They put their hands through holes in a screen 30 cm apart, and Emily spun a coin to determine whether she would hold her hands just above their left or right hand. The aim was to show whether the healers were aware of the kinds of human energy fields through which they claim to heal. Accuracy would have to be well above 50 per cent to demonstrate sensitivity, but was only 47 per cent in the first trial and 41 per cent in the second. Emily's mother believed that the healers took part because they did not feel threatened by a child, and experts praised this simple and novel way of gaining evidence that casts strong doubt on the healers' claims. Previously, complicated, lengthy and expensive trials had compared patients' healing rates after therapeutic touch and more orthodox treatments (Rosa et al. 1998).

In another project, care leavers aged 16 years and older investigated experiences of young people leaving care in five British cities. This group is highly over-represented among the homeless and prison population. The young researchers chose the research topics and questions during five residential meetings, and interviewed 80 young care leavers and 22 social work staff. They undertook full qualitative analysis of the results and made recommendations based on these. They wrote and launched the report and talked to the media and to local authorities about the work, besides making a video (West 1997). Another project combined different teams with a central research group, and flexible use of core questions on 12 research sites. A key coordinating worker liaised with one practitioner and two young people on each site, and all of them made up the research group which took overall control over methods and editing of reports. They identified the main themes and 20 questions per theme. They worked mainly in schools, but also with groups of refugees and homeless young people (Kenny and Cockburn 1997). Young people aged 8–18 become skilled investigative reporters and editors, publishing their work in mainstream television and press through *Headliners* (formerly *Children's Express*). Their website (www.headliners.org) archives over 1,200 reports, including, for example, one on Kenyan children's peer-led education on HIV/AIDS (Parry-Davies and Akerbousse 2006).

Research and play

A striking aspect of children's research is the combining of work and play. Young researchers use 'ice-breaking' sessions to help one another to feel confident and relaxed, genuinely included, more willing to listen to one another and to risk sharing ideas with less fear of being dismissed (Treseder 1997). The UNCRC connects rights to engage in cultural life with the right to play (article 31) resonating with the way play methods can enhance children's research imagination. For example, talking about 'let's pretend' and making maps with drawings and photographs can involve young children in planning improvements in playgrounds and nurseries (Clark and Moss 2001). The play approaches help research teams to enjoy being together as well as working together, and help to sustain the enthusiasm of children who are usually unpaid volunteers. Young children can be good at listening, questioning, challenging, keeping to the point, and helping each other to learn and develop ideas (O'Kane, this volume). For example, adults with young children select topics and ideas and note them in words or pictures on large sheets and everyone has coloured sticky dots to put beside the most popular items. This provides an instant relatively anonymous evaluation for everyone to see at a glance. It is one of several democratic, quick and fun ways to assess opinions. Very young or pre-literate children can contribute detailed data through their songs and dreams, by models, drawings or maps about their daily mobility and routines and environment (Boyden and Ennew 1997; Hart 1992).

Research and work

It has been argued that children's work mirrors adults' work, in being mainly either physical or mental labour. European and north American societies tend to identify work, and therefore research, with mental effort. In cultures where the emphasis is more on physical work, the next examples could be seen as action research, because knowledge is gained through learning from difficulties, planning projects, collecting and applying new knowledge, publicizing the research products (food and news) and testing public responses. In one example, during their monthly meetings, street boys in New Delhi realized that they spent 75 per cent of their money on food and they planned their project. Twelve boys, aged 7 to 17, took an intensive ten-day course on cooking, nutrition, cleanliness, looking after customers and book-keeping, and they had help with renting a space for a restaurant. They took half pay at first, saying 'you can't expect to be an over-night success in this business, one has to bear losses for a while … and try very hard'. They gave free food to some street children, learned Chinese cooking to expand the menu, and planned to raise money to buy a van to take food to an area where there are many street children, financed by selling snacks in public places (ISCA 1995: 239). In a comparable example, in Sarajevo in 1993, 18 editors aged 10 to 13 years ran a radio programme, Colourful Wall, with an estimate audience of 80 per cent of all the local citizens. They conducted polls of children's views and based their programme planning on the results. They had 15 press centres through the city to which children brought news items, and when the phones were working these were phoned through to the radio station. Many schools were closed at the time, and many children were injured and bereaved. The programme carried education, entertainment and psychological support for them, with counsellors, a personal column section and a daily slot on children's rights. The young disc jockeys were especially popular and, like the New Delhi boys, were keen to evaluate and expand their work.

Practical and ethical problems for child researchers

However, problems and questions arise for child researchers, as they do for adult 'lay' researchers (Pratt and Loizos 1992) and for children who are the subjects of research (Alderson and Morrow 2004). How can young researchers work with adults on reasonably equal, informed and unpressured terms? How much responsibility is it fair to expect children to carry and how much should adults intervene to support them or to control the research? How can adults avoid exploiting or manipulating children, as in the participation ladder mentioned earlier? How much time can children be expected to give to research beyond the work they may already do at school, at home or outside the home, or begging? Should they be paid and, if so, how much, and in cash or in kind? There can be further problems with research expenses, and access to research meetings for children who have to have an adult escort. When research is conducted through schools, teachers may need to be, or insist on being, involved and this can set up new adult-child power imbalances to attend to. When child researchers seem to be over-impressed with, for example, the views of officials which they have collected, should adults encourage them to be more critical? Who should have final control over the data and any reports, the children or adults or both jointly? And even when all the complex arrangements have been made and children arrive to give their thoroughly researched presentations to world summits, they may be silenced and ignored (John 2003: 202–8; *Children's Express* 2001).

Losing the plot

In June 2006, the Government's Every Child Matters and Youth Matters website with the National Youth Agency showcased best examples of 'What's Changed: Making a positive contribution'. One example reported young people's concerns about 'perceived stereotyping' of them by the police. After meeting with the police, the young people agreed to research, plan and present a training day for police officers. The young people said, 'We came up with the idea to get involved with police and break down some barriers between them and the kids and some of the prejudices that some officers may have towards teenagers.' They used role play, discussions and open evaluation recorded on video. Thirteen police community support officers (PCSOs, not real police officers) attended the day, but the website report shifted into assuming that the problem was in the young people's misperceptions. 'Outcomes' listed that young people appreciated meeting police 'on a level playing field'. 'It's nice to be talking to a copper and them not taking my details.' The 'what has changed' section recorded that 'young people involved in the project have since met the PCSOs within their community role and feel happy to interact with uniformed officers. Other young people are changing their perceptions and beginning to accept PCSOs as "real people"' www.nya.org.uk, accessed 18th June 2006. The example illustrates how easily young people's research can be twisted into serving the opposite aims to the original ones. Adults' critical reflexivity must be central to research with children (Punch 2002).

I have mentioned just a few from many potential complications to show that working with child researchers does not simply resolve problems of power, exploitation or coercion. Indeed it may amplify them, and so working methods need to be planned, tested, evaluated and developed with the young researchers. One advantage is that there is often more time to talk with child researchers than with child research subjects, and to turn problems into opportunities for children and adults to increase their skill and knowledge.

Conclusion: Working with child researchers

Although there is a growing literature on children as researchers, they are still an under-estimated, under-used resource. Just as research about women has become far more insightful because women are involved as researchers, the scope of research about children could be expanded by involving children as researchers in many methods, levels and stages of the process. When I interview disabled or black people, I find that although we discuss difficulties that arise from discrimination, we are also partly papering over the cracks of these very differences in order to try to hold equal respectful relationships. In contrast, when black researchers talk with black interviewees their common experiences of these differences can enable them to explore them much more deeply (Scott 1998) and this shared exploration can apply to children's research about children.

Children are the primary source of knowledge about their own views and experiences. They can be a means of access to other children, including those who may be protected from strange adult researchers. The novelty and immediacy of children's research reports can attract greater publicity and interest in using the findings than much adult research does. Doing research helps children (perhaps disadvantaged ones especially) to gain more skills, confidence and perhaps determination to overcome their disadvantages than adult researchers working on their behalf could give them. Adult researchers have noted their surprise at child researchers' competence, and their plans to do more complicated work, and to work with younger children in future. Adult researchers frequently emphasize the value of listening to children, and this point is made more effectively when children can express themselves through doing and publicly reporting their own research.

Research sponsors and funders promote research by children when they increasingly adopt policies of consulting 'consumers' of all ages, and when they follow UNCRC guidance that research and services should be 'child-focused', strongly and directly influenced by children. As more children's research is published, the dangers of ignoring their views, and the benefits of working with them become more obvious, although the dangers of token involvement and of misreporting their views also increase. Funders, from the ESRC to Rowntree, expect researchers to work closely with user groups, from inception to the implementation stages of research, although they may not fully fund these often complicated and expensive stages. Consulting children as the largest 'user group' of research affecting them can redress inter-generation imbalances of power, but critical awareness of continuing structural inequalities and prejudices is vital. As the examples have shown, work by young researchers can open up new directions for research, and respect children's rights, or it can be misrepresented to produce the opposite effects.

A booklet for young people 'whose sense of adventure and idealism is the only hope for more voluntary action in future against unsavoury acts towards man and Nature' quotes Gandhi: 'My humble occupation has been to show people how they can solve their own difficulties' (Oza 1991). Child researchers can increase understanding of their lives and interests, concerns and capacities, their needs, ingenuity and originality within the contexts of their family, community and environment. Their work can demonstrate how children can have unique and valid perspectives and insights, to inform social policy so that they can share in solving their own difficulties. However, a key question is: how can adults get beyond the power constraints and expose the intricacies of power in relations between adults and children? Research by children with its emphasis on addressing power before, during and after the formal research stages, with its use of potentially partly subversive games, and its expansion beyond thinking into shared doing, can offer useful approaches.

Notions of childhood vary, and we cannot easily transfer experiences, structures and attitudes across cultures. Child researchers tend to be more adventurously involved in poor and war-torn countries, in adult work as well as research. Children cannot simply set up restaurants in the UK as they can in New Delhi. The limitations in Europe and north America for research by children seem to lie less therefore in children's (in)competencies, than in adults' limiting attitudes, in constraints, and concern for protection over participation rights. However, the evidence of child researchers' activities and achievements, as well as their research findings, are likely to promote more respectful and realistic appreciation of their abilities and rights as social actors. This appreciation and respect can be catalysts, expanding adult funding and support for the stages, levels and methods of research in which children and young people can be active.

Acknowledgments

I am grateful to all the children, young people and adults who have helped to inform this chapter, and to everyone who contributed many more examples of research by children than I could include here.

References

Alderson P. (2000) *Young Children's Rights*, London: Jessica Kingsley/Save the Children.
Alderson. P. and Goodey. C (1998) *Enabling Education: Experiences in Special and Ordinary Schools*, London: Tufnell Press.

Alderson. P. and Montgomery. J. (1996) *Health Care Choices: Making Decisions with Children*, London: Institute for Public Policy Research.

Alderson, P. and Morrow, V. (2004) *Ethics, Social Research and Consulting with Children and Young People*, Barkingside: Barnardo's.

Alderson, P., Sutcliffe, K. and Curtis, K. (2006) 'Children as partners with adults in their medical care', *Archives of Disease in Childhood* 91: 3000–3.

Barry, M. (2005) *Youth Policy and Social Inclusion: Critical debates with Young People*, London: Routledge.

Boyden. J. and Ennew. J. (1997) *Children in Focus; A Manual for Participatory Research with Children*, Stockholm: Radda Barnen.

Butler, M. (1998) 'Negotiating place', in S. Steinberg and J. Kincheloe (eds) *Students as Researchers*, London: Falmer.

CCSE (no date) *Citizenship Education*, No. 31, Leicester: Centre for Citizenship Studies in Education.

Children's Express (2001) 'They feel they don't have a voice' *CRIN News*, 5 February, www.crin.org, accessed 28.2.2001.

Clark, A. and Moss, P. (2001) *Listening to Young Children. The Mosaic Approach*, London: National Children's Bureau/Joseph Rowntree Foundation.

Cockburn, T., Kenny, S. and Webb, M. (1997) *Moss Side Youth Audit: Phase 2, Indicative Findings in Employment and Training*. Manchester: Metropolitan University.

Ennew, J. and Plateau, D.P. (2004) *How to Research the Physical and Emotional Punishment of Children: A Manual for Participatory Research*, Bangkok: Save the Children Alliance.

Gerard, Nikita, Kathleen, Michael, Chris, Siobhan, John, Steven, Jamie, Alan, Mary, Jane, Paddy, Bridgit and Mark (2002) *Learning from our Lessons. A Handbook Written by Children in Residential Care about our Experiences of Secondary School*, Dublin: The Children's Research Centre, Trinity College.

Hart, R. (1992) *Children's Participation*, London. Earthscan/ UNICEF.

Hart, R. (2002) 'Factfile Guide to participatory research', *CRIN News*, 16: 23.

Hood, S. (2002) *The State of London's Children Report*, London: Office of Children's Rights Commissioner for London.

Hood, S. (2004) *The State of London's Children Report*. London: Greater London Assembly.

ISCA, International Save the Children Alliance (1995) *UN Convention on the Rights of the Child Training Kit*. London: Save the Children.

James, A. and Prout, A. (eds) (1997) *Constructing and Reconstructing Childhood*, London: Falmer/Routledge.

John, M. (2003) *Children Rights and Power*, London: Jessica Kingsley.

Kellett, M. (2005) *How to Develop Children as Researchers*, London: Paul Chapman, and see http://childrens-research-centre.open.ac.uk, accessed 29.1.2007.

Kenny. S. and Cockburn, T. (1997) *The Moss Side Youth Audit: Final Report*. Manchester: Metropolitan University.

Keogh, A.F. and Whyte, J. (2005) *Second Level Student Councils in Ireland: A Study of Enablers, Barriers and Support*. Dublin: The Children's Research Centre, Trinity College.

Khan, S. (1997) *A Street Children's Research*. London: Save the Children/ Dhaka: Chinnamul Shishu Kishore Sangstha.

Kirby, P. and Bryson, S. (2002) *Measuring the Magic: Evaluating and Researching Young People's Participation in Public Decision Making*, London: Carnegie Young People Initiative.

Kirby, P., Lanyon, C., Cronin, K. and Sinclair, R. (2003) *Building a Culture of Participation: Involving Children and Young People in Policy, Service Planning, Delivery and Evaluation*, London: Department for Education and Skills.

Klocker, N. (2006) 'An example of "thin" agency: child domestic workers in Tanzania', in E. Robson, R. Panelli and S. Punch (eds) *Young Rural Lives*, London: Taylor & Francis.

Lansdown, G. (2005) *Can You Hear Me? The Rights of Young Children to Participate in Decisions Affecting Them*, The Hague: Bernard van Leer Foundation.

Michael, Chris, Nikita, Gerard, Kathleen, Siobhan, Mark, Paddy, May Jane, Bridget, Alan, Jamie, Steven and John (2002) *Learning from our Lessons. A Handbook Written by Children in Residential Care about our Experiences of Secondary School*, Dublin: The Children's Research Centre, Trinity College.

Miller. J. (1997) *Never Too Young*, London: National Early Years Network. Save the Children.

Nairn, K., Higgins, J. and Sligo, J. (in press) 'Youth researching youth', *Teachers College Record*.

NICCY – Northern Ireland Children's Rights Commissioner's Office www.niccy.org, accessed 29.1.2007.

Noyes, J. (1999) *The Voices and Choices of Children on Long-term Ventilation*, London: Stationery Office.

OCRCL – Office of the Children's Rights Commissioner for London (2001) *Sort It Out!* London: OCRCL.

Oza, D. (1991) *Voluntary Action and Gandhian Approach*, New Delhi: National Book Trust India.

Parry-Davies, E. and Akerbousse, G. (2006) 'Are young people the solution to the Africa HIV/AIDS epidemic?' www.headliners.org accessed 29.1.2007.

Pratt, B. and Loizos. P. (1992) *Choosing Research Methods: Data Collection for Development Workers*, Oxford: Oxfam.

Punch, S. (2002) 'Research with children: the same or different from research with adults?' *Childhood* 9 (3): 322–3.

Qvortrup. J., Bardy, M., Sgritta, G. and Wintersberger, H. (eds) (1994) *Childhood Matters: Social Theory, Practice and Politics*, Aldershot: Avebury.

Rosa, E., Sarner, L. and Barrett, S. (1988) 'A close look at therapeutic touch', *Journal of American Medical Association* 279: 1005–10.

Save the Children (2007) Video/DVD *Involving young people in doing evaluations* (s.emerson@savethechildren.org.uk).

Scott, P. (1998) 'Caribbean people's experience of diabetes', in S. Hood, B. Mayall and S. Oliver (eds) *Critical Issues in Social Research: Power and Prejudice*, Buckingham: Open University Press.

Smyth, M. (2004) 'Using participative acting research with war-affected populations', in M. Smyth and E. Williamson (eds) *Researchers and Their 'Subjects'*, Bristol: Policy Press.

Treseder, P. (1997) *Empowering Children and Young People: A Training Manual for Promoting Involvement in Decision-Making*, London: Save the Children/ Children's Rights Office.

UNICEF (1989) *Convention on the Rights of the Child*, New York: UNICEF.

UNICEF (2006) *Child and Youth Participation Resource Guide*, CD chongkolnee@unicef.org.

Warrington, C. (2006) *Children's Voices, Changing Futures: The Views and Experiences of young Gypsies and Travellers*, Ipswich: Ormiston Children and Families Trust.

Wellard, S., Tearse, M. and West, A. (1997) *All Together Now: Community Participation for Children and Young People*, London: Save the Children.

West, A. (1997) 'Learning about leaving care through research by young care leavers', *Learning from Experience: Participatory Approaches in SCF*, London: Save the Children.

Willow, C. (1997) *Hear! Hear! Promoting Children's and Young People's Democratic Participation in Local Government*, London: Local Government Information Unit.

Willow, C. (2002) *Participation in Practice: Children and Young People as Partners in Change*, London: Children's Society.

Index

Lightning Source UK Ltd.
Milton Keynes UK

171057UK00002B/47/P

9 780415 416849